T0211060

Lecture Notes in Computer Science 10461

More information about this series at http://www.springer.com/series/7409

Mounir Mokhtari · Bessam Abdulrazak
Hamdi Aloulou (Eds.)

Enhanced Quality of Life and Smart Living

15th International Conference, ICOST 2017
Paris, France, August 29–31, 2017
Proceedings

Editors
Mounir Mokhtari
Institut Mines Telecom/CNRS IPAL
Singapore
Singapore

Hamdi Aloulou
Institut Mines Télécom
Paris
France

Bessam Abdulrazak
Dep. d'informatique/Fac. des sciences
Université de Sherbrooke
Sherbrooke, QC
Canada

ISSN 0302-9743 ISSN 1611-3349 (electronic)
Lecture Notes in Computer Science
ISBN 978-3-319-66187-2 ISBN 978-3-319-66188-9 (eBook)
DOI 10.1007/978-3-319-66188-9

Library of Congress Control Number: 2017949518

LNCS Sublibrary: SL3 – Information Systems and Applications, incl. Internet/Web, and HCI

Printed on acid-free paper

This Springer imprint is published by Springer Nature
The registered company is Springer International Publishing AG
The registered company address is: Gewerbestrasse 11, 6330 Cham, Switzerland

Preface

This year we are celebrating the 15th anniversary of ICOST, a conference which has succeeded in bringing together a community from different continents over a decade and a half and has raised society's awareness of frail and dependant people's quality of life.

ICOST has so far been hosted in France (2003), Singapore (2004), Canada (2005), Northern Ireland (2006), Japan (2007), USA (2008), France (2009), South Korea (2010), Canada (2011), Italy (2012), Singapore (2013), USA (2014), Switzerland (2015), and China (2016). Following these 14 annual events, covering the three continents of Europe, Asia and North America, the 15th International Conference on Smart Homes and Health Telematics (ICOST'2017) will be hosted in France by the Institut Mines-Télécom/CNRS IPAL (UMI 2955).

ICOST provides a premier venue for the presentation and discussion of research in the design, development, deployment, and evaluation of Smart Urban Environments, Assistive Technologies, Chronic Disease Management, Coaching, and Health Telematics Systems. ICOST brings together stakeholders from clinical, academic, and industrial backgrounds along with end users and family caregivers to explore how to utilize technology to foster independent living and offer an enhanced quality of life. ICOST 2017 invites participants to present and discuss their experience in design, development, deployment, and evaluation of assistive and telehealth systems, as well as ethical and policy issues. The conference features a dynamic program incorporating a range keynote talks, of technical, clinical, or industrial focus, oral and poster presentations; and demonstrations and technical exhibits.

The theme of the conference this year is "IoT for Enhanced Quality of Life and Smart Living" focusing on the quality of life of dependent people, not only in their homes, but also in an outdoor living environment, to improve mobility and social interaction in the city. Extending the living space with suitable support from ICTs in terms of smart transportation, mobility, interaction, and socialization is the scientific challenge that the ICOST community has decided to tackle. ICTs are not limited only to end-users with special needs, but also to caregivers and relatives in charge of taking care of dependent and elderly people. To be more effective and impactful, technologies in different areas, such as IoT (Internet of Things), big data analytics, smart mobility… should target all stakeholders.

ICOST 2017 is proud to extend its hospitality to an international community consisting of researchers from major universities and research centers, people from industry and users from 18 different countries. We would like to thank first the authors for submitting their current research work and the Program Committee members for their commitment in reviewing submitted papers. ICOST proceedings have now reached over 150000 downloads, which puts their download figures in the top 25% of Springer's LNCS.

We are very pleased to host world-renowned keynote speakers from multiple backgrounds, coming from Canada, Finland, Singapore, and France, and we are extremely honored by the confidence of the sponsors in this conference.

We are looking forward to welcoming you to France! We wish you all a pleasant stay in Paris, and a memorable and rich experience at ICOST 2017.

July 2017

Mounir Mokhtari
Bessam Abdulrazak
Hamdi Aloulou

Organization

General Chair

Mounir Mokhtari	Institut Mines Télécom/CNRS IPAL, Singapore

Scientific Committee

Christian Roux	Institut Mines Télécom, France
Carl K. Chang	Iowa State University, USA
Sumi Helal	University of Florida, USA
Z. Zenn Bien	Korea Advanced Institute of Science and Technology, South Korea
Ismail Khalil	Johannes Kepler University, Austria
Chris Nugent	University of Ulster, UK
William Cheng-Chung Chu	Tunghai University, Taiwan
Mounir Mokhtari	Institut Mines Télécom, CNRS LIRMM, France/CNRS IPAL, Singapore
Daqing Zhang	Institut Mines Télécom/TELECOM SudParis, France
Hisato Kobayashi	Hosei University, Japan
Bessam Abdulrazak	Université de Sherbrooke, Canada
Yeunsook Lee	Yonsei University/The Korean Gerontological Society, South Korea
Tatsuya Yamazaki	National Institute of Information and Communications Technology, Japan
Cristiano Paggetti	I+ S.r.l, Italy
Nick Hine	University of Dundee, UK

Program Committee

Chair

Bessam Abdulrazak	Université de Sherbrooke, Canada

Co-chair

Hamdi Aloulou	Institut Mines Télécom, CNRS LIRMM, France

Members

Salim Hima	ESME-SUDRIA, France
Patrice C. Roy	NICHE Research Group, Dalhousie University, Canada
Philip Yap	Khoo Teck Puat Hospital, Singapore
Étienne André	Université Paris 13, LIPN, CNRS, UMR 7030, France
Shijian Lu	Institute for Infocomm Research, Singapore

Iyad Abuhadrous	Palestine Technical College, Palestine
Vigouroux Nadine	IRIT, Toulouse, France
Janet Light	University of New Brunswick, Canada
Hicham Zabadani	American University in Dubai, UAE
Hamid Mcheick	University of Quebec at Chicoutimi, Canada
Manfred Wojciechowski	University of Applied Sciences Dusseldorf, Germany
Yves Demazeau	CNRS LIG, France
Hongbo Ni	Northwestern Polytechnical University, China
Laurent Billonnet	University of Limoges, France
Fulvio Mastrogiovanni	University of Geneva, Switzerland
Kaori Fujinami	Tokyo University of Agriculture and Technology, Japan
Ye-Qiong Song	LORIA - University of Lorraine, France
Mahmoud Ghorbel	Faculty of Sfax, Tunisia
Hisato Kobayashi	Hosei University, Japan
Yan Liu	Advanced Digital Sciences Center, Singapore
Stefanos Kollias	University of Lincoln, UK
Mark Donnelly	University of Ulster, UK
Belkacem Chikhaoui	Prospectus Laboratory, University of Sherbrooke, Canada
Abdenour Bouzouane	Université du Quebec à Chicoutimi, Canada
David Menga	EDF R&D, France
Farah Arab	Université Paris 8, France
Joaquim Bellmunt	Institut Mines Télécom, France
Ibrahim Sadek	Institut Mines Télécom, France
Salim Hima	ESME-SUDRIA, France
Kim Jongbae	University of Pittsburgh, USA
Gang Pan	Zhejiang University, China
Jutta Treviranus	OCAD University, Canada
Charles Gouin-Vallerand	Télé-Université du Québec, Canada
Diane Cook	Washington State University, USA
Mi Jeong Kim	Kyung Hee University, South Korea
Jeffrey King	Elster Solutions LLC, USA
Abdallah Mhamed	Télécom SudParis, France

Organizing Committee

Chair

Hamdi Aloulou	Institut Mines Télécom, CNRS LIRMM, France

Members

Philippe Fraisse	University of Montpellier, CNRS LIRMM, France
Angela Saenz	CNRS IPAL, Singapore
Firas Kaddachi	Univeristy of Montpellier, CNRS LIRMM, France

Fabien Clavier	CNRS IPAL, Singapore
Joaquim Bellmunt	Institut Mines Télécom, CNRS IPAL, Singapore
Antoine de Marassé Enouf	CNRS IPAL, Singapore

Media and Webmaster

Hamdi Aloulou	Institut Mines Télécom, CNRS LIRMM, France

Sponsors

Image and Pervasive Access Lab, CNRSUMI 2955, Singapore
Institut Mines Télécom, Paris, France
National Center for Scientific Research, France
University of Sherbrook, Canada
University of Montpellier, France

Invited Talks

Teaching Our Machines to be Smart, Not Prejudiced

Jutta Treviranus[1,2]

[1] Inclusive Design Research Centre (IDRC), Toronto, Canada
[2] Faculty of Design at OCAD University, Toronto, Canada

Abstract. Before an intelligent machine can be of help, it has to understand us. There is nothing more frustrating than negotiating with a machine that does not recognize our request, or that misunderstands our intent. Machine learning models and algorithms depend upon data analytics. Data analytics is biased toward dominant patterns, not outliers. People with disabilities and other minorities are outliers. Artificial intelligence has been heralded as a promising technology to assist individuals with disabilities. Intelligent machines have been envisioned as personal assistants, companions and smart environments to remind, prompt, guide, alert to risk and assist with daily functions. More urgently, intelligent machines are making a host of important decisions that affect our lives from predicting loan and credit worthiness, academic potential, terrorist intent, to future employment performance. Before the promise can be fully realized, and the prejudice averted, we must train our machines to be inclusive. This will benefit everyone. Intelligence that understands diversity and stretches to encompass the outliers is better at predicting risk and opportunity, more capable of processing the unexpected, more adaptable, and more dynamically resilient.

Machine Learning for Image Processing in Healthcare

Roger Zimmermann

MMRL Lab, NUS, Singapore

Abstract. Many aspects of healthcare are undergoing rapid evolution and facing many challenges. Computer vision and image processing methods have progressed tremendously within the last few years. One of the reasons is the excellent performance that machine learning algorithms are achieving in many the fields of image processing, especially through deep learning techniques. There exists various application areas where computer-based image classification and object detection methods can make meaningful contributions. Yet, these data-intensive methods encounter a unique set of challenges in the medical domain – which often suffer from a scarcity of large public datasets and still require reliable analysis with high precision. This talk will present some recent work in the area of image analytics for cervical cancer screening in the context of low resource settings. The work is in collaboration with Dr. Pamela Tan from Singapore's KK Hospital and MobileODT, a medical device and software-enabled services company. In this joint project, our group's work focuses on machine learning algorithms for the medical analysis of cervix images acquired via unconventional consumer imaging devices like smartphones, based on their appearance and for the purpose of screening cervical cancer precursor lesions. The talk will present our methodology and some preliminary results.

Invited Papers

Interpretation of Activity Data Collected with Accelerometers

Timo Jämsä[1,2], Maarit Kangas[1,2], Maisa Niemelä[1], Petra Tjurin[1], and Raija Korpelainen[2,3,4]

[1] Research Unit of Medical Imaging, Physics and Technology, University of Oulu, 90014 Oulu, Finland
[2] Medical Research Center Oulu, University of Oulu and Oulu University Hospital, 90220 Oulu, Finland
[3] Center of Life Course Health Research, University of Oulu, 90014 Oulu, Finland
[4] Department of Sports and Exercise Medicine, Oulu Deaconess Institute, 90100 Oulu, Finland
{Timo.Jamsa,Maarit.Kangas,Maisa.Niemela, Petra.Tjurin}@oulu.fi
Raija.Korpelainen@odl.fi

Abstract. Interpretation of activity data collected with accelerometers strongly depends on the purpose and health outcome in question and there is no single solution. Instead, a wide range of activity parameters have been presented, In addition, e.g. sensor location, sampling rate, acceleration range, pre-processing, analysis algorithm, and selected thresholds define the outcome. This paper overviews some approaches and algorithms for recording physical activity and sedentary behavior, applying data collected with an accelerometer on the wrist and waist in daily life.

Keywords: Accelerometer • Wearable • Algorithms • Physical activity • Inactivity • Sedentary

Introduction

Physical activity (PA) has been shown to be a key factor for good health and wellbeing. Therefore, recording and analysis of daily PA has become one of the main streams in the wearable devices. A wide range of PA monitors are currently available for research and as consumer devices. Interpretation of activity data collected with accelerometers strongly depends on the purpose and health outcome in question, and there is no single best solution. Instead, a wide range of activity parameters have been presented. In addition, e.g. sensor location, sampling rate, acceleration range, pre-processing, analysis algorithm, and selected thresholds define the outcome [1]. From the research perspective, it is important to understand the wide variation in algorithms and applications for PA monitoring.

Monitoring Physical Activity

The most simple PA measurement method is recognition of walking or running steps, for instance in order to follow whether the recommendation of 10 000 daily steps is fulfilled or not. However, to obtain more detailed information on physical activity or sedentary behavior, more advanced methods are needed.

The acceleration magnitude of individual steps is an important descriptor of e.g. osteogenic exercise (exercise that prevents osteoporosis). This is because bone adapts to mechanical loadings. We have developed algorithms focused on the magnitude, slope, area and energy of acceleration signal during individual steps, as measured with a waist-worn accelerometer [2, 3]. In those studies, we were able to present osteogenic threshold of 4 g or 100 g/s for improving bone density. We also defined the daily impact score [4], which combines accumulated daily impacts at various intensity levels. Using similar approach, focusing on different intensity bands of acceleration, we were able to define PA intensity thresholds also for osteoarthritis [5], and lipid, insulin and glucose metabolism [6]. Since the peak impact loads during vigorous activities may range above 10 g, the operating acceleration range of the device may have significant results in intensity-based data recordings [7].

Physical activity monitors are typically calibrated for estimates of energy expenditure, given as metabolic equivalents (MET). METs are typically analyzed within predefined epochs (e.g. 15–60 s), and counted as daily accumulation of PA in different MET levels. However, there is a large variation in the MET values given by different PA monitors with different attachment sites, algorithms and thresholds [8]. Thus, some caution is needed when comparing results of the time spent on different activity levels in different studies.

Physical inactivity has been shown to be an independent risk factor for morbidity. Thus, algorithms for detecting long-term sitting and interruption of sedentary behavior are needed. Using wrist-worn accelerometer and MET-based assessment of sedentary behavior (1-2 MET), we showed significant underestimation in self-reported sitting time by (8 h 49 min vs. 10 h 35 min) [9]. We developed machine learning algorithms for classifying daily activities. Using bagged tree prediction, we were able to recognize different activities with an overall accuracy of 96.5%, and sitting with sensitivity of 92.2% and specificity of 99.2% [10].

We have also found relationship between acceleration signal and body weight change [11]. This suggests potential of using accelerometric signal for weight control. The highest association ($r = 0.89$) was obtained with the parameter describing the 3D orientation of the acceleration vector.

Conclusions

We have presented here some possibilities and challenges in objective measurement of PA. In spite of the existing challenges (see more e.g. in [1, 7]), wearable devices offer a feasible way of collecting activity data in large populations [8, 12]. They may also be effective in motivating people for more active behavior [13].

Acknowledgments. The authors acknowledge the contributions of the researchers and students in our team, especially Dr Riikka Ahola, as well as all our collaborators and funding sources during the different studies. We also thank all study participants in various studies during the years.

References

1. Sievänen, H., Kujala, U.M.: Accelerometry – Simple, but challenging. Scand. J. Med. Sci. Sports **27**, 574–578 (2017)
2. Jämsä, T., Vainionpää, A., Vihriälä, E., Korpelainen, R., Leppäluoto, J.: Effects of daily physical activity on proximal femur. Clin. Biomech. **21**, 1–7 (2006)
3. Heikkinen, R., Vihriälä, E., Vainionpää, A., et al.: Acceleration slope of exercise-induced impacts is a determinant of changes in bone density. J. Biomech. **40**, 2967–2974 (2007)
4. Ahola, R., Korpelainen, R., Vainionpää, A., Jämsä, T.: Daily impact score in long-term acceleration measurements of high-impact exercise. J. Biomech. **43**, 1960–1964 (2010)
5. Multanen, J., Nieminen, M.T., Häkkinen, A., et al.: Effects of high-impact bone exercise on bone and articular cartilage: a 12 months randomized controlled quantitative magnetic resonance imaging study. J. Bone Miner. Res. **29**, 192–201 (2014)
6. Herzig, K.-H., Ahola, R., Leppäluoto, J., Jokelainen, J., Jämsä, T., Keinänen-Kiukaanniemi, S.: Light physical activity determined by a motion sensor decreases insulin resistance, improves lipid homeostasis and reduces visceral fat in high-risk subjects: PreDiabEx study RCT. Int. J. Obesity **38**, 1089–1096 (2014)
7. Ziebart, C., Giangregorio, L.M., Gibbs, J.C., et al.: Measurement of peak impact loads differ between accelerometers – Effects of system operating range and sampling rate. J. Biomech. **58**, 222–226 (2017)
8. Leinonen, A.-M., Ahola, R. Kulmala, J., et al.: Measuring physical activity in free-living conditions: Comparison of three accelerometry-based methods. Front. Physiol. **7**(681), 1–9 (2016)
9. Niemelä, M. Ahola, R., Pyky, R., et al.: Self-reported versus measured physical activity and sedentary behavior in young men. Liikunta Tiede **53**(2–3), 73–79 (2016)
10. Tjurin, P., Niemelä, M., Huusko, M., Ahola, R., Kangas, M., Jämsä, T.: Classification of physical activities and sedentary behaviour using raw data of 3D accelerometer. IFMBE Proc. **65**, 872–875 (2017)
11. Vihriälä, E. Rinta-Paavola, A., Sorvoja, H., Jämsä, T., Myllylä, R.: Relationship between weight change and changes in 3D acceleration signals generated by walking. J. Mech. Med. Biol. **15**, 1550080, 1–15 (2015)
12. Niemelä, M., Kangas, M., Ahola R. et al.: Self-evaluated and objectively measured physical activity and sitting time in relation to self-rated health at the age of 46. In: Fifth International Conference on Ambulatory Monitoring of Physical Activity and Movement (2017)
13. Jauho, A.-M., Pyky, R., Ahola. R., et al.: Effect of wrist-worn activity monitor feedback on physical activity behavior: a randomized controlled trial in Finnish young men. Prev. Med. Reports **2**, 628–634 (2015)

Health Smart Homes...and Beyond

Norbert Noury

University Lyon/INL CNRS 5270, France

The ageing process is generally characterized by a decline in the main bio-physiological capacities of individuals and is visible by a significant reduction in activities and of the social and family roles [1]. Nevertheless, to have less activities does not come necessarily with less involvement in the one conserved [2].

Due to the various costs of the placement in retirement houses, psychological, social and also financial, people prefer to stay in their own home when they get aged. This is the place which they are the more familiar with, where they can develop or maintain their already existing network of relationships with their relatives and peers. In addition, this is the place where they still can take, or participate to, decisions - on the internal organization and on the internal architecture. In short this is the place which can allow people to maintain a beneficial projection in their future, a "project of life" at short and longer term.

Therefore, to face the increase span in longevity, the main policy makers acting in the domain of gerontechnology - researchers in various fields of public Health and ICT, industrial partners, business planners, as well as politicians - must actively envisage new ways to satisfy the needs for an independent living at home.

With aging, the elderly person will naturally reduce his activities. This corresponds to a normal physiological process due to the loss in musculo-skeletal strength and aptitudes. This may be a "normal" senescence with slow reduction in possible activities and their intensities. This can also be more "pathological" if the subject reduces his activities fearing "accident-prone" situations, such as aggression or a fall; with direct consequences on reduced socialization and isolation. Although in a most optimistic way, ageing can also be "optimal" if the subject accepts and adapts to his new evolving situation.

The main thesis in this presentation is that it is possible to allow for this more optimistic way of aging with the use of information technologies as "enablers". With the collection of various information directly on the field, then the use of data fusion mechanisms to produce higher level information on the trends (trajectory) of Health, also with the production of adapted feedbacks which will motivate and accompany the person (coaching); This should also address the two other types of actors in home, that are the professionals and the informal carers.

Therefore, the introduction of technologies in the personal home, and in the professional activities, must be questioned in terms of acceptations to avoid the risk of rejection [3]. But the ICT are prone to be intrusive and will modify the relationships and interactions to others and to places. Therefore we must envisage the impact of the introduction of ICT in home, that is we must select tools and metrics and to measure this impact.

The major source of information we can collect at home comes from the monitoring of the activities of the subject in terms of variety and intensity. Again we need some metrics. What do we need to measure and what do we do with the collected information?

We base our knowledge on the concept of homeostasis. This is a natural process to regulate our internal physiological parameters in order to face external variations (e.g. thermoregulation of internal central temperature, adaptation of cardiac frequency to efforts, regulation of arterial pressure, regulation of blood concentrations in oxygen and carbon dioxide, etc.). It was evidenced by the French Physiologist Claude Bernard that the adaptation of homeostasis is an expression of good health as it shows how the human system dynamically adapts to face pathological aggressions.

In the French project AILISA we started with the development of a basic sensing technology, based on a network of sensors to measure selected physiological parameters, parameters on ambient conditions and in addition eventually parameters of activities. We proposed the diagrams "ambulatograms" [4] to visualize the daily mobility and we were the first to uncover the "circadian rhythms of activities" [5, 6]. We have found that the technology we have placed at home has not been rejected by the people. But also that the technology should not be too demanding to the end user; the physiological devices were rapidly neglected because they needed too much interactions from users.

In the project MAPA, promoted by the French Company Orange Labs, we adopted a less intrusive approach by using a technology already in place. A simple meter of the electrical energy was modified in order to produce indicators of the kind of activities performed. We discovered that with this very unobtrusive technology we could detect some pathological trends of activities [7]. This was also a confirmation that the main information collected are not on the absolute values (static) but in their variations (dynamic).

The domain of Health Smart homes is not new as it started to develop in the mid-90s. Still we must make the statement of his very limited deployment. So it is still worth questioning on the means for introducing technologies in the home. Was it a failure in acceptation, in motivation, or we did not access the right levers (politics, industrial, business makers)? Thus, in our discussion we will attempt to bring some elements of responses, but modestly no solution will be proposed.

As a conclusion we want to consider Health Smart Homes not only as a problem to be solved in itself, but furthermore as a broader paradigm of the more and more complex problems humans will have to solve in the near future. Obviously, more and more problems are a complex mix of different points of views from science, technology, usages, ergonomics, and sociology. From the ergonomic point of view we must be more prospective. What we learn is that we need to work together, to share our knowledge, to expand our own understanding, to be more integrative, also more flexible and modest.

References

1. Lelièvre, E., Bonvalet, C. (eds.): Family Beyond Household and Kin. Life Event Histories and Entourage, a French Survey, p. 198. Springer (2016)
2. Clément, S., Rolland, C., Thoer-Fabre, C.: Usages, normes, autonomie: analyse critique de la bibliographie concernant le vieillissement de la population. In: Plan Urbanisme Construction Architecture, Paris, vol. 177, p. 240 (2007)
3. Czaja, S.J., Charness. N., Fisk, A.D., Hertzog, C.: Factors predicting the use of technology. Psychol. Aging **21**(2), 333–352 (2006)
4. Noury, N. et al.: Monitoring behavior in home using a smart fall sensor and position sensors. In: Proceedings of the IEEE-EMBS Microtechnologies in Medicine and Biology, Lyon, pp. 607–610, October 2000
5. Virone, G., Noury, N., Demongeot, J.: A system for automatic measurement of circadian activity deviations in telemedicine. IEEE-TBME **49**(12), 1463–1469 (2002)
6. Le Bellego, G., Noury, N., Virone, G., Mousseau, M., Demongeot, J.: Measurement and model of the activity of a patient in his hospital suite. IEEE TITB **10**, 92–99 (2006)
7. Noury, N., Berenguer, M., Teyssier, H., Bouzid, M.-J., Giordani, M.: Building an Index of human activity from the activity on the residential electrical power line. IEEE-TITB **15** (5), 758–766 (2011)

Contents

Well-Being Technology

Biomedical and Health Informatics

Activity and Recognition

Short Contributions

Well-Being Technology

Smart Assistive Technologies to Enhance Well-Being of Elderly People and Promote Inclusive Communities

Rebeca I. García-Betances[1], María Fernanda Cabrera-Umpiérrez[1](✉), Juan Bautista Montalvá Colomer[1], Miguel Páramo Castrillo[1], Javier Chamorro Mata[2], and María Teresa Arredondo[1]

[1] Life Supporting Technologies (LifeSTech), Superior Technical School of Telecommunication Engineers, Universidad Politécnica de Madrid (UPM), Avenida Complutense no 30, Ciudad Universitaria, 28040 Madrid, Spain
{rgarcia,chiqui,jmontalva,mparamo,mta}@lst.tfo.upm.es
[2] Consorcio Regional de Transportes de Madrid (CRTM), Plaza del Descubridor Diego de Ordás, no 3, planta baja, 28003 Madrid, Spain
javier.chamorro@crtm.es

Abstract. Within the framework of the H2020 IN LIFE project we have designed and developed two ICT services related to independent living and travel that support home activities, communication, mobility and socialization. A brief overview of the Spanish pilot, in which these solutions will be tested, is presented describing the inclusion and exclusion criteria, use cases, actors, as well as the services that will be tested. The manuscript also presents the description of functionalities and characteristics of the developed ICT services.

Keywords: AAL · Mild cognitive impairment · Elderly people · Assistive technologies · Well-being · ICT services · Inclusive communities

1 Introduction

Rising population longevity calls for increasing the quality and efficacy of health care and social support services demanded by the growing elderly population sector [1]. In particular, elderly people affected by mild cognitive impairment (MCI) might benefit from assistive technologies [2]. As MCI and early dementia entails memory decline and impairments in daily functioning ability that gradually worsen, ICT solutions that help them to improve their well-being, as well as promote communities more inclusive and adapted to their specific needs are needed. This manuscript is organized as follow. Section 1 presents the introduction describing the context in which the designed solutions are based, and a brief overview of the Spanish pilot approach in which they will be tested. Sections 2 and 3 describe the two ICT services designed and developed to address the needs of people with cognitive disabilities and/or reduced mobility in two areas: independent living and travel support. Finally, Sect. 4 presents the conclusion and the future work that is planned to be accomplished.

M. Mokhtari et al. (Eds.): ICOST 2017, LNCS 10461, pp. 3–12, 2017.
DOI: 10.1007/978-3-319-66188-9_1

1.1 IN LIFE Project Context

Following the challenges proposed by the H2020 call on "Advancing active and healthy ageing with ICT: ICT solutions for independent living with cognitive impairment" (PHC-20-2014) the IN LIFE project aims to "*prolong and support the independent living of seniors with cognitive impairments, through interoperable, open, personalized and seamless ICT services that support home activities, communication, health maintenance, travel, mobility and socialization tasks, with novel, scalable and viable business models, based on feedback from large-scale and multi-country pilot applications*" [3]. The specific objectives of the IN LIFE project are:

- To connect a wide range of adaptable ICT solutions for elderly with various cognitive impairments, into a common open reference architecture, to allow their interconnection and enhance their interoperability.
- To instantiate applications, services and business models to different geographical and sociocultural backgrounds, user group types (i.e. early dementia, moderate dementia, etc.), as well as lifestyles (i.e. living at home alone or with spouse, living at elderly home, traveling, etc.).
- To provide tools and systems for services adaptation and personalization, to meet the different needs and wants of each individual in a dynamic way, allowing services to evolve together with the users' health and condition.
- To provide tools and instructions to carers of people with cognitive impairments and/or dementia in order to support communication and functioning in daily life.
- To estimate the return of investment of the different business models and connected services through pilots in 6 sites Europe wide and highlight best practices for relevant viable business and financial models for their uptake and instantiation per region and market.
- To issue key guidelines on the proper and ethical application of the proposed business models, to guarantee the respect of users' wants, lifestyle, personal data and personal beliefs.
- To study the scalability and sensitivity of the tested business models and cases and provide guidelines on their optimal application in different financial, sociocultural and healthcare contexts.

The IN LIFE project is starting to conduct six pilots in six different sites: UK, Sweden, The Netherlands, Spain, Greece, and Slovenia. All sites cover holistically multiple services for elderly citizens with cognitive impairments, but each has different focus areas and diversity in ICT solutions offered for Ambient Assisted Living (AAL). IN LIFE will be able to ensure a good spread of test participants in terms of age, family status, socioeconomic status, location and ethnicity, by conduct long-terms tests with over 2100 users, in total; 1.200 with cognitive impairment and over 600 carers. Table 1 shows the main user groups targeted. This stratification of users allows to easily identify the needs and requirements using an extended evaluation framework that will address separately each user group and will be flexible to accommodate the potential transition of users from one group to the next.

In addition, other type of users will be stakeholders with an interest in IN LIFE solutions, but not with a direct involvement in day-to-day care provision. Some main

Table 1. IN LIFE main user groups.

User group	Description
Mild Cognitive Impairment (MCI)	Elderly who have lost cognitive functioning on at least one aspect with no sign of dementia and still functioning in daily activities
Early and later stages of Dementia	People that have been diagnosed with dementia but they are still maintaining some aspects of their daily functions (early signs of dementia are apparent) and people have been diagnosed by specialists and might be under medication
Cognitive impairment as a co-morbid condition	People with other conditions and diseases with cognitive impairment and other conditions as co-condition
Caregivers	Either formal (i.e. healthcare, social), or informal (i.e. family members and friends) that need to be empowered with knowledge and tools to support the elderly at their everyday life activities

stakeholders related to the IN LIFE approach are: (1) regulatory authorities on local, national or international level; (2) user interest organizations; (3) standardization organizations; and (4) public bodies, insurance companies and care organizations. The evaluation method will follow a longitudinal evaluation framework for a long-term evaluation characterized by a dynamic user-centered approach, in which the idea is to compare everyday living experiences of people with cognitive impairment with and without the IN LIFE system. It will focus on three main dimensions: (D1) QoL & Health Status; (D2) Sustainability of Health and Care systems; and (D3) Innovation & Growth. Each dimension will be addressed measuring different primary and secondary indicators. D1 will measure the Health related Quality of Life (HRQOL) including: physical activity, cognitive decline, functional status, fall, nutrition, and mental health. D2 will address change in resources or unit for resources, including: comparison of hospital care vs. home care, potential for care process improvement and cost gains, and the positive and viable Rol and SRol. Finally, D3 will measure innovation indicators such as: number of implemented technologies, and number of deployed technologies to users.

1.2 Spanish Pilot Description

Each pilot site tests a number of IN LIFE services that are different for each site but all represent important daily activities. In the case of the Spanish pilot we (Universidad Politécnica de Madrid), together with the Regional Transport Consortium of Madrid (CRTM) and the Matia Gerontological Institute (INGEMA), will test the following services: (1) daily functions assistant; (2) activity monitoring and coaching; (3) virtual gaming; public transport support; (4) care giving monitoring and supervision; and (5) caregiver scheduling and reminding.

The Spanish pilot will test two application modules, one for independent living support called "Daily Function Assistant module" and other for travel support called "Public Transport Support module," that is described in the following sections. These solutions will be tested with 220 elderly users with cognitive impairments, 60 health care professionals, 120 informal carers and 11 stakeholders. In total 431 users will test the proposed solutions. Also different use cases will be evaluated combining different functionalities of the applications. Table 2 shows the defined use cases for the Spanish pilot.

Table 2. Defined use cases for the Spanish pilot.

	Use case	Description	Primary and Secondary actor (s)
Independent living support	Home environment control with NFC pictograms	Control of domotic house appliances (lights, doors, blinds and media player) using pictograms	Healthy Elderly; Elderly with MCI; Early Dementia; Elderly at home
	Make a call with NFC pictograms	Making a call choosing the image of the person	Healthy Elderly; Elderly with MCI; Early Dementia; Elderly hospitalized and at home; Family members & Informal caregivers
	Send SMS messages with NFC pictograms	Composition of a SMS message using the desired pictograms. Send the message choosing the image of the person	Healthy Elderly; Elderly with MCI; Early Dementia; Elderly hospitalized and at home; Family members & Informal caregivers
	Smartphone functionalities control with NFC pictograms	Control a subset of elementary smartphone functionalities (battery status, date) and management of settings (silent mode de/activation, toggle Wi-Fi, etc.) using pictograms	Healthy Elderly; Elderly with MCI; Early Dementia; Elderly hospitalized and at home
Travel support	Favorite Journeys Database Arrangement	User and carer registration into the Server by means of a username and password. Both of them have to be able to create, consult and update the data User manages his/her own database of favorite routes, analyzes the routes and the possible critical points in its itinerary, and assigns them one or more checking points	Healthy Elderly; Elderly with MCI; Elderly at home; Family members & Formal and Informal caregivers; User interest organizations; Public bodies, insurance companies and care organizations

(continued)

Table 2. (*continued*)

	Use case	Description	Primary and Secondary actor (s)
	Personalized Journeys Database Arrangement	The final user and the caregiver make out the list of preferred routes giving them some symbols for easier and quick recognition	Healthy Elderly; Elderly with MCI; Elderly at home; Family members & Formal and Informal caregivers; User interest organizations; Public bodies, insurance companies and care organizations
	Personal journey navigation and tracking	Increase or create confidence in the Public Transport Network. Increase of his/her journeys/week ratio to expand his/her personal autonomy and experience in social relationships	Healthy Elderly; Elderly with MCI; Elderly at home; Family members & Formal and Informal caregivers; User interest organizations; Public bodies, insurance companies and care organizations

The inclusion and exclusion criteria defined are the same for all pilot sites, but each site will use their own diagnostic tools for categorizing and allocating users in different groups. The inclusion criterion is defined as follows:

- Mini Mental State Examination (MMSE) score or equivalent: 18–26.
- Cognitive impairment diagnosis after complaints, with not physiological measurements indicating Alzheimer's Disease (AD) (just Mild Cognitive impairment; MCI), unless stated otherwise [4].
- Good functional level.
- Still independent in most daily activities (Index of Activities of Daily Living - IADL)
- Diagnosis from specialists.

For the exclusion criteria we have defined the following rules:

- Participants with psychiatric or substance abuse.
- Only comorbid conditions stated in the recruitment will be included.
- Participants who cannot consent will not be included in the study unless stated otherwise in their pilots' objectives and covered by their ethics approval.

Also other exclusion criteria relate to: (1) other medication intake; (2) history of alcohol, drug abuse; and (3) history of psychiatric illnesses; will be followed.

2 Daily Function Assistant

The Daily Function Assistant is a tool that enables users to be assisted in their daily living activities by means of the NFC technology. It is composed by two components: (1) scanning a tag to perform an action; and (2) recording a tag to configure a desired functionality. In the first case, the users can trigger a pre-defined action only by scanning the smart tag related to the action. For example, Fig. 1 shows a user scanning a smart tag already configured to "call Alison". The user scans the smart card and the smartphone automatically calls Alison. There are many possibilities depending on the actions and functionalities previously recorded in the smart tag.

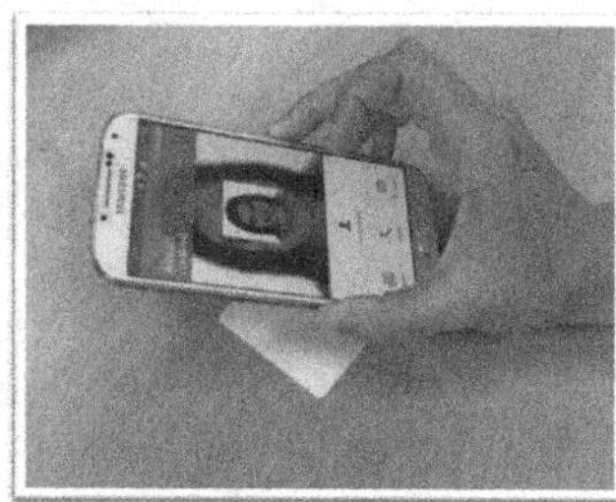

Fig. 1. Make a call example.

The recording application, designed for Android smartphones, allows to create physical smart tags that automatizes a wide set of functions addressing different options such as: identifying objects, controlling the phone, making a call or communicate and express needs or emotions. Those actions can be configured so the user just needs to naturally scan one of these tags in order to automatically trigger an action. Figure 2 shows the main menu of the recording application.

Within the recording application, users have eight types of functionalities in order to create a smart tag:

1. *Mobile settings*: users can put the device in Normal, Silent or Vibration mode, know the date and time, the device battery level, switch on and off the Wi-Fi and Bluetooth, and increase/decrease the volume;
2. *Contacts*: users can record a number into a tag, or record any number by typing or choosing it from the contact list;
3. *Pictograms*: there is a set of pre-defined Alternative and Augmentative Communication (AAC) tags with pictograms that represent an action, a need or a feeling [5]. Users could also create personalized pictograms by choosing an image from the device gallery or by taking a photo. With these pictograms users can compose a text in natural language by scanning them (limited to two pictograms);
4. *Music*: users can control the open VLC media player once it has been configured;
5. *Reminders*: users can create and define reminders. They are able to store a text or configure a voice alarm;

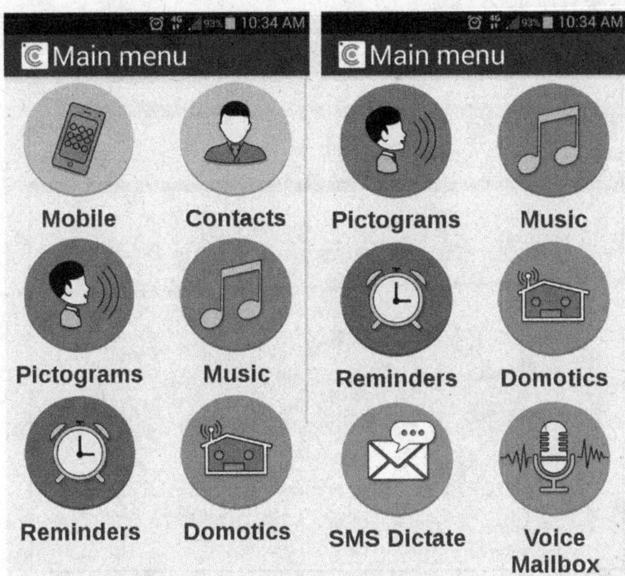

Fig. 2. Recording smart tags - main menu.

6. *Domotic controls*: pictograms that can automate a domotic action targeting the UPM's Living Lab domotic system;
7. *SMS Dictate*: after composing a text, the user can scan a contact tag and an SMS with the composed message will be sent;
8. *Voice mailbox*: allows to create a private communication channel from one to many users, where they cloud store voice messages that are saved on the cloud;

3 Public Transport Support

Regarding the travel support approach, we have developed an application to provide public transport support, called MY ROUTES. MY ROUTES is an on-route assistant composed by a Web-based portal and an Android mobile application for guiding persons with reduced mobility (due to cognitive impairments related to age, illnesses, foreign language, and/or other issues related to accessibility) while travelling by public transport, specifically inside the Madrid bus network.

3.1 The Web-Based Portal

The Web-based Application allows the carer and/or the end user to configure usual routes they use on daily basis and register them using a map interface similar to Google maps (see Fig. 3). The configured routes will be kept in the server protected and recovered by means of registry and password through the IN LIFE portal.

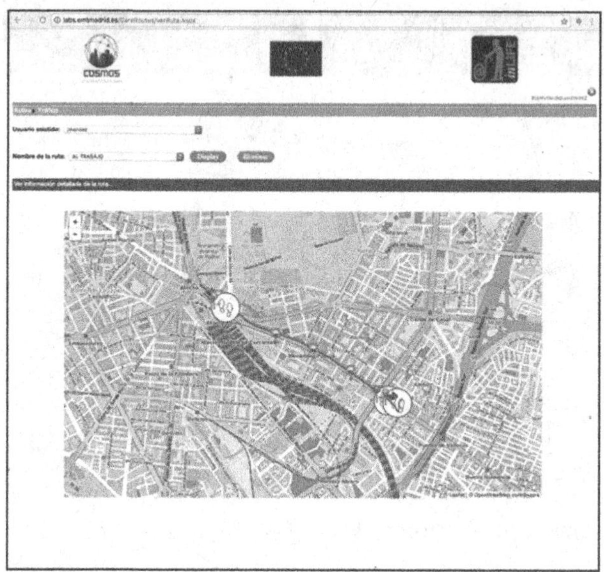

Fig. 3. Web-based portal.

The following are the options and functionalities endorsed within the application:

- Favorite routes (origin-destination) contain on-foot and on-board bus laps including bus changes.
- Favorite routes will be registered and associated to a particular user and features (time laps, days of week, duration, etc.).
- There is no restriction in the number of favorite routes.
- Favorite routes can be classified by an assorted number of personal utilities, for example: day of week, period of the day and number of invocations.
- The carer could use "Check-in" points to monitor the journey. These points can be defined by the user, the carer or both. Also, there are several "check points" already defined such as: route start and end point; and the stop where the user takes or leave the bus. The carer will be notified during the entire user's journey while on-route about their performance, and will be notified also by SMS if any contingency occurs.
- The selected routes could be visualized anytime on the Web Portal.

3.2 Mobile Application

The mobile application allows people with reduced mobility, to travel using the public transport with the confidence of not getting lost. The application will guide the users in their journey indicating which is the bus they need to take and the stop where they need to get off in order to reach the desired destination. Also, using the Wi-Fi access inside the bus, the application provides different resources to get essential information regarding the current state of the trip, such as the next stop or the remaining time to

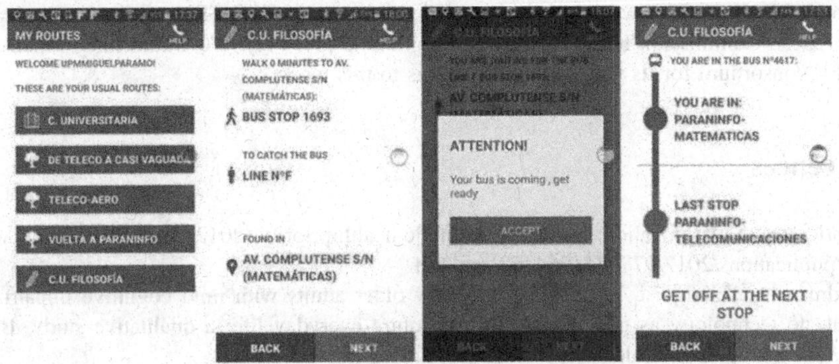

Fig. 4. MY ROUTES application screen shots.

reach the destination, etc. Using the smartphone GPS, the application sends the position of the user to the Web-based portal, so the carer obtains also information about the user's journey.

Figure 4 presents some screen shots of the functionalities of the mobile application listed below:

- The users can choose one route among their favorite routes.
- The chosen route is shown on users' mobile smartphone, showing all the stops in an accessible and easy to understand way.
- The tracking starts at the beginning of the initial point of the journey (first checking-point), including walking to the nearer stop.
- Every 30 s the mobile application checks the position of the user and verify if he/she is correctly located and follows the track of the chosen route.
- The carer will be informed about every deviation from user's destination. If any deviation occurs the user will also receive a SMS through the mobile smartphone notifying the deviation. This SMS message will include user's actual position.
- If the user is approaching the end of the route, he will be advised to get off the bus 200 m before the last stop.

4 Conclusions and Future Work

The Daily Function Assistant and the Public Transport Support modules have been technically tested and different versions have been released, in order to follow an iterative development cycle. The current final releases are widely compatible with different commercial Android devices and the different available versions of OS. Also different elements of the user interfaces were improved according to the recommendations from the end-users' organization in order to increase the usability of the overall solutions. The developed solutions are currently being tested within the IN LIFE project specifically in the Spanish pilot site, which will last at least 10 months. After the end of all IN LIFE pilots, different types of analysis (e.g. cost-effectiveness, cost-benefit, usability, effect on care provision and QoL, etc.) will be conducted and published accordingly.

Acknowledgments. This work has been carried out as part of IN LIFE, a project co-funded by the European Commission under the H2020 Programme (643442). We would like to thank the IN LIFE consortium for its valuable contributions to this work.

References

1. World Health Organization: Dementia: a public health priority (2012). http://whqlibdoc.who.int/publications/2012/9789241564458_eng.pdf
2. Hedman, A., Lindqvist, E., Nygård, L.: How older adults with mild cognitive impairment relate to technology as part of present and future everyday life: a qualitative study. BMC Geriatr. **16**, 73 (2016). doi:10.1186/s12877-016-0245-y
3. Panou, M., Cabrera, M.F., Bekiaris, E., Touliou, K.: ICT services for prolonging independent living of the elderly with cognitive impairments-IN LIFE concept. In: Studies in Health Technology and Informatics Assistive Technology. Studies in health technology and informatics Assistive Technology, vol. 217, September 2015. IOS Press (2015). ISBN 978-1-61499-565-4 (print) | 978-1-61499-566-1. doi:10.3233/978-1-61499-566-1-659
4. Anna Ekström, Ulrika Ferm, Christina Samuelsson. Digital communication support and Alzheimer's disease. Dementia. Sage journals. 1–21 (2015). ISSN: 1471-3012. Online ISSN: 1741-2684. doi:10.1177/1471301215615456
5. Montalvá Colomer, J.B., Cabrera-Umpiérrez, M.F., Ríos Pérez, S., Páramo del Castrillo, M., Arredondo Waldmeyer, M.T.: Developing an augmentative mobile communication system. In: Miesenberger, K., Karshmer, A., Penaz, P., Zagler, W. (eds.) ICCHP 2012. LNCS, vol. 7383, pp. 269–274. Springer, Heidelberg (2012). doi:10.1007/978-3-642-31534-3_41. ISBN: 978-3-642-31533-6. ISSN:0302-9743

Mining User Experience Dimensions from Mental Illness Apps

Jamil Hussain and Sungyoung Lee(✉)

Department of Computer Engineering, Kyung Hee University Seocheon-dong, Giheung-gu, Yongin-si, Gyeonggi-do 446-701, Republic of Korea
{jamil,sylee}@oslab.khu.ac.kr

Abstract. Mental illness is prevalent, the primary cause of disability worldwide, and regardless of the extensive treatment choices. Mobile apps provide greater support for depression treatment that eliminates the communication barriers. This perspective can be dropped with poor application design. Our goal is to mining the user experience (UX) dimensions from top-n mental illness apps reviews that will help to design the better application for persons with severe mental illness (SMI) and cognitive deficits. In this paper, we extracted the key UX dimension from a huge corpus of mental illness apps reviews using unsupervised Latent Dirichlet Analysis (LDA). Finally, LDA uncovered 20 UX dimensions that need to consider for mental illness app design in order to promote the positive UX by reducing the cognitive load of app end users.

Keywords: Mobile application · Cognitive impairment · mHealth · mHealth design · Severe mental illness · User experience · Usability

1 Introduction

Mental illness, the major contributor in disability worldwide. Mental illness is the fifth greatest contributor to the global burden of disease. It disrupts the individual's mood, cognitive and language styles, ability to work and routine activities. Some individuals might not even know what's going on, especially in the initial episode of psychosis [1]. Globally, medical resources are utilized to overcome the consequences of mental illness by strengthening health system, including mobile health (mHealth) applications. mHealth can offer different services such as self-assessment, self-help support, notification to promote positive behavior, symptoms monitoring, therapy, education how to cope with SMI, skills training, gamification for user engagement, and much more [2, 3].

However, these features benefits may be drop with poor app design. Research shows [4] that the usability of website application heavily depends on the user ability, so called mental model. Mental model is a cognitive representation of ideas, beliefs, image, and verbal that leads to form user experience [5]. These representations of user perception explain cause and effect and conduct us to expect certain results, and move us to act in certain ways. Cognitive abilities strongly bound by the application usage, such as researching, reading and task completion. The study found that person with depressive disorder have neurocognitive deficits such as lack of perception and attention, which

M. Mokhtari et al. (Eds.): ICOST 2017, LNCS 10461, pp. 13–20, 2017.
DOI: 10.1007/978-3-319-66188-9_2

deals with object relationship, and episodic memory, which deals with the learning process, and recall from learning experience [6].

A standard website design model is already published [7, 8] that focus on website design such as content organization, hypermedia, links organization and its deeps level, and pages distribution and its styling. Few studies focus on accessibility issues for the persons with cognitive deficits [5, 9, 10]. However, we need design model for mHealth that cover the all aspects of user's having depressive disorder.

There are thousands of mental illness apps having user reviews are available at distribution platforms such as iTune and google play store. User reviews contain useful information related to usability and user experience, which is freely available at anywhere, anytime [11].

In this study, we attempted to extract important information of user experience design from mental illness apps reviews that influence the positive user experience of mental illness apps for the persons with SMI problem.

The rest of the paper is structured as follows. In Sect. 2, the proposed framework is described. Section 3 is about the implementation, results and validation of study. Finally, Sect. 4 concluded the study.

2 Method

We use the following framework to extract the UX dimension from the mental illness apps as shown in Fig. 1, which described the overall process used in the study.

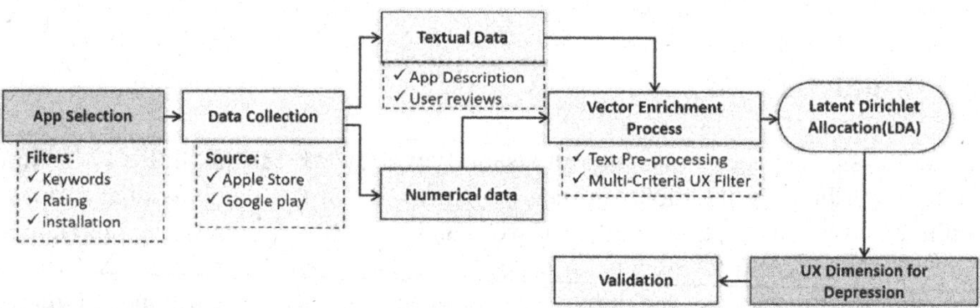

Fig. 1. Framework of UX dimension extraction from depression apps for depression application design

2.1 Apps Selection

For mining the user experience (UX) dimension, we made the selection of applications in 4 steps using systematic review [12]. First, downloaded the mHealth application repository [13] having comprehensive details of health and fitness apps collected from iTune and google play store. Second, exclusion using keywords (mental illness, depression, and stress)filters. Third, for top n apps selection, other filters such as average rating, user rating, and number of installing/download used. Forth, 5 coders manually review the description of filtered apps and apply further inclusion criteria using the MARS scale

[14], which having four dimensions: engagement, functionality, aesthetic and information quality. Apps are included that's related to mental illness, depression, stress, anxiety, and bipolar disorder for future study. The selection process is shown in Fig. 2.

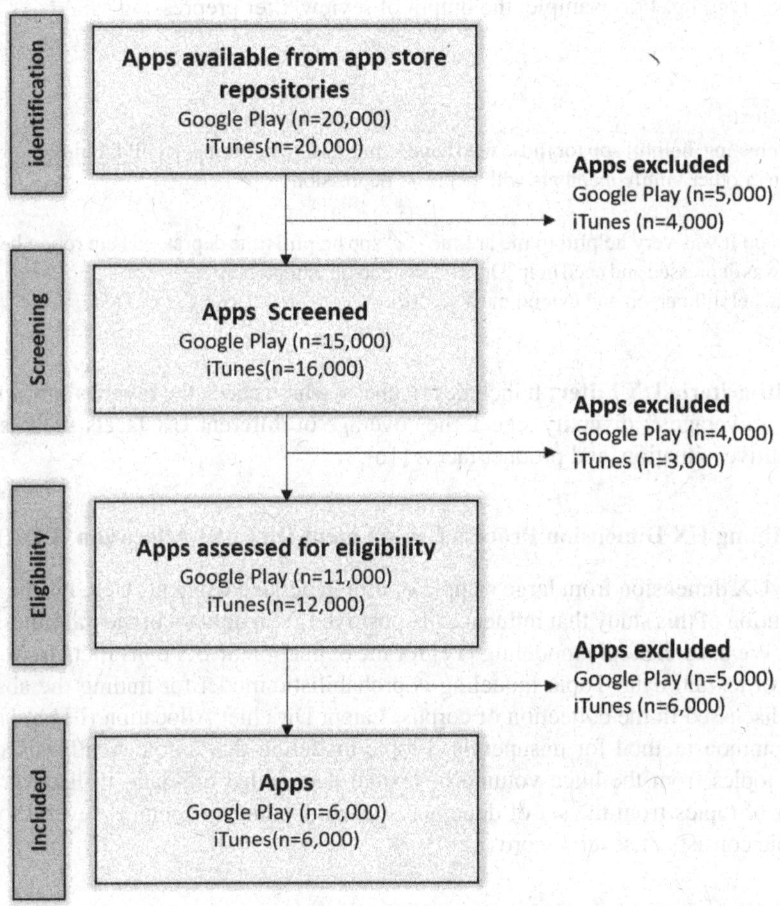

Fig. 2. Selection criteria process flow chart

2.2 Data Collection

We developed the crawler program that's collected user reviews from selected applications. We used Breadth-First search starts from the first app in the selected list, and crawled all app page by paring the HTML tag to extract the app's information such as app description, rating. Next at each app description page, we collected all user reviews against that app. Finally, the collected data are stored as dataset for text analysis.

2.3 Vector Enrichment Process

- **Text Pre-processing:** text pre-processing includes English word filter, spell checker and auto correction, tokenization, stop words removal, stemming, and Part-of-speech (POS) tagging. For example, the output of review after prepressing as:

Review text	Pre-processing
"An interesting, helpful app for those who have children or other family members with depression"	"interesting helpful app child family member depression"
"Great app It was very helpful to me at time when I was depressed and need help. Dr. Robert is a very helpful person and extend me a great help"	"app helpful time depressed help robert helpful person extend help"

- **Multi-criteria UX Filter:** It includes richness, which check the reviews subjectivity [15]; coverage & diversity, check the coverage of different UX facets such as user cognitive, situation, and product facets [16].

2.4 Mining UX Dimension Process Using Latent Dirichlet Allocation (LDA)

Mining UX dimension from large sample of user generated Content (UGC) is the main contribution of this study that influence the positive UX in domain of mental illness app design. We used the topic modeling [17] for the extraction of UX constructs from huge corpus of textual data. Topic modeling is probabilistic model for finding the abstract topics discussed in the collection of corpus. Latent Dirichlet Allocation (LDA) [18] is most common method for unsupervised topic modeling that automatically discovers hidden topics from the huge volume of textual data called big-data. It discovers the number of topics from the set of documents, each documents contains several topics, and topic consists of several words.

3 Results

In this section we described the extracted dimensions of UX for mental illness application. We validated the extracted dimensions by comparative analysis with prior studies on depression application. Topic modeling is performed using KNIME, which provide the open source analytics platform [19]. The workflow created based on proposed framework, includes corpus reading, text preprocessing, multi-criteria UX filters, and topic extractor (LDA) components as shown in Fig. 3.

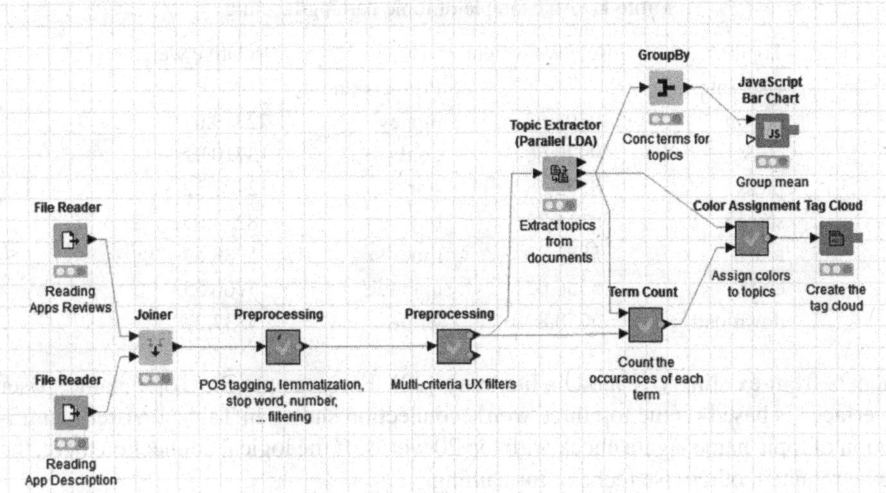

Fig. 3. KnimeLDA workflow

3.1 Dimension of UX for Mental Illness Application

We apply the LDA for the extraction of effective UX dimension from the collected mental illness apps description and user reviews. The LDA extract 20 topics and each topic having 30 words with the relative weight. The word cloud of extracted words is shown in Fig. 4.

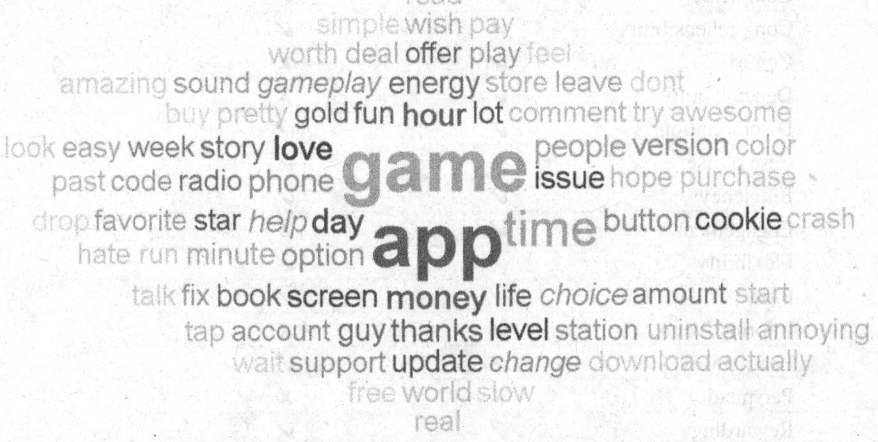

Fig. 4. Word cloud of apps description and user reviews

For Topic labeling (naming), peer reviews was conducted by using the word connection among the topic words. Labels are barrows from our prior work, developed UX

Table 1. An example of topic naming/labeling

Topic	Relative weight		Relative weight
User interface		Pro version	
button	30702.62	money	22219.07
click	9930.66	gold	13710.02
press	8373.58	star	12487.22 3
screen	8115.33	buy	8254.09
touch	5881.83	time	5988.69
error	5356.02	upgrade	5766.55
download	5050.8	waste	5337.27

models from existing UX models literature [20]. For example the Topic name "User Interface" is based on the top three words connection shown in Table 1. After identification of topic name, again check with top 20 words. If the logical connection there, the name retained, otherwise recheck for naming.

Table 2. A comparison of dimensions between LDA analysis and prior studies.

Dimensions/Constructs	LDA Analysis	Prior studies
Accessibility	✔	✘
Attachment	✔	✘
Competence	✔	✘
Complexity	✔	✔
Comprehensibility	✘	✔
Context	✔	✘
Dependability	✔	✘
Disorientation	✔	✔
Ease of use	✘	✔
Efficiency	✔	✔
Engagement	✔	✘
Flexibility	✔	✔
Flow	✔	✔
Informativeness	✔	✘
Learnability	✔	✔
Perspicuity	✘	✘
Rewarding	✔	✔
Satisfaction	✔	✔
Simplicity	✔	✔
Stimulation	✔	✘

Notes: ✔ = included; X = not included. Jaccard coefficient: 0.45. We compared the dimensions derived from LDA with the FEDM [2, 5].

3.2 Validation

We compared the extracted dimension using LDA analysis with existing studies on mHealth application UX dimension. We used the Jaccard coefficient similarity [21] to check the degree of dimension overlapping. The Jaccard coefficient is calculated as

$$JC = \frac{|D_{LDA} \cap D_{Ex}|}{|D_{LDA} \cup D_{Ex}|} \tag{1}$$

Where D_{LDA} dimension is extracted using automatic LDA analysis and D_{EX} is dimension mentioned on existing studies.

The higher the Jaccard coefficient's value, the higher the degree of overlap between the two sets of dimensions. The Jaccard coefficient of our study is 0.45 as shown in Table 2.

This concludes that our study inferred new latent variables or dimensions from the app description and reviews that have been ignored by earlier studies. We claim that our study outcomes are more reliable for generalization due to a large corpus textual data.

4 Conculsion

In this paper, we propose a framework for the extraction of UX dimension for mental illness app in mHealth domain. For Latent dimension extraction, our proposed LDA identifies important dimensions that are not found using traditional methods such as interviews and questionnaires in mheath domain. Our work have some limitations such as, our model ignores infrequent words, that might be very important in mhealth apps, and need large coupes of textual data for better results.

Acknowledgments. This work was supported by the Industrial Core Technology Development Program (10049079, Develop of mining core technology exploiting personal big data) funded by the Ministry of Trade, Industry and Energy (MOTIE, Korea).

References

1. Hussain, J., Ali, M., Bilal, H.S.M., Afzal, M., Ahmad, H.F., Banos, O., Lee, S.: SNS based predictive model for depression. In: Geissbühler, A., Demongeot, J., Mokhtari, M., Abdulrazak, B., Aloulou, H. (eds.) ICOST 2015. LNCS, vol. 9102, pp. 349–354. Springer, Cham (2015). doi:10.1007/978-3-319-19312-0_34
2. Stoll, R.D., Pina, A.A., Gary, K., Amresh, A.: Usability of a smartphone application to support the prevention and early intervention of anxiety in youth. Cogn. Behav. Pract. (2017)
3. Shen, N., Levitan, M.-J., Johnson, A., Bender, J.L., Hamilton-Page, M., Jadad, A.A.R., Wiljer, D.: Finding a depression app: a review and content analysis of the depression app marketplace. JMIR MHealth UHealth. **3**, e16 (2015)
4. Dalal, N.P., Quible, Z., Wyatt, K.: Cognitive design of home pages: an experimental study of comprehension on the World Wide Web. Inf. Process. Manag. **36**, 607–621 (2000)

5. Rotondi, A.J., Sinkule, J., Haas, G.L., Spring, M.B., Litschge, C.M., Newhill, C.E., Ganguli, R., Anderson, C.M.: Designing websites for persons with cognitive deficits: Design and usability of a psychoeducational intervention for persons with severe mental illness. Psychol. Serv. **4**, 202 (2007)
6. Vinogradov, S.: Cognition in schizophrenia: impairments, importance, and treatment strategies. Am. J. Psychiatry **160**, 404–405 (2003)
7. Leavitt, M.O., Shneiderman, B.: Research-based web design & usability guidelines. US Department of Health and Human Services (2006)
8. Board, Access: Electronic and information technology accessibility standards (2000). Accessed 13 Dec 2000
9. Friedman, M.G., Bryen, D.N.: Web accessibility design recommendations for people with cognitive disabilities. Technol. Disabil. **19**, 205–212 (2007)
10. Stjernswärd, S., Hansson, L.: User value and usability of a web-based mindfulness intervention for families living with mental health problems. Health Soc. Care Community **25**, 700–709 (2017)
11. Guo, Y., Barnes, S.J., Jia, Q.: Mining meaning from online ratings and reviews: tourist satisfaction analysis using latent Dirichlet allocation. Tour. Manag. **59**, 467–483 (2017)
12. Bardus, M., van Beurden, S.B., Smith, J.R., Abraham, C.: A review and content analysis of engagement, functionality, aesthetics, information quality, and change techniques in the most popular commercial apps for weight management. Int. J. Behav. Nutr. Phys. Act. **13**, 35 (2016)
13. Xu, W., Liu, Y.: mHealthApps: a repository and database of mobile health apps. JMIR MHealth UHealth **3**, e28 (2015)
14. Stoyanov, S.R., Hides, L., Kavanagh, D.J., Zelenko, O., Tjondronegoro, D., Mani, M.: Mobile app rating scale: a new tool for assessing the quality of health mobile apps. JMIR Mhealth Uhealth **3**(1), e27 (2015). doi:10.2196/mhealth.3422. This Artic. Discusses Dev. Psychom. Prop. Mob. Appl. Rate Scale MARS Eval. Qual. Mob. Health Appl.
15. Chenlo, J.M., Losada, D.E.: An empirical study of sentence features for subjectivity and polarity classification. Inf. Sci. **280**, 275–288 (2014)
16. Liang, Y., Liu, Y., Loh, H.T.: Exploring online reviews for user experience modeling. In: DS 75-7: Proceedings of the 19th International Conference on Engineering Design (ICED 2013), Design for Harmonies, vol. 7. Human Behaviour in Design, Seoul, Korea, 19–22 August 2013
17. Zou, J., Xu, L., Yang, M., Zhang, X., Yang, D.: Towards comprehending the non-functional requirements through developers' eyes: an exploration of Stack Overflow using topic analysis. Inf. Softw. Technol. **84**, 19–32 (2017)
18. Blei, D.M., Ng, A.Y., Jordan, M.I.: Latent Dirichlet allocation. J. Mach. Learn. Res. **3**, 993–1022 (2003)
19. KNIME | Open for Innovation. https://www.knime.org/
20. Hussain, J., Lee, S.: Identifying user experience (UX) dimensions from UX literature reviews. 한국정보과학회학술발표논문집, pp. 323–324 (2016)
21. Niwattanakul, S., Singthongchai, J., Naenudorn, E., Wanapu, S.: Using of Jaccard coefficient for keywords similarity. In: Proceedings of the International Multiconference of Engineers and Computer Scientists, p. 6 (2013)

Unobtrusive Technological Approach for Continuous Behavior Change Detection Toward Better Adaptation of Clinical Assessments and Interventions for Elderly People

Firas Kaddachi[1(✉)], Hamdi Aloulou[1], Bessam Abdulrazak[2], Philippe Fraisse[1], and Mounir Mokhtari[3]

[1] Montpellier Laboratory of Informatics, Robotics and Microelectronics (LIRMM), Montpellier, France
{firas.kaddachi,hamdi.aloulou,philippe.fraisse}@lirmm.fr

[2] University of Sherbrooke, Quebec, Canada
bessam.abdulrazak@usherbrooke.ca

[3] Institut Mines-Telecom (IMT), Paris, France
mounir.mokhtari@mines-telecom.fr

Abstract. Behavior change indicates continuous decline in physical, cognitive and emotional status of elderly people. Early detection of behavior change is major enabler for service providers to adapt their services and improve the quality of life of elderly people. Nowadays, existing psychogeriatric scales and questionnaires are insufficient to observe all possible changes at a daily basis. Therefore, we propose a technological approach for behavior change detection, that employs unobtrusive ambient technologies to follow up elderly people over long periods. In fact, we study significant behavior change indicators (*e.g.,* sleep impairments, visits and go out) and investigate statistical techniques that distinguish transient and continuous changes in monitored behavior. Furthermore, we present a preliminary validation of our approach through results based on correlations between our technological observations and medical observations of two-year nursing home deployment.

Keywords: Behavior change detection · Elderly people · Unobtrusive technologies · Statistical analysis techniques

1 Introduction

Detecting behavior change in early evolution stages is keystone for better adaptation of provided services to elderly people and improvement of their quality of life. In fact, aging process is associated with significant behavior change and continuous decline in physical and cognitive capacities. Existing psychogeriatric methods diagnose limited number of possible changes at assessment time and in

M. Mokhtari et al. (Eds.): ICOST 2017, LNCS 10461, pp. 21–33, 2017.
DOI: 10.1007/978-3-319-66188-9_3

assessment place [1]. We propose a technological approach for behavior change detection that uses unobtrusive technologies to monitor elderly people over long periods in their living environment and detect possibilities of long-term changes in their behavior.

Behavior change is a continuous modification or transformation in the way and manner of executing activities of daily living [2]. Behavior change is associated with mobility impairments [3], memory troubles [4], eating difficulties [5], and problematic management of household and personal finances [6, 7].

Early detection of behavior changes is major enabler to adapt provided services and change treatments [8]. Significant information on behavior change allows to conduct more advanced medical assessments, change medical equipment, improve nutritional program and adapt living environment. This delays the negative evolution of their autonomy problems and enhances their quality of life at home [9].

We propose in this paper a technological approach for behavior change detection that targets long-term changes at temporal scale (*i.e.*, compared to past habits). We employ unobtrusive ambient technologies (*e.g.*, movement sensors) to monitor elderly people without affecting their privacy and interfering with their natural behavior.

Compared to our previous work [10], we (i) investigate a new bootstrap-based technique that differentiates between transient and continuous changes, (ii) study new behavior change indicators such as sleep impairments, visits and go out, and (iii) discuss new results based on correlations between our technological observations and medical observations of nursing-home team such as mobility, nutrition and cognition problems.

Following, Sect. 2 presents state of the art behavior change detection methods. Sections 3 and 4 introduce our behavior change detection methodology and implementation approach. Section 5 discusses second validation of our approach. Section 6 concludes this paper.

2 Related Work

Psychologists and geriatrics often use scales and questionnaires for behavior change detection, whereas researchers propose technological methods to detect behavior changes, using environmental technologies (*e.g.*, movement sensors, bed sensors, cameras and microphones) and wearable technologies (*e.g.*, smart phone, smart watch and neurosensors).

Following, we discuss existing psychogeriatric and technological methods for behavior change detection (Table 1). In fact, psychogeriatric methods are often used in the medical field, but present certain inconveniences (*e.g.*, hard to recall all past events at assessment time). Furthermore, technological methods has been successfully integrated in the medical field, but (i) mainly focus on short-term change detection, (ii) retrospectively detect changes in advanced stages, (iii) consider changes at population scale, or (iv) use inconvenient technologies (Table 1).

Table 1. Comparison of behavior change detection methods

	Psychogeriatric methods [3–6, 11]	Technological methods [12–25]	Our proposed approach
Automated detection	no	yes	yes
Objective observation	yes/no	yes	yes
Unobtrusive monitoring	no	yes/no	yes
Long-term changes	yes	yes/no	yes
Early changes	yes/no	yes/no	yes
Personal changes	yes	yes/no	yes

2.1 Psychogeriatric Methods

In the medical field, formal scales and questionnaires are often used to diagnose abnormal behavior changes. Clinicians ask patients to reply to given questions or perform required tasks, such as "How many falls did you have in the last six months?" [6] and "Could you please get up and walk three meters away!" [3]. Analyzing elderly people replies and their task execution allows to determine possible behavior changes.

Among existing psychogeriatric scales, Get-up-and-Go scale is used to detect mobility impairments [3]. Mini Mental State Examination (MMSE) is applied to diagnose memory troubles [4]. Clinicians evaluate nutritional status with Mini Nutritional Assessment (MNA) [5]. They also diagnose autonomy problems with Autonomie Gerontologique et Groupes Iso-Ressources (AGGIR) [6]. Behavioral anomalies such as aggressiveness and anxiety are investigated using Behavioral Pathology in Alzheimer's Disease (BEHAVE-AD) [11].

These psychogeriatric assessments identify significant behavior change indicators. However, it is often difficult for elderly people to recall all past events at assessment time and move to assessment place at a daily basis. Their anxiety increases if they are not able to provide the right answers. Possible assessment inaccuracies can also occur due to subjective evaluation.

Our proposed approach employs technologies to remotely and unobtrusively monitor elderly people in their living environment at a daily basis. Unobtrusive ambient technologies do not affect elderly people privacy and do not interfere with their natural behavior. Therefore, our objective technological observations usefully enrich medical observations.

2.2 Technological Methods: Short-Term Change Detection

Technological solutions are proposed to detect short-term changes, such as falls, wandering at night, showering for too long and leaving the wash-room tap on [12–15]. In order to detect these anomalies, researchers apply classification and semantic techniques to analyze data collected from real deployments using wearable and environmental sensors.

Whereas these technological methods study snapshots of behavior in specific time periods, the novelty of our approach is studying overall behavior over long periods to identify long-term changes. Clinicians and caregivers are not only interested in diagnosing short-term anomalies, but also in analyzing their long-term evolution; e.g., diagnosing not only falls, but also investigating changes in fall frequency over months.

2.3 Technological Methods: Retrospective Change Detection

Further technological solutions are developed to retrospectively detect long-term changes after they occur; e.g., invite elderly people to a reflection session after six months of monitoring using electronic pillbox to either confirm their own-confidence in medication adherence or re-assess it [16], and invite clinicians to review bed sensor data and investigate potential correlations with health events (*e.g.*, falls, emergency room visits and hospitalizations) after they occur [17].

Whereas these technological methods retrospectively detect changes in advanced stages of their evolution, our proposed approach targets behavior changes in early stages of their evolution. In fact, early detection of behavior changes enables better adaptation of provided services and provides significant information for more advanced medical assessments and interventions [8].

2.4 Technological Methods: Population-Scale Change Detection

Further studies compare behavior of different populations for change detection. They investigate influence of mild cognitive impairments (MCI) on sleep quality using pressure mats [18], computer use using mouse events [19] and medication adherence using electronic pillbox [20]. It was reported that MCI patients have less disturbed sleep, use less frequently computers and present more risk of medication non-adherence than elderly people with higher cognitive function.

Whereas these technological methods compare different populations to identify segments of populations that show potential risk and require close monitoring, our proposed approach analyzes personal behavior and detects changes compared to past habits. In fact, personal change detection enables personalized health assessments and interventions.

2.5 Technological Methods: Obtrusive Change Detection

Researchers use wearable technologies to inspect personal behavior changes; e.g., wearable bracelets with RFID reader to detect changes in coffee making [21] and neurosensors placed on the scalp to detect wandering and falls from bed during sleep [22]. Furthermore, they study global video and audio statistics to identify changes in interpersonal interactions in nursing home [24], and apply online-based questionnaires to identify mental state changes toward depression [25].

These technological methods use obtrusive technologies (*e.g.*, wearable sensors, cameras, microphones and online-based questionnaires) to collect precise information on elderly people behavior. However, elderly people often reject wearable sensors and can not operate them [26], and refuse to complete daily questionnaires [25]. Furthermore, cameras and microphones capture video and audio sequences that affect the privacy. Therefore, our proposed approach uses unobtrusive technologies (*e.g.,* movement sensors) that are deployed in the environment, do not affect the privacy and do not interfere with the natural behavior.

3 Proposed Behavior Change Detection Methodology

We propose a technological behavior change detection methodology that analyzes elderly people behavior over long periods, in order to identify long-term behavior changes associated with continuous decline in their physical and cognitive abilities.

Fig. 1. Examples of behavior change indicators

Based on internationally-validated psychogeriatric scales, we identify significant behavior change indicators (*e.g.,* physical, cognitive, nutritional and social activities) (Fig. 1), that can be monitored via unobtrusive ambient technologies. We analyze these indicators considering different dimensions (*e.g.,* quantity, duration, time and place metrics) to distinguish between transient and continuous behavior changes. In order to validate detected changes, we correlate them with health records (*e.g.,* hospitalizations, falls, diseases and medication change) and context information (*e.g.* weather conditions).

3.1 Behavior Change Indicators

We have investigated internationally-validated psychogeriatric scales (*e.g.,* AGGIR [6], MNA [5] and NPI [27]) to identify significant behavior change indicators that can be monitored via unobtrusive ambient technologies (*e.g.,* movement, contact, proximity, vibration and pressure sensors for indoor monitoring, and beacons for outdoor monitoring).

Among these behavior change indicators (Fig. 1), we identify significant **activities of daily living** that require important physical and cognitive efforts from elderly people, such as managing household, preparing meals, dressing and hygiene [6,7]. We also consider **motor behaviors**, such as moving indoors and outdoors, getting up, turning around and walking [3]. Furthermore, **cognitive tasks** (*e.g.*, learning, language and managing financial situation) are associated with temporal orientation, spatial orientation, attention, calculation and construction [4]. In addition, we study **social behaviors**, (*e.g.*, communicating with others, using means of transport and shopping) [6,7], **nutritional activities** (*e.g.*, serving oneself and eating) [5], and **mood and emotions** [28] that correlate with physical and cognitive functions.

3.2 Analysis Metrics

We analyze behavior change indicators considering different dimensions (*e.g.*, quantity, duration, time and place metrics) to quantify way and manner of performing these identified indicators. Quantifying these indicators enables to distinguish transient and continuous changes.

Quantity refers to number and amount of behavior execution (*e.g.*, number of friend visits decreases due to social isolation). **Duration** is related to length of behavior execution (*e.g.*, duration of preparing meals increases due to cognitive impairments). **Time** refers to start and end times of behavior execution (*e.g.*, sleep hours are irregular due to sleep troubles). **Place** describes where behavior is executed (*e.g.*, detected falls outdoors become more frequent due to fear of going outside).

3.3 Correlation Variables

In order to validate detected changes in our technological observations, we correlate them with significant health records and context information. Whereas **health records** (*e.g.*, falls, diseases and hospitalizations) increase the probability of behavior changes [6], **context information** (*e.g.*, changing one's house and family status) allow better understanding of detected behavior changes. In fact, correlating our technological observations with medical and context observations is essential to evaluate the relevance of detected changes.

4 Implementation Approach

We integrate our behavior change detection approach in our ambient assisted living platform UbiSMART [10,13].

UbiSMART analyzes data collected by environmental sensors to identify anomalies in monitored behaviors and provides new services for elderly people (*e.g.*, sending notifications to caregivers in case anomalies are detected) (Fig. 2). Following, we discuss the implementation phases of our behavior change detection approach:

- **Deployment** refers to installing our hardware infrastructure in the living environment (*e.g.*, environmental sensors, gateways and internet access points).

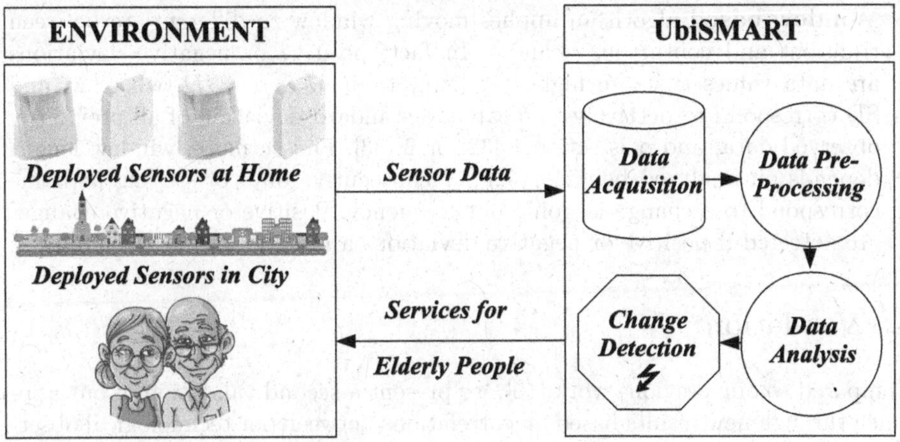

Fig. 2. Implementation phases of our behavior change detection approach

- **Data Acquisition** consists in transmitting environmental sensor data via internet to our remote database for permanent storage.
- **Data Pre-Processing** is essential to extract significant inferred data from raw sensor data (*e.g.*, movement sensor data allow to infer activity periods).
- **Data Analysis** applies statistical algorithms to analyze inferred data and differentiate between transient and continuous changes.

In order to analyze data, we investigate statistical algorithms that are robust to outliers and detect continuous changes at a daily basis as early as possible. Following, we discuss three algorithms investigated in our research; cusum-based [29,30], bootstrap-based [31] and window-based [32,33] algorithms. These algorithms apply different filters on detected deviations and identify changes with different granularity:

- **CUSUM-based** algorithm consists of a reference phase and an analysis phase [29,30]. In the reference phase, initial data enable to compute reference parameters that will condition change detection in the analysis phase (*e.g.*, mean and standard deviation). In the analysis phase, cumulative sums for positive and negative deviations are recursively computed to identify continuous changes.
- **Bootstrap-based** algorithm uses an iterative combination of a CUSUM analysis and a bootstrapping analysis (*i.e.*, random re-ordering of data) [31]. In the CUSUM analysis, cumulative sums of differences between data values and data mean are computed to determine the magnitude of the change. In the bootstrapping analysis, 1000 bootstraps are generated by randomly re-ordering original data values to detect a change if at least 95% of these bootstraps have a lower magnitude of change. For each detected change point, data is divided into two new segments and the bootstrapping analysis is repeated to detect additional change points.

- **Window-based** algorithm applies moving window to differentiate between transient and continuous changes. In fact, positive or negative deviations are data values that are higher or lower than $M \pm \alpha * SD$, where M and SD correspond respectively to mean and standard deviation of all previously observed data, and α is set to 1 [32] or 2 [33]. Furthermore, window length depends on analyzed behavior; e.g., 7 consecutive days of staying at home correspond to a change in going out frequency. Positive or negative changes are detected if positive or negative deviations are consecutively detected.

5 Validation

Compared to our previous work [10], we present a second validation of our approach through new results based on correlations between our technological observations and medical observations of two-year nursing-home deployment. In fact, we investigate new behavior change indicators (*e.g.,* sleep impairments, visits and go out) that are monitored via movement sensors (Fig. 3). In order to evaluate the relevance of detected behavior changes, we correlate them with significant health records such as mobility, cognition and nutrition problems.

Fig. 3. Deployment of movement sensors in nursing home rooms

5.1 Data Collection

During two years, we deploy movement sensors in bedrooms and bathrooms of 9 elderly people living in a french nursing home and having an average age 88 years (Table 2).

We employ Marmitek MS13E movement sensors (Fig. 3) that use X10 communication protocol with a frequency of 433 Mhz. In fact, these movement sensors are fired each 10 s after movements are detected within a range of 30 meters. They have 1 year battery life and embedded light sensors that configure movement sensing during light and darkness periods. Furthermore, we simply define an activity period as a period of consecutive movement sensor firings, that are transmitted with time difference less than 1 minute.

Table 2. Resident gender, age and monitoring period

Resident	Gender	Age	Period (months)
A	M	90	5
B	M	89	5
C	M	81	14
D	F	84	11
E	F	95	12
F	F	85	23
G	F	87	23
H	F	92	8
I	F	92	14

5.2 Data Analysis

Collected movement sensor data allow to (i) analyze behavior of elderly people over long periods, (ii) study significant indicators of behavior change (e.g., sleep impairments, room entries, visits and go out) that are associated with physical and cognitive impairments [3,6], and (iii) detect significant possibilities of changes in analyzed behavior by applying different statistical change detection techniques (Sect. 4).

Daily activity periods enable to analyze **sleep impairments** by selecting all sensors and limiting time interval at night (*e.g.*, from 0 h to 6 h). Furthermore, they allow to follow-up **entries to specific rooms** at home by selecting specific sensor (*e.g.*, kitchen, living room, bedroom, bathroom or toilet). In fact, we measure daily duration of all activity periods when person is **alone at home** (*i.e.*, visit and go out periods are not considered, because they have an increasing and a decreasing influence on activity periods respectively).

We analyze social activities at a monthly basis by computing **visit** and **go out** days. Whereas visits are detected based on parallel activity periods in different rooms at home, go out is detected based on long inactivity periods (*e.g.*, we set minimum go out duration to 6 hours, in order to discard sleep periods where few periodic movements are detected even when elderly people are lying in bed).

5.3 Results and Discussion

In order to evaluate the relevance of detected behavior changes (*e.g.*, changes in sleep impairments, room entries, visits and go out), we study their correlation with medical-team observations:

- **Sleep impairment** changes are associated with anxiety periods, health problems (*e.g.*, pain in leg and respiratory problems) and medication change; e.g., two decreasing changes are detected in sleep impairments of resident C on

2016-02-29 and 2016-06-03 and are associated to less anxiety felt by resident C months after undesired entry to nursing home on 2015-09-10 (Fig. 4).
- **Room entry** changes are associated with health problems (*e.g.*, cold and cough, pain in leg and respiratory problems), depression periods and nutritional problems (*e.g.*, weight loss); e.g., a decreasing change is detected in room activity periods of resident B on 2015-07-16 due to pain in leg, and an increasing change is detected in room activity periods of resident F due to wandering periods associated with Alzheimer on 2016-04-07.
- **Visit and go out** changes are associated with caregiver visits when health problems occur (*e.g.*, heart problems and anxiety periods), and go out with family members for dinner and local events; e.g., a decreasing change in visits and an increasing change in go out are detected in same month 2016-05 for resident E after several invitations to family events.

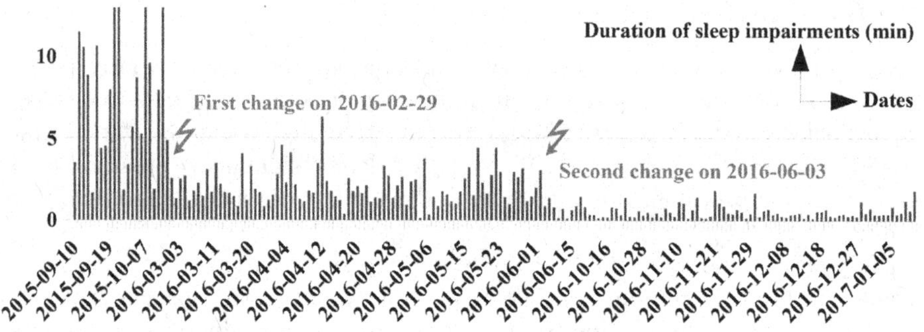

Fig. 4. Detected changes in daily evolution of sleep impairments for resident C

Based on medical-team evaluation, we determine the relevance of detected behavior changes (*i.e.*, the percentage of detected changes that are relevant to medical assessments and interventions). Whereas the precision of bootstrap-based algorithm is 68.55%, the precision of cusum-based and window-based (1SD with W = 3 and 2SD with W = 1) is 19.45%, 23.65% and 11.4% respectively. Considering that the bootstrapping analysis enables more precise recognition of continuous changes, bootstrap-based algorithm is more robust to outliers and detects relevant changes that are missed by cusum-based and window-based algorithms.

6 Conclusion

We propose in this paper a technological approach for behavior change detection that targets long-term behavior changes detected via unobtrusive ambient technologies. In fact, we monitor elderly people over long periods to identify continuous behavior changes associated with continuous decline in physical and cognitive abilities.

In order to validate our technological observations, we correlate them with real medical observations of two-year nursing home deployment. Using unobtrusive movement sensors deployed in bedrooms and bathrooms of nursing home residents, we collect real data on significant behavior change indicators (*e.g.*, sleep impairments, room entries, visits and going outside). Using statistical change detection techniques, we differentiate between transient and continuous behavior changes. Based on medical team feedback, 68.55% of detected changes are significantly correlated with their medical observations (*e.g.*, mobility, cognition and nutrition problems).

In the context of the European project City4Age [34], we are improving our behavior change detection. The City4Age project investigates data generated by technologies deployed in urban areas, in order to provide new adaptable services for elderly people. The objective is to capture frailty of elderly people, and provide subsequent individualized interventions.

Acknowledgement. We give our special thanks to Saint Vincent de Paul nursing home in Occagnes, France. Our deployment in this nursing home is also supported by VHP inter@ctive project and the Quality Of Life chair.

Our work is part of the European project City4Age that received funding from the Horizon 2020 research and innovation program under grant agreement number 689731.

References

1. Holsinger, T., et al.: Does this patient have dementia? JAMA **297**(21), 2391–2404 (2007)
2. Cao, L.: In-depth behavior understanding and use: the behavior informatics approach. Inf. Sci. **180**(17), 3067–3085 (2010)
3. Mathias, S., et al.: Balance in elderly patients: the "get-up and go" test. Arch. Phys. Med. Rehabil. **67**(6), 387–389 (1986)
4. Cockrell, J.R., Folstein, M.F.: Mini-mental state examination. Principles and Practice of Geriatric Psychiatry, pp. 140–141 (2002)
5. Vellas, B., et al.: The mini nutritional assessment (mna) and its use in grading the nutritional state of elderly patients. Nutrition **15**(2), 116–122 (1999)
6. Lafont, S., et al.: Relation entre performances cognitives globales et dépendance évaluée par la grille aggir. Revue d'épidémiologie et de santé publique **47**(1), 7–17 (1999)
7. Barberger-Gateau, P., et al.: Instrumental activities of daily living as a screening tool for cognitive impairment and dementia in elderly community dwellers. J. Am. Geriatr. Soc. **40**(11), 1129–1134 (1992)
8. Boockvar, K.S., Lachs, M.S.: Predictive value of nonspecific symptoms for acute illness in nursing home residents. J. Am. Geriatr. Soc. **51**(8), 1111–1115 (2003)
9. Ridley, S.: The recognition and early management of critical illness. Ann. R. Coll. Surg. Engl. **87**(5), 315 (2005)
10. Kaddachi, F., et al.: Technological approach for behavior change detection toward better adaptation of services for elderly people. BIOSTEC **2017**, 96 (2017)

11. Reisberg, B., et al.: Behavioral pathology in alzheimer's disease (behave-ad) rating scale. Int. Psychogeriatr. **8**(S3), 301–308 (1997)
12. Bourke, A.K., et al.: Fall detection algorithms for real-world falls harvested from lumbar sensors in the elderly population: a machine learning approach. In: 2016 IEEE 38th Annual International Conference of the Engineering in Medicine and Biology Society (EMBC), pp. 3712–3715. IEEE (2016)
13. Aloulou, H., et al.: Deployment of assistive living technology in a nursing home environment: methods and lessons learned. BMC Med. Inform. Decis. Mak. **13**(1), 42 (2013)
14. Singtel: Monitor and watch you elderly family members' daily activities with singtel's smart home solutions (2017). https://www.singtelshop.com/smarthome-yuhua
15. SeniorHome: Eva est une plateforme logicielle qui fonctione sur la base de capteurs repartis dans le domicile (2017). http://seniorhome.fr/
16. Lee, M.L., Dey, A.K.: Sensor-based observations of daily living for aging in place. Pers. Ubiquit. Comput. **19**(1), 27–43 (2015)
17. Rantz, M., Skubic, M., Miller, S., Krampe, J.: Using technology to enhance aging in place. In: Helal, S., Mitra, S., Wong, J., Chang, C.K., Mokhtari, M. (eds.) ICOST 2008. LNCS, vol. 5120, pp. 169–176. Springer, Heidelberg (2008). doi:10.1007/978-3-540-69916-3_20
18. Hayes, T.L., et al.: Sleep habits in mild cognitive impairment. Alzheimer Dis. Assoc. Disord. **28**(2), 145 (2014)
19. Kaye, J., et al.: Unobtrusive measurement of daily computer use to detect mild cognitive impairment. Alzheimer's Dement. **10**(1), 10–17 (2014)
20. Hayes, T.L., et al.: Medication adherence in healthy elders: small cognitive changes make a big difference. J. Aging Health (2009)
21. Hodges, M.R., Kirsch, N.L., Newman, M.W., Pollack, M.E.: Automatic assessment of cognitive impairment through electronic observation of object usage. In: Floréen, P., Krüger, A., Spasojevic, M. (eds.) Pervasive 2010. LNCS, vol. 6030, pp. 192–209. Springer, Heidelberg (2010). doi:10.1007/978-3-642-12654-3_12
22. Avvenuti, M., et al.: Non-intrusive patient monitoring of alzheimer's disease subjects using wireless sensor networks. In: World Congress on Privacy, Security, Trust and the Management of e-Business. CONGRESS 2009, pp. 161–165. IEEE (2009)
23. Tolstikov, A., et al.: Eating activity primitives detection-a step towards ADL recognition. In: 10th International Conference on e-health Networking, Applications and Services. HealthCom 2008, pp. 35–41. IEEE (2008)
24. Allin, S., et al.: Toward the automatic assessment of behavioral distrubances of dementia (2003)
25. Magill, E., Blum, J.M.: Personalised ambient monitoring: supporting mental health at home. Advances in home care technologies: Results of the Match project, pp. 67–85 (2012)
26. Demiris, G., et al.: Older adults' attitudes towards and perceptions of smart home technologies: a pilot study. Med. Inf. Internet Med. **29**(2), 87–94 (2004)
27. Cummings, J.L., et al.: The neuropsychiatric inventory comprehensive assessment of psychopathology in dementia. Neurology **44**(12), 2308–2308 (1994)
28. Parmelee, P.A., Katz, I.R.: Geriatric depression scale. J. Am. Geriatr. Soc. **38**, 1379–1379 (1990)
29. Page, E.: Continuous inspection schemes. Biometrika **41**(1/2), 100–115 (1954)
30. Mesnil, B., Petitgas, P.: Detection of changes in time-series of indicators using cusum control charts. Aquat. Living Resour. **22**(2), 187–192 (2009)

31. Taylor, W.A.: Change-point analysis: a powerful new tool for detecting changes. preprint http://www.variation.com/cpa/tech/changepoint.html (2000)
32. Bland, J.M., Altman, D.G.: Comparing methods of measurement: why plotting difference against standard method is misleading. Lancet **346**(8982), 1085–1087 (1995)
33. Krishef, C.H.: Fundamental Approaches to Sigle Subject Design and Analysis. Krieger, Malabar (1991)
34. City4Age: Elderly-friendly city services for active and healthy aging (2016). http://www.city4ageproject.eu/

Biomedical and Health Informatics

Extracting Heartbeat Intervals Using Self-adaptive Method Based on Ballistocardiography(BCG)

Hongbo Ni(✉), Mingjie He, Guoxing Xu, Yalong Song, and Xingshe Zhou

School of Computer Science, Northwestern Polytechnical University, Xi'an 710072, China
{nihb,zhouxs}@nwpu.edu.cn, hmj2008mhxy@163.com,
alan19920930@163.com, 290165336@qq.com

Abstract. Ballistocardiogram (BCG) could reflect mechanical activity of cardiovascular system instead of ECG. And it is often acquired by sensitive mattress or chair without any constraints and limitations, but it contains many noise because of the impact of body and acquired equipment, those questions make heart rate detection difficult from the original BCG. In the paper, we propose an adaptive method which is used to extract heartbeat intervals (RR), and the method acquire automatically input parameters of Ensemble Empirical Mode Decomposition (EEMD) algorithm, and then decompose BCG signal using EEMD algorithm, and select adaptively decomposition component of BCG signal, whose periodicity is in accordance with the cardiac cycle completely as the target signal. Furthermore we detect the peak points and calculate the heartbeat intervals series using the target signal. In the result, the proposed method is tested using the BCG datasets from 18 subjects, including 8 females and 10 males (age 20–72). Finally, the heart rate from BCG will be compared with ECG, and the results are satisfactory and have a high accuracy.

Keywords: Ballistocardiogram · Ensemble empirical mode decomposition · Heartbeat intervals

1 Introduction

Cardiovascular disease (CVD) seriously affect the health of the elderly as the major cause of death. The World Health Organization reported that about 17.3 million people died from CVD in 2008 and the total is 30% of global deaths [1]. In recent years, as the growth of the total number of the elderly, the number of CVD deaths is expected to reach 23.6 million by 2030 [1].

Ballistocardiogram (BCG) originally was discovered in the late 19th century [2], which also could reflect the cardiac mechanical activity instead of Electrocardiogram (ECG). With the development of transducer technology, many investigators turn to apply the embedded sensors bed-frame or mattress to collect the BCG signal. The researchers [3, 8, 9] set up a smart chair embedded with EMFi-film sensors to detect BCG signal. P.F. Migeotte et al. [4] get BCG signal based on acceleration sensor. The researches [5–7] design a non-intervention mattress perception system based on piezoelectric transducer or optical fiber sensor to acquire BCG signal. As known, the RR

M. Mokhtari et al. (Eds.): ICOST 2017, LNCS 10461, pp. 37–47, 2017.
DOI: 10.1007/978-3-319-66188-9_4

intervals or heart rate variability can be extracted based on BCG signal, and the patients will not be attached with any electrodes on the surface of the skin, and there will not be any interference for the patients. However, BCG signal contains a lot of noises because of the effect of the body and acquired equipment, that makes it difficult to extract RR intervals from the BCG signal difficult. Therefore, there are many researcher in the pervasive computing community pay more attention to it.

In our paper, we propose a self-adaptive algorithm to extract RR intervals based on BCG signal. The method contains three main steps. Firstly, the input parameters of EEMD algorithm adaptively is acquired and decompose BCG signal using EEMD. Secondly, the target signal is selected automatically from the decomposition component of BCG signal, and the target signal is that its periodicity agree with the cardiac cycle completely. Finally, the peak points of target signal is detected and then we can obtain the heartbeat intervals series automatically.

The paper contains four main sections. Section 1 introduce the background knowledge and the purpose of the paper. Section 2 mainly introduce the related works about extracting RR intervals. Section 3 presents the BCG data acquired system and a novel heartbeat cycle extraction method. Section 4 test the algorithm performances based on BCG datasets from eighteen participants, and explain the experimental result. Section 5 make a summary for the paper.

2 Related Works

Many works have been completed in the matter of extracting RR intervals. Postolache O.A. et al. [9, 10, 20] design a wheelchair embedded sensors, the wheelchair can acquire BCG signal, the author use wavelet filtering and independent component analysis to remove BCG artifacts and obtain the heart rate based on wavelet transform. Mack D.C. et al. [21] develop a BCG-based sleep monitoring system, and the system can analyze noninvasively physiological signals, the system uses bidirectional recursive to filter BCG signal noise, and uses an improved variable threshold method to detect peaks. Krej M. et al. [22] acquire BCG signal based on fiber-optic vital signs sensor, and use band-pass filter, quadratic function to process BCG signal, and then use an improve search windows to detect the heartbeat peaks.

C. Bruser et al. [7] extract features from the shape of a single heartbeat, and train the feature using an unsupervised learning techniques, and then detect the occurrence of individual heartbeats in the signal using the learning parameter, and obtain beat-to-beat interval length information. C. Bruser et al. [23] design a force-sensor bed to acquire BCG signal and use a sliding window to get the intervals. Jin J. et al. [11] first use wavelet transform to remove some noise of BCG signal and then employ threshold method to get the RR intervals. Shin J.H. et al. [12] complete the heartbeat detection in two stages. Firstly, the BCG template was constructed by the expert with an empirical analysis of BCG signal and measurement device, and secondly the correlation function calculates an accuracy of template with BCG signal using a local moving window. The researcher [13, 14] preprocess the BCG signal, such as normalizing and filtering the BCG signal, and combine the threshold and power operation for BCG data to extract heartbeat intervals. Algunaidi M. et al. [15] firstly get the range of heart rate based on a lot of heartbeat data statistic, and then set the sliding window length according to the range, and get the heartbeat intervals based on sliding windows. Choi B.H. et al. [16] firstly acquire BCG signal based on a load-cell-installed bed, and combine sliding window and threshold method to get the RR intervals.

Singh B. et al. [17] propose an improved adaptive length sliding window method to get heartbeat cycle. X. Cao et al. [18] firstly decompose the BCG signal based on EEMD algorithm, and then select decomposition component seven of BCG signal as the target signal, the target signal is that whose periodicity agrees with the cardiac cycle completely, and then use the target signal to extract RR interval.

Comparing to the works discussed above, the research in this paper combine with the characteristics of biological signal that it is nonlinear and non-stationary, and improve EEMD method, and then complete to adaptively extracting the RR intervals.

3 Methods

3.1 Data Collection Platform

A nonintrusive sleep sensing system is used to collect BCG signal, which consists of a micro-movement sensitive mattress, the analog-digital (A/D) converter and a terminal PC, the system is shown in Fig. 1. The mattress is embedded with two hydraulic pressure sensors (oil tubes), one is located at the upper part of the mattress to sense the pressure of the heartbeat, the other is placed in the leg regions, and the mattress can make sure there is enough area for various subjects' physical sizes, and BCG signal is sampled with 100 Hz. The original pressure signal is recorded using micro-movement sensitive mattress, converting to digital signal by the A/D converter. Finally, we can acquire some kinds of physiological parameters datasets from the system, such as Ballistocardiogram, respiration and so on. In this work, we pay more attention to analyze the cardiac vibrations of subjects, so we only select BCG signal as our original datasets.

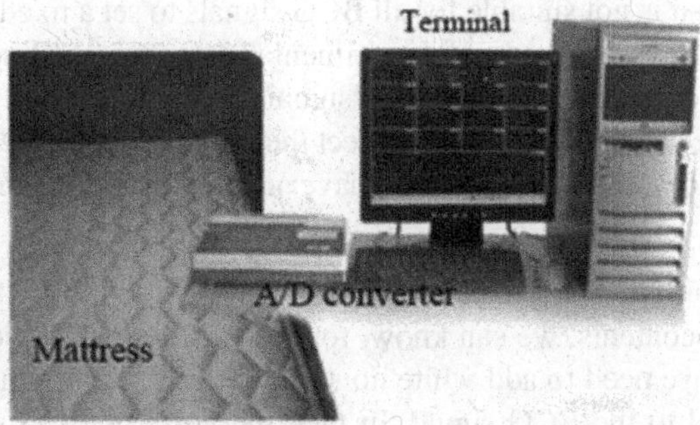

Fig. 1. Micro-movement sensitive mattress sleep monitoring system.

3.2 Signal Processing

3.2.1 Theoretical Basis and Existing Issues

Norden E. Huang came up with a method of Hilbert-Huang Transformation (HHT) in 1998 [16] which is used for analyzing nonlinear and non-stationary signals based on Empirical Mode Decomposition (EMD) and Hilbert Spectral Analysis (HSA), and the method has already been applied to many scientific research areas, including biological signal analysis. But the EMD exists many questions, such as mode mixing problem. To solve the problem, Huang propose an improved method named Ensemble Empirical Mode Decomposition (EEMD). The method is generally used for non-stationary signal, such as physiological signal.

In this paper, we will use the EEMD algorithm as a basis to deal with BCG signal, and try to solve some issues still exist, as follows:

(1) The EEMD algorithm contains two important parameters: Nstd and NE. The Nstd is the ratio of standard deviation of amplitude of the white noise signal and BCG signal, and NE is the number of iterations in the program. According to Huang theory [19], the Nstd is often set based on the working experience, so the experimental results is under the influence of parameters settings.
(2) BCG signal is different due to diverse sleep posture, person and also data acquire equipment. Different BCG signal need to set various parameters when is decomposed using EEMD. So it will be difficult to set the parameters according to different kinds of the BCG signal.
(3) X. Cao et al. [18] deal with BCG signal based on EEMD, and then select decomposition component seven as the target signal to extract RR interval, but because the BCG signal exists difference with distrinct persons, it leads to the decomposition component six or others but not seven agree with the cardiac cycle. The situation is also shown in the paper [19]. The method is suitable if we just analyze small amounts of data, but if we use it in an automatic heartbeat extraction system, it will reduce the accuracy of heartbeat cycle. Meanwhile, the decomposition effects of EEMD related to input parameters of EEMD, and the parameters is affected by BCG signal. So it is not suitable for all BCG signals to set a fixed parameter value. In order to improve accuracy of experimental data, we must select the suitable decomposition component as the target signal.
(4) Because the NE value is large, it will affect the program time efficiency. We should find a way to decease the NE value and have no effect on the decomposition effects.

3.2.2 Solving Problem Method

Based on the above contents, we can know, for the BCG signal, if we want to remove the noise perfectly, we need to add white noise signal whose amplitude is equal to the noise of BCG signal to the BCG signal. In fact, the noise of BCG signal is the high frequency information of BCG signal. So if we know the high frequency information of BCG signal, we can get the amplitude of white noise. Meanwhile, if we can extract the high frequency information that we want to remove from BCG signal, we can also calculate the parameters Nstd, and then we can complete adaptively to set the parameters Nstd of the EEMD method.

In order to remove the noise of BCG signal, we need to know that which frequency bands should be extracted as high frequency signal. According to medical field knowledge, the heart rate is 40–200 beats/min, and the maximum and minimum heart rate value is often athletes. Its corresponding frequency range is 0.67 Hz–3.33 Hz. So we should extract the high frequency signal whose frequency band is larger than 3.33 Hz.

Many methods can be used to extract high frequency information of BCG signal, such as EMD algorithm, high-pass filtering and multi-resolution wavelet transform. For the EMD algorithm, its time efficiency is relatively poor. For the high-pass filtering method, it needs to manual input the filter parameter value, different the parameter value will have different effect on the filter result. For the multi-resolution wavelet transform, it can extract high frequency detail signal adaptively, however, multi-resolution wavelet transform need to select wavelet basis.

In order to know about whether wavelet basis have seriously effect on Nstd value, we select BCG signal for 16 persons to test and select three different series of wavelet bases, they are respectively db, sym and bior, the sym and bior are select randomly, and db is often used for the wavelet decomposition of the BCG signal [39–41]. The experimental results are shown in Table 1, optional argument is Nstd parameter range that they are chose based on the artificial experience, the range is best for decomposition effect. From the Table 1, we can observe that the wavelet basis almost have no effect on Nstd value.

Table 1. The adaptive parameters compared with optional parameters.

Subject	Optional Argument	Adaptive Argument		
		db6	Sym6	bior2.8
S1	0.33–0.62	0.5115	0.5118	0.5269
S2	0.30–0.40	0.3215	0.3247	0.3233
S3	0.90–0.99	0.9820	0.9796	0.9789
S4	0.48–0.67	0.5942	0.5978	0.6012
S5	0.50–0.62	0.5648	0.5564	0.5571
S6	0.30–0.41	0.3357	0.3327	0.3460
S7	0.56–0.76	0.6340	0.6332	0.6156
S8	0.77–0.79	0.7837	0.7863	0.7896
S9	0.51–0.57	0.5367	0.5355	0.5396
S10	0.66–0.88	0.7753	0.7738	0.7745
S11	0.45–0.49	0.4702	0.4689	0.4712
S12	0.59–0.80	0.6228	0.6236	0.6230
S13	0.40–0.86	0.5863	0.5936	0.6083
S14	0.39–0.55	0.4352	0.4340	0.4279
S15	0.66–0.71	0.6904	0.6897	0.6920
S16	0.35–0.45	0.3975	0.3947	0.3898

Therefore we decide to select the multi-resolution wavelet transform to extract the high frequency signal. But we must know which decomposition scales is our need. In order to solve this problem, we randomly select an original BCG signal and a target signal, it is shown in the Fig. 2. Then we deal with the BCG signal using multi-resolution wavelet transform and get the high frequency detail signal, and then we handle the BCG signal, the target signal and the high frequency detail signal with Fourier transform. The result is shown in the Fig. 3.

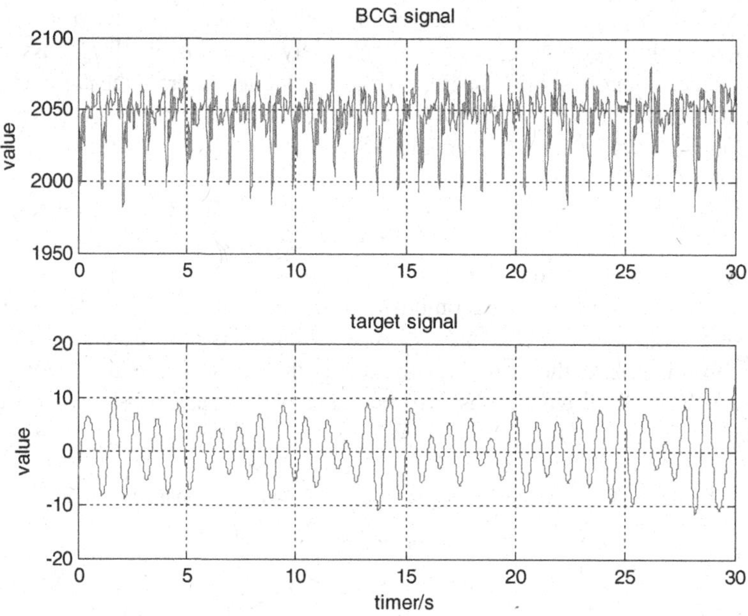

Fig. 2. The original signal and the target signal.

From the Fig. 3, we can observe that the frequency bands of the target signal is about 0–3 Hz, being consistent with the range of human heart rate. Meanwhile, so we will treat the frequency bands signal which is larger than 3 Hz as the noise signal, namely, these signals are high frequency signal that we need. From the Fig. 3, we can observe that the decomposed scale 1–4 of BCG signal is out of the bands of the heart rate of human, so we select them as the noise signal, and we should extract these high frequency signal. In order to facilitate the operation, we choose to reconstruct the decomposed scale 1–4 high frequency signal. Then we will treat the reconstructed high frequency signal as the adding white noise signal, and then compute the parameter Nstd. Now, we can complete adaptively setting of the parameters Nstd.

According to the part Theoretical Basis and Existing Problems, we know EEMD have two parameters, now we solve how to get the NE value. According to the statistical rules proposed by Huang [19], the relation of Nstd and NE is shown in the formula 1, e is decomposition error value, and which is generally set for 1%.

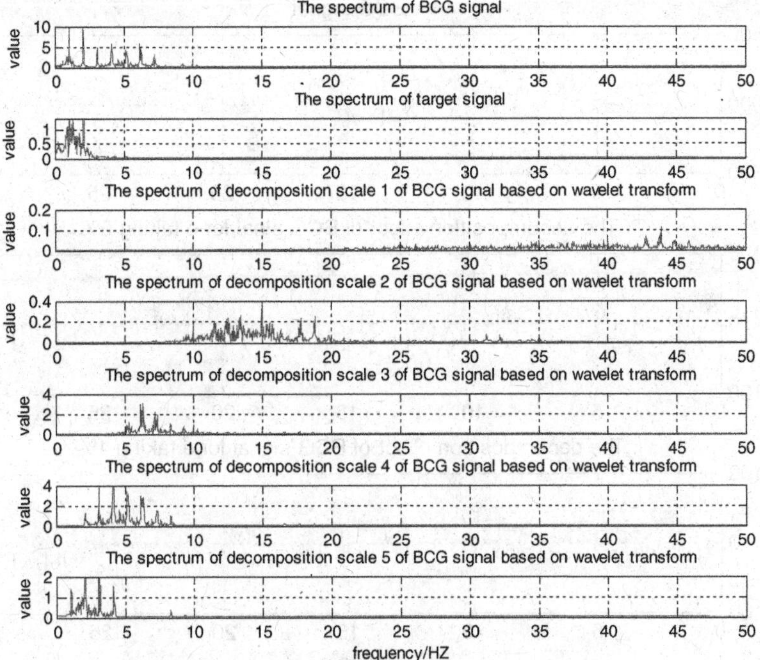

Fig. 3. The result of FFT of signal.

$$e = \frac{Nstd}{\sqrt{NE}} \tag{1}$$

However, it is not appropriate for BCG signal to let the e take 1% based on experiments experience. According to a lot of experiments, we find that it is suitable for the e taking 5%. In order to explain the question, we select an example randomly, we decompose the BCG signal using EEMD algorithm for e taking 1% and 5%, the decomposition result is shown in the Fig. 4. Although the theoretical decomposition error value is increased when e is 5%, from the Fig. 4, we can perceive that the decomposition effect is practically no difference. The Nstd value is 0.3 in this experiment, according to the formula 1, the NE value will be 900 for e being 1% and 36 for e taking 5%. So it is more suitable to set e for 5% and decreases the running time of the program. Now, we can complete adaptively setting of the parameters NE.

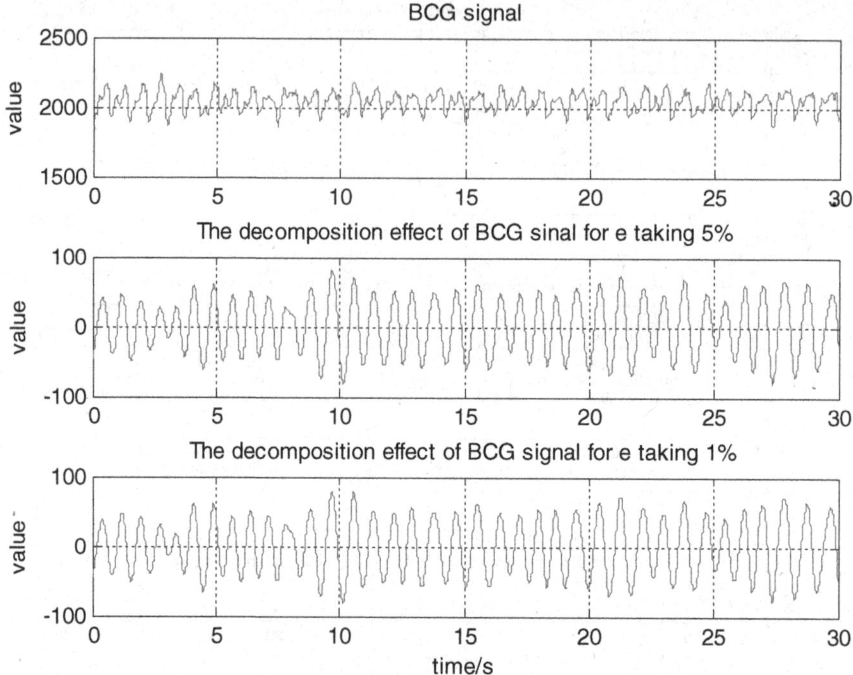

Fig. 4. The decomposition effect of the BCG signal with different e value

4 Results

In this study, we have performed experiments on each individual dataset using BCG signals from eighteen subjects, including ten males and eight females (age 20–72). The RR interval series were obtained using the proposed method.

In the procedure of extracting RR intervals, we firstly need to detect the peak points, so the procedure can be regarded as event detection, so it is possible to appear the situation that the heartbeat peak points is identified incorrectly (False Positive) and the heartbeat peak points can't be identified correctly(False Negative). In order to evaluate performance of this method. We collect the statistic data of TRR, F.P, F.N, Total Error, and calculate the accuracy value. The formula is as follow, and the statistic content is shown in the Table 3.

$$Total\ Error = TP + TN \tag{2}$$

$$Accuary = (Total\ Error/T_{RR}) * 100\% \tag{3}$$

From the Table 2, we can observe that the total error event number from the AHE algorithm is less than the total error event number from the RDS algorithm, and from the parameter Accuracy, it also reflects that the AHE algorithm has a higher accuracy and reliability for extracting the heartbeat intervals than the FDS algorithm.

Table 2. The performance comparison of the method.

Method	T_{RR}	Error			Accuracy [%]
		F.P	F.N	Total Error	
AHE	53692	273	262	535	99.00
FDS	53692	1879	3759	5638	89.49

In the Sect. 3, we know that we set e for 5% based on a lot of experiment experience, and we can improve the time efficiency of the program, so in order to evaluate time efficiency of the AHE algorithm, we start to give a test, and set e for 1% for the FDS algorithm, the result was shown in the Table 3.

Table 3. The time performance comparison of methods.

Data(min)	T_{cost}(s)	
	AHE	FDS
1	5.62	22.95
5	37.32	151.22
10	118.94	453.55
30	1054.47	4029.27

In the research filed, we often use five-minute or ten-minute datasets (such as ECG, BCG) to extract RR intervals and analyze heart rate variability. So, in this experiment, four kinds of different time-length datasets are respectively arranged to complete the test. From the Table 3, we can observe clearly that the time performance of algorithm AHE is greatly improved.

5 Conclusion

Cardiovascular disease affects seriously the health of the elderly all over the world. This study presents a novel adaptive method to obtain RR intervals based on BCG datasets. The algorithm firstly complete to acquire automatically input parameters of EEMD algorithm based on wavelet transform and signal reconstruction, and secondly complete to signal decomposition based on EEMD, and select adaptively the target signal, finally, complete to detect the peak points and calculate the heartbeat intervals series using the target signal. In brief, the method complete to adaptively extract heartbeat intervals series based on datasets.

In the result, the proposed method is tested using the BCG datasets from eighteen subjects, including eight females and ten males (age 20–72). The results of heart rate from BCG will be compared with ECG. From the Sect. 3, we can observe the precision of heart rate value from BCG is high and the accuracy of the method is 99%.

Acknowledgments. This work was supported by the China Scholarship Council, and is supported by the Key Project of National Found of Science of China (61332013) and Fundamental Research Grant of NWPU (3102015JSJ0010).

References

1. WHO: Cardiovascular Diseases (CVDs). Geneva, Switzerland: World Health Organization (2013)
2. Giovangrandi, L., Inan, O.T., Wiard, R.M., et al.: Ballistocardiography—a method worth revisiting. In: 2011 Annual International Conference of the IEEE Engineering in Medicine and Biology Society, EMBC, pp. 4279–4282. IEEE (2011)
3. Junnila, S., Akhbardeh, A., Barna, L.C., et al.: A wireless ballistocardiographic chair. In: 28th Annual International Conference of the IEEE Engineering in Medicine and Biology Society. EMBS 2006, pp. 5932–5935. IEEE (2006)
4. Migeotte, P.-F., Tank, J., Pattyn, N., Funtova, I., Baevsky, R., Neyt, X., Prisk, G.K.: Three dimensional ballistocardiography: methodology and results from microgravity and dry immersion. In: Proceedings of the 33rd Annual International Conference of the IEEE EMBS, Boston, MA (2011)
5. Chung, G.S., Lee, J.S., Hwang, S.H., Lim, Y.K., Jeong, D.-U., Park, K.S.: Wakefulness estimation only using ballistocardiogram: nonintrusive method for sleep monitoring. In: Proceedings of the 32nd Annual International Conference of the IEEE EMBS, Buenos Aires, Argentina (2010)
6. Paalasmaa, J.: A respiratory latent variable model for mechanically measured heartbeats. IOP Phys. Meas. **31**(10), 1331–1344 (2010)
7. Bruser, C., Stadlthanner, K., de Waele, S., Leonhardt, S.: Adaptive beat-to-beat heart rate estimation in ballistocardiograms. IEEE Trans. Inf. Tech. in Biomed. **15**(5), 778–786 (2011)
8. Koivistoinen, T., Junnila, S., Varri, A., Koobi, T.: A new method for measuring the ballistocardiogram using EMFi sensors in a normal chair. In: Proceedings of the 26th Annual International Conference of the IEEE EMBS, San Francisco, CA (2004)
9. Postolache, O., Girao, P.S., Postolache, G., Pereira, M.: Vital Signs Monitoring System Based on EMFi Sensors and Wavelet Analysis. IEEE IMTC, Warsaw (2007)
10. Postolache, O., Girão, P.S., Postolache, G.: New approach on cardiac autonomic control estimation based on BCG processing. In: Canadian Conference on Electrical and Computer Engineering, 2007. CCECE 2007, pp. 876–879. IEEE (2007)
11. Jin, J., Wang, X., Li, S., et al.: A novel heart rate detection algorithm in ballistocardiogram based on wavelet transform. In: Second International Workshop on Knowledge Discovery and Data Mining. WKDD 2009, pp. 76–79. IEEE (2009)
12. Shin, J.H., Choi, B.H., Lim, Y.G., et al.: Automatic ballistocardiogram (BCG) beat detection using a template matching approach. In: 30th Annual International Conference of the IEEE Engineering in Medicine and Biology Society. EMBS 2008, pp. 1144–1146. IEEE (2008)
13. Smrcka, P., Jirina, M., Trefny, Z., et al.: New methods for precise detection of systolic complexes in the signal acquired from quantitative seismocardiograph. In: 2005 IEEE International Workshop on Intelligent Signal Processing, pp. 375–380. IEEE (2005)
14. Akhbardeh, A., Kaminska, B., Tavakolian, K.: BSeg ++: a modified blind segmentation method for ballistocardiogram cycle extraction. In: 29th Annual International Conference of the IEEE Engineering in Medicine and Biology Society. EMBS 2007, pp. 1896–1899. IEEE (2007)
15. Algunaidi, M., Ali, M.A.M.: Threshold-free detection of maternal heart rate from abdominal electrocardiogram. In: 2009 IEEE International Conference on Signal and Image Processing Applications (ICSIPA), pp. 455–458. IEEE (2009)
16. Choi, B.H., Chung, G.S., Lee, J.S., et al.: Slow-wave sleep estimation on a load-cell-installed bed: a non-constrained method. Physiol. Measur. **30**(11), 1163 (2009)

17. Singh, B., Nagarkoti, S.K., Kaushik, B.K.: A modified algorithm for maternal heart rate detection using RR interval. In: 2011 International Conference on Emerging Trends in Networks and Computer Communications (ETNCC), pp. 39–42. IEEE (2011)
18. Cao, X., Guo, H., Tang, J.: Heart rate extraction of ballistocardiogram based on hilbert-huang transformation. In: Long, M. (ed.) World Congress on Medical Physics and Biomedical Engineering, vol. 39, pp. 619–622. Springer, Berlin (2013)
19. Wu, Z., Huang, N.E.: Ensemble empirical mode decomposition: a noise-assisted data analysis method. Advances in adaptive data analysis **1**(01), 1–41 (2009)
20. Postolache, O.A., Girao, P., Silva, M.B., et al.: Physiological parameters measurement based on wheelchair embedded sensors and advanced signal processing. IEEE Trans. Instrum. Measurem. **59**(10), 2564–2574 (2010)
21. Mack, D.C., Patrie, J.T., Suratt, P.M., et al.: Development and preliminary validation of heart rate and breathing rate detection using a passive, ballistocardiography-based sleep monitoring system. IEEE Trans. Inf Technol. Biomed. **13**(1), 111–120 (2009)
22. Krej, M., Dziuda, L., Skibniewski, F.W.: A method of detecting heartbeat locations in the ballistocardiographic signal from the fiber-optic vital signs sensor. IEEE J. Biomed. Health Inf. **19**(4), 1443–1450 (2015)
23. Bruser, C., Kortelainen, J.M., Winter, S., et al.: Improvement of force-sensor-based heart rate estimation using multichannel data fusion]. IEEE J. Biomed. Health Inf. **19**(1), 227–235 (2015)

Novel Unobtrusive Approach for Sleep Monitoring Using Fiber Optics in an Ambient Assisted Living Platform

Ibrahim Sadek(✉), Joaquim Bellmunt, Martin Kodyš, Bessam Abdulrazak, and Mounir Mokhtari

Image and Pervasive Access Laboratory, CNRS UMI 2955, Singapore, Singapore
ibrahim.sadek@ipal.cnrs.fr

Abstract. Sleep plays a vital role in a person's health and well-being. Unfortunately, most people suffering from sleep disorders remain without diagnosis and treatment since the current sleep assessment systems are cumbersome and expensive. As a result, there is an increasing demand for cheaper and more affordable sleep monitoring systems in real-life environments. In this paper, we propose a novel non-intrusive system for sleep quality monitoring using a microbend fiber optic mat placed under the bed mattress. The sleep quality is assessed based on different parameters. Moreover, the sensor has been integrated into an existing Ambient Assisted Living framework to be validated in real scenarios. Three senior female residents participated in our study and the sleep data was collected over a one-month period in a home-living situation. The proposed system shows accurate and consistent results with a survey collected from each participant showing their sleep patterns and other in-home activities.

1 Research Context

Technological progress allows us to take better care of ourselves and our relatives with less effort. Furthermore, we observe an emergence of *Zero-Effort Technologies* (ZET) [1]. They represent technological solutions that provide a service without requiring any form of active participation of the user. Their main paradigm is to leverage on unobtrusive observations of daily activities and on smart use of available information. *Ambient Assisted Living* (AAL) platforms, which is a specific type of ZET, target improving the quality of life – of both the monitored person and their caregivers. Such a platform aims at empowering people who may be at risk without assistance, especially the elderly. It contributes to users' autonomy in their own living space rather than leaving them completely dependent on others (e.g. a nursing home).

In this paper, we focus on sleep monitoring as a substantial vector of quality of life. Sleep is one of the critical physiological human needs. Humans spend a third of their lives sleeping. As advised, amongst others, by the *U.S. National Institutes of Health*, sleep deficiency can lead to fatal health problems. Currently,

M. Mokhtari et al. (Eds.): ICOST 2017, LNCS 10461, pp. 48–60, 2017.
DOI: 10.1007/978-3-319-66188-9_5

sleep assessments and evaluation tools are burdensome, expensive, and time-consuming. An unobtrusive method, which can provide a sleep monitoring daily is ballistocardiography (BCG). BCG records the mechanical activity of the body generated during each heartbeat. Multiple sensors are commonly used to record the BCG signal such as piezoelectric sensors, electromechanical sensors, fiber optic sensors. In addition to load cells, and pressure pads, these sensors can be integrated with chairs, beds, and cushions or even in weighing scales [2].

This work's contribution consists of a design and integration of a novel sleep quality monitoring model into an Ambient Assisted Living (AAL) platform using a microbend fiber optic sensor. This sensor is a suitable choice for unconstrained sleep monitoring as it is highly sensitive to pressure changes induced by the ballistic forces of the heart, and it does not require close contact with the body. It is also relatively small, lightweight, and affordable. Additionally, it improves sleep activity assessment previously based on motion sensor as presented by Bellmunt *et al.* [3].

The paper is organized in the following way. First, we discuss the technical state of the art of bodily signals processing to extract medical values as well as its inclusion in AAL platforms. Second, we present our methodology; introduce the microbend sensor and its specifications. Next, we introduce our AAL framework and the sensor integration. Fourth, we discuss the process to retrieve the values and the key items in sleep monitoring. Finally, we validate the complete system in real scenarios, and discuss the results.

2 Related Work in Sleep Monitoring

Healthcare systems worldwide are struggling with significant challenges, i.e., rapid growth in aging population, increased number of people with chronic and infectious diseases, rising costs, and inefficiencies in health-care systems. As a response to these challenges, the healthcare community is seeking for novel non-invasive solutions that can improve the quality of healthcare for the patient while maintaining the cost of the service provided. To achieve this goal, early diagnosis, prevention, and a more efficient disease management system are highly needed [2]. For example, the sleep disordered breathing (SDB), also known as obstructive sleep apnea (OSA), is one of the most common clinical disorders that can affect elderly people. The patient with OSA will need to stay in a specialist sleep clinic for the whole night to be diagnosed with multiple sensors attached to his/her body to monitor different vital signs besides sleep activates. Therefore, non-intrusive and less-expensive sleep diagnostic modalities are very important for long-term monitoring.

A thin air-filled cushion is introduced by Watanabe *et al.* [4] to detect sleep staging. Sleep data from eight university students were collected over 27 overnight recordings, where the cushion is placed between the bed and the mattress. For validation purposes, the students went to bed at a specific time at night. The proposed system provided heartbeat, respiration, snoring, and body movements.

Kortelainen *et al.* [5] proposed to use an Emfit foil sensor to monitor sleep stages by placing the sensor under the bed mattress. The sleep data was recorded from nine female subjects in a sleep laboratory. The recorded data consisted of heart rate, respiratory rate, and body movements.

Matar *et al.* presented [6] an application for gesture recognition in sleep monitoring. The authors used a pressure mattress covering the whole surface of the bed. The raw data is collected from the pressure sensors. Afterward, the movement is classified through a supervised learning method. Although these systems might be consistent with the gold standard methods, an intermediate training phase is required. Thus, they might not be applicable to real-life deployment. On the other hand, Paalasmaa *et al.* [7] provided a fully automated web application for home-based sleep monitoring using a piezoelectric film sensor, which can be placed under the mattress topper, the sensor can provide heart rate, respiratory rate, and body movements. The proposed approach was validated with 40 patients in a sleep clinic.

Finally, Rosales *et al.* [8] used a hydraulic bed based sensor to monitor sleep quality of four subjects over two to four months in-home living conditions. The hydraulic sensor was placed under the bed mattress, and they estimated the sleep quality based on the heart rate using two different methods. The contribution of this work is superior to other related works in the literature since authors deployed the system in real-life conditions without any constraints of in-lab environments. As we can see above, few approaches in existing literature dedicated to unobtrusive sleep monitoring in-home living situations.

To conclude, we position our research as one of the deployable solutions, which computes some medical parameters during the sleep time of an individual.

3 Methodology

We propose to use a microbend fiber optic sensor (FOS) to detect sleep parameters, and its integration into a user-friendly AAL IoT platform that observes and computes activities of daily living of an individual. First, second and third, we explain the principle of the used sensor, we introduce our AAL platform, and we present the integration of the sensor into the platform. Fourth, the algorithm processing the sensor data is provided. Finally, we adjust the key sleep items to the International Classification of Functioning, Disability, and Health (ICF)[1] model presented by the World Health Organization. The mathematical approach homogenizing the aggregated data is provided.

Figure 1 summarizes a deployment of the presented system in user's home.

3.1 Unobtrusive Sensor Selection

As described above, the BCG signal is used to analyze the sleep data through a microbend FOS. The fundamental principle is based on the light intensity

[1] http://www.who.int/classifications/icf/en/.

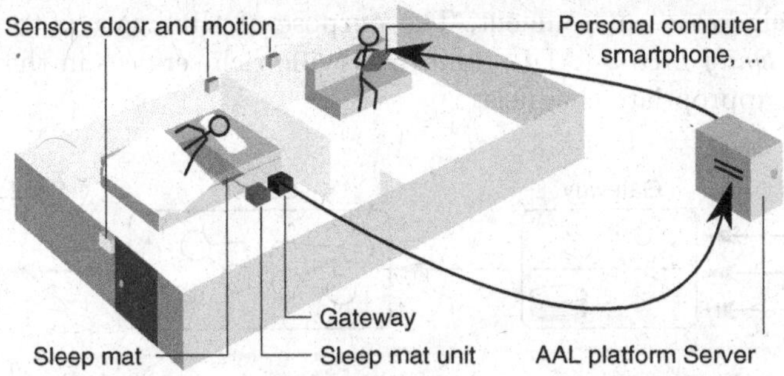

Fig. 1. Overview of our unobtrusive monitoring in a living space.

modulation induced by microbending in multimode fibers, which is used as a transduction mechanism for detecting pressure. A 10-meter loop of graded-index multimode fiber is sandwiched between two layers of tuned grating structures that subject the fiber to mechanical perturbation when there is a pressure applied as shown in Fig. 2(a). The pressure causes the transmission modes in the multimode fiber to be coupled into the loss mode, reducing the amount of light received by the photodetector. Hence, the detected light is converted to current by the photodetector, which is, in turn, converted into a voltage using a transimpedance amplifier. The signal is filtered via a 20 Hz low-pass filter and then digitized by a 16-bit analog-to-digital converter with a sampling frequency of 50 Hz [9,10].

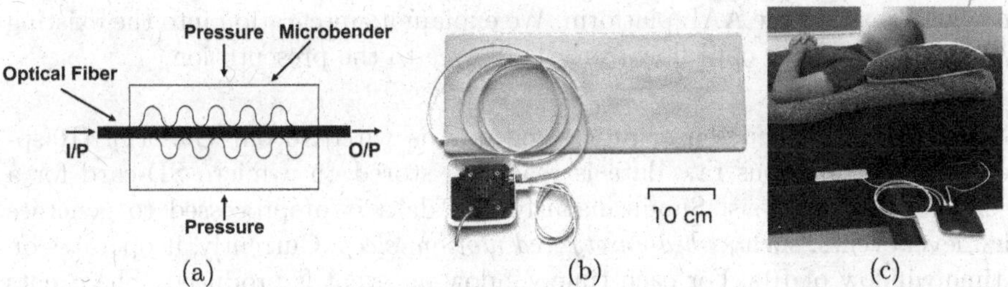

Fig. 2. (a) Longitudinal section of the microbend fiber optic sensor, (b) Sleep mat and processing box. (Mat dimensions: 20 cm × 50 cm × 0.5 cm) (c) Sleep mat positioned under the mattress.

3.2 UbiSmart Design

UbiSmart is a web-enabled AAL platform intended for large-scale deployments following the approach presented by Bellmunt *et al.* [11]. Key features [12] are *plug & play* ability, privacy protection as there is no sound and no image recording, easy interaction for end-users, and generic architecture. This AAL platform is able to transform any environment into a smart space in five minutes, enabling an unobtrusive assessment of indoor as well as outdoor activities of dependent people in their home environment. The purpose of UbiSmart is to detect the *Activities of Daily Living* (ADL), and to provide rich services in the right context through appropriate channels.

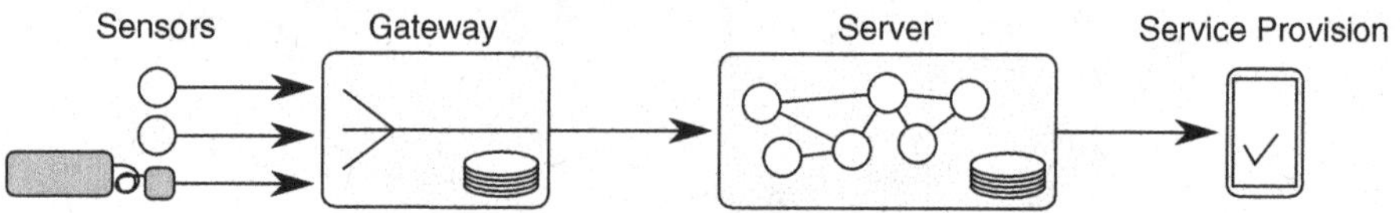

Fig. 3. Simplified view of UbiSmart AAL platform with sleep mat and its processing unit as a sensor.

The framework is composed of three main parts (Fig. 3), in data flow order: (1) **Gateway**, "smart home in a box" – sensors (motion sensors, contact sensors and the newly integrated bed sensor for sleep monitoring) and a gateway (Raspberry Pi); (2) **Server** – receives formatted inputs from the gateway, and processes them using semantic reasoning following the approach presented by Aloulou and Bellmunt *et al.* [3,13]; (3) **Service Provisioning** – responsive user interfaces on the web or on hand-held devices that allow users to receive notifications or interact with the platform.

3.3 Integration of Microbend Fiber Optic Sensor

The sleep mat equipment is considered as another sensor that contributes to the knowledge base of the AAL platform. We explain its integration into the existing system following the data flow from the source to the presentation.

Collection. The bed sensor-processing unit is wired to our *Gateway* (Raspberry Pi). Voluminous raw data is read and stored on a micro SD-card for a deeper off-line analysis. Simultaneously, the data is preprocessed to generate high level events, such as *bed empty, bed motion, sleep.* Currently, it operates on a time window of 10 s. For each time window an event is produced. The events are then sent to the *Server* as a structured sensor data using MQTT protocol over an Internet connection [3].

Reasoning. *Server* handles the received structured information (event). The bed sensor will appear in the *home description* interface as available for association to a house. If confirmed, this association is stored in the knowledge base (KB). Any subsequent events are then inserted into the KB of the associated house, allowing to the reasoning engine to be aware of bed occupancy with respect to our ontology (Listing 1.1). Coupled with the information from other sensors and sources, it provides an accurate contextual information. In parallel, the raw data is processed every 5 min to extract information about the occupant's respiratory effort and heart rate. This information is also inserted into the KB.

Listing 1.1. Simplified sample of our knowledge base in *Notation3* – sleep monitoring model featuring basic ontology, rule, instantiation and conclusions. (Note that not all the objects have been declared in the code sample.)

```
## Workspace definition ##
@prefix rdf: <http://www.w3.org/1999/02/22-rdf-syntax-ns#>.
@prefix qol: <http://www.ubismart.org/n3/qol-model#>.
@prefix hom: <http://www.ubismart.org/n3/home#>.

## INFERENCE RULE ##
{?se qol:hasLastUpdate true. ?se qol:indicateSleep true. ?se qol:attachedTo ?b. ?b a qol:Bed.}
=> {hom:user qol:believedToDo hom:sleepOnBed}.

## EXCERPT FORM KNOWLEDGE BASE ##
hom:bed rdf:type qol:Object.
hom:sleep rdf:type qol:Activity.
hom:bed qol:locatedIn hom:house.
hom:sensor_sleepmac_b8_27_eb_10_1c_79 rdf:type qol:Sensor.
hom:sensor_sleepmac_b8_27_eb_10_1c_79 rdf:type hom:SleepMatSensor.
hom:sensor_sleepmac_b8_27_eb_10_1c_79 qol:id "sleepMac_b8_27_eb_10_1c_79".
hom:sensor_sleepmac_b8_27_eb_10_1c_79 qol:attachedTo hom:bed.
hom:SleepMatSensor qol:hasPossibleState _:b1.
hom:SleepMatSensor qol:hasPossibleState _:b2.
_:b1 qol:hasValue "bed_empty".
_:b2 qol:hasValue "bed_motion".
_:b2 qol:hasValue "sleep";
    qol:indicateSleep "true"^^xsd:boolean.

## CONCLUSIONS ##
hom:sensor_sleepmac_b8_27_eb_10_1c_79 qol:hasValue "sleep".
hom:user qol:believedToDo hom:sleepOnBed.
```

Presentation. *Service provisioning* through our simple responsive web interface *Life Tiles* Fig. 4 allows us to give the user an instant feedback about bed occupancy and continuously updated information about the occupant's respiratory effort and heartbeat. Other indicators show aggregated information about activities out of the scope of this paper.

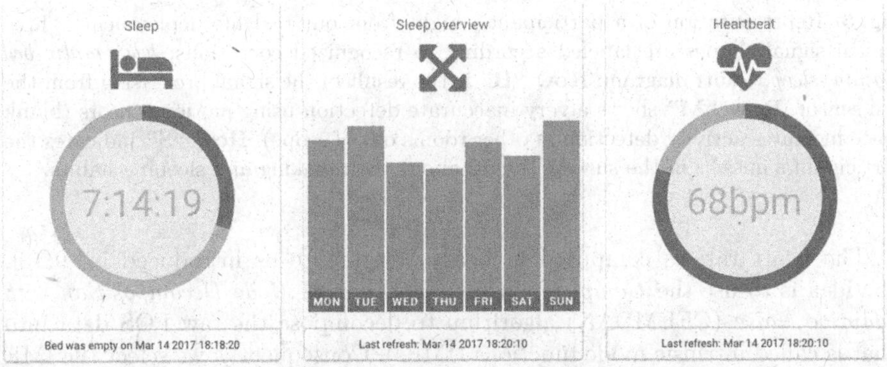

Fig. 4. UbiSmart user interface is organized in tiles and it provides following information: daily quantity of sleep (selected day) with updated bed occupancy status that changes the color of the icon and status line; aggregated week overview of sleep quantity; and heartbeat information.

3.4 Fiber Optic Data Processing

The sleep data is stored in 5-minutes chunks on a Micro SD-Card embedded in the processing unit. Then it is sent to a cloud-based server for data processing. Subsequently, the resident bed state is determined using a sliding window w with a size of 1500 samples, i.e., 30 s. Thereafter, three-bed states are recognized, as illustrated in Fig. 5. First, if the standard deviation (SD) of the window is greater than 0.7 of the mean SD of all windows, the status is considered as a *bed motion* (Fig. 5). Second, if the SD of the window is smaller than a predetermined threshold, the status is regarded as a *bed empty* (Fig. 5). Finally, in other cases, the state is identified as a *sleep* (Fig. 5). Algorithm 1 summarizes the bed state data processing.

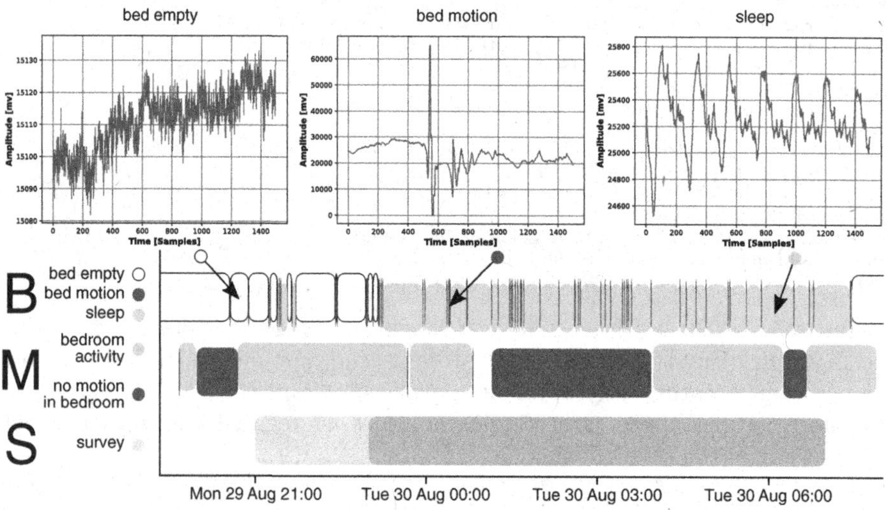

Fig. 5. Representation of a participant's night from our real life deployment. Three typical signal shapes are labeled according to recognized conditions: *bed empty*, *bed motion*, *sleep*. Gantt diagram: **Row "B"** is the result of the signal processing from the bed sensor. **Row "M"** shows a very inaccurate detection using motion sensors (blank space indicates activity detection in other rooms out of scope). **Row "S"** indicates the participant's answer in the survey Table 2 about their waking and sleeping habits.

The heart rate is computed in beats per minute as introduced in [9,10]. The idea is to use the *Complete Ensemble Empirical Mode Decomposition with Adaptive Noise* (CEEMDAN) algorithm to decompose the raw FOS data into what is called intrinsic mode functions (IMFs). Consequently, we select the IMF that matches the heart beats.

We employed the CEEMDAN algorithm as implemented in the *libeemd* package [14]. The algorithm is applied with a noise standard deviation of 0.25, an ensemble size of 250, S number of 4, while the number of siftings is 50.

The 5th IMF is selected for heart rate estimation because each local maximum shows an agreement with heart beats. Heart rate is computed using a sliding time window of a size 10 s.

The respiratory rate is computed in breaths per minute using a sliding time window of a size 20 s, where the raw FOS data is filtered using Chebyshev type I bandpass filter with frequency limits of 0.03 and 0.4 Hz. Then, a simple peak detector is utilized for respiratory peak detection.

Algorithm 1. Sleep mat data processing

Input: $W = \{w_1, w_2, \ldots, w_N\}$, T = 10
Output: state

```
for i = 1,...,N do
    Compute S(i) = SD(w_i)
end for
Compute M = mean(S)
for j = 1,...,N do
    if SD(w_j) > 0.7 * M then
        state = bed motion
    else if SD(w_j) < T then
        state = bed empty
    else
        state = sleep
    end if
end for
```

3.5 Sleep Monitoring Parameters Computation

In this paper, we focus on the sleep performance using a single fiber optic sensor placed under the mattress. To make sense of the collected data, we have conceived a sleep model based on the current literature. As mentioned in Sect. 3, we have identified six key sleep parameters following the ICF model, which can be computed using the collected data. Table 1 presents these six items with its description and its correspondence within the ICF model.

The generated dataset per user results to be very heterogeneous. While items as **Bed Time** or **Wake Up Time** are computed in time scale, others as **Heart rate** are expressed as a natural number. Moreover, some items are represented on a much smaller scale than the sleep time. Therefore, the system processes these values to reduce its range and homogenizes them into the same scale. Consequently, the collected datasets have been normalized using the zero normalization (Z_{Norm}), or standardization, to reduce the large trend of the data.

Let x_{id} be the observation for an item i in a day d. This value x_{id} is then standardized using a Z_{Norm} with the previous days' observations. The values will be in the range of -1 *to* 1,

Table 1. Sleep items computed during our study. Each item is represented by its code in the IFC model and its description.

Sleep parameter	ICF code	Unit	Daily computation
Sleep time	b1340	Time	Amount of deep sleep time
Night movement	b1342	Time	Movement during sleep time
Wake up time	b1343	Time	Time when the user wakes up
Bed time	b1343	Time	Time when the user goes the bed
Respiration functions	b440	Breaths/Min	respiratory effort during sleep time
Heart rate	b4100	Beats/Min	Heart rate during sleep time

$$\widehat{x_{id}} = Z_{\text{Norm}} = \frac{x_{id} - \mu_{id}}{\sigma_{id}}$$
$$-1 \leq \widehat{x_{id}} \leq 1 \quad (1)$$
$$\text{where: } \mu_{id} = mean(\mathbf{x_i}), \quad \sigma_{id} = SD(\mathbf{x_i}) \quad \text{and} \quad \mathbf{x_i} = \{x_{ij} \mid 0 \leq j \leq d\}$$

The standardization highlights the outliers within a dataset. On daily basis, the system produces reference items' values for each user. The proposed solution aims to detect spontaneous and unexpected abnormalities. For this purpose, the system applies the Bland-Altman analysis, which is employed to find unpredictable or aberrant values. As a person might change his behavior in a long-term deployment, the system computes the average value μ, and the standard deviation σ, for a given day d based on all previous observations. This procedure helps to evolve the boundaries of normality for each parameter adding dynamism to the Bland-Altman analysis.

4 Results and Discussion

The proposed solution was deployed in real conditions for 30 days in order to validate our approach. During the deployment in participants' homes, our system recorded data, and they were post-processed and evaluated. The objective of this validation was to study the reliability of the sleep monitoring and the performance of the entire system in a distant real deployment. At the same time, this deployment allows us to validate the interconnectivity of different sensors, the communication between the gateway and the server, and presentation of results in real time.

The sleep data is continuously acquired from three HDB[2] flats with elderly female residents, where the FOS sleep mat shown in Figs. 2(b) and (c) is placed under the bed mattress. However, one of the residents prefers to sleep on the

[2] http://www.hdb.gov.sg *Housing & Development Board* is a Singaporean governmental organization responsible for public housing, on their website, HDB claims: "HDB flats are home to over 80% of Singapore's resident population".

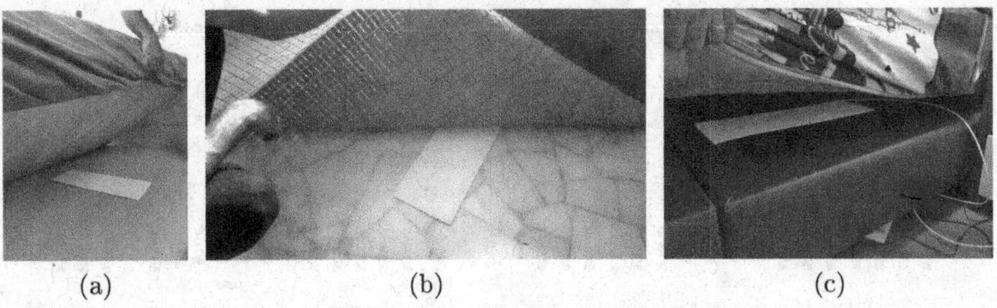

Fig. 6. Sleep mat integration at the three HDB apartments; (a) 1st home with mat under bed mattress, (b) 2nd home with mat under sleeping rug, (c) 3rd home with mat under bed mattress.

floor thus the sleep mat is placed under the sleeping rug. Before data collection, a survey is collected from the residents to indicate their sleep habits and other social activities as presented in Table 2. Figure 6 (a), (b), and (c) show sleep mat deployment in the three HDB apartments.

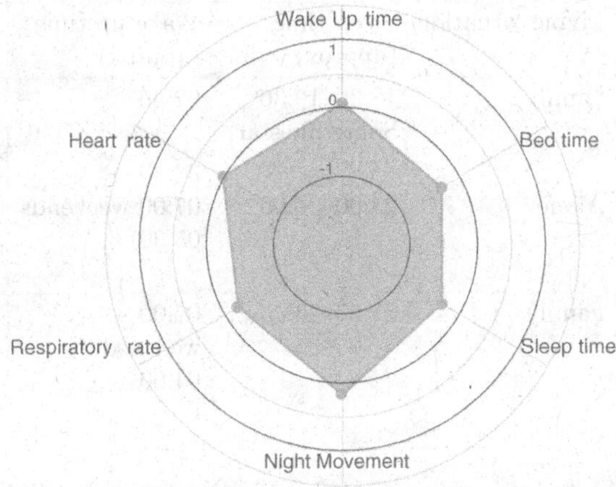

Fig. 7. Sleep chart model for 1st resident.

We observed a notable improvement in terms of detection of bed activity compared to the previous approach using motion sensors. Figure 5 presents a sample of the processed data. In Fig. 7 the user is characterized in a multidimensional spider graph. The values are computed on daily basis, normalized and compared to its statistical components, arithmetic mean and standard deviation following Bland-Altman analysis to detect outliers. This graph allows us to observe whether sleep performance has remained within a range of normality. The heart rate and the respiratory rate are computed and updated each hour. Figure 8(a) represents the result of the evolution of the *bed activity* along our

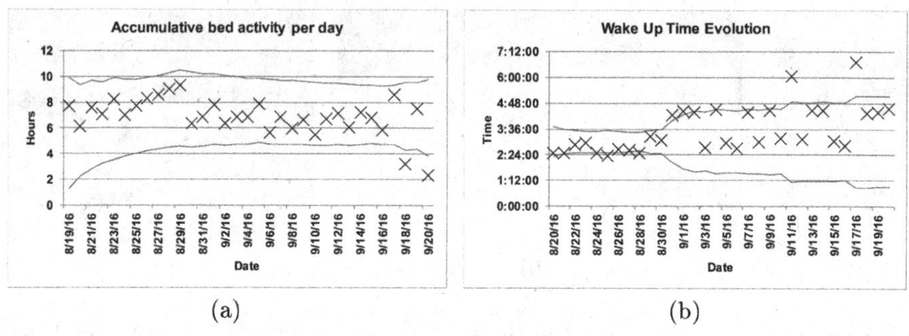

(a) (b)

Fig. 8. Sleep data analysis for 1st resident; (a) Bed activity, (b) Wake up time.

deployment. Each day is represented by its value and the range of normality represented by $\mu \pm \sigma$.

Table 2. Age and sleep profile of each independent resident (no chronic diseases or disabilities are reported).

	Age	Living situation	Sleep time (approx)	Wake up time (approx)	Nap
Resident#1	68	Family	18:30–19:30 Sometimes at 22:00	02:30	2–3 times 14:00–15:00 pm 30 min
Resident#2	69	Alone	23:00–00:00	07:00 weekends 05:30	1–2 times 14:00–15:00 30–60 min
Resident#3	65	Family	21:00–23:00	07:00 wednesday 04:00	Not reported

In order to validate our aggregated values, we performed individual interviews to understand the individual lifestyle of each participant. Table 2 presents an abstract of the results of the personal interviews. For instance, we detected that resident 1 started his bed activity very soon in the evening, and they woke up around 2.30 am. At first, it seemed to be an aberration in our measurement. However, in the survey, the resident confirmed her sleeping time matched our results. Thus, we could validate our inferred values.

5 Conclusion

In this paper, we presented a novel unobtrusive method for sleep monitoring using fiber optics in an Ambient Assisted Living platform, featuring a concise user interface. Our system was tested for 30 days in a real deployment in three flats in Singapore. Personal interviews confirmed the results of our post-processing.

Subsequently, the signal processing was implemented to be performed in real-time. The sleep mat was wired to our gateway in the user's place. The gateway processes the raw data, extracts bed events, and sends them to the server. At the same time, it stores the raw data and sends them to a dedicated cloud API for a deeper processing in order to extract the proposed sleep parameters. The outputs are used by both our reasoning engine, and served in our platform's new responsive interface adapted for hand-held devices. The reasoning engine is operating on an ontology and provides context for each event that occurs.

We also described the most-recent post-processing, including other vital-signs monitored by the same optic fiber technology.

The overall results contribute to a quantification of the residents' behaviors and to a measurement of their quality of life.

References

1. Mihailidis, A., et al.: Zero effort technologies: considerations, challenges, and use in health, wellness, and rehabilitation. Synth. Lect. Assistive Rehabil. Health Preserv. Technol. **1**(2), 1–94 (2011)
2. Koenig, S.M., et al.: Sleep and Sleep Assessment Technologies. Humana Press, Totowa (2008)
3. Bellmunt, J., et al.: Agile framework for rapid deployment in ambient assisted living environments. In: Proceedings of the 18th International Conference on Information Integration and Web-Based Applications and Services. iiWAS 2016, pp. 410–413. ACM, New York (2016)
4. Watanabe, T., Watanabe, K.: Noncontact method for sleep stage estimation. IEEE Trans. Biomed. Eng. **51**(10), 1735–1748 (2004)
5. Kortelainen, J.M., et al.: Sleep staging based on signals acquired through bed sensor. IEEE Trans. Inf. Technol. Biomed. **14**(3), 776–785 (2010)
6. Matar, G., et al.: Internet of Things in sleep monitoring: an application for posture recognition using supervised learning. In: 2016 IEEE 18th International Conference on e-Health Networking, Applications and Services (Healthcom), pp. 1–6, September 2016
7. Paalasmaa, J., et al.: Unobtrusive online monitoring of sleep at home. In: 2012 Annual International Conference of the IEEE Engineering in Medicine and Biology Society, pp. 3784–3788, August 2012
8. Rosales, L., et al.: Heart rate monitoring using hydraulic bed sensor ballistocardiogram1. J. Ambient Intell. Smart Environ. **9**(2), 193–207 (2017)
9. Sadek, I., et al.: Sensor data quality processing for vital signs with opportunistic ambient sensing. In: 2016 38th Annual International Conference of the IEEE Engineering in Medicine and Biology Society (EMBC), pp. 2484–2487, August 2016
10. Sadek, I., et al.: Continuous and unconstrained vital signs monitoring with ballistocardiogram sensors in headrest position. In: IEEE-EMBS International Conferences on Biomedical and Health Informatics, pp. 289–292, February 2017
11. Bellmunt, J., Tiberghien, T., Mokhtari, M., Aloulou, H., Endelin, R.: Technical challenges towards an AAL large scale deployment. In: Geissbühler, A., Demongeot, J., Mokhtari, M., Abdulrazak, B., Aloulou, H. (eds.) ICOST 2015. LNCS, vol. 9102, pp. 3–14. Springer, Cham (2015). doi:10.1007/978-3-319-19312-0_1

12. Aloulou, H., Abdulrazak, B., Endelin, R., Bentes, J., Tiberghien, T., Bellmunt, J.: Simplifying installation and maintenance of ambient intelligent solutions toward large scale deployment. In: Chang, C.K., Chiari, L., Cao, Y., Jin, H., Mokhtari, M., Aloulou, H. (eds.) ICOST 2016. LNCS, vol. 9677, pp. 121–132. Springer, Cham (2016). doi:10.1007/978-3-319-39601-9_11
13. Aloulou, H., Mokhtari, M., Tiberghien, T., Biswas, J., Kenneth, L.J.H.: A semantic plug&play based framework for ambient assisted living. In: Donnelly, M., Paggetti, C., Nugent, C., Mokhtari, M. (eds.) ICOST 2012. LNCS, vol. 7251, pp. 165–172. Springer, Heidelberg (2012). doi:10.1007/978-3-642-30779-9_21
14. Luukko, P.J.J., et al.: Introducing libeemd: a program package for performing the ensemble empirical mode decomposition. Computational Statistics **31**(2), 545–557 (2016)

Intent-Context Fusioning in Healthcare Dialogue-Based Systems Using JDL Model

Muhammad Asif Razzaq, Wajahat Ali Khan, and Sungyoung Lee(✉)

Department of Computer Science and Engineering, Kyung Hee University, Seocheon-dong, Giheung-gu, Yongin-si, Gyeonggi-do 446-701, Republic of Korea
{asif.razzaq,wajahat.alikhan,sylee}@oslab.khu.ac.kr

Abstract. A revolutionized wave of intelligent assistants has emerged in daily life of human over the recent years, therefore huge progress has been witnessed for development of healthcare assistants having the capability to communicate with users. However, the conversational complexities demand building more personalized and user-oriented dialogue process systems. To support human-computer dialogue process many models have been proposed. Considering personalization aspect, this research work presents novel Context-aware Dialogue Manager (CADM) model with its foundation based on well-known JDL fusion model. The proposed model addresses modern techniques for multi-turn dialogue process, by identifying dialogue intents, contexts and fusing personalized contexts over them. The model also maintains the dialogue context for progressing complex and multi-turn dialogue. It also helps using intent-context relationship in identifying optimized knowledge source for accurate dialogue expansion and its coherence. CADM functionality is discussed using support of Intelligent Medical Assistant in healthcare domain, which has the speech-based capability to communicate with users.

Keywords: Intent recognition · Context identification · Intent-context fusioning · Ontology

1 Introduction

In this era of digital world, dialogue based systems have been introduced in human daily life in several forms. They can be conversational systems, virtual assistants, robots or chat-bots. They are useful in a wide range of applications ranging from daily life entertainment to healthcare. Most important is that, they have the capabilities of conversational interaction with underlying speech and language understanding. In healthcare domain, intelligent medical assistants have also been introduced for personalized-care and assistance services. Intelligent medical assistants provide interactive and seamless dialogue process to its users for health related queries. However, there is still a need for devising an efficient mechanism for identifying dialogue intents and management of context for multi-turn dialogue process. In order to proceed with dialogue strategy, another important task is to choose proper system of actions, with underpinning reference

M. Mokhtari et al. (Eds.): ICOST 2017, LNCS 10461, pp. 61–72, 2017.
DOI: 10.1007/978-3-319-66188-9_6

of appropriate knowledge-base for effective question answering. To strengthen the decision of responsive system actions, recognition and maintenance of dialogue context from on-going multi-turn dialogue can provide effective mechanism for selecting suitable knowledge-base for efficient dialogue response.

2 Motivation

Most of the proposed Dialogue manager lack insights regarding conversational dialogue contexts. In this study besides, identification of dialogue intents, we also focused on observing their relations with dialogue contexts so that effective dialogue management process can be performed. Based on current state of the art, we figured out some of the key limitations, challenges and proposed our solutions as mentioned in Table 1. The main contributions of this paper depends on identified limitations.

Table 1. Limitations, challenges and solutions

Current focus	Limitations & challenges	Solutions
Intent recognition [5]	Lack semantic relationships for accurate intent identification	• Context-aware dialogue ontology development • Ontological modeling for intent identification
Context management	Little or no attention given to maintain and coalesce dialogue contexts, their switching & expansion	• Semantic mappings amongst intent and contexts • Design SPARQL queries to interact with ontological model for text/speech based dialogue process
Intent-context fusioning [8]	Lack of personalization effect	Besides dialogue context additionally inclusion of personalization contexts like location, environmental etc.
Appropriate knowledge sources referral	Crawls web, searches all repositories by dialogue manager for efficient answers	Model prioritized knowledge sources information
Response generation	Lack context-aware personalized response	Fusioning of personalized contexts with response

The rest of the paper is organized as follows. Section 3 describes survey work that is related to the topic of this paper. Section 4 describes the component level insights of architecture for Context-aware dialogue manager which we proposed. Section 5 implementation of CADM in healthcare domain. Finally, main conclusions and future road map are presented in Sect. 6.

3 Related Work

In last decade dialogue based management systems such as virtual assistant, chat-bots, healthcare assistants have gained popularity with dialogue management aiming to provide good interaction. Intents identified during conversational dialogue are closely related to context, which includes not only external environmental contexts like time, location, temperature but also personal daily life contexts. The relationship between context and intent is complicated, which exhibits complex co-occurring and sequential correlation [11]. Context itself also consists of numerous heterogeneous entities collected from various sources, and these entities mostly are of diverse in nature. Therefore, it is challenging to model the context-intent relationship. Moreover, to track users' intent-context relationship in real-time is even more challenging as personal assistants have to pay attention to the personalized contexts. An overview of intent recognition approaches [7], relationship among different states belonging to different objects in an area of interest for given point in time have been sketched. In this study authors suggested that inclusion of additional dialogue states have impact on recognizing more sub-intentions, which leads to the proper task completion for intention recognition in dialogue process. The Dialogue State Tracking Challenge (DSTC) also provides a forum in dialogue state tracking in spoken dialogue systems. For instance, DSTC-5 mainly refers to track dialogue states based on sub-dialogue segments for TourSG dataset [4]. In this challenge, most researchers based on hypothesis contributed several results for the each turn for a given sub-dialogue by considering dialogue context history. Researchers are more focused with how to make robots for more engaging to people [1] using different methods to exploit use of sensors for identifying the physical contexts. This work aims at contextualizing the additional information conveyed during the interaction with a robot, by using information enrichment techniques. In this study, researchers rely on semantic techniques to extract from users' inputs information related to their moods, to the main entities and concepts they were mentioning, to the topic they are talking about and to other information such as time or money expressions. In the work by [3] have highlighted the importance of *understanding intentions* in context is an essential human activity during conversation. Similar likelihood will be considered as important as for any robot if its functionality is required in any social domains. The development of context-based fusion system mainly relies on the quality of fused inputs and their usage for domain-adapted solutions [9]. In this fused input role of context is non-trivial in modern fusion systems which is specifically addressed in Joint Directors of Laboratories- Model (JDL). The JDL model, in order to gain adaptability and improved performance supports object recognition by exploiting physical context, and estimate intents using linguistic conversational analysis.

3.1 Information Fusion Model

Our investigation for finding state of the art in the field of information fusion have considered work presented by [6] in which they highlighted different

Table 2. Information fusion models and their features

Category	Model	Features
Information-based models	• Joint Directors of Laboratories (JDL) • Data Feature Decision (DFD)	Based on the abstraction of the data generated during fusion process
Activity-based models	• Boyd control loop • Intelligence cycle • Omnibus model	Based on activities that must be performed by fusion system, activities and correct sequence of execution are explicitly specified
Role-based models	• Object oriented model • Frankel-Bedworth architecture	Based on fusion roles and their relationships

data/information fusioning techniques required for intent recognition and context determination. The findings are reported in Table 2.

3.2 JDL Model

The US Joint Directors of Laboratories (JDL) Data Fusion Sub-Group initially proposed JDL Model for data fusion and introduced its functions in 1985 which was later updated in 1998 [10]. In the study [9] Snidaro et al., provided comprehensive status of context-based information fusion systems and explored novel context exploitation dynamics and architectural aspects such as incorporation of Contextual Information in JDL Model. The study demonstrated and differentiated *functions* into *fusion levels* by providing important distinction among information fusion processes. The derived JDL Model relates refinements for parameters of interest at 5 levels. Data source are responsible for providing input to the JDL model, it can be of any form, like sensory, human interaction or any other system [6]. DBMS provides data management support required to process within in JDL data fusioning whereas human-computer interface

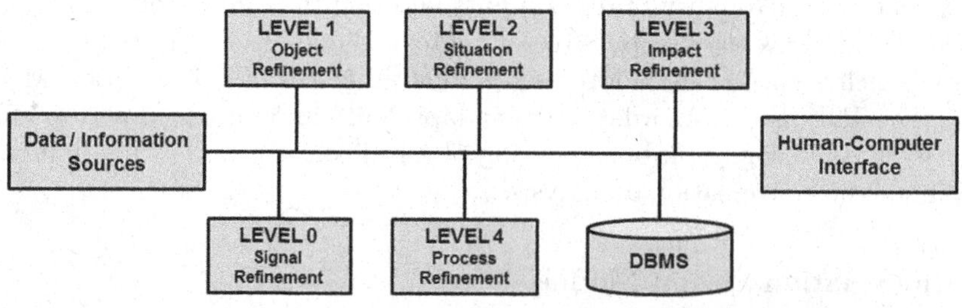

Fig. 1. JDL data fusion model derived from 1999 revision [10]

provides interface to interact with system in obtaining the desired fused results as shown in Fig. 1. The details for layers are as under.

- *Level 0 (Signal Refinement):* This level is for estimation, association, characterization and prediction for signals. Several preprocessing tasks related to data, such as normalization, missing values, incomplete data sets, and filtration of low quality measurements are performed in this level.
- *Level 1 (Object Refinement):* This level on the basis of inferences from observation performs estimation and prediction for entity states. This level performs key role for transforming data into consistent structure with objects identification based on inference.
- *Level 2 (Situation Refinement):* To identify a situation a contextual description of the relationship among entities and observations by using a-priori knowledge and environmental information is obtained in this level.
- *Level 3 (Impact Refinement):* To deal with the impact of effects on situations or predicted actions i.e. evaluate the current situation and predict possible threats.
- *Level 4 (Process Refinement):* This is responsible for data acquisition and source allocation to support mission objectives. It also monitors the system performance according to the specified goals.

4 CADM: Context Aware Dialogue Manager

The proposed model Context-aware dialogue manager (CADM) is based on JDL fusion model. Special attention has been considered while designing CADM and associated its work-flow corresponding to the layers of JDL Model.

4.1 CADM: Component Level Details

This proposed model disclosed herein, comprises of a subcomponents for modeling the user dialogue with system. This study covers the domain of dialogue-based systems, where system communicate with user through speech. This system can be Intelligent Medical Assistant (IMA) or health assisted robot facilitating users to interact using conversation for healthcare issues, diagnosis, appointments etc. The subsequent sections describe the component level details.

Sub-dialogue Builder: The sub-dialogue builder is responsible for conversion of entities obtained from speech language understanding into ontological form as per Context-aware Ontology (CADO). This component holds capability to complete sub-dialogue as there can be some noise and some keyword might be missing from SLU (Fig. 2).

- *Utterance Mapper:* The Utterance Mapper a component, which is responsible for generating ontological models for sub-dialogue entities. These entities are obtained from speech language understanding. Utterance mapper transforms

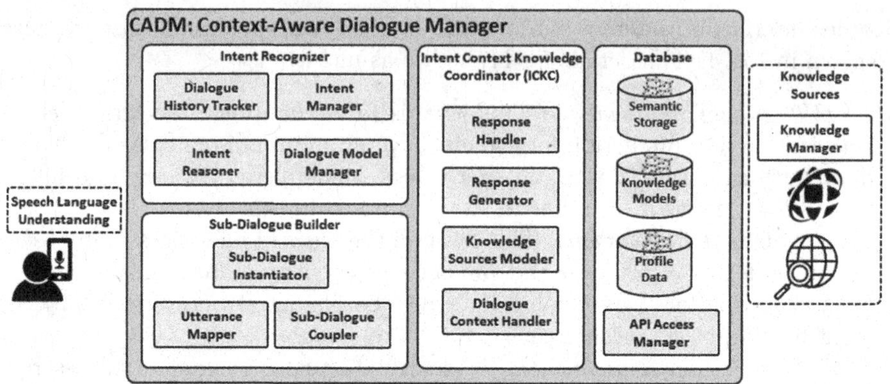

Fig. 2. Context aware dialog manager architecture

these entities into corresponding ontological model concepts called utterance triples. It also converts meta-data like user information and time into ontological form. These utterance triples are stored in semantic storage using Dialogue Context Handler which coordinates with database storages.

- *Sub-Dialogue Coupler:* The Sub-Dialogue Coupler is responsible to receive the utterance triples and arrange relevant utterance triples obtained from utterance mapper, which might have been received with delay or missing due to some noise or misunderstanding from speech language understanding. This component retrieves the concurrent utterance triples from semantic storage through dialogue context handler.
- *Sub-Dialogue Instantiator:* The sub-dialogue instantiator creates new ontological instance called *apparent sub-dialogue instance*, linking similar and non-similar utterance triples obtained from sub-dialogue coupler. Once the apparent sub-dialogue instance is created, it is given to dialogue model manager.

Intent Recognizer: The Intent Recognizer component provides diverse functionalities by verifying the apparent sub-dialogue instance, identifying context history, and inferring intents before routing the desired information to the knowledge sources. Its working is dependent on coordination of Dialogue Model Manager, Dialogue History Tracker, Intent Reasoner and Intent router.

- *Dialogue Model Manager:* The apparent unclassified sub-dialogue model is received Dialogue Model Manager. This component verifies the apparent unclassified sub-dialogue model semantically and syntactically verses CADO through Dialogue context handler. Once the apparent unclassified sub-dialogue context is validated, this instance is provided to intent reasoner.
- *Intent Reasoner:* The Intent Reasoner identifies the Intent of apparent unclassified sub-dialogue instance. This classification of the apparent unclassified sub-dialogue based instance into conversational intent is based on inference functionalities provided by the CADO. Using the ontological reasoner such

as Pellet[1], an automatic classification is performed over apparent unclassified sub-dialogue instance. This apparent unclassified sub-dialogue instance is compared by the definitions of different intents to determine whether these conditions complies with the intent definition or not. In affirmative case, the apparent unclassified sub-dialogue is considered to be inferred to be part of intent. This intent reasoning process gets triggered whenever dialogue model manager sends verified apparent unclassified sub-dialogue instance to intent recognizer. Otherwise, if the intent membership could be classified than this apparent unclassified sub-dialogue instance is delivered further without intent identification to find out the response from the knowledge sources. In both the cases intent information along-with sub-dialogue information is passed to the dialogue history tracker.

- *Dialogue History Tracker:* Dialogue consists of several sub-dialogues, with each sub-dialogue can have different or same intents. Monitoring and keeping dialogue consistent with context, dialogue history tracker performs key role based on current apparent unclassified sub-dialogue model. This previously contextual state is retrieved using SPARQL queries from semantic storage. This component activates the model enrichment process, by identifying if there exist certain intent/context for apparent unclassified sub-dialogue model. This component retrieves contextual information from profile data. This component helps in use for adaptation like user interest, previous contexts obtained from profile data. It basically refines the criteria by fusing additional information to the intents, like profile information, which helps for creating appropriate response generation.
- *Intent Manager:* After the intent has been identified, the sub-dialogue and intent is provided to intent manager. Intent manager before notifying has two more tasks to perform, i.e. fusing the personal context and identifying the knowledge source for further dialogue action. Intent manager requests knowledge source modeler. This component has the capability to respond, based on sub-dialogue model and intent using SPARQL. The determined intent plays vital role in identifying the appropriate knowledge source. This knowledge source information is modeled in the repository Knowledge models. The obtained knowledge source information, intent along with sub-dialogue information is referred to knowledge source for reply. Our system works for healthcare domain, in which entities are gathered from user using speech based devices. This information based on entities, intents and appropriate knowledge source is forwarded to Knowledge Manager, a component for coordinating Knowledge sources which helps in expanding dialogue using further questioning or response generation by knowledge sources.

Intent-Context Knowledge Coordinator: This component Intent-Context Knowledge Coordinator provides full functionalities support to CADM. This component supports coordination between sub-dialogue builder, Intent Recognizer and Database Storage. It coordinates for storing newly mapped utterances,

[1] https://www.w3.org/2001/sw/wiki/Pellet.

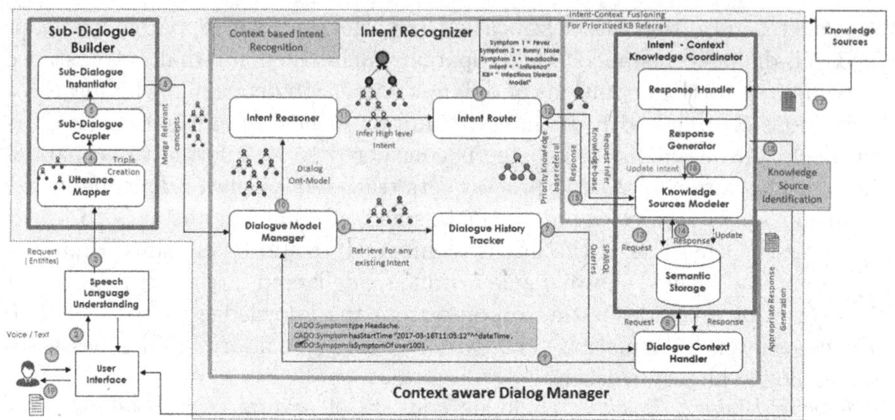

Fig. 3. Context aware dialog manager detailed work-flow

retrieval and loading of CADO, and also persistence of updation to the knowledge source mappings with intents. Besides all, It also facilitates for generation of responses and helps in dialogue progress. The sub components include terminology definitions, communication mechanism using SPARQL query language among components and Database Storage infrastructure (Fig. 3).

- *Dialogue Context Handler:* The Dialogue Context Handler provides interaction and management facilities with Context-aware dialogue ontology (CADO) model stored in semantic storage. This component is responsible for providing three types of supports to CADM. It provides management facilities for inter-component interaction. It performs CADO loading into memory so that the concerned components can readily use it. It also holds automatic extension to the CADO once some extension is required in terms of CADO terminology, Intent-concept mapping etc. The extended CADO is evolved in terms of new definitions and rules determining new or updation of existing intents. The Dialogue Context Handler ensures ease of use for the latest CADO by respective components of systems as discussed in different sections.
- *Knowledge Source Modeler:* The component Knowledge Source Modeler play two major roles. One of them is identifying and optimizing prioritized knowledge source model amongst various knowledge models stored in Knowledge Model Database storage. The Intent Manager, for identifying prioritized knowledge source referral based on identified conversational intent, generates this request. The second key role is to persist the knowledge source model information and its relationship with intents so that it can be made available for conversational intents for the management of dialogue process.
- *Response Handler:* The component Response Handler gets triggered, when Knowledge Manager gathers information based on the input generated by the Intent Manager or if unnecessary delays incurs. This component takes care of two important aspects, one of which is handling the response based

on information gathered from the knowledge manager and other is to engage user if relevant response generation gets delayed.
- *Response Generator:* Based on the responses delivered by Response Handler, this component initiates dialogue response which is forwarded to text to speech component.

Storage: Several storage strategies were considered in CADM discussed briefly as under.

- *Semantic Storage:* The Semantic Storage is a database storage, which provides persistence to the CADO. This includes both the CADO definition terminologies and rules. Since sub-dialogue are modeled using CADO and intent is inferred over them. The semantic storage follows triple storage framework mechanism, in which all sub-dialogue concepts, intents are converted into triples. The read/write interactions among sub-dialogue triples are supported by dialogue context handler component in the ICKC layer.
- *Knowledge Models:* The Knowledge Models storage provides facility to knowledge model information and their relationships with conversational intents. This involves intervention from Ontology Engineer Expert for verification because of the criticality of health domain. These knowledge models are not in detail but holds meta-data information with intent relationships only. The detailed information resides with Knowledge Sources. Whenever new Knowledge source is added, or intents definition needs to be related to the knowledge source, this information is passed by Knowledge Manager to the Knowledge sources Modeler via Response Handler which updates.
- *Profile Data:* The necessary information pertaining to user lies with Profile Data storage. As this study targets health related conversation management, so this repository will have information like past medical history, allergies, nutrition choices etc. This personal information enriches the intent and is fused while retrieved through dialogue history tracker.
- *API Access Manager:* This component is activated when user's contexts like location, environmental information such as weather, temperature needs to be determined. Just like personal information additionally the on demand contextual and environmental information collected via API Access Manager which provides access to external applications in the Knowledge Sources.

4.2 CADM and JDL Model

The survey conducted by Snidaro et al. [9] provides several existing definitions of context in literature with highlighting the most important evidences for inclusion of Contextual Information in different domains. It provides a comprehensive overview how contextual information fusion can play important role in the domains like mobile and pervasive computing, healthcare, image processing, artificial intelligence knowledge-based systems etc. They provided insights to various techniques applied to all levels of JDL model and categorized levels into Low-Level Fusion and High-Level Fusion. Low-level included Level 0 and Level 1 whereas high-level included Level 2, Level 3 and Level 4. They provided detail description over the importance of contextual information in high-level fusion processes (Level 2–4). They separated knowledge representation, intent assessment, decision making and process refinement functions by introducing extensive context discover, adaptation and learning techniques. For knowledge representation and establishing the relationship among multi-domains they highlighted the role of ontologies for context representation. Level 3–4 fusion is mostly concerned with high-level contextual knowledge extraction from low level fusion processing [2] in particular Level 3 for intent prediction and Level 4 for process control, mission management and source requirement determination in knowledge based systems.

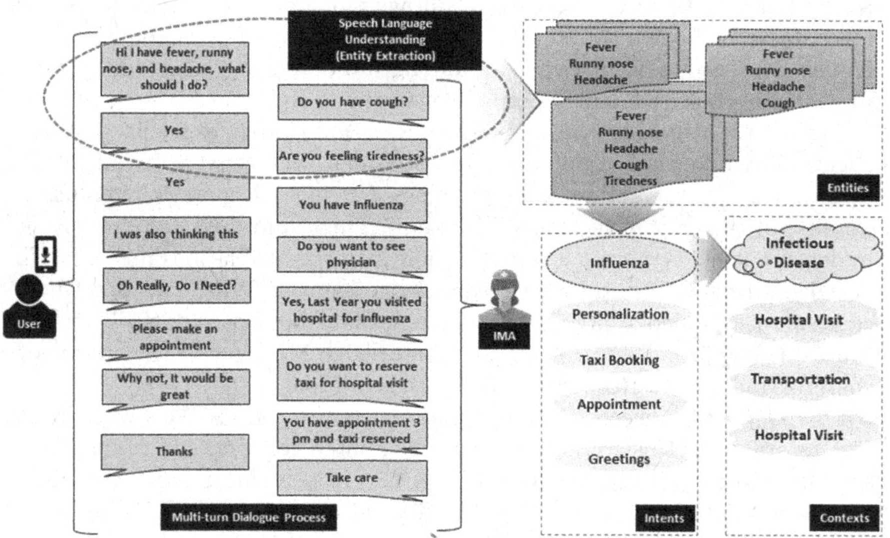

Fig. 4. Intent-context recognition based on entities in IMA

5 Case Study: Intelligent Medical Assistant (IMA)

In conversational and dialogue based systems most of the examples are tailored to the characteristic of particular problem related to specific domain. However less importance was given to design a dialogue manager which fulfills all requirements for Information Fusion prescribed by JDL Model. In this study, we proposed a generalized CADM which works based on JDL Model. The components are designed in a sense that they comply with the JDL functionalities distinguishing all entities separately like Intent, context and knowledge information. We demonstrate use of speech based utility in healthcare domain, in which patients are provided voice enabled functionalities like interacting with Intelligent agent. We consider Intelligent Medical Assistant (IMA). IMA has capability to respond user and interact based on questions and queries. The information obtained in the form of text/speech is semantically annotated based on CADO, Intent of dialogue are determined, and context is maintained through out the process as discussed in detail in previous sections. Taking in accounts user's present context, like health conditions, past medical history, location, weather information, past conversational context, transportation, communication type, real-time response generation is considered by CADM. Using the services of CADM in IMA, monitors the dialogue context and user context for appropriate response generations from knowledge sources as mentioned in Fig. 4. The CADM is carefully designed and as a test case tailored especially for IMA to keep the reliability, consistency, and relevancy of dialogue of user with IMA. By highlighting the key aspect that intent-context fusioning can play vital role in modern dialogue based systems by intent estimation through linguistic conversation analysis and context determined over it.

6 Conclusions and Future Work

In this paper context-aware dialogue manager (CADM) model is proposed in compliance with JDL for enrichment and completeness for effective conversational service. The presented case study CADM in *Intelligent Medical Assistant* (IMA) indicated the feasibility and usability of proposed model for conversation with user end-to-end. We demonstrated the interaction of different components and their inputs/outputs. We also highlighted the importance of determining intents, identify context and fusing them each other for appropriate responses from knowledge sources. As a future work, we aim to develop CADM with underlying context-aware dialogue ontology (CADO). We plan to evaluate CADM for different domains and measure its correctness, real-time responses and dialogue confidence.

Acknowledgment. This work was supported by the Industrial Core Technology Development Program (10049079, Develop of mining core technology exploiting personal big data) funded by the Ministry of Trade, Industry and Energy (MOTIE, Korea).

References

1. Alonso-Martín, F., Castro-González, A., Luengo, F.J.F.D.G., Salichs, M.Á.: Augmented robotics dialog system for enhancing human-robot interaction. Sensors **15**(7), 15799–15829 (2015)
2. Azimirad, E., Haddadnia, J.: The comprehensive review on JDL model in data fusion networks: techniques and methods. Int. J. Comput. Sci. Inf. Secur. **13**(1), 53 (2015)
3. Kelley, R., Tavakkoli, A., King, C., Ambardekar, A., Nicolescu, M., Nicolescu, M.: Context-based Bayesian intent recognition. IEEE Trans. Autonom. Ment. Dev. **4**(3), 215–225 (2012)
4. Kim, S., D'Haro, L.F., Banchs, R.E., Williams, J.D., Henderson, M., Yoshino, K.: The fifth dialog state tracking challenge. In: Proceedings of the 2016 IEEE Workshop on Spoken Language Technology (SLT) (2016)

5. Labidi, N., Chaari, T., Bouaziz, R.: Towards an automatic intention recognition from client request. In: Nguyen, N.-T., Manolopoulos, Y., Iliadis, L., Trawiński, B. (eds.) ICCCI 2016. LNCS, vol. 9875, pp. 163–172. Springer, Cham (2016). doi:10.1007/978-3-319-45243-2_15
6. Noughabi, H.A., Kahani, M., Behkamal, B.: SemFus: semantic fusion framework based on JDL. Innovations and Advances in Computer, Information, Systems Sciences, and Engineering, vol. 152, pp. 583–594. Springer, New York (2013). doi:10.1007/978-1-4614-3535-8_49
7. Schlenoff, C., Kootbally, Z., Pietromartire, A., Franaszek, M., Foufou, S.: Intention recognition in manufacturing applications. Robot. Comput. Integr. Manuf. **33**, 29–41 (2015)
8. Smirnov, A., Levashova, T., Shilov, N.: Patterns for context-based knowledge fusion in decision support systems. Inf. Fusion **21**, 114–129 (2015)
9. Snidaro, L., García, J., Llinas, J.: Context-based information fusion: a survey and discussion. Inf. Fusion **25**, 16–31 (2015)
10. Steinberg, A.N., Bowman, C.L.: Revisions to the JDL data fusion model. In: Handbook of Multisensor Data Fusion: Theory and Practice, 2nd edn., pp. 45–67. CRC Press (2008)
11. Sun, Y., Yuan, N.J., Wang, Y., Xie, X., McDonald, K., Zhang, R.: Contextual intent tracking for personal assistants. In: Proceedings of the 22nd ACM SIGKDD International Conference on Knowledge Discovery and Data Mining, pp. 273–282. ACM (2016)

Unhealthy Dietary Behavior Based User Life-Log Monitoring for Wellness Services

Hafiz Syed Muhammad Bilal, Wajahat Ali Khan, and Sungyoung Lee(✉)

Department of Computer Engineering, Kyung Hee University, Seocheon-dong, Giheung-gu, Yongin-si, Gyeonggi-do 446-701, Korea
{bilalrizvi,wajahat.alikhan,sylee}@oslab.khu.ac.kr

Abstract. Unhealthy behavior, constitutes of unhealthy diet, smoking, physical inactivity and alcohol intake, increases the risk of chronic diseases and premature mortality. These unhealthy behaviors can be avoided by little intention and guidance. Diet is an influential factor of healthcare. Healthy and balanced diet selection is related to the better life expectancy and decreases the chances of chronic diseases. The Ubiquitous computing revolutionized the wellness domain towards user centric preference based health management. In this study we proposed a method for monitoring and indication of users' unhealthy nutrition consumption. We evaluated 3 different timings of indication to user for induction of healthy dietary pattern. The "location and time based indication" depicts very promising result of 78% in the adoption of healthy diet pattern and has positive impact on the intake of fat nutrient in diet.

Keywords: Life-log · Automatic monitoring · Unbalanced diet · Unhealthy situation · Wellness

1 Introduction

Today in wellness domain, technology focuses to improve personal health and socio-economic conditions through self –quantification from innovative and smart gadgets. According to theoretical model, wellness was introduced in 1990s [1, 2] as Wheel of Wellness. The initial high level wellness models were defined and categorized into nutrition knowledge, stress management, physical fitness and environmental & social awareness [3]. The wellness is a concerning target of healthcare domain to avoid and prevent the diseases with the development of innovative user centric platform. The platforms are capable to digitize health and wellness domain and provide wellbeing services and recommendations [4]. Good physical health, proper food, freedom to live, social interaction and safety define the human wellbeing [5]. So active routine, balanced diet, proper hydration, leisure and finance are ingredients of healthy lifestyle [6].

M. Mokhtari et al. (Eds.): ICOST 2017, LNCS 10461, pp. 73–84, 2017.
DOI: 10.1007/978-3-319-66188-9_7

1.1 Consequences of Unhealthy Behavior

Multiple research have shown that specific unhealthy behaviors, including smoking, physical inactivity, higher alcohol intake and, unbalanced diets are associated with an increased risk of cardiovascular disease, cancer and premature mortality [7]. Practicable improvements in lifestyle behaviors are likely to have a significant impact at both the individual and population level. The health status of the population can simply be measured from mortality rate, where unhealthy behaviors have been associated with a higher risk of lifestyle diseases [8]. Diet is an influential health agent and bad diet pattern is among the prominent causes of premature death and chronic disease [9]. The diet constitutes of multiple nutrients in different proportions. It is quite difficult to calculate multiple attribute to all variations in dietary pattern. According to the FSC (Australia New Zealand Standards Code) [16] the recommended balanced diet for an average adult is as shown in Table 1.

Table 1. Nutrition requirements of average adult

	Component	Quantity per day
Average adult-requirements	Energy	2000 Calories
	Protein	50 g
	Fat	70 g
	Carbohydrates	310 g
	Sugars	90 g
	Sodium (salt)	2.3 g
	Dietary Fiber	30 g

1.2 Wellness Applications for Human Activity Analysis

Currently, the designing trend of healthcare and wellness applications changes to manage and analyze the users' temporal activity data to identify healthy and unhealthy lifestyle pattern [11]. The identified patterns may help to understand and diagnose the root cause of any undesired health issues. Instead of reactive approach to cure and manage diseases, these applications are focusing on proactive personalized health approach. Multiple ubiquitous applications are available i.e. 7 min Workout, LoseIt, Noom Coach and etc. These applications are used to quantify and log user activities, and calories consumption to empower users for visualization. In the upcoming portions we have discussed Mining Minds platform, Nutrition focused lifelog monitor architecture and evaluation methodology.

2 Mining Minds: In a Nutshell

Context based health informatics is a fruit of technology revolution for community [14]. The emerging software technology has reshaped the world through big data infrastructure and deep learning techniques to analyze the buried pattern under pile of data. Our ongoing project, Mining Minds MM [11, 12] is providing a platform to educate, engage and trigger the users on the basis of preferences and context to support for leading long healthy lifestyle. It is possible because of the use of state of the art technologies and emerging electronic gadgets. The concepts, from curation of raw sensory data to services orchestration, make the platform capable to manage the current requirements of user centric model in healthcare and wellness domains [13].

Mining Minds platform provides interface to communicate and gather multimodal data generated from different sensors to capture the temporal and spatial information along with activities. The key attributes time, place and activity are used to understand the user context and support to generate context based personalized wellness recommendations [12]. To cope with the challenges of personalized wellness, platform consists of five layers Data Curation Layer (DCL), Information Curation Layer (ICL), Service Curation Layer (SCL), Knowledge Curation Layer (KCL) and Supporting Layer (SL) respectively.

The SL is in-charge of the interaction with users and providing analytical reports on the basis of customer's requirement in a graphical manners. The granularity of analytics depends on the access level permission of users. Comprehensive view of the habits, activities and classification is provided to wellness stakeholders on the demand base and access right to understand and make decision for improvement [14, 15].

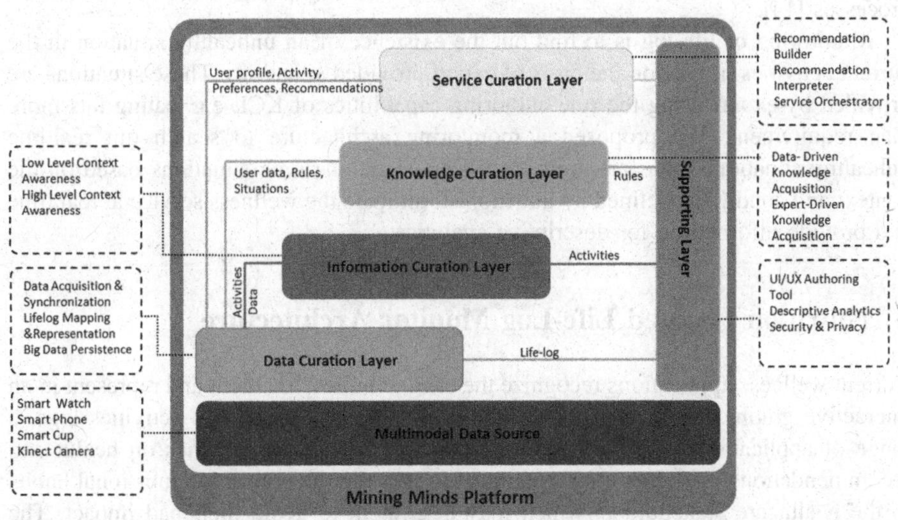

Fig. 1. Mining Minds Platform

The SCL is the orchestrator of personalized recommendation services in push and pull mode. In push mode the indication for recommendation is generated by platform while in pull mode the user requests for recommendations. The knowledge based personalized recommendation are provided by exploring demographic, physiological, health status, context and preferences information [14] (Fig. 1).

The KCL provides a data driven and an expert driven knowledge acquisition authoring environment to expert. Experts can transform their experiences and wellness knowledge in to rules through authoring environment. These rules guide about the unhealthy context based situation in the life-log and provide remedies to avoid unhealthy patterns in term of actions [15]. So the rules are then transformed into executable guidelines to highlight monitoring situations and the recommendation for action plan. Besides authoring environment the experts are supported through data driven approach which consists of machine learning algorithm to facilitate through previous information and knowledge.

ICL recognize user's activities and context from multimodal sensory data through hierarchical models. It consists of multiple recognizers for activity, emotion and location respectively. These recognizers provides the low level context awareness. The fusioning of low level context supports to recognize various high level context. It is the essential layer of MM platform to manage the activity context, e.g. sitting in office. These low level and high level contexts play an essential role for defining the lifestyle pattern [15].

DCL is the foundation service in the MM platform. It provides the ability to continuously sense and manage the raw sensory data from multimodal data sources. The data acquisition is device independent and can support large induction of sensors which helps to identify richer context [4]. It provides data curation through data acquisition and synchronization, data representation and mapping and big data storage processes [14].

Monitoring of life-log is to find out the existence of an unhealthy situation in the current activities of user on the basis of expert provided situations. These situations are provided by expert using the rule authoring capabilities of KCL e.g. eating fats more than requirement. We proposed a monitoring architecture to search out realtime unhealthy situation. It has an ability to filter out the alarming situations based on the context and conditions defined by nutritionist, intimate the wellness service at real time and provide information for descriptive analytics.

3 Nutrition Focused Life-Log Monitor Architecture

Current wellness applications recognize the user activities, log them and represent in an interactive graphical manner [11]. In addition to present the user's activities logs, a range of applications also provides the impact of co-related activities on health and recommendations [10]. It is more beneficial to indicate the unhealthy nutritional habits to the healthcare stakeholders which may help them to avoid their bad impact. The proactive approach towards healthy lifestyle drive us to construct a nutrition focused Life-log Monitor (LLM). The LLM, shown in Fig. 2, constitutes of three major components. These components manage the rules related to unhealthy habits provided by experts, monitor the life-log under the guidance of these rules and indicate the wellness services instantly. The three main components are Monitor Event Configurator, Constraints Configurator and Situation Event Detector.

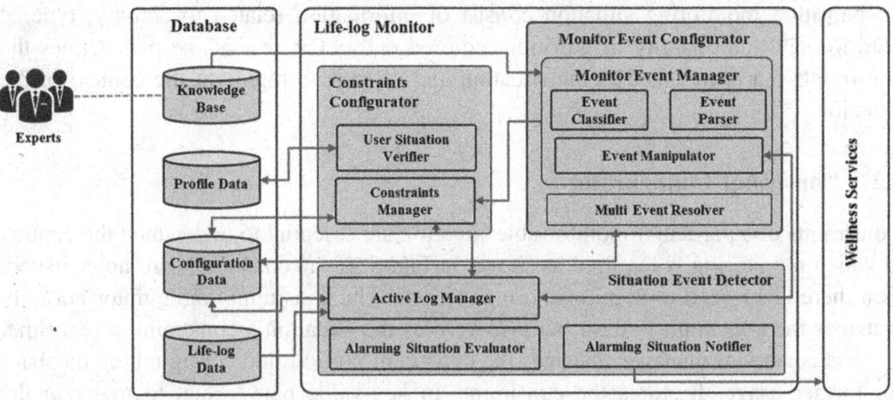

Fig. 2. Nutrition focused Life-log Monitor architecture

3.1 Monitor Event Configurator

Nutritionists are the expert to provide guidelines for identification of the alarming micro nutrition intake with respect to the context of the user. These guidelines are authored through authoring environment and share in common configuration format. The monitor event configurator is responsible for extracting the monitoring situations from a common configuration format as shown in Fig. 3. The situations are parsed and classified into monitoring situations and situation constraints. The monitoring situation constitutes of nutrition and its quantity for a particular day. The Event manipulator map the monitoring situation in configuration data for further access.

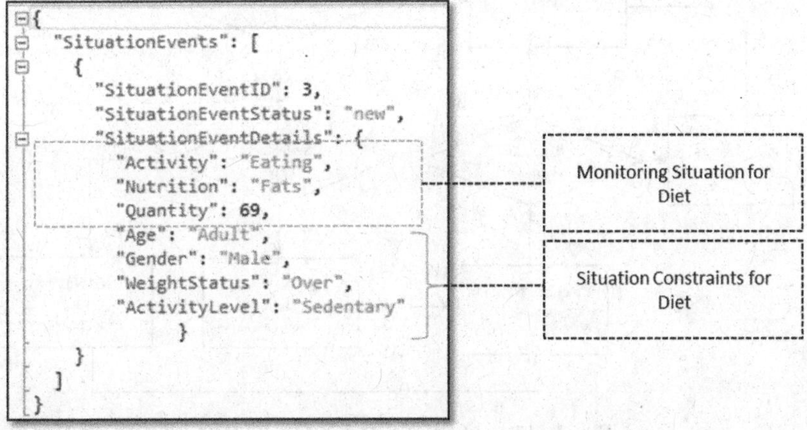

Fig. 3. Common configuration format for complete Situation

Nutrition monitoring situation consist of information related to activity, type of nutrition and the quantity of nutrition required daily. The rest of the part defines the constraints that are related to the situation and support to highlight the context of the situation.

3.2 Constraint Configurator

Constraints of a particular monitor-able situation are essential to understand the context in which monitoring is required as shown in Fig. 3. If the constraints are not satisfied, then there is no need to monitor those situations. The constraint configurator not only manages the constraint portion but also verifies the situation's constraint at real time.

The constraint manager manages the constraint portion into configuration database for further usage. It stores the constraints in key-value pair format to maintain the dynamicity for handling multiple constraints.

The User Constraint Verifier (UCV) is activated whenever a monitor-able activity is detected. It searches the user profile to verify the constraints to satisfy the context of the situation. It communicate all those situations whose context are matched for further detection and monitoring.

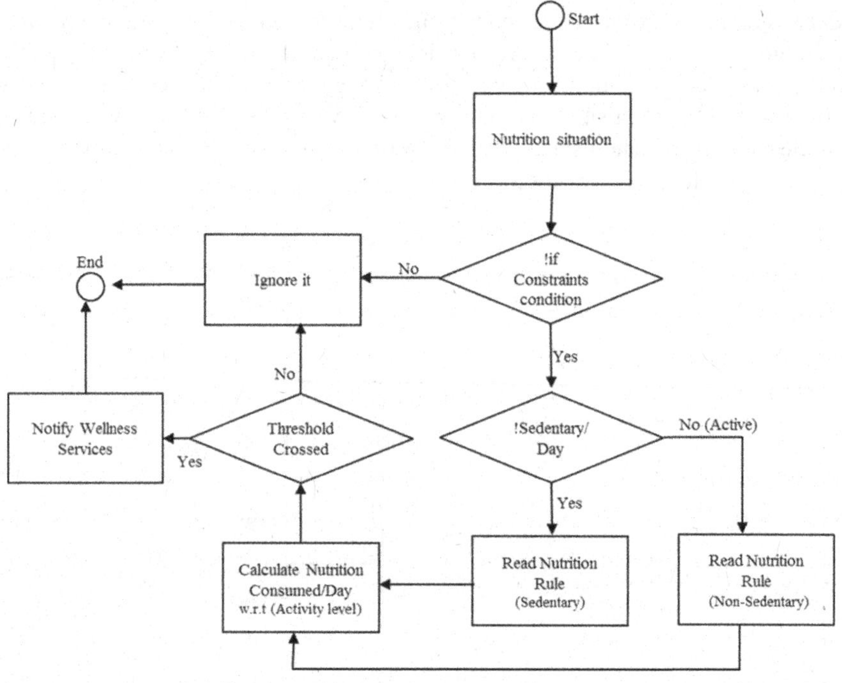

Fig. 4. Flow chart of Life-log Monitoring

3.3 Situation Event Detector

The identification of an unhealthy diet depends on the intake of the amount of nutrients in a whole day till current time. Monitoring of such situation is performed by Situation Event Detector (SED), which is key component of the LLM. It identifies the situation when amount of nutrients cross the threshold values with respect to some context. These situations are identified by the guidelines provided by the expert in the form of rules. The situation detection task is performed by Alarming Situation Evaluator (ASE) which map the intake nutrients with the defined target. While indication in a particular communication format is performed by the Alarming Situation Notifier (ASN).

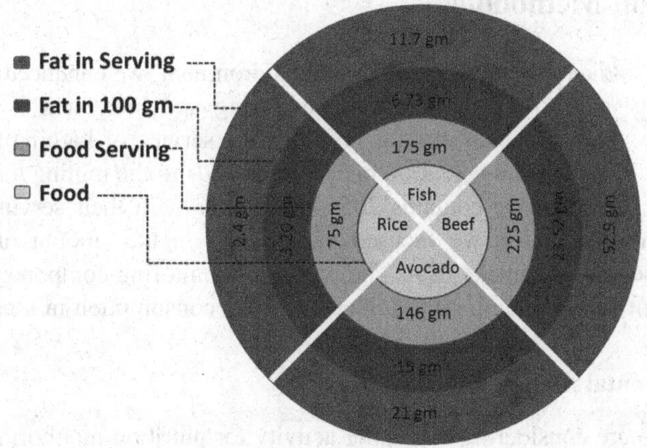

Fig. 5. Amount of Nutrient serving

ASE identify the abnormal nutrition situation by comparing the quantity of nutrition accumulated in the whole day as shown in Fig. 4. For the accumulation of nutrients we used the information extracted by the guide lines of United States Department of Agriculture [18]. It provides about the amount of nutrient per 100 g of food. It converted nutrient amount into serving amount with the help of information extracted about serving [19] as shown in Fig. 5.

It also perform analysis of user behavior in-term of sedentary or active in a particular day as per the information extracted from Canadian Physical Activity guidelines [17] as shown in Fig. 6. The ASE handover the unhealthy nutrition situation to ASN for the conversion of the nutrition and user information into common communication format and send it to the wellness services for indication and recommendations.

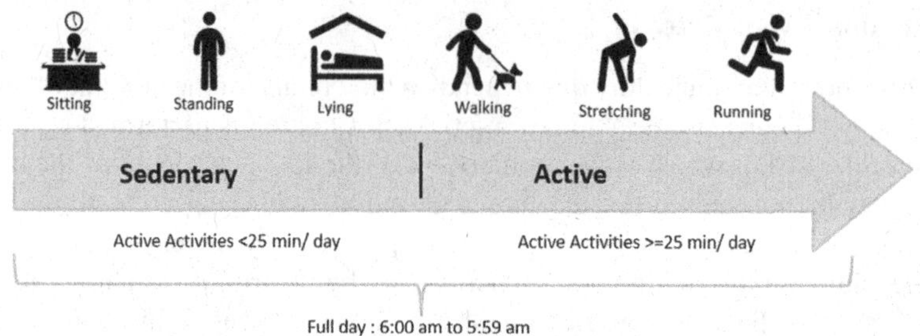

Fig. 6. Activities for Behavior Identification

4 Evaluation Methodology

To evaluate the indication for nutrition in real environment, we enhanced our previous work of activity monitoring to nutrition monitoring and integrated it with Mining Minds platform. The MM platform has provided the service of logging food through picture and tag. The user can take food picture and sends to the mining minds platform with food tag. Our database contains 2055 food items with their serving amount of nutrients. In this evaluation we focused particularly on the amount of fat nutrient required by a person and intake of it. The nutrition monitoring component manipulate the food nutrient for maintaining the log and nutrient consumption in a particular day.

4.1 Experimental Setup

In this work we are considering the eating activity for nutrition monitoring along with physical activities, so that we can validate monitoring of nutrition quantity intake for two different kinds of user i.e. the sedentary and the active one. We have 10 adult volunteers of different ages and gender. All of them have different height and weight. Through BMI calculation we can see there are three main groups of people on the basis of weight, as shown in Table 2.

Table 2. Volunteers detail involved in experiment

Subject	Age	Gender	Height (cm)	Weight (kg)	BMI	Weight status
S1	33	Male	178	92	29	Over
S2	27	Male	173	73	24.4	Normal
S3	28	Female	168	72	25.5	Over
S4	29	Female	164	56	20.8	Normal
S5	24	Male	179	69	21.5	Normal
S6	25	Male	176	75	24.2	Normal
S7	24	Male	165	48	17.5	Normal
S8	28	Female	165	64	23.5	Normal
S9	23	Male	165	66	24.2	Normal
S10	39	Male	180	86	26.5	Over

The Mining Minds platform has high accuracy to identify different activities: sitting, standing, lying, walking, stretching, running and eating [15]. Our nutrition expert provides the amount of nutrition required in different groups of people. The adults can be divided into 12 groups on the basis of gender, weight status, and activity level with the recommended fat amount (gm) per day as shown in Table 3.

Table 3. Situations for monitoring the activities

Sr.#	Age group	Gender	Weight status	Activity level	Recommended fat
1	Adult	Male	Over	Sedentary	69 g
2	Adult	Male	Over	Active	72 g
3	Adult	Male	Normal	Sedentary	70 g
4	Adult	Male	Normal	Active	82 g
5	Adult	Female	Over	Sedentary	60 g
6	Adult	Female	Over	Active	70 g
7	Adult	Female	Normal	Sedentary	66 g
8	Adult	Female	Normal	Active	78 g
9	Adult	Male	Under	Active	85 g
10	Adult	Female	Under	Active	74 g
11	Adult	Male	Under	Sedentary	69 g
12	Adult	Female	Under	Sedentary	61 g

We have recorded the activities of the volunteers as a whole for 3 weeks with minimum of 4 days in a week. The indication is provided on the basis of food that they logged and the location detection with respect to time.

4.2 Evaluation Criteria

The performance of the LLM is monitored on the basis of the feedback gathered from the volunteer as well as the log saved by them regarding the fat intake a whole day. These volunteers are students, about 30% enjoy their meals in the lab and rest take meal either at home or restaurant. The timing for the breakfast is between 7:00 am to 10:00 am, for lunch is 12:00 pm to 3:00 pm and for dinner is 6:00 pm to 10:00 pm.

In the 1st week duration MM platform only recorded the food log without creating any indication and recommendation of food. In this duration volunteers had recorded all the food stuff that they took in the whole day. The breakfast, lunch and dinner were recorded very well but there was issue regarding other supplementary food stuff (like chocolates, biscuits, chips). In next 2 weeks, LLM started monitoring and indicated the volunteers about the food on the basis of required fats and fats already consumed by them. The indication is produced to the wellness service whenever the amount of nutrient particularly fats crossed threshold value for a particular day i.e. 6:00 am to 5:59 am. Moreover if the amount of nutrient crossed the threshold value with a particular meal then after that indication is also generated.

4.3 Experimental Result Analysis

LLM starts monitoring of the nutrients as soon as user logged the food. It manipulates the physical activity status of the user to identify the sedentary or active status. Then check for the threshold with respect to the category of user for nutrient. We have evaluated the effectiveness of indication in three different scenarios:

(i) Start of Meal time,
(ii) Food Logging time,
(iii) Location and Meal time based

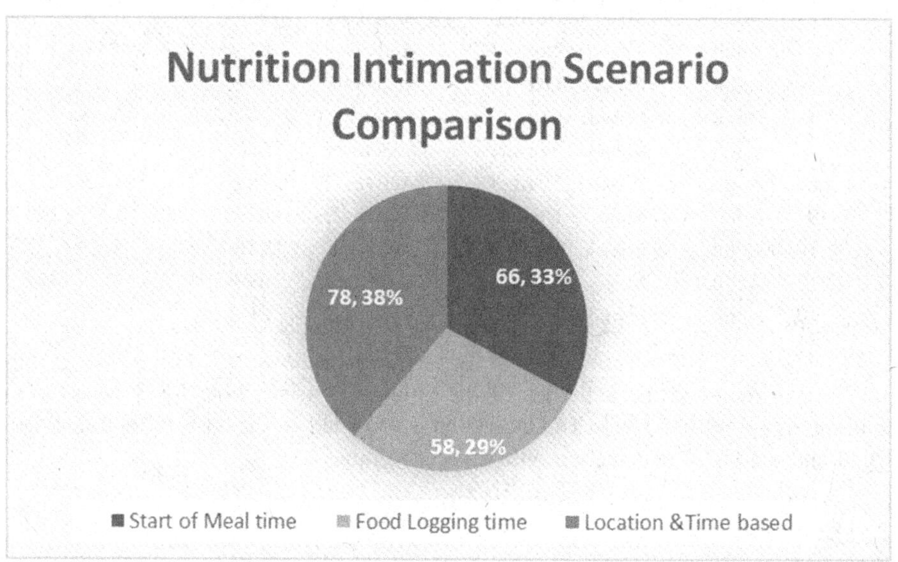

Fig. 7. Nutrition Intimation Scenario Comparison

After analysis of the food log, it is observed that the indication of nutrition on the basis of location and time is quite effective as shown in Fig. 7. While the indication at the food logging time is the least effective. According to the volunteers' feedback, they have to remember about the food recommendation for long period of time. According to the analysis, we divided the volunteers into 3 categories which were overweight, normal weight and underweight groups and all of these were under the category of sedentary activity level. The result shows that there is an impact of indication that improved the intake of fats amount of all three categories, but the change in overweight category is little higher as shown in Fig. 8.

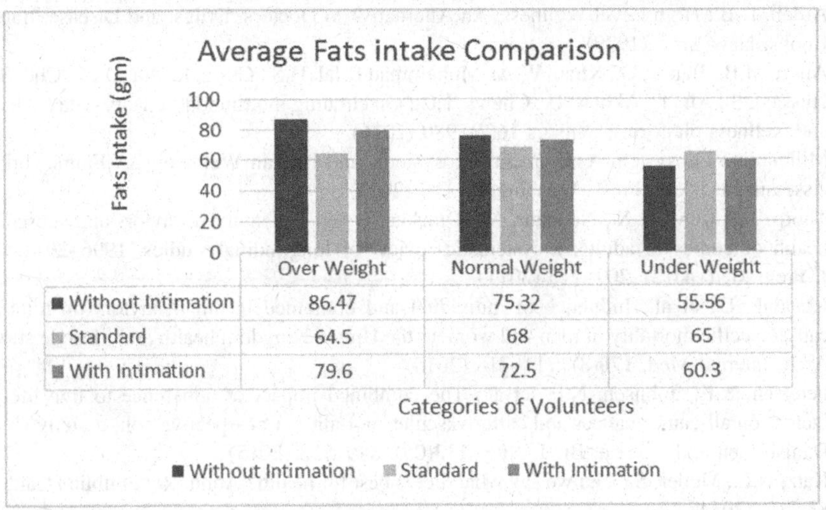

Fig. 8. Fats Intake Comparison chart

5 Conclusion and Future Work

The designed LLM monitors the fat nutrient and indicate about the target values to the user recommended by the expert rules. The push based methodology of indication supports the users to adopt healthy dietary behavior proactively. It is a new approach to monitor nutrition and push information instead of waiting for the user or expert to examine the daily diet. This technique can support the wellness applications to become proactive to avoid the bad impact of unhealthy behavior. The precautionary approach can be adopted for more effective way to reduce weight and maintain balanced diet for longer period. Currently, the LLM monitors diet for sedentary and active adult persons with respect to gender and weight status. In wellness domain the diet has a big influence on diabetic, cardiac and hypertensive patients. In future we will extend the LLM for monitoring and intimating the dietary pattern for chronic disease patients.

Acknowledgments. This work was supported by the Industrial Core Technology Development Program (10049079), Develop of mining core technology exploiting personal big data) funded by the Ministry of Trade, Industry and Energy (MOTIE, Korea) and this research was supported by Basic Science Research Program through the National Research Foundation of Korea (NRF) funded by the Ministry of Science, ICT and Future Planning (2011-0030079).

References

1. Sweeney, T.J., Witmer, J.M.: Beyond social interest: Striving toward optimum health and wellness. Individ. Psychol. **47**, 527–540 (1991)
2. Witmer, J.M., Sweeney, T.J.: A holistic model for wellness and prevention over the lifespan. J. Couns. Dev. **71**, 140–148 (1992)

3. Ardell, D.B.: High Level Wellness, An Alternative to Doctors, Drugs, and Disease. Bantam Books, New York (1979)
4. Amin, M.B., Banos, O., Khan, W.A., Muhammad Bilal, H.S., Gong, J., Bui, D.M., Cho, S.H., Hussain, S., Ali, T., Akhtar, U., Chung, T.C.: On curating multimodal sensory data for health and wellness platforms. Sensors **16**(7), 980 (2016)
5. Millennium Ecosystem Assessment: Ecosystems and Human Wellbeing: A Framework for Assessment. Island Press, Washington, DC (2003)
6. Thorp, A.A., Owen, N., Neuhaus, M., Dunstan, D.W.: Sedentary behaviors and subsequent health outcomes in adults: a systematic review of longitudinal studies, 1996–2011. Am. J. Prev. Med. **41**(2), 207–215 (2011)
7. Kvaavik, E., et al.: Influence of individual and combined health behaviors on total and cause-specific mortality in men and women: the United Kingdom health and lifestyle survey. Arch. Internal Med. **170**(8), 711–718 (2010)
8. Petersen, K.E., Johnsen, N.F., et al.: The combined impact of adherence to five lifestyle factors on all-cause, cancer and cardiovascular mortality: a prospective cohort study among Danish men and women. Br. J. Nutr. **113**(05), 849–858 (2015)
9. Katz, D.L., Meller, S.: Can we say what diet is best for health? Annu. Rev. Public Health **35**, 83–103 (2014)
10. Azumio: Argus quantify your day-to-day (2015). http://www.azumio.com/s/argus/index.html
11. Ahmad, M., Amin, M.B., Hussain, S., Kang, B. H., Cheong, T., Lee, S.: Health Fog: a novel framework for health and wellness applications. J. Supercomputing, 1–19 (2016)
12. Banos, O., Amin, M.B., Ali Khan, W., Ali, T., Afzal, M., Kang, B. H., Lee, S.: Mining minds: an innovative framework for personalized health and wellness support. In: 2015 9th International Conference on Pervasive Computing Technologies for Healthcare (PervasiveHealth), pp. 1–8. IEEE (2015)
13. Khan, W.A., Amin, M.B., Banos, O., Ali, T., Hussain, M., Afzal, M., Hussain, S., Hussain, J., Ali, R., Ali, M., Kang, D,: Mining minds: journey of evolutionary platform for ubiquitous wellness
14. Ali, R., Afzal, M., Hussain, M., Ali, M., Siddiqi, M.H., Lee, S., Kang, B.H.: Multimodal hybrid reasoning methodology for personalized wellbeing services. Comput. Biol. Med. **69**, 10–28 (2016)
15. Banos, O., Amin, M.B., Khan, W.A., Afzal, M., Hussain, M., Kang, B.H., Lee, S.: The Mining Minds Digital Health and Wellness Framework
16. Australia New Zealand Food Standard Code (FSC). http://www.foodstandards.gov.au/code/Pages/default.aspx
17. CSEP: Canadian Physical Activity Guidelines (2017). http://csep.ca/CMFiles/Guidelines/CSEP_PAGuidelines_adults_en.pdf
18. USDA Food Composition Database. https://ndb.nal.usda.gov/ndb/
19. Portions per Person. https://www.cookipedia.co.uk/recipes_wiki/Portions_per_person

Activity and Recognition

Activity Recognition Enhancement Based on Ground-Truth: Introducing a New Method Including Accuracy and Granularity Metrics

Hamdi Aloulou[1,2(✉)], Romain Endelin[1,2], Mounir Mokhtari[1,2,3], Bessam Abdulrazak[4], Firas Kaddachi[2], and Joaquim Bellmunt[1,3]

[1] Institut Mines Telecom, Paris, France
{hamdi.aloulou,romain.endelin,mounir.mokhtari}@mines-telecom.fr
[2] Laboratory of Informatics, Robotics and Microelectronics, Montpellier, France
firas.kaddachi@lirmm.fr
[3] Image and Pervasive Access Laboratory, Singapore, Singapore
joaquim.bellmunt@ipal.cnrs.fr
[4] University of Sherbrooke, Sherbrooke, Canada
bessam.abdulrazak@usherbrooke.ca

Abstract. The uncertainty associated with existing sensing technologies and reasoning methods affects the outcome of the activity recognition process (e.g., accuracy, precision, granularity). The activity recognition process is even challenging when switching from laboratory towards real deployments, where scenarios are not predefined and more complex. Therefore we propose a novel method to improve the activity recognition outcome, by finding a proper balance between accuracy and granularity. The method has been validated through the deployment of UbiSMART (an AAL framework) in 45 scenarios of ageing in place. We discuss in this paper our method and the validation results.

Keywords: Ambient assisted living · Activity recognition · Semantic reasoning · Quality insurance · Ground-truth acquisition

1 Introduction

The acceptance of Ambient Assisted Living (AAL) solutions by stakeholders is a critical factor for the success and large use of such systems. Different criteria influence the acceptance of AAL solutions such as the usability, usage, usefulness. According to EN ISO 9241-11 [8], usability is defined as the degree of suitability of use of a system, a prototype, or a service in a particular application environment to achieve specific goals in a satisfactory and efficient manner. In this perspective, context-awareness and activity recognition are critical components leading to the acceptability and usability of AAL solutions.

Context-awareness and activity recognition are necessary to trigger adequate services on appropriate media, given a certain situation/context. An example can

M. Mokhtari et al. (Eds.): ICOST 2017, LNCS 10461, pp. 87–98, 2017.
DOI: 10.1007/978-3-319-66188-9_8

be to send an alert when a risk/dangerous situation is detected. Thus, fault inferences (i.e., lack of accuracy and granularity) in activity recognition are among the most critical issues we have identified in our experience with AAL. An inaccurate system generates a number of misleading reactions affecting the acceptability of the solution, whereas a coarse-grained system can possibly be accurate, but hardly useful.

Following, we present our approach to improve the activity recognition outcome based on collected ground-truth data. The approach adopts a hierarchical representation of activities and introduces two metrics "Accuracy" and "Granularity" in the activity recognition process. Section 2 illustrates the problems of fault inferences. Section 3 positions our contribution within the literature. Section 4 introduces our method to quantify the accuracy of a reasoning engine. Section 5 discusses our method to optimize the decision-making. We also introduce in this section a score of quality for activity recognition. Section 6 presents the validation of our method. Finally, Sect. 7 concludes the paper.

2 Granularity and Accuracy Issues in Activity Recognition

We propose to introduce the use of two metrics "accuracy" and "granularity" in the activity recognition process to improve its outcome and reduce fault inferences. For clarity purpose, it is important to distinguish the concepts of *granularity* and *accuracy*: The granularity represents who much precise an activity recognition engine was; for instance, a fine-grained inferred activity would be "on the phone with his daughter," and a coarse-grained activity would be "in the living-room." Therefore, we assign a granularity level to each specific activity. On the other hand, accuracy is defined in the literature [7] as the confidence that the inferred activity matches the reality (i.e., the confidence of having a correct inference). We use accuracy to determine the ability of an activity recognition engine to properly detect a specific activity. A system with 99% of accuracy would be considered highly accurate, whereas another system with 20% would be considered inaccurate.

From our experience, we can deduce that the more fine-grained an activity is, the less accurate it will be. To illustrate this, Fig. 1 represents two chains of hierarchical activities (one in circles and one in triangles). Activities on the upper left corner are the most fine-grained (for example eating pasta), however, they are difficult to infer and therefore they have low accuracy. On the other side, activities on the lower right corner are easy to infer (for example located in the kitchen) and therefore have the highest accuracy. However, they are too coarse-grained to provide appropriate services for the end-user. Therefore, our method presented in this paper intends to find the best balance between granularity and accuracy, in order to improve the outcome of the activity recognition process.

Following we discuss existing works on the evaluation and validation of reasoning engines, with techniques used to collect ground-truth and the employment of the "Accuracy" metric to evaluate the activity recognition engines outcome.

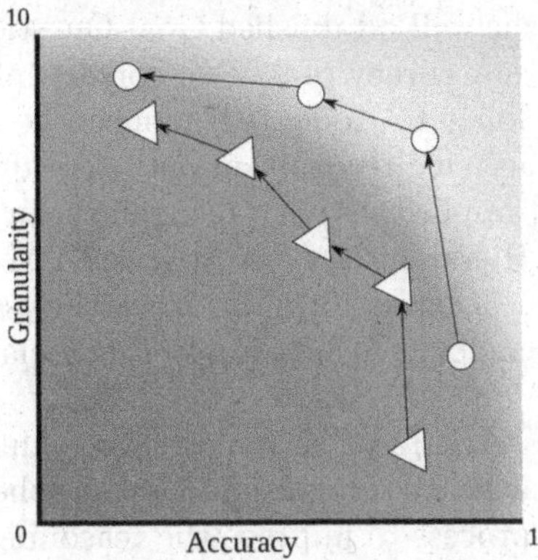

Fig. 1. Illustrating the relation between accuracy and granularity for activity recognition

3 Related Works

A large number of AAL solutions prototypes exist around the world [3,14,17]. Nevertheless only few of them involve long-term deployments with real data gathering [15]. Yet, we witness recently a shift in AAL research, from laboratory experiments towards real deployments. This shift is accompanied by the creation of several databases that enable researchers to share the real-world deployment recorded data. CASAS[1] is an example of these databases.

The limitation in the number of AAL solutions aiming for long-term deployment is a big burden towards the validation of the accuracy of such solutions. We believe that the availability of databases for real-world deployment records will promote the development and validation of approaches to improve accuracy of AAL solutions. In addition, a key step towards wide acceptance of AAL solutions is the evaluation and validation of reasoning engines [1]. The legacy approach for assessing elderly people Activities of Daily Livings (ADLs), whether by direct observations [10] or by questionnaires [6,13], are very instructive, but they lack practical applications towards activity recognition in the AAL. These solutions are difficult to put in place in nursing homes and especially in personal residences for end-users living independently as the observations are limited to specific points of time when caregivers are available. They are based on a manual process which is tedious and time-consuming. Thus, some technological solutions should be put in place to easily collect elderly people ADLs and directly introduce them in the evaluation and improvement process of the AAL solution accuracy.

Several researchers have been interested in accuracy using the datasets gathered from the real-world deployment [4,5,9]. For example, Cook [5] has used CASAS datasets to perform machine-learning methods for activity recognition; the results of her team were around 75% on rich training datasets. Kleinberger et al. [11] performed a thorough validation of their system, measuring its

[1] http://ailab.wsu.edu/casas/datasets.html.

accuracy with the use of the well-established Goal-Question-Metric (GQM) approach [2]. They observe an accuracy of 92% of correct inferences on average for simple ADLs such as "Going to Toilet." Kadouche et al. used Support Vector Machine (SVM) for activity recognition and they obtained an accuracy of 88% [9]. Chung et al. [4] applied activity recognition in an application targeting nursing home. Using Hierarchical Context Hidden Markov Model (hchmm), they obtain a recognition accuracy of 85%. Nevertheless, their activity recognition process relies on cameras, which is often associated with acceptability issues.

These approaches use "Accuracy" as a metric to evaluate the performance of their reasoning engine in activity recognition. On the other hand, the results are not used in a systematic process to improve the reasoning approach or methodology. The method we propose in this paper uses both metrics accuracy and granularity in an iterative process to gradually improve the reasoning engine outcome without changing the approach used or bringing new sensing technologies and complicate the deployment. In addition, researches to improve activity recognition have been supported by the development of novel algorithms based on Artificial Neural Network, Naive Bays, Support Vector Machine, etc. [16]. The method we introduce in this paper to improve the activity recognition outcome is reasoner-agnostic. It can be applied with any approach for activity recognition (e.g., machine-learning, ontological reasoning).

We believe that accuracy and granularity are key criteria in the validation of the activity recognition outcome, since accuracy is an indicator of the reliability of an AAL system and granularity is an indicator of its usefulness. We also believe that using these two indicators in an iterative process of activity recognition will improve the reasoning engine outcome. Our method improves the decision-making process on the output of the reasoning (i.e., the set of activities possibly being performed by the end-user), through accuracy, granularity, and score of the reasoning engine.

4 Measuring Accuracy of a Rule Engine

We discuss in this section the measurement of the deployed solution accuracy. As an example of inaccurate inference, the system infers that the end-user "*Watches TV*" at 14:00, whereas we know from direct observations that he actually "*Takes a Nap.*" There is a need to know how accurate a reasoning engine is, in order to improve the quality of activity recognition. Thus, there is a need to measure the confidence towards the fact that an activity is actually being performed, given that it has been inferred. To obtain this confidence, we first need to enrich our datasets with real observations (*ground-truth*), in order to confront inferred activities with observed ones. The relation between real activities, sensor events, and inferred activities can be summarized in Fig. 2. Following we discuss the process of gathering ground-truth and measuring the accuracy of activities.

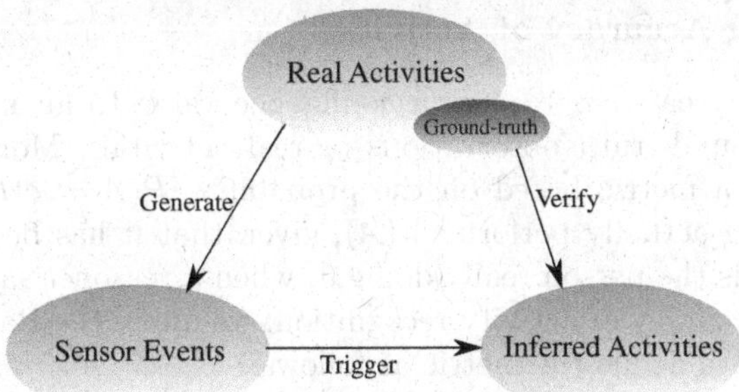

Fig. 2. Relation between Real Activities, Inferred Activities, and Sensor Events

4.1 Gathering Ground-Truth

The most straightforward method to gather ground-truth is to perform direct observation in a real-world environment. A human observer regularly observes and records what end-users do. The result is a list of punctual observations of activities over a period of time. Through this method, we can be certain that the observations represent a real situation. However a bias may be introduced by the sampling periods: the observers are more likely to perform the ground-truth acquisition only at specific hours of the day (e.g., in morning time for nurses), ending up with an heterogeneous density of data, that must be translated later in the measurement process. The ground-truth acquisition is a manual process, and it is not immune to human errors. This manual process is time-consuming, which restricts observers recruiting.

This method may also have logistic difficulties and acceptance issues, particularly in the case of collecting data linked to end-user living independently. We have experienced this situation ourselves in individual houses. A solution would be to ask caregivers to perform acquisition, but it would only bring little benefit, as caregivers would actually influence the environment they observe. In fact, in this situation, ground-truth acquisitions would take place in a multi-user situations (i.e., end-user and caregiver), in which the acquired data sensors cannot be considered linked only to the end-user.

We have provided a dedicated mobile application which sends a quick questionnaire when the system wants to verify the reasoning output or a risky situation is detected. This solution was used by our collaborating nursing home's caregivers and helped to semi-automatically collect ground-truth data without seriously affecting the caregivers daily routines. It also allowed integrating data directly into our process of activities accuracy measurement.

Another approach to overcome the limitations of the direct observation by human would be using cameras. This method is rich in data, however, we did not consider it due to acceptability and privacy concerns.

4.2 Measuring Accuracy of Activities

One goal of our research is to give a confidence value to an inferred activity based on our ground-truth observations of real activities. More precisely, we are interested in a metric based on the probability $P(A = a|I = a)$ that an activity a is being actually performed (A), given that it has been inferred (I). In other words: "is the person really doing a, when a reasoner says a?" In order to measure the accuracy of activity recognition, we apply the Bayes equation of probability [12]. We define the metric as follows:

$$P(A = a|I = i) = \frac{P(A = a \cap I = i)}{P(I = i)} = \frac{|a \cap i|}{|A \cap I|P(I = i)} = \frac{|a \cap i| \sum_{X \in I} duration(X)}{|A \cap I| \sum_{x \in i} duration(x)} \quad (1)$$

where:
$|a \cap i|$ is the number of occurrences when i is inferred and a is observed
$|A \cap I|$ is the number of observations made while inferring an activity
$\sum_{X \in I} duration(X)$ is the total duration covered by our inferences
$\sum_{x \in i} duration(x)$ is the total duration when i is inferred

In the case when the activity has never been observed or never been inferred, we set accuracy value of this activity as 0.

5 Improving the Decision-Making Process by Introducing a Score of Quality

We believe that the accuracy metric can be helpful to evaluate the quality of a reasoning engine. By coupling accuracy with granularity, and introducing hierarchical activities models, we propose a systematic method to improve the activity recognition outcome and help the reasoner to conclude with more effective inferences.

5.1 Introducing Granularity to the Reasoner

The reasoner may infer "Takes Shower" whereas the ground-truth shows a faulty inference, as the end-user "Goes to Toilet." It could also infer "Is Busy", which is not an adequate inference for a service delivery. These two cases are caused by an irrelevant granularity. In fact, in some cases, the reasoner tends to be too fine-grained, and leads to an inaccurate inference. The reasoner could infer a slightly less precise activity with more accuracy.

Generally, a human observer intuitively adjusts his conclusions to the expected level of granularity. He also measures the risks of being inaccurate when he makes fine-grained conclusions. Our approach is to apply the same process for decision-making in activity recognition, so that the system will minimize the risk of inaccuracy and maximize granularity. Thus, we represent granularity in our model as a value ranging from "1" to "10," determined by an expert. "1" would be an extremely coarse-grained activity and "10" would be an extremely fine-grained one. We argue that introducing granularity into the model as an arbitrary value is acceptable because an acceptable granularity is a non-functional requirement of a system, which is by nature arbitrary.

5.2 Introducing Hierarchical Activities

"Takes Shower" and "Goes to Toilet" can both be generalized as "Is in the Bathroom." In other words, "Is in the Bathroom" is a parent activity of "Takes Shower" and "Goes to Toilet." More generally, activities exist at different granularities, and can be modeled as hierarchies. With a hierarchical model, several activities are inferred at a given time, and a person can be both "Going To Toilet" and "In the Bathroom." When an activity occurs, all of its generalizations occur, recursively. Similarly, we can affirm that when an activity occurs, some of its specializations may occur too. An example of a hierarchical model is presented in Fig. 3, and the generalization inference goes from right to left.

Hierarchical models are richer than linear models, and the ability to infer activities on several layers has powerful applications when combined with granularity and accuracy. In a hierarchical model, an activity always has a higher granularity than its parent. On the other hand, an activity always has a lower accuracy than its parent: if an activity is accurate, its parent will always be accurate, but if an activity is not accurate, its parent will sometimes be accurate. Following this logic, we created a formal process to perform accurate inferences while being as fine-grained as possible. The reasoning process is similar to a tree exploration, where the system starts by reasoning on the most coarse-grained activities (i.e., the activities with no parent) to its specializations (more fine-grained). In this path (parent → kid), the reasoning checks whether the context can be valid or not (for of each specialization). This process can be executed recursively across specializations until the inference of a chain of activities, from coarse-grained to fine-grained (Fig. 1). We expect that with this process, a system converges towards the activity that has the best balance between granularity and accuracy.

5.3 Measuring Performance of the Reasoning Engine

We propose to formalize the process of inferring activities with the right level of granularity. Therefore, we introduced a score of quality of activity recognition that enables the reasoner to converge towards the activity having the best balance of accuracy vs. granularity. Our proposed process starts by giving each activity a score, that is based on its accuracy and granularity. Then, the decision-making engine selects the activity with the best score. The system uses a weighted geometric mean of accuracy and granularity (Eq. 2) to measure

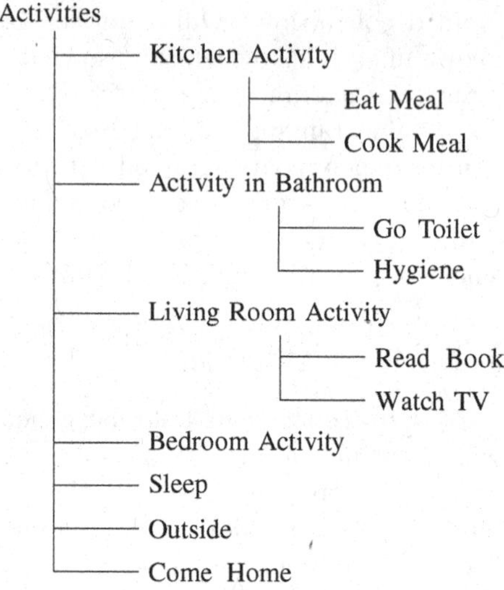

Fig. 3. A hierarchical set of activities

score. The advantage of a geometric mean is that a marginally low value of either granularity or accuracy has a dramatic impact on the resulting score, and an accuracy of 0% will result in a score of 0.

$$Score(a) = \left(accuracy\,(a)^{A} \times (0.1 \times granularity\,(a))^{G}\right)^{\frac{1}{A \times G}} \quad (2)$$

Where:

A is the weight given to accuracy
G is the weight given to granularity
The 0.1 factor normalizes granularity in range [0, 1]

A and G are to be defined by experts. However, there is no objective criteria to set them. From our empirical experience, we choose to give more importance to accuracy than to granularity and we set $A = 3$ and $G = 1$. The goal is to have the most useful sets for the end-user experience. We also propose to run reasoners with various values of A and G, and ask end-users which reasoner generates the most useful conclusions.

6 Validation

Our proposed method was validated using our AAL framework Ubiquitous Service MAnagement & Reasoning sysTem (UbiSMART). UbiSMART was deployed in a real environment where several scenarios of aging in place were performed. The first version did neither include the hierarchical activities approach, nor the metrics of Accuracy and Granularity. We have updated UbiSMART in order to support accuracy and granularity. The new UbiSMART reasoner can be executed in two different ways:

1. **In calibration mode:** we execute the reasoner in order to measure the accuracy of all activities in hierarchical chain. We expect the reasoner to return all possible valid inferred activities, without making a conclusion. The result of the calibration mode is used as an input for the production mode. The calibration mode is run only at the first phases of deployment. Once the reasoner has converged towards stationary accuracy values, there is no need to run calibration mode anymore.
2. **In production mode:** we execute the reasoner in order to infer a single activity at a given time. In this case, accuracy measurement is predefined and calculated during the calibration mode. The production mode is the mode used by UbiSMART framework to deliver adaptable services.

We use the same collected datasets to run the UbiSMART's reasoner, before and after applying the proposed method. We have experimented our system in the environment represented in Table 1 and with the activities summarized in Table 2.

Table 1. Topology of the experiment

Room	Bedroom	Bathroom	Living Room	Kitchen	Entrance
Sensors	Motion sensor	Motion sensor	Motion sensor	Motion sensor Door sensor (fridge)	Motion sensor Door sensor (main door)

6.1 Introducing Validation Metrics

We propose four metrics to validate our proposed method. The first metric is the Recall R (e.i. total measured accuracy vs. ground-truth) as defined in Eq. 3. R is useful to measure the exact accuracy of the reasoning, given that we have a ground-truth on the executed dataset. R is similar to the measured accuracy of an activity (Eq. 1), but it is measured on all activities at once (A), not on a specific activity. It is defined as the number of times the system inferred correctly (based on ground-truth observations), divided by the total number of activities that are both inferred and observed.

$$R(A) = \frac{|\{groundtruth(a) = inferred(a) | a \in A\}|}{|groundtruth(A) \cap inferred(A)|} \tag{3}$$

Three other metrics have been introduced: the average value of accuracy ($\bar{A}$), granularity ($\bar{G}$) and score ($\bar{S}$) for the inferred activities (Eq. 4). These three metrics provide an estimation of accuracy, granularity, and score of reasoning engine in a dataset, even in the absence of ground-truth. $\bar{A}$ is not to be confused with the total measured accuracy R. $\bar{A}$ is an indicator that can be obtained at any time, whereas R is exact, but requires ground-truth to be measured.

$$\bar{X}(act) = \frac{\sum_{a \in act} (X(a) \times d(a))}{\sum_{a \in act} d(a)} \quad (4)$$

where: X = accuracy — granularity — score; act = activities; d = duration

6.2 Results

We run UbiSMART reasoning engine in both modes (i.e., calibration and production). Table 2 presents accuracy, granularity and score values for each activity, after the calibration mode. Score is calculated using Eq. 2 from Sect. 5.3, with an accuracy weight $A = 3$ and a granularity weight $G = 1$. For comparison, a second score is calculated, using $A = 1$ and $G = 1$. We observe that activities that are coarse-grained but extremely accurate, such as "*Kitchen Activity*", are more valued with a higher value of A. With $A = 3$, it has a score of 79.5%, whereas it only has a score of 63.2% with $A = 1$. On the opposite, a more fine-grained and less accurate activity, such as "*Cook Meal*" has a score of 64.5% with $A = 3$, and 69.3% with $A = 1$. When both "*Kitchen Activity*" and "*Cook Meal*" are inferred, the reasoner will conclude with "*Kitchen Activity*" if $A = 3$, and with "*Cook Meal*" if $A = 1$.

We run the reasoner four times in production mode: with $(A = 3, G = 1)$ and with $(A = 1, G = 1)$, in both case *before* and *after* running the calibration (Table 3). Without calibration, each activity has a default accuracy of 10%, and scores are calculated accordingly. With $(A = 3, G = 1)$, we measure $T = 93.8\%$ after the calibration, whereas R was only 63.4% before the calibration (+30.4%). $\bar{G}$ has decreased from 6.75 to 4.15 (−2.60), and $\bar{A}$ has increased from 55.5% to 89.4% (+33.9%). This illustrates the trade-off between accuracy and granularity. With $(A = 1, G = 1)$, the calibration impact is less significant. R happens to increase by 3.3%. $\bar{A}$ decreases by 11.8%, and $\bar{G}$ increases by 0.26. This is explained by the fact that with $A = 1$, the reasoner is not allowed to decrease much granularity in favor of accuracy. Thus, it will tend to be as fine-grained as possible, which is similar to its default behavior, without the method introduced in this paper. Finally, we notice that $\bar{S}$ increases with both values of (A, G): +16.5% with $(A = 3, G = 1)$ and +1.7% with $(A = 1, G = 1)$. This is inherent to the method we propose, which always selects the activity with the maximal score among all the inferred activity.

Table 2. Scores of the original UbiSMART reasoner

Activity	Kitchen Activity	Cook Meal	Bathroom Activity	Go Toilet	Living Room Activity	Read book	Bedroom Activity	Sleep
Accuracy	100%	60%	100%	50%	100%	50%	100%	100%
Granularity	4	8	4	8	4	8	6	7
Score A = 3, G = 1	79.5%	64.5%	79.5%	56.2%	79.5%	56.2%	88%	91.5%
Score A = 1, G = 1	63.2%	69.3%	63.2%	63.2%	63.2%	63.2%	77.5%	83.7%

Table 3. Results with $(A = 3, G = 1)$ and $(A = 1, G = 1)$, *before* and after the calibration

Sample	A	G	Total Accuracy	Average Accuracy	Average Granularity	Average Score
Before calibration	*3*	*1*	63.4%	55.5%	6.75	56.9%
After calibration			93.8%	89.4%	4.15	73.4%
Before calibration	*1*	*1*	63.4%	67.3%	5.56	59%
After calibration			66.7%	55.5%	5.82	60.7%

7 Conclusion

We have introduced in this paper our research on improving the activity recognition decision-making process in developing AAL solutions. This research has been motivated by the feedback we had from our real deployment in a nursing home and three individual houses. The observations from this real deployment brought our attention to the faulty results of our reasoning engine and stressed the need for a systematic method to evaluate reasoning engines in order to improve the activity recognition process.

We argue that an efficient systematic method to evaluate reasoning engines has to include ground-truth from deployment environment (e.g., elderly people house). Therefore, we proposed a method that includes observing ground-truth as an input for measuring the accuracy of a reasoning engine. We also introduce for the first time granularity and score of the quality of a reasoning engine. The score is derived from accuracy and granularity. Our method effectively leads to conclude on the most reasonable activity (i.e., the activity with the best balance between granularity and accuracy). We found that by giving more importance to accuracy over granularity, our reasoner infers more coarse-grained activities, in order to be more accurate.

Acknowledgments. This research project has been supported by the Quality Of Life Chair supported by Foundation Telecom of the Institut Mines-Telecom in France, La Mutuelle Generale and REUNICA which figure among the major health-care insurance companies in France. The work is also supported by the grand emprunt VHP inter@ctive project. We also wish to acknowledge the support of the Saint-Vincent-de-Paul nursing home and its director Brigitte Choquet, who kindly let us deploy our system within their environment.

References

1. Abdulrazak, B., Malik, Y.: Review of challenges, requirements, and approaches of pervasive computing system evaluation. IETE Tech. Rev. **29**(6), 506–522 (2012)
2. Basili, V.R.: Software modeling and measurement: the goal/question/metric paradigm (1992)

3. Biswas, J., et al.: Activity recognition in assisted living facilities with incremental, approximate ground truth. In: Geissbühler, A., Demongeot, J., Mokhtari, M., Abdulrazak, B., Aloulou, H. (eds.) ICOST 2015. LNCS, vol. 9102, pp. 103–115. Springer, Cham (2015). doi:10.1007/978-3-319-19312-0_9
4. Chung, P.C., Liu, C.D.: A daily behavior enabled hidden markov model for human behavior understanding. Pattern Recogn. **41**(5), 1572–1580 (2008)
5. Cook, D.J.: Learning setting-generalized activity models for smart spaces. IEEE Intell. Syst. **2010**(99), 1 (2010)
6. Fillenbaum, G.G.: Multidimensional Functional Assessment of Older Adults: The Duke Older Americans Resources and Services procedures. Psychology Press, London (2013)
7. Jahn, A., David, K.: Improved activity recognition by using grouped activities. In: 2016 IEEE International Conference on Pervasive Computing and Communication Workshops (PerCom Workshops), pp. 1–5. IEEE (2016)
8. Jokela, T., Iivari, N., Matero, J., Karukka, M.: The standard of user-centered design and the standard definition of usability: analyzing ISO 13407 against ISO 9241–11. In: Proceedings of the Latin American Conference on Human-Computer Interaction, pp. 53–60. ACM (2003)
9. Kadouche, R., Abdulrazak, B., Mokhtari, M., Giroux, S., Pigot, H.: Semantic matching framework for handicap situation detection in smart environments. J. Ambient Intell. Smart Environ. **1**(3), 223–234 (2009)
10. Katz, S., Ford, A.B., Moskowitz, R.W., Jackson, B.A., Jaffe, M.W.: Studies of illness in the aged: the index of adl: a standardized measure of biological and psychosocial function. JAMA **185**(12), 914–919 (1963)
11. Kleinberger, T., Jedlitschka, A., Storf, H., Steinbach-Nordmann, S., Prueckner, S.: An approach to and evaluations of assisted living systems using ambient intelligence for emergency monitoring and prevention. In: Stephanidis, C. (ed.) UAHCI 2009. LNCS, vol. 5615, pp. 199–208. Springer, Heidelberg (2009). doi:10.1007/978-3-642-02710-9_23
12. Koch, K.-R.: Bayes' Theorem. Bayesian Inference with Geodetic Applications. LNES, vol. 31, pp. 4–8. Springer, Heidelberg (1990). doi:10.1007/BFb0048702
13. Lawton, M.P.: Scales to measure competence in everyday activities. Psychopharmacol. Bull. **24**(4), 609–614 (1987)
14. Memon, M., Wagner, S.R., Pedersen, C.F., Beevi, F.H.A., Hansen, F.O.: Ambient assisted living healthcare frameworks, platforms, standards, and quality attributes. Sensors **14**(3), 4312–4341 (2014)
15. Mokhtari, M., Aloulou, H., Tiberghien, T., Biswas, J., Racoceanu, D., Yap, P.: New trends to support independence in persons with mild dementia-a mini-review. Gerontology **58**(6), 554–563 (2012)
16. Slim, S.O., Atia, A., Mostafa, M.-S.M.: An experimental comparison between seven classification algorithms for activity recognition. In: Gaber, T., Hassanien, A.E., El-Bendary, N., Dey, N. (eds.) AISI 2015. AISC, vol. 407, pp. 37–46. Springer, Cham (2016). doi:10.1007/978-3-319-26690-9_4
17. Yared, R., Abdulrazak, B., Tessier, T., Mabilleau, P.: Cooking risk analysis to enhance safety of elderly people in smart kitchen. In: Proceedings of the 8th ACM International Conference on Pervasive Technologies Related to Assistive Environments, p. 12. ACM (2015)

Activity Model for Interactive Micro Context-Aware Well-Being Applications Based on ContextAA

Victor Ponce(✉) and Bessam Abdulrazak

Université de Sherbrooke, 2500, boul. de l'Université, Sherbrooke, QC, Canada
{Victor.Ponce,Bessam.Abdulrazak}@USherbrooke.ca

Abstract. Representing people activities in smart environments is an important aspect of supporting people well-being. Improving activity representation enables exploiting the semantics of people's actions. We propose a novel activity model that facilitates the representation based on the ContextAA micro context-aware programming approach. In this approach, applications contain a self-described semantics in an ontic knowledge, and autonomic components interpret the knowledge to augment the interaction and adaptation of pervasive smart environments. In this paper, we present our model which integrates the semantics of the activity as an essential part of the ontic knowledge. We also present the programming constructs designed to facilitate building micro context-aware applications, and the components implemented to reduce the activity semantics to a minimal self-described context capable of being deployed in our ContextAA micro smart environment platform.

Keywords: Activity model · Micro context-awareness · Semantics · Ontic

1 Introduction

People dynamicity is an important aspect of pervasive computing systems because of the increasingly need for supporting people activities with technologies. This aspect is more relevant in well-being assistance for elderly people, where activities range from dynamic to unknown, due to the continuous decline of the cognitive abilities/health conditions of this population. For example, an elderly person can prepare a meal today, but not tomorrow because of a sudden change due to stress, requiring performing another activity such as walking. Dynamic/unknown activities also require executing in diverse environments, from smart homes to smart cities, demanding an immediate extension of the limits of computational spaces. For well-being assistance, domain experts (e.g., physicians, caregivers) are required to become programmers to build applications to support dynamic people activities. Thus, domain experts, who are non-technical users, require manipulating activities that can change regularly, and smart environments must provide functionalities for an appropriate interaction and adaptation to dynamic user activities in diverse spaces.

Smart environment systems include, in the first instance, mechanisms to interpret the *knowledge* of the current situation (i.e., user conditions, activity, environment

M. Mokhtari et al. (Eds.): ICOST 2017, LNCS 10461, pp. 99–111, 2017.
DOI: 10.1007/978-3-319-66188-9_9

context) [21]. These systems use the *knowledge* to adapt the environment based on the user requirements (e.g., goals, preferences, habits) defined in the context-aware applications. In general, these applications contain a limited representation of the situation, limiting the scope of these applications. Consequently, context-aware applications have been relegated to be only an additional tool for specific situations. Moreover, the actual process for building applications is time-consuming. These processes mainly apply programming language constructs, originally designed for technical people (e.g., software developers). On the other hand, pre-defined solutions in app stores and service provision in the cloud (e.g., sensing-as-a-service) facilitate programming for simple situations(e.g., IF This Then That(IFTTT) [20] and cloud providers for integrating and reacting with smart sensors/appliances). These pre-defined solutions promote the use of context-aware applications by non-technical users (e.g., physician, home user). These users can install/access software components and use applications/services for supporting specific needs. Both traditional approaches (i.e., programming languages and pre-defined solutions) are designed for general purpose, reducing the possibility of interchange context beyond domain boundaries, and limiting the expressiveness for domain experts. We believe that domain experts can improve the expression of the knowledge of the situation based on their expertise. They can recognize situations by efficiently combining past experiences with available and external resources, and create an enriched model for providing support to end-users. Therefore, we focus on easing the process of defining applications that represent daily activities, attempting to answer the following question: *Can programming language constructs support domain experts to increase knowledge representation of dynamic activities, for improving the interaction and adaptation of context-aware applications?*

We propose in this paper an *activity model* that considers the activity semantics as an essential aspect of describing applications that support people actions. We mainly focus on the expression and relationship between the activity terminology (e.g., concepts, domain) and the activity elements (e.g., environment context, rules) necessary to create well-being applications. These expressions and relationships enable to increase domain-experts involvement in describing applications by appropriately defining activities. Our research adopts the micro context-aware approach proposed in our ContextAA platform [1]. In ContextAA micro context-awareness, autonomic components incorporate a self-described context into their *ontic knowledge*(local knowledge that can be seen as a local ontology) which is analyzed to produce proper responses [16]. Following the micro context-aware approach, our model facilitates creating dynamic micro context-aware applications. These applications contain the activity semantics expressed in ContextAA's ontic knowledge to augment the system interaction and adaptation.

The rest of the paper is structured as follows. In Sect. 2, we summarize the approaches to model the semantics of activities. In Sect. 3, we present our approach for representing activities. In Sect. 4, we introduce our activity model for creating dynamic context-aware applications, and an action machine to reduce these applications. In Sect. 5, we describe our implementation to validate our model. Finally, we present the conclusions and future work in Sect. 6.

2 Related Work

The Activity modeling is an essential aspect of designing the interaction and adaptation of computational systems for supporting people actions. It is the basis to apply methods for activity recognition, e.g., interpreting activity based on primitive actions [17] (i.e., a model of user activity as a composition of primary actions such as move, ingest, grasp, speak). Activity modeling enables generating activity related context for improving adaptation [10], as well as, building applications and user interfaces in diverse domains, e.g., health care [2], smart homes [11], human-robot interaction [19], Ambient Assisted Living(AAL) [15], and computer games [3]. Diverse approaches for activity modeling have been proposed in the literature. They range from using (1) mechanisms to infer unknown elements in the model to (2) allow creating a complete model through an expressive representation:

(1) The approaches for manipulating unknown elements (i.e., discriminative, generative and pattern matching representations [7]) introduce variables, data sets, and mathematical models to link known and unknown activity elements, e.g., a discriminative representation which associate activity elements to activity labels for activity recognition [12], therefore it is not considered at this stage of our work.
(2) The approaches for expressive representation simplify the manipulation of known activity elements and facilitate the development by non-technical users. They exploit the activity semantics and enable describing activity elements and relationships for a subsequent utilization of the semantics to interpret activities. They integrate diverse methods to express the semantics of activities:
    (i) The logic formalism: They employ a set of logical rules defined to represent the activities, e.g., action maps [4] which include a formalism based on Event-Condition-Action(ECA) rules and the time relation between actions, altogether to describe activities (i.e., an action's behavior - a set of linked actions in the action map).
    (ii) The ontological description logic/language: Ontologies offer a standard solution for categorizing activity elements (e.g., domain concepts, actions, rules), incorporating knowledge. Ontologies enrich semantics with logic formalisms to express the relationship between elements. E.g., an approach based on an ontological implementation with a description logic (DL) activity representation [6]. In this approach, the authors use DL-based descriptions (i.e., OWL, RDF) for modeling and infer everyday activities and the way a user is performing an activity. Another approach for describing the relation between ontology elements is using a language, e.g., the semantic web rule language (SWRL) to model and infer the relationship between people, locations, events, activity and time [22].
    (iii) Domain-specific languages, and natural language: Domain-specific languages allow the representation of activities, enriching the semantics, e.g., using the Asbru language [18] which contains a Backus-Naur Form(BNF) grammar to model tasks. Using the Asbru language, the authors model hierarchical ADLs, including activities (i.e., ADLs) and sub-activities (i.e., tasks in an ADL) [13]. Likewise, natural language is an approach for

representing activities through grammatical relations such as a representation based on lexical sources (e.g., Wikipedia) or case frames - i.e., natural language cases of diverse categories (e.g., agent, objective, localization, source, goal) to represent a hierarchy of actions for describing activities [8].

The previous expressive approaches enable to represent the semantics of the activities and related elements, and the expressiveness depends on the methods. The drawback in expressive approaches is that the model is fixed to the expressiveness of the rules, requiring combining the model with other approaches to support complex problems (e.g., recognize an activity related to an unknown sensor input). For these complex problems, diverse approaches use heuristic, probabilistic, statistical and pattern matching methods [2, 6, 7]. Even though expressive approaches are not for complex problems, they are appropriate to describe well-being applications. Thus, we consider simpler problems where an expressive representation style enables describing complete situations. Then, domain experts can increase their involvement for an appropriate definition of activities. In the following section, we present our proposal for simplifying the expression of activities for domain experts.

3 Methodology

We propose an activity model (that represents activity terminology and elements) and an action machine (that computes the elements) to facilitate application development by domain experts. The output of the action machine includes a self-described context that contains the semantic of the activity. We validate our model by implementing programming constructs, i.e., semantic elements to represent terminologies such as concepts and conditions. The design of our model attempts to facilitate the development through simplifying the manipulation of the constructs. The constructs are part of our semantic framework for micro context-aware applications (called AmI-DEU-Semantics: Ambient Intelligence Domain Expert User Semantics) [14]. Our framework facilitates the use of the constructs, programming the action machine, and deploying applications to our ContextAA micro context awareness platform. Using our framework, the activity model becomes part of the ontic knowledge of the smart environment component, which allows to augment the interaction with the system and enhance the adaptation to user needs (Fig. 1).

We adopt the logic formalism to represent the activity conditions (part of the elements). We disregard the use of languages because they incorporate terms that overload domain experts. We only consider a set of terms (i.e., keywords) that enable to describe the activity semantics. Finally, we target dynamic activities whose knowledge is diverse. Thus, we disregard an ontology-based model. We represent the activity semantics in an ontic knowledge which is complete only for each dynamic activity.

Three steps were needed to reach the goal of enabling application development by domain experts:

(a) Exploring the activity conceptualization: we analyzed the Activity Theory (AT) [9]. The theory expresses that an activity is decomposed hierarchically into actions and operations within an activity system. Actions are processes which obey conscious goals. Operations are methods for accomplishing actions, obeying the conditions to attain an action goal. The activity system interrelated elements (i.e., subject, object, community, tool, rules, and the division of labor) to produce an outcome. Although domain experts are who define the activity outcome in our approach, we analyzed the AT elements in context-aware applications to determine the elements required to model the activity domain.

(b) Designing our model: we classified the activity elements. We found that a relevant aspect to increase the semantics is to consider the activity domain because it allows expressing the significance of the activity through the relationship between concepts and activity elements. Then, we defined the elements of our model, designing programming constructs to represent the elements and an action machine to compute the elements.

(c) Reifying the model: we validated our model through an implementation. We implemented micro context-aware programming constructs to define the activity domain and to build application flows. We also implemented the action machine that enables the reduction of an application flow to assignments, i.e., smart environment actions. The assignments contain a standard set of attributes, the conditions to check for executing the actions, and a reduced ontic knowledge required to interpret the activity in the smart environment. Afterward, the smart environment can provide an autonomous interaction/adaptation to support users (e.g., an elderly person).

In the following section, we address our conceptual model which capitalizes the activity domain and the expression of user activities by domain experts.

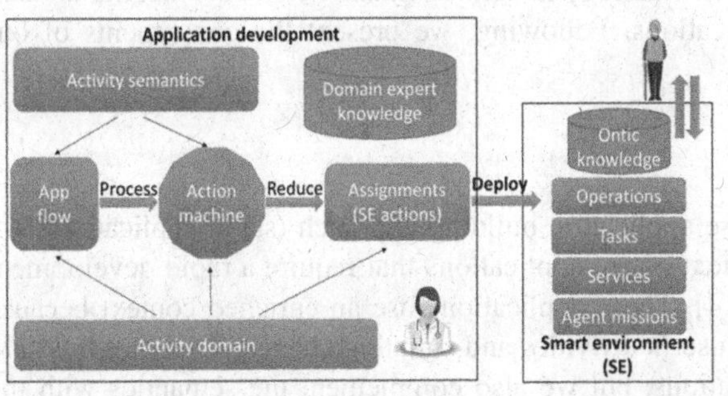

Fig. 1. Activity model

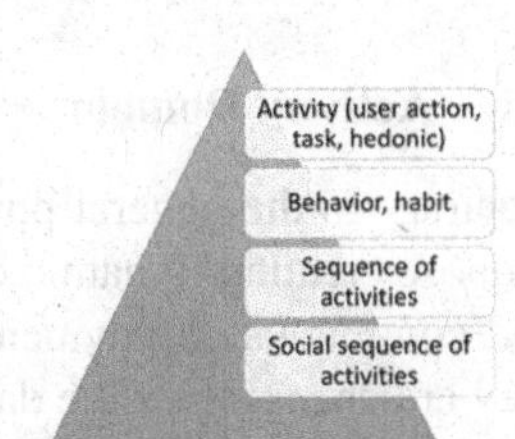

Fig. 2. Activity hierarchy

4 Activity Model

We propose a hierarchical classification to organize and facilitate the description of activities (Fig. 2). A hierarchical organization enables decomposing the activity model into diverse levels of sub-models that simplify the manipulation of activity elements [8, 13]. The atomic level in the hierarchy comprises a set of user actions. A user action is an event, a step, or a process that is performed to achieve the activity or part of the activity. When an action is part of an activity, we define it as a task – a piece of work assigned, undertaken or attempted. Note that a task can comprise one action, if the activity is only to perform such action, e.g., trash the garbage.

The Activity can be seen as the solution logic to represent what a user does, i.e., current action, task or activity. Note that an activity can comprise one action/task if the intention is only to perform such action/task, e.g., tell me the time. Regarding computational semantics, the previous hierarchy is the primary classification for our model because we can define a category of activities and algorithms based on a set of actions/tasks/activities. Regarding computational processing, user actions are equivalent to processing units (i.e., system actions), and the hierarchy comprises a set of user actions that can be semantically expressed by domain experts and reduced by the system. Examples of activity-based applications that we envisage facilitating developing include: (a) Hedonic: based on user preferences/profile involving goals for well-being, e.g., maintain comfort indoor, check health conditions; (b) behavior: a pattern of activities; (c) habit: an established behavior; (d) sequence of activities: an arrangement of activities, e.g., a plan to prepare a meal; and (e) social activity/sequence of activities: activity/sequence of activities performed by two or more people. The previous examples involve activities for both single users and multiple users. We focus in this paper on single users as a first step to finding challenges for multiple users.

Activity expression is challenging because it not only depends on user actions, it also depends on the user profile, i.e., health conditions, preferences, emotions. Our approach adopts an *expressive representation* (Sect. 2) to exploit human intelligence to express activities, facilitating domain experts (e.g., a practitioner) to build activity flows, i.e., applications. We envisage the hierarchy classification for defining "templates" of activities. We also consider domain experts as the "user" of the model, and we exploit the activity domain terminology to define semantic elements that the domain expert will use to build applications. Following, we present the constituents of our model.

4.1 Activity Domain

Contrary to the general purpose application building approach (static application), we propose creating dynamic context-aware applications that require a rapid development and continuous deployment [14]. These applications use an enriched context because they are changing as the daily user's activities and situation change. Thus, we not only consider actions in the applications, but we also complement the semantics with the description of the activity domain. The complemented semantics enables improving system capacities to match the context with the significance of the activity, involving related concepts and relationships. Applications' domain description also facilitates matching user profile with activity concepts and their associations. Regarding the diverse aspects of domain modeling [5], we only model the concepts of the activity domain due to the dynamicity of activities. In our model, we consider concepts with two kinds of direct associations: (a) part-whole relations, e.g., "living room" contains "temperature sensor," and (b) weighted relations, e.g., "user" prefers "leisure" with a 0.8 weight. These two aspects enable domain experts to define applications with detailed goals/activities constraints involving simultaneous/sequential actions.

4.2 Activity Semantics

The Activity domain terminology together with the concept associations (part-whole and weighted relations) enable defining the activity semantics of our model. The semantics enable domain experts to describe simple flows of actions to represent *simple activities*. To do so, domain experts describe the "environment" of the activity required to perform smart environment actions (i.e., activities, tasks, and user actions), as well as, describing the activities based on user preference/profile (i.e., hedonic activities). For *complex activities* (i.e., activities regarding behavior, habit and sequence of activities), our approach is to enable domain experts to describe the activity based on a flow of context/actions to create complex flows. In any case, a flow can include a timing configuration for repetition, considering either an interval (e.g., every hour), an interval between times (e.g., every hour between 9 and 12 on Saturday), or at a given moment (e.g., at 12 on Monday to Friday). Another aspect is that an activity can include a priority to distinguish between two overlapped activities, and actions must include the order to define the predilection of executions.

The activity semantics enables generating the **activity net** (Definition 1) which is the reification of the model. The activity net represents the connection between application flows and concepts, including the relationships, attributes, values, and conditions. Each path of the flow is self-contained, including weights and conditions of the transition, enabling having the required context in each step of the flow. The end of each flow must have actions to execute when all the conditions in the paths are satisfied.

Definition 1. An activity net in an activity domain D is a triple N = (APP, A, P) where APP is a set of applications, A is a set of actions and P $\subset$ (APP$\times$ A) is a set of paths. An executable action in a path pa $\in$ A is a triple pa = (•c, a, c•), where a is an action, •c is the input context of a, and c• is the output context of a.

In Definition 1, the concepts of an activity domain are part of the input/output context. We disregard the state because an application flow defines a set of non-connected actions with context. Thus, the state of the activity net is independent of the paths. It only depends on the action's context, regarding concepts, weights, conditions and configuration (e.g., priority). The activity net is envisioned to define applications to deploy in an autonomous smart environment (i.e., a runtime platform) capable of interpreting the context. An action path *pa* is "followed" when all its conditions are satisfied regarding its input context •c, and its context values gathered in the smart environment. Upon the "followed" path *pa*, an action a is executed, and the values in the output context c• become part of the most recent context in the current path *pa*. A reduction process transforms the activity netto assignments for deploying in a smart environment. The reduction is performed in the action machine (Fig. 1).

4.3 Action Machine

Application flows can contain a plethora of attributes, overmatched conditions, and redundant paths for relating activities. For example, a domain expert can define an application to go for a walk, and an application to notify to bring a medicine if going outside. Thus, both application regards outdoor context. The main functionality of the action machine is to reduce all activities to a set of independent assignments corresponding to smart environment actions (Definition 2). Each assignment is a self-contained context which includes the conditions and the required environment context (defined in the paths of the application flow). The key design aspect of the action machine is to create independent assignments with their ontic knowledge, able to be deployed in a smart environment (Fig. 3).

Definition 2. An assignment is defined by $\alpha = (O, APP, A, P, X, \{X_a\}_{a \in A}, \{G_p\}_{p \in P}, \{U_a\}_{a \in A})$ where:

- $O \subseteq M$, M is the set of all contexts. O is the ontic knowledge which contains the context of α (i.e., concepts, relations, and environment).
- (APP, A, P) is an activity net.
- $X \subseteq O$ is a set of variables representing the attributes of the conditions
- For each action $a \in A$, X_a is the set of condition variables of the action a.
- For each path $p \in P$, G_p is a predicate defined over X.
- For each action $a \in A$, $U_a \subseteq O$ is the set of variables updated by a (i.e., context with new values).

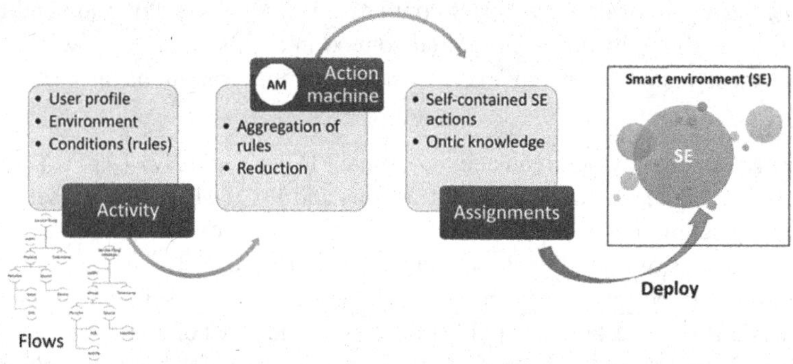

Fig. 3. Action machine

In Definition 2, the predicate G corresponds to the condition to check before executing an action of the assignment. However, G is not mandatory, e.g., a notification at the beginning of the application where the action "display a message" is executed, updating the variable U_{ai} = "new message." Similarly, an activity can define triggers to execute based on a) timing, e.g., display a message every day; or (b) initial conditions either if $X \in D$ (e.g., display a message if temperature $\geq 35°$ at home) or $X \in O$ (e.g., display a message if temperature $\geq 35°$ everywhere). In any case, an assignment α_i considers the nearest context, matching the ontic context with the available context in the smart environment when deployed.

4.4 Model Validation

We implemented the proposed model as part of our semantic framework for micro context-aware applications [14]. The framework includes the computation of semantic elements (i.e., context-based value types) developed to build applications. The semantic elements include basic data types (e.g., numbers, Boolean, text), composite data types (e.g., functions, lists, maps) and semantic entities (abstract computational entities, e.g., concept type, service type). We defined new semantic entities which enable creating activity flow (i.e., applications). Afterward, we implemented the action machine on top of the semantic framework to reduce the application flows, and to create self-contained assignments (smart environment actions). In the following section, we describe the implementation of our model.

5 Programming Constructs and Components

We implemented our model to create interactive applications that run in smart environments in a micro context-aware approach [1]. Components in micro context-awareness are autonomic computing-based and include a *Context* representation and an ontic knowledge to analyze and interpret the environment for producing proper responses. The implementation adopts our Context-based programming constructs [14] which allow defining new semantic elements to describe activities. The programming constructs inherit from the unique abstract value type CTerm (Context Term) defined as a tuple *CTerm = (type, context)* where type = n {v} is a *Context* that contains a unique token representing the type of term, and context = n {v} is a *Context* that contains the self-description of the element, e.g., aTerm = (type, context) where **type** = TERM_TYPE {Concept}; and **context** = concept_id {name {a_name} relation {name {a_relation_name} weight {a_weight} … } …}.

We distinguish the programming constructs through keywords, e.g., TERM_TYPE, APP_PATH. The keywords allow a high-level processing of the semantic. However, when deploying to the smart environment, the deployment process transforms the assignments to ContextAA *Context* representation, discarding keywords.

The implementation is in C++, based on template programming and the Standard Template Library (STL). The main semantic elements that we defined are Concept and Application. The element Concept enables the definition of activity domain. The element Application involves other semantic elements to define the flow of the activity (i.e., Entity, Condition, Action). Following we describe the implementation.

5.1 Semantic Repository

We store the semantic elements in a singleton repository. It is implemented as a symbol table R = (idx, aTerm) where idx is an index and aTerm is a CTerm value type containing a semantic element (i.e., Concept, Activity, Entity, Condition, Action). We implemented a mutex synchronization for accessing to the repository, dynamic casts for polymorphisms (i.e., CTerm → semantic element), and add/delete/query methods.

5.2 Activity Domain

The semantic element Concept represents any activity domain concept and its associations between concepts. Its definition is *CTermConcept = (uid, name, List_attribute, List_relation)* where ***uid*** is a unique identification of the concept; ***name*** is the concept name (meaningful token); ***attribute*** = (name, value), where *name* is the name of the attribute; and *value* is the value of the attribute; and ***relation*** = (type, description, weight), where *type* is the relation category which can be a part-whole or a weighted relation; *description* is to add information about the relation; and *weight* is a value between [0,1] to determine the preference degree for weighted relations.

We reified the activity domain concepts and associations as a directed acyclic graph $A = (T, P)$. The node set T is a set of Concepts of the domain $\{\tau_1, \ldots, \tau_n\}$, and a set of edges P is a set of relations $\{(\tau_1, \tau_2) : \tau_1, \tau_2 \in T\}$.

5.3 ActivityNet

The activitynet (Definition 1) represents the semantic of the applications. Its definition is a tuple *CTermActivity = (uid, name, List_property, List_element, priority)* where ***uid*** is a unique identification of the element; ***name*** is the activity name (meaningful token); ***property*** = (category, temporization), where *category* is the "type" of activity which value can be hedonic (to consider preference degrees) or goal-based (best match in concepts and relations); and *temporization* represents the schedule for repetition of the activity; ***element*** = (entity | condition | action), represents the next element in the flow, where *entity* = (uid, name, List_property, List_element); *condition* = (uid, name, List_property, List_element); and *action* = (uid, name, List_property, order), where order defines the sequence or predilection for execution; and ***priority*** defines the predilection for the application.

Each path of the activity net contains a sequence of elements which describe an action. A *condition* element enables the decomposition of an action path into context validations to accomplish the action. It allows to describe operators on strings and numbers (e.g., greater than, is true), as well as, their combination with programming statements (e.g., else) and logical operators to create complex rules (i.e., and, or).

We implemented the activity net as a directed acyclic graph $\Gamma = (E, \Pi)$. The node set E is a set of semantic elements $\{\varepsilon_1, \ldots, \varepsilon_n\}$, $\varepsilon \in$ {"Application", "Entity", "Condition", "Action"}. The set of direct edges Π is the set $\{(\varepsilon_1, \mu, \varepsilon_2) : \varepsilon_1, \mu, \varepsilon_2 \in E \; M \times E\}$, where M is the set of all contexts. An edge $\varepsilon_1 \xrightarrow{\mu} \varepsilon_2 = (\pi_1, \mu, \pi_2)$ in the edge set Π expresses that the environment surrounding the element $\varepsilon_1$is affected by the context μ, and all together form the environment surrounding the element ε_2. Thus, μ represents the payload context, and the union of the payloads is part of the ontic knowledge. The graph element "Application" is root/start nodes (i.e., a node with no parents), and the element "Action" is a leaf node (i.e., a node with no children).

5.4 Action Machine

We implemented the action machine on top of our framework (i.e., AmIDEU-Semantics) for managing the activity semantics. The output of the machine is a set of assignments (Definition 2) corresponding to the actions of the activity net composed of the set of conditions to accomplish the action. Algorithm 1 shows the recursion implemented in the action machine to reduce the Activity Net to a set of assignments.

Since our model is based on a flow of actions starting from the root node (application starts), Algorithm 1 accumulates the context of all paths and create an assignment with the accumulated context. A relevant case is the element "condition" (Algorithm 1 line 9) where it is necessary to accumulate all paths from the root (i.e., "Application") to the current node (i.e., "Condition"). Then, the set of conditions of each assignment becomes the context to be evaluated in the path to achieve the action.

Algorithm 1: Activity reduction

```
1:  Input:Semantic repository R, Activity graph Γ;Output: Assignments α
2:  for each CTermActivityappin R do
3:      for all path_x (paths of app) doReduceActivity(path_x, app, ϕ)end for
4:  end for
5:  Void Function ReduceActivity(currentPath, currentActivity, currentEnvironment)
6:  Add currentEnvironment to •c_currentPath
7:  for all ctx (components of currentPath) do
8:      if ctx.term_type == "entity" then Add ctx.properties to•c_currentPath
9:      else if ctx.term_type == "condition" then
10:         for all element (Γ elements of all paths between currentActivity and ctx.currentElement) do
11:             Add element.properties to •c_currentPath
12:         end for
13:         ReduceActivity(ctx.condition_path_true, currentActivity, •c_currentPath)
14:         if exist ctx.condition_path_else then
15:             ReduceActivity(ctx.condition_path_else, currentActivity, •c_currentPath)
16:         end if
17:     else if ctx.term_type == "action" then
18:         Add ctx.properties to c•_currentPath; Add (•c_currentPath, c•_currentPath) to α
19:     else if ctx is a path then ReduceActivity(ctx.nextPath, currentActivity, ϕ)
20:     end if
21: end for
```

6 Conclusion and Future Directions

We presented in this paper our activity model designed to facilitate domain experts to build applications in the micro context-aware programming approach. Our model focuses on providing the semantic elements for creating meaningful descriptions, enriching the context of activities, improving the assessment and adaptation of the pervasive smart environment to support user activities. Our activity model facilitates the description of the activity domain using semantic elements designed to represent concepts and its relations. The semantic elements enable creating flow descriptions aimed at providing computational interaction in daily activities. The action machine reduces the flows to self-described assignments which contain the conditions, actions and activity terminology.

As a future work, we are increasing the operations to facilitate the modeling of complex activities, e.g., for context matching, and for validations on data types. We are also working on an UI to represent the semantic elements for making our approach useful/usable to domain experts, as well as, for conducting user tests.

References

1. Abdulrazak, B., Roy, P., Gouin-Vallerand, C., Belala, Y., Giroux, S.: Micro context-awareness for autonomic pervasive computing. Int. J. Bus. Data Commun. Networking **7**(2), 48–68 (2011)
2. Acampora, G., Cook, D.J., Rashidi, P., Vasilakos, A.V.: A survey on ambient intelligence in health care. Proc. IEEE. Inst. Electr. Electron. Eng. **101**(12), 2470–2494 (2013)
3. Ang, C.S., Zaphiris, P., Wilson, S.: Computer games and sociocultural play: an activity theoretical perspective. Games Cult. **5**(4), 354–380 (2010)
4. Aztiria, A., Augusto, J.C., Basagoiti, R., Izaguirre, A., Cook, D.: learning frequent behaviours of the user in intelligent environments. IEEE Trans. Syst. Man Cybern. Syst. **43**(6), 1265–1278 (2013)
5. Bjorner, D.: Software Engineering 3: Domains, Requirements, and Software Design. Texts in Theoretical Computer Science. An EATCS Series. Springer, New York (2006)
6. Chen, L., Nugent, C.D., Wang, H.: A knowledge-driven approach to activity recognition in smart homes. IEEE Trans. Knowl. Data Eng. **24**(6), 961–974 (2012)
7. Kim, E., Helal, S., Cook, D.: Human activity recognition and pattern discovery. IEEE Pervasive Comput. **9**(1), 48–53 (2010)
8. Kojima, A., Tamura, T., Fukunaga, K.: Natural language description of human activities from video images. Int. J. Comput. Vis. **50**(2), 171–184 (2002)
9. Leontyev, A.N.: Activity and consciousness. Philos. USSR, pp. 1–192, (1977)
10. Li, X., Tao, X., Lu, J.: Improving the quality of context-aware applications: An activity-oriented context approach. In: Proceeding International Symposium on the Physical and Failure Integrated Circuits, IPFA, pp. 173–182 (2013)
11. Lu, C.-H., Ho, Y.-C., Chen, Y.-H., Fu, L.-C.: Hybrid user-assisted incremental model adaptation for activity recognition in a dynamic smart-home environment. IEEE Trans. Hum.-Mach. Syst. **43**(5), 421–436 (2013)
12. Minor, B., Cook, D.J.: Forecasting occurrences of activities. Pervasive Mob. Comput. **38**, 77–91 (2016)
13. Naeem, U., Bigham, J., Wang, J.: Recognising activities of daily life using hierarchical plans. In: Kortuem, G., Finney, J., Lea, R., Sundramoorthy, V. (eds.) EuroSSC 2007. LNCS, vol. 4793, pp. 175–189. Springer, Heidelberg (2007). doi:10.1007/978-3-540-75696-5_11
14. Ponce, V., Roy, P., Abdulrazak, B.: Dynamic domain model for micro context-aware adaptation of applications. In: Proceedings of the 13th IEEE International Conference on Ubiquitous Intelligence and Computing, pp. 98–105 (2016)
15. Rashidi, P., Mihailidis, A.: A survey on ambient-assisted living tools for older adults. IEEE J. Biomed. Heal. Inform. **17**(3), 579–590 (2013)
16. Roy, P., Abdulrazak, B., Belala, Y.: Quantifying semantic proximity between contexts. In: Bodine, C., Helal, S., Gu, T., Mokhtari, M. (eds.) ICOST 2014. LNCS, vol. 8456, pp. 165–174. Springer, Cham (2015). doi:10.1007/978-3-319-14424-5_18
17. Schank, R.C.: The Forteen Primitive Actions and Their Inferences, March 1973
18. Shahar, Y., Miksch, S., Johnson, P.: The Asgaard project: A task-specific framework for the application and critiquing of time-oriented clinical guidelines. Artif. Intell. Med. **14**(1–2), 29–51 (1998)
19. Sukthankar, G., Geib, C., Bui, H.H., Pynadath, D., Goldman, R.P.: Plan, Activity, and Intent Recognition: Theory and Practice. Newnes (2014)

20. Ur, B., McManus, E., Pak Yong Ho, M., Littman, M.L.: Practical trigger-action programming in the smart home. In: Proceedings of the 32nd annual ACM Conference on Human factors in computing systems - CHI 2014, pp. 803–812 (2014)
21. Ye, J., Dobson, S., McKeever, S.: Situation identification techniques in pervasive computing: a review. Pervasive Mob. Comput. **8**(1), 36–66 (2012)
22. Zhang, S., McCullagh, P., Nugent, C., Zheng, H., Black, N.: An ontological framework for activity monitoring and reminder reasoning in an assisted environment. J. Ambient Intell. Humaniz. Comput. **4**(2), 157–168 (2013)

Ambient Assisted Robot Object Search

Dennis Sprute[1,2(✉)], Aljoscha Pörtner[1,2], Robin Rasch[1], Sven Battermann[1], and Matthias König[1]

[1] Bielefeld University of Applied Sciences, Campus Minden, 32427 Minden, Germany
dennis.sprute@fh-bielefeld.de
[2] Faculty of Computer Science, Otto-von-Guericke University Magdeburg, 39106 Magdeburg, Germany

Abstract. In this paper, we integrate a mobile service robot into a smart home environment in order to improve the search of objects by a robot. We propose a hierarchical search system consisting of three layers: (1) local search, (2) global search and (3) exploration. This approach extends the sensory variety of the mobile service robot by employing additional smart home sensors for the object search. Therefore, the robot is no more limited to its on-board sensors. Furthermore, we provide a visual feedback system integrated into the smart home to effectively inform the user about the current state of the search process. We evaluated our system in a *fetch-and-delivery* task, and the experimental results revealed a more efficient and faster search compared to a search without support of a smart home. Such a system can assist elderly people, especially people with cognitive impairments, in their home environments and support them to live self-determined in old age.

1 Introduction

Service robots can support elderly in their home environments by undertaking common tasks, such as picking and placing objects, opening doors or preparing meal [1]. Furthermore, they are used in the health-care sector, e.g. as social robots to support elderly people [2]. A certain problem is the search of objects, e.g. shoes or key rings. This is especially interesting for elderly people since they often misplace objects and do not find them again, e.g. people with dementia suffer from a disturbance of their cognitive functions [3]. Besides, the search of objects is exhausting for elderly people due to their mobility restrictions.

Therefore, mobile service robots provide an opportunity to assist elderly in the task of object search. Robots have been used in several works to find objects in an environment, e.g. Deyle et al. [4] use ultra-high frequency radio-frequency identification (UHF RFID) tags to localize objects and Kunze et al. [5] use cameras on a robot in a *fetch-and-delivery* task. In general, these mobile robots are equipped with sensors, such as cameras, to detect and recognize objects and to navigate autonomously inside the environment. A major drawback of these

M. Mokhtari et al. (Eds.): ICOST 2017, LNCS 10461, pp. 112–123, 2017.
DOI: 10.1007/978-3-319-66188-9_10

approaches is the limitation of the robots perception to their on-board sensors. They can only use their own sensors to perceive the environment resulting in a large search space.

By integrating a mobile service robot into a smart home, we overcome this limitation and extend the sensory variety of the robot. This will make the task of object search more efficient and faster because the robot's search space can be reduced by employing information from the smart home. In order to interact with the system, we present a human-robot interface that is based on two components: (1) a smartphone application is used to select a certain object to be searched for and (2) a lighting concept is proposed to give the user visual feedback about the current state of the search process.

The remainder of this paper is structured as follows. In the next section, we give an overview of existing works in the area of robots in smart environments as well as human-robot interaction using colored lighting. Subsequently, we present our new system to enhance the task of robot object search in a smart home. We evaluated our system concerning its efficiency and search time and describe the experimental results in the following section. Finally, we summarize our work and point out work for the future.

2 Related Work

The integration of robots into smart environments is referred to as network robotic systems or ubiquitous robots. This term was coined by Kim et al. [6] and describes the embedding of robotics into a ubiquitous space that features a high connectivity between several heterogeneous devices. A concrete implementation of this vision is implemented by Saffiotti et al. [7] in form of their PEIS-ecology. Physically Embedded Intelligent Systems (PEIS) comprise different components like sensors, actuators, mobile robots or smart appliances, that are integrated into a joint space. Leveraging the cooperation of these components enables the development of advanced robotic applications that are based on a distributed system instead of a highly autonomous robot. Furthermore, Rusu et al. [8] followed the ubiquitous robotics paradigm by introducing a service robot that autonomously operates in a sensor-equipped kitchen. It is equipped with several sensors like RFID tags and accelerometers on objects, light sensors and cameras. Enabling a communication between these devices yields a network robotic system capable of performing complex tasks by extending the system's perception capabilities. A more recent system is shown by Li et al. [9] who introduce a multi-robot architecture for ambient assisted living based on the Robot Operating System (ROS) framework [10]. It allows autonomous navigation of robots and their collaboration inside a smart environment. This environment consists of a collection of different sensors, especially cameras to observe the scene. Chamberlain et al. [11] propose a distributed visual object detection service, that uses cameras mounted in the robot's environment, and applied it to the task of robot path planning. High-level object information is extracted directly on the camera nodes to reduce network bandwidth.

For the design of ambient intelligence interfaces, Kleinberger et al. [12] suggest unobtrusive and ambient interfaces to enhance usability. A critical factor for the design of interaction strategies is visual communication, e.g. color and light. Studies considering color are carried out with children [13,14] or adults [15] and show a clear connotation of colors, e.g. bright colors (positive) and dark colors (negative). An overview of the expressivity and meaning of light illumination intensity patterns is given by Harrison et al. [16]. Some of the described paradigms and technologies can already be found partially in today's human-robot interaction (HRI) strategies. Examples are the color-based communication of intents of a UAV [17] for end-to-end HRI, the communication of "moods" using a LED strip for the research on robot anthropomorphism [18] or the use of color lighting to induce empathy between human and robot [19]. Another field of application is the use of expressive lights for an indication of a robots actual state [20]. Finally, colored light of a smart home lamp is utilized to automatically adapt to the user's current activity [21].

3 Our Approach

In this section, we present our novel approach to optimize the object search by robots inside a smart home. Therefore, we first of all give an overview of the system architecture and its components. Then we describe the task of global object localization and explain our new hierarchical search system in detail. Finally, we introduce our solution to the challenge of an adequate interaction interface between the users and the proposed system.

3.1 System Architecture

The system consists of several components that are depicted in Fig. 1. A tablet PC with a simple user interface is used as an interaction device for the user to initiate a search task and to get information about the current status of the system. In addition, a controllable light installation is integrated into the environment to provide visual feedback to the user. We also integrate a mobile service robot in order to fetch and deliver specified objects. Furthermore, we use cameras, e.g. a camera on a robot or integrated into the home environment, as primary sensors to perceive the environment. Each camera node is related to a global coordinate frame G. The homogeneous transform between a camera coordinate frame C_i and the global coordinate frame G is denoted as ${}^{G}T_{C_i}$. These transformations are static for cameras that are integrated into the environment, while the transformation for the robot's on-board camera changes dynamically when the robot is moving. Since all cameras are related to the global coordinate frame G, we can transform coordinates between all cameras. Furthermore, each camera node is calibrated, i.e. the intrinsic camera parameters are known. These can be used to obtain depth information of the objects.

All these components are connected to a central system controller which handles the interactions between the components. The robot as well as the smart cameras communicate via TCP/IP using the Robot Operating System (ROS) framework [10], while the tablet PC uses a web service to interact with the system controller. The ZigBee communication protocol is employed to wirelessly control the smart lighting.

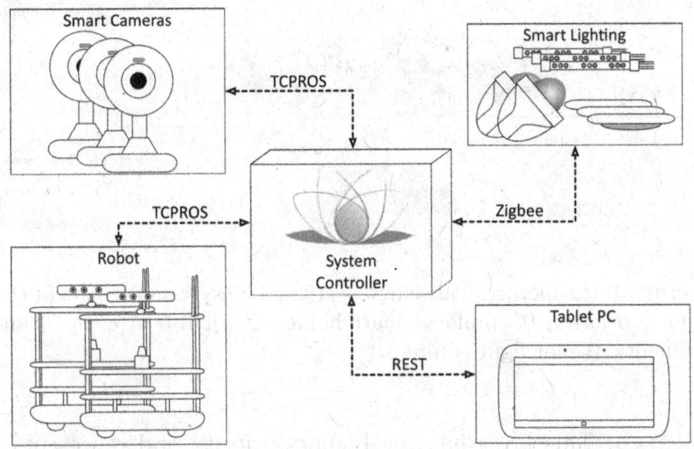

Fig. 1. Overview of the system architecture with its different components and communication links.

3.2 Global Object Localization

In order to localize objects inside a smart home, we encode several objects with different visual markers. For this purpose, we use ArUco markers [22] that provide 2D image features mapped to a unique ID. We equipped each object, e.g. shoe or key ring, with a unique and fixed-size visual marker that can be identified by the camera system. Since each camera node is calibrated, we can estimate the 3D pose of the marker with respect to the camera C. To determine the marker's pose $\boldsymbol{p}$ with respect to the global coordinate frame G, we apply the following formula:

$$^{G}\boldsymbol{p} = {^{G}T_C} \cdot {^{C}\boldsymbol{p}} \tag{1}$$

with $^{G}T_C \in SE(3)$ being a homogeneous transform between the coordinate frames G and C.

3.3 Hierarchical Search System

In this subsection, we describe our novel hierarchical search system that we apply in order to efficiently localize an object, that the user is searching for. The structure is visualized in Fig. 2.

The proposed search system mainly consists of three hierarchically arranged layers with the highest priority on the top:

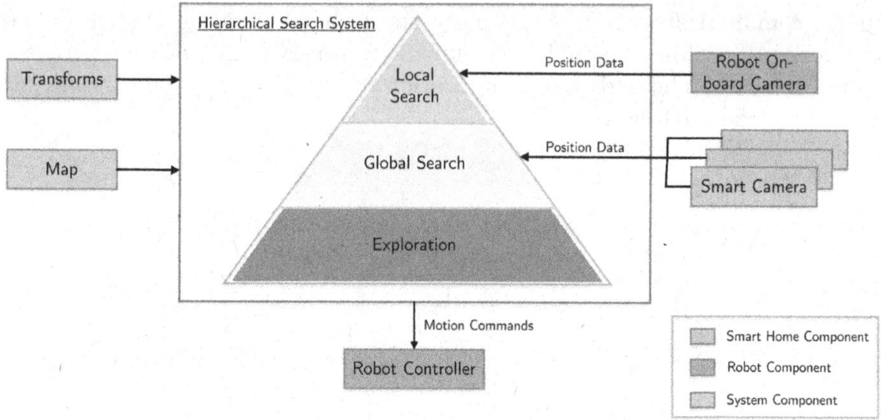

Fig. 2. Structure of the hierarchical search system. The system consists of three layers with descending priority. It employs smart home (blue), robot (orange) and system (gray) components. (Color figure online)

1. **Local search:** This layer has the highest priority and represents the case when the object is in the field of view of the robot's on-board camera. In this case, the robot exactly knows the position of the object with respect to itself. Therefore, we apply visual servoing technique to guide the robot directly to the object.
2. **Global search:** If the robot is not able to localize the object using its on-board camera, we apply a global search by additionally employing the smart cameras integrated into the environment. Note that the smart cameras perform the computer vision steps necessary for object recognition locally on an embedded device. Thus, only the position data of the object are transmitted over the network and not the high-resolution images. This saves network bandwidth and distributes the computing capacities onto several nodes. The robot uses the given map of the environment and the position data as input for a common path planning algorithm in order to create a navigation function to the goal position. Due to camera calibration inaccuracies, the object position data provided by the smart cameras are not that accurate as the data provided by the robot's on-board camera. Thus, the priority of this layer is lower than the previous layer.
3. **Exploration:** If the object can neither be localized by the robot's on-board camera nor by the smart home cameras, the robot starts performing a search based on an exploration algorithm. This is the case if the object is not in the robot camera's field of view and if the smart cameras do not cover the whole environment, e.g. due to occlusion of furniture. In the exploration case, the hierarchical search system degrades to a standard approach for object search.

In order to produce valid motion commands for the robot controller, the system depends on a given map and a transformation tree that describes the homogeneous transforms between the different components, such as cameras and the robot.

The main advantage of this hierarchical search system is the efficient and fast search of objects. This advantage essentially originates from the integration of a mobile service robot into a smart home environment with additional sensors. We utilize the smart home's cameras to localize objects in the environment and to guide the robot close to the object. Once in the proximity of the object, the robot can switch to its local search to precisely fetch the object. Without the use of the smart home components, the robot would exhaustively explore the environment until it finds the object.

3.4 Human-Computer/Human-Robot Interaction

The system's interaction strategy is founded on a multi-modal interaction, that is based on vision, touch and hearing. The system interface can be separated into two phases: the *input* and the *output* or *feedback* phase.

The input phase of the system describes the phase where the user is the active part of the interaction while the user calls on the system to fetch and deliver the specified object. This *task* is defined by the user via a mobile application and a tablet PC as interaction device. As it is a first prototype, the mobile application is tailored to the specific use case but already takes the simple handling of the system into account. This includes big and intuitive software buttons depicted by icons of their corresponding objects in the real world as well as animations for every status transition of the system. The second phase of the system is the output or feedback phase. This phase uses the visual and auditory perception of the user and is independent of the mobile application and the tablet PC because the input method can be replaced by other methods, e.g. voice or gesture control. Therefore, the system uses the smart environment as well as the robot itself for the interaction. The smart environment comprises a controllable light installation as described in Sect. 3.1. The current feedback system consists of four animations associated with four system states (Table 1).

Table 1. Animations, system status and their meaning used for the ambient visual feedback system.

Animation	State	Meaning
Pending	Waiting for instructions	The system is ready to accept control commands.
Search	Searching	The system is searching for an object.
Error	Error occurred	The system cannot find the defined object or is not ready to accept control commands.
Finished	Object delivered	The object has been delivered to the last known position of the user

These four system states have been selected based on the questions of their advantage for the user. In other words, how can an animation empower the system's expressiveness, reveals the internal state to a non-technical user and as a consequence improves the transparency of the system. The animations are illustrated by characteristic illumination intensity patterns and colors (Fig. 3). The four animations are:

1. **Pending:** This animation applies if the system is ready to accept *fetch-and-delivery* tasks. The light behavior is called *Transmission with fixed Brightness* and indicates that the system is active [16]. The light iterates through the colors by altering the hue value of the HSV color space.
2. **Search:** This animation applies if the system searches for the object using the hierarchical search system described in Sect. 3.3. The light behavior is called *Staircase Continuous* and is characteristic for a *system bootup* [16]. The color shown during this phase is a *light yellow-red* which should represent positive emotions and indicate interest [13,23]. Additionally, for a better differentiation between the global and local search, the robot beeps whenever it switches between the global and local search phase.
3. **Error:** This animation applies if the system fails to achieve the goal. The major reason for this state is the non-findability of an object. The light behavior is called *staircase blink* and is a characteristic pattern for the indication of an error [16]. The color shown during this phase is a *dark blue-purple* which should represent negative emotions and indicate sadness [13,23].
4. **Finished:** This animation applies if the system has finished its task and has delivered the object successfully. The light behavior is called *Beacon* which is a characteristic representation for a notification [16]. The color shown during this phase is a *light green* which should represent positive emotions and indicate joy [13,23].

Beside the previously described emotional aspect, the different animations have a practical aspect, e.g. the animation *Finished* also indicates the completion of the task and therefore helps the user to understand when the user can take the object without system interference.

4 Experimental Results

In this section, we describe our experiments in order to evaluate the proposed hierarchical search system concerning its search time and efficiency compared to a simple robot exploration approach. In contrast to our system, the simple exploration approach uses only its on-board camera and no smart home cameras.

4.1 Experimental Setup

We evaluated our system in a 6.1 m $\times$ 3.5 m lab environment that was equipped with two smart cameras. A map of the environment was built a priori, and the camera poses were related to the map. The cameras' fields of view covered most

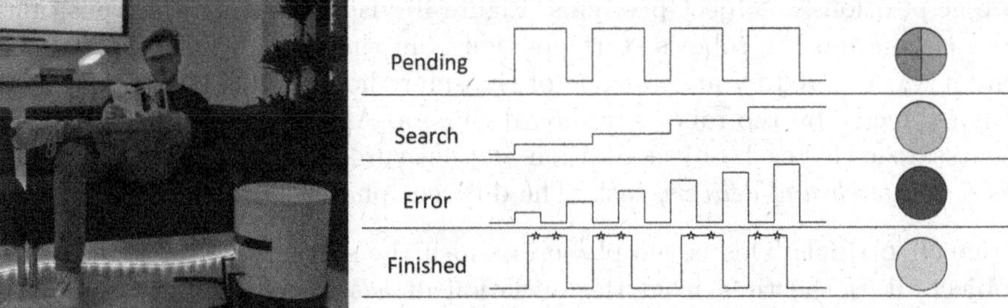

(a) Illuminated robot and light installation

(b) Light behavior and color sequences (Intensity ranges from *Off* to *High* and stars indicate an additional short blink)

Fig. 3. Realization of the visual feedback system. (a) shows an image of the robot and its illumination. (b) shows the different light behaviors and color sequences during the feedback animations. (Color figure online)

of the environment to demonstrate the effectiveness of the hierarchical search system. We deployed a TurtleBot 2 equipped with a laser range finder, a monochrome camera and a gripper as mobile service robot platform. Additionally, we installed different colored lights, such as lamps and LED strips, to realize the proposed visual feedback system. A tablet PC was used to initiate an object search task. Figure 4a depicts a 3D model of the environmental setup including the mobile service robot, the light installations and the smart cameras.

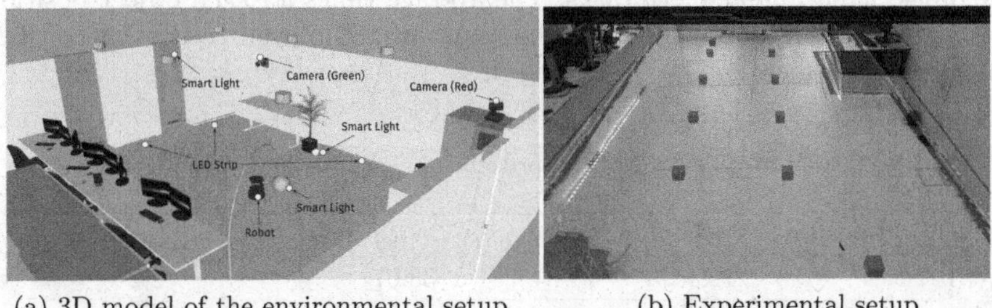

(a) 3D model of the environmental setup

(b) Experimental setup

Fig. 4. Setup for the evaluation of the search time and efficiency. (a) shows a model of the lab environment with the robot inside the smart environment. (b) gives an overview of the lab environment and the object positions depicted as red cubes. The image was taken from the red camera shown in the 3D model. (Color figure online)

In order to demonstrate the advantage of using a smart home environment in an object search task, we compared our hierarchical search system with an approach that does not use additional smart home cameras. Therefore, we used a frontier-based exploration algorithm [24] to explore the map and search for objects. We selected a robot start position in the lab environment and chose ten different positions as object positions. Figure 4b visualizes the object positions as red cubes, and the robot's start position is in the bottom left corner. Each position was covered by at least one of the smart home cameras' fields of view but not directly by the robot's on-board camera. Afterwards, we initiated five object searches for each object position and measured the time for the different phases of a *fetch-and-delivery* task. The different phases are:

1. **Search object:** This is the phase in which the system tries to localize the object. It is the time from the initiation of a search task up to the first detection of the marker either by the smart home cameras or the robot's on-board camera.
2. **Move to object:** This is the phase in which the robot moves to the specified object. The time is measured from the first localization of the object up to arriving at the object.
3. **Deliver object:** This is the phase in which the robot delivers the object at its start position.

The combination results in 50 trials for our proposed ambient assisted object search system. In order to demonstrate the importance of the smart home integration, we performed the same 50 trials (same robot start position and object locations) using the frontier-based exploration algorithm [24] without the use of smart home cameras.

4.2 Search Time

While conducting the experiments for both approaches, we measured the overall time of the *fetch-and-delivery* tasks. The average times for each object position are shown in Table 2 dependent on the approach. The average is based on five trials per object location.

Table 2. Search time for both approaches in seconds and speedup factor

Object position	Without smart home [s]	With smart home [s]	Speedup
1	72.18	33.07	2.2
2	98.30	38.76	2.5
3	110.34	37.76	2.9
4	104.11	41.17	2.5
5	135.11	48.60	2.8
6	130.81	47.58	2.8
7	166.45	57.30	2.9
8	168.78	56.40	3.0
9	75.72	38.58	2.0
10	112.03	41.23	2.7
Average			2.6

The overall times for the *fetch-and-delivery* tasks show significant speedups (between 2.0 and 3.0) compared to the exploration approach. Our proposed hierarchical search system provides a 2.6× speedup on average over the exploration-based search.

4.3 Efficiency

We assess the efficiency of both approaches by analyzing the time distribution of the three phases of a *fetch-and-delivery* tasks. The efficiency results for both approaches are shown in Fig. 5. The left figure depicts the efficiency results for the object search without smart home cameras based on the frontier-based exploration algorithm [24]. Each bar shows the time distribution for the different object positions. The results show that the search of the objects takes the major part of the overall time because the robot only uses its on-board camera and has to explore large areas of the environment. Thus, the phase *Move to object* only takes a constant small part of the overall time (5–6 s) since the object is in the robot camera's field of view. Additionally, the time to deliver the object at the initial position depends on the distance between both locations. The times in phase *Deliver object* are equal in both approaches (with and without smart home). In contrast to the exploration approach, the experimental results for our hierarchical search system employing smart home cameras are shown in Fig. 5b. It is apparent that the time distribution of the three phases differs from the previous approach. For our approach, the *Search object* phase only takes minimal time due to the fast object localization by the smart home cameras. This makes our system more efficient because the robot can directly move to the position of the object instead of exploring large areas of the environment. Therefore, the time to move to the object and the time to deliver the object is equally distributed due to the same path. These results demonstrate the efficiency of the proposed hierarchical search system and the improvement over the exploration-based search system.

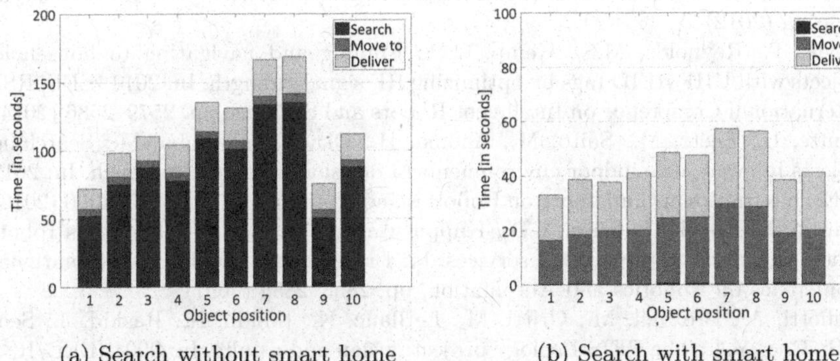

(a) Search without smart home (b) Search with smart home

Fig. 5. Time distribution for both approaches. Different colors denote different phases of a *fetch-and-delivery* task. Note the different scaling for both figures. (Color figure online)

5 Conclusions and Future Work

We proposed a novel object search system integrated into a smart home environment. It is based on a hierarchical search approach that utilizes a robot's on-bard camera as well as smart cameras integrated into the environment in order to localize objects. Our experimental results revealed a more efficient and faster object search compared to a standard robot search based on an exploration algorithm. Furthermore, we presented a visual feedback system as part of the smart home to inform the user about the current state of the search process. The whole system has the potential to support self-determined living in old age.

In the future, we will remove the visual markers attached to the objects and replace the marker-based localization system by a sophisticated object recognition system. This will enable the deployment in real-life scenarios. Additional work should also focus on a more dynamic and robust system. This should be achieved by a dynamic negotiation and task allocation system based on a multi-agent modeling approach. Besides, we are interested in the effect of the visual feedback animations on the users, especially elderly people. Thus, we plan to conduct a comprehensive study to investigate the effect.

Acknowledgement. This work is financially supported by the German Federal Ministry of Education and Research (BMBF, Funding number: 03FH006PX5).

References

1. Xu, Y., Qian, H., Wu, X.: Household Service Robotics. Intelligent Systems Series. Elsevier Science (2014)
2. Gross, H.M., Mueller, S., Schroeter, C., Volkhardt, M., Scheidig, A., Debes, K., Richter, K., Doering, N.: Robot companion for domestic health assistance: implementation, test and case study under everyday conditions in private apartments. In: 2015 IEEE/RSJ International Conference on Intelligent Robots and Systems (IROS), pp. 5992–5999 (2015)
3. World Health Organization: Dementia: a public health priority. World Health Organization (2012)
4. Deyle, T., Reynolds, M.S., Kemp, C.C.: Finding and navigating to household objects with UHF RFID tags by optimizing RF signal strength. In: 2014 IEEE/RSJ International Conference on Intelligent Robots and Systems, pp. 2579–2586 (2014)
5. Kunze, L., Beetz, M., Saito, M., Azuma, H., Okada, K., Inaba, M.: Searching objects in large-scale indoor environments: a decision-theoretic approach. In: 2012 IEEE International Conference on Robotics and Automation, pp. 4385–4390 (2012)
6. Kim, J.H., Lee, K.H., Kim, Y.D., Kuppuswamy, N.S., Jo, J.: Ubiquitous robot: a new paradigm for integrated services. In: Proceedings 2007 IEEE International Conference on Robotics and Automation, pp. 2853–2858 (2007)
7. Saffiotti, A., Broxvall, M., Gritti, M., LeBlanc, K., Lundh, R., Rashid, J., Seo, B.S., Cho, Y.J.: The PEIS-Ecology project: vision and results. In: 2008 IEEE/RSJ International Conference on Intelligent Robots and Systems, pp. 2329–2335 (2008)
8. Rusu, R.B., Gerkey, B., Beetz, M.: Robots in the kitchen: exploiting ubiquitous sensing and actuation. Robot. Auton. Syst. **56**(10), 844–856 (2008)

9. Li, R., Oskoei, M.A., Hu, H.: Towards ROS based multi-robot architecture for ambient assisted living. In: 2013 IEEE International Conference on Systems, Man, and Cybernetics, pp. 3458–3463 (2013)
10. Quigley, M., Conley, K., Gerkey, B., Faust, J., Foote, T.B., Leibs, J., Wheeler, R., Ng, A.Y.: ROS: an open-source robot operating system. In: ICRA Workshop on Open Source Software (2009)
11. Chamberlain, W., Leitner, J., Drummond, T., Corke, P.: A distributed robotic vision service. In: 2016 IEEE International Conference on Robotics and Automation (ICRA), pp. 2494–2499 (2016)
12. Kleinberger, T., Becker, M., Ras, E., Holzinger, A., Müller, P.: Ambient intelligence in assisted living: enable elderly people to handle future interfaces. In: Stephanidis, C. (ed.) UAHCI 2007. LNCS, vol. 4555, pp. 103–112. Springer, Heidelberg (2007). doi:10.1007/978-3-540-73281-5_11
13. Boyatzis, C.J., Varghese, R.: Children's emotional associations with colors. J. Genet. Psychol. **155**(1), 77–85 (1994)
14. Terwogt, M.M., Hoeksma, J.B.: Colors and emotions: preferences and combinations. J. Gen. Psychol. **122**(1), 5–17 (1995)
15. Hemphill, M.: A note on adults' coloremotion associations. J. Genetic Psychol. **157**(3), 275–280 (1996)
16. Harrison, C., Horstman, J., Hsieh, G., Hudson, S.: Unlocking the expressivity of point lights. In: Proceedings of the SIGCHI Conference on Human Factors in Computing Systems, CHI 2012, pp. 1683–1692. ACM (2012)
17. Monajjemi, M., Mohaimenianpour, S., Vaughan, R.: UAV, come to me: end-to-end, multi-scale situated HRI with an uninstrumented human and a distant UAV. In: 2016 IEEE/RSJ International Conference on Intelligent Robots and Systems (IROS), pp. 4410–4417 (2016)
18. Rea, D.J., Young, J.E., Irani, P.: The Roomba mood ring: an ambient-display robot. In: 2012 ACM/IEEE International Conference on Human-Robot Interaction, pp. 217–218. ACM (2012)
19. Kim, E.H., Kwak, S.S., Kwak, Y.K.: Can robotic emotional expressions induce a human to empathize with a robot? In: IEEE International Symposium on Robot and Human Interactive Communication (RO-MAN), pp. 358–362 (2009)
20. Baraka, K., Paiva, A., Veloso, M.: Expressive lights for revealing mobile service robot state. In: Reis, L.P., Moreira, A.P., Lima, P.U., Montano, L., Muñoz-Martinez, V. (eds.) Robot 2015: Second Iberian Robotics Conference. AISC, vol. 417, pp. 107–119. Springer, Cham (2016). doi:10.1007/978-3-319-27146-0_9
21. Sprute, D., König, M.: On-chip activity recognition in a smart home. In: 12th International Conference on Intelligent Environments (IE), pp. 95–102 (2016)
22. Garrido-Jurado, S., Munoz-Salinas, R., Madrid-Cuevas, F., Marín-Jiménez, M.: Automatic generation and detection of highly reliable fiducial markers under occlusion. Pattern Recogn. **47**(6), 2280–2292 (2014)
23. Terada, K., Yamauchi, A., Ito, A.: Artificial emotion expression for a robot by dynamic color change. In: 2012 IEEE RO-MAN: The 21st IEEE International Symposium on Robot and Human Interactive Communication, pp. 314–321 (2012)
24. Yamauchi, B.: A frontier-based approach for autonomous exploration. In: 1997 IEEE International Symposium on Computational Intelligence in Robotics and Automation, CIRA 1997, Proceedings, pp. 146–151 (1997)

Visual Confusion Recognition in Movement Patterns from Walking Path and Motion Energy

Yan Zhang[1], Georg Layher[1], Steffen Walter[2], Viktor Kessler[1], and Heiko Neumann[1(✉)]

[1] Institute of Neural Information Processing, Ulm University, James-Franck-Ring, 89081 Ulm, Germany
heiko.neumann@uni-ulm.de

[2] Department for Psychosomatic Medicine and Psychotherapy, Ulm University Hospital, Frauensteige 6, 89075 Ulm, Germany

Abstract. For elderly people healthcare in ambient living environments, recognizing confusion states in an automatic and non-contact manner is essential. In this work we provide a visual approach to confusion recognition consisting of behavior monitoring and movement pattern analysis. To collect data for evaluation, we created a dataset from a search experiment. After extracting and analyzing the movement patterns, we achieved a recognition rate of 89.6% when cross-validating over different subjects and 88.9% when testing on a new set of samples. To our knowledge, we are the first to investigate confusion recognition using visual information. Our work shows that the mental confusion can be effectively recognized based on the movement pattern.

Keywords: Confusion recognition · Elderly people healthcare · Behavior monitoring · Movement pattern analysis

1 Introduction

Compared with young generations, elderly people often suffer from motor dysfunction, perception decline, cognitive impairment and so on. Such disabilities can cause confusion, which severely impairs their daily lives and necessitates effective assistance. In addition, continuous confusion is an early sign of mental disorders such as dementia and Alzheimer's disease. Thus recognizing confusion from their daily behaviors is essential for healthcare and treatment at early stages. In the US National Library of Medicine *confusion* is defined as: *the inability to think as clearly or quickly as you normally do. You may feel disoriented and have difficulty paying attention, remembering, and making decisions.*[1] According to this definition, a person who suffers from confusion will behave in a less efficient manner. For example, loss of attention can cause irrelevant actions; disorientation makes walking towards targets difficult. Thus we conjecture that mental confusion can be recognized based on movement patterns.

[1] https://medlineplus.gov/ency/article/003205.htm.

M. Mokhtari et al. (Eds.): ICOST 2017, LNCS 10461, pp. 124–135, 2017.
DOI: 10.1007/978-3-319-66188-9_11

We aim to solve the problem of confusion recognition for elderly people in ambient living environments such as smart home or intelligent hospitals. Instead of using wearable sensors like smart wristbands, we propose a visual method that only uses visual stream recordings from a camera network, which usually costs less and operates in a non-contact manner. Such visual methods incorporate two aspects: (1) behavior monitoring which extracts the walking trajectories and estimates the motion energy; (2) movement pattern analysis involving feature extraction and classification. In addition, we created a dataset for confusion behavior recognition through a search experiment, in which we artificially intervened cognitive processes of the participants. We then used this dataset to evaluate our proposed methods. This paper is organized as follows: In Sect. 2, we briefly recapitulate some related work. In Sects. 3 and 4, we introduce the two processing steps of our vision-based method respectively. In Sect. 5, we present our experiments for data collection and method evaluation. In the last section, we discuss our results and make a conclusion.

2 Related Work

In ambient environment systems, activity recognition is one of the most important and challenging problems which is solved relying on different sensors like cameras, accelerometers and gyroscopes [17]. Numerous advantages of visual sensors and vision-based methods have been reported [12]. For example, visual signals provide in-depth contextual information of the scene and visual sensors are non-contact and hence do not interfere daily activities of the users.

Activity recognition is performed in a hierarchical manner [1]. At the coarse level, behavior analysis is usually based on long-term observations and features like walking trajectories [14] and motion energy [11]. Walking path estimation and person tracking in indoor environments can be solved by 3D tracking algorithms, e.g. [5,22]. At finer levels, more complex spatiotemporal features are used to perform action recognition [16] or special action detection [20]. In addition, activities can be analyzed using either sequential approaches or space-time approaches [1]. In sequential approaches like dynamic time warping or hidden Markov modeling, the input visual stream is regarded as a sequence of observations, from which the activity is recognized if its characteristic sequential pattern is discovered. In space-time approaches like Bag-of-Words methods [10], the video is treated as a 3D volume in the spatiotemporal space, from which sparse or dense features are extracted and the activity is recognized based on their statistics.

In this work, we focus on the coarse level behavior analysis and use a space-time approach which first extracts a bag of local movement patterns and then classifies the behaviors based on the local feature statistics. To avoid expensive computation and the risk of inappropriate 3D grid selection, our method performs tracking in each individual view, triangulates the corresponding points within regions of interests and then associates the 3D location using a linear Kalman filter.

3 Behavior Monitoring via Spatiotemporal Visual Sequence Analysis

Our behavior monitoring approach estimates the walking path and the motion energy over time, based on a synchronized and calibrated camera network. Considering elderly people that live alone, it also assumes that only one person appears in the scene and interacts with some objects, while the background is static. Our approach consists of three stages: (1) initialization, (2) bounding box tracking in each individual view and motion energy estimation and (3) locating the person in the 3D world. Dense optical flow fields are computed for every two successive frames using the Horn-Schunck method [9]. Initialization is only performed once at the beginning. Afterwards, the step (2) and the step (3) alternate to update the internal states with new input frame recordings.

Initialization. A bounding box is generated using the optical flow magnitude. When the person moves, the optical flow is more significant over the person than other image regions. By thresholding the flow magnitude and performing image opening, one can obtain a binary mask which covers the moving part of the person. Then the bounding box is the minimal rectangle containing all the non-zero elements in the mask map.

Within such bounding boxes, interest points are detected within each bounding box using *FAST* [19] and described by *FREAK* [2]. Then these detected points are matched and triangulated to obtain a 3D point cloud. The cloud centroid is regarded as the initial 3D location.

Bounding Box Tracking and Motion Energy Estimation. The 2D bounding box in each individual view is tracked by a linear Kalman filter assuming constant velocity, the observation of which incorporates the location and the size of the bounding box. When a new frame is captured, the optical flow is first computed. Given the previous bounding box location $\boldsymbol{l}_{t-1}$ and the current flow magnitude m_t, the current location observation $\boldsymbol{l^o}_t$ is selected at the minimum of a potential

$$\phi(\boldsymbol{l^o}_t) \propto \phi(\boldsymbol{l}_{t-1}) \cdot \phi(m_t), \tag{1}$$

where the potential function $\phi(\cdot)$ is obtained by binary map generation, distance transform and Gaussian smoothing. The binary map of a location has only one non-zero element which covers that location, and the binary map of the flow magnitude is obtained via thresholding and image opening as in the initialization step. The distance transform approximates the inverse probability and the Gaussian smoothing is used to remove high-frequencies in the potential map. Simultaneously, the current size observation $\boldsymbol{s^o}_t$ of the bounding box is computed according to the previous 3D locations and previous size $\boldsymbol{s}_{t-1}$. Once obtaining $\boldsymbol{l^o}_t$ and $\boldsymbol{s^o}_t$, the linear Kalman filter is updated to generate the current estimates $\boldsymbol{l}_t$ and $\boldsymbol{s}_t$. In the calibrated camera network, one camera is located at the origin of the 3D world whose capturing view is regarded as the base view. When tracking bounding boxes in other views, the current bounding box location $\boldsymbol{l}_t$ is only selected along a epipolar line, which corresponds to the bounding box center in the base view.

After estimating the bounding boxes from all views, the current motion energy is calculated by the averaged optical flow magnitude within these bounding boxes.

Localization in the 3D World. 3D location of the subject is tracked by a linear Kalman filter assuming constant velocity as well, which is used to stabilize the 3D tracking process and generate smooth trajectories. The observation of the current 3D location is obtained by triangulating the bounding box centers from all views. The walking path is obtained by projecting the 3D location to the ground, thus, discarding information along the vertical direction. Figure 1 illustrates a tracking result.

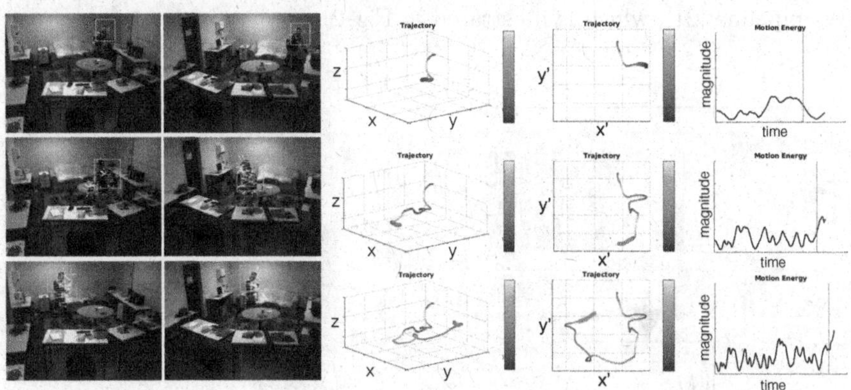

Fig. 1. This figure illustrates our behavior monitoring based on two synchronized cameras where the person walks surrounding the round table clockwise. **The rows** represent three time instances in a selected video. **The first two columns** show two sample image pairs from the frame sequences. The optical flow, bounding boxes and the 3D location projections (the red dots) are displayed. **The third and fourth columns** show the 3D trajectory and the walking path respectively, where the color denotes the speed and the thick segments denote the locations in the newest 20 frames. One should note that the focal plane of the camera is not parallel to the ground. **The fifth column** illustrates the motion energy, where the motion energy in the newest 20 frames is highlighted in red and the x-axis denotes the time stamp in terms of frames. (Color figure online)

4 Movement Pattern Analysis and Behavior Recognition

Behavior analysis is based on the walking path and the motion energy. Influenced by time-varying cognitive processes such as motivation changes, loss of attention and confusion, different actions and movements occur in an alternating or even random manner. This nature makes creating consistent sequential patterns difficult. Therefore, we regard the entire sequence as a 3D spatiotemporal volume and represent this volume using a bag of local patterns while ignoring their temporal orders. From a psychological perspective, we assume that the cognitive process of the person retains stable for a short time and we hence extract local movement patterns over a short time window. Then the global behavior is described by the occurrence of some characteristic local movement patterns. For example, a person without confusion tends to walk fast and the walking path contains more straight segments; a disorientated person, on the other hand, generates a walking path with some circular segments. Based on these considerations, we propose movement pattern analysis which consists of four steps: (1) extracting local movement patterns, (2) detecting characteristic movement patterns, (3) representing the long-term behavior by their occurrence and (4) labeling the behavior using a classifier. Steps (2) and (3) can be regarded as a *Bag-of-Words* (BoW) pipeline [21], which is illustrated in Fig. 2.

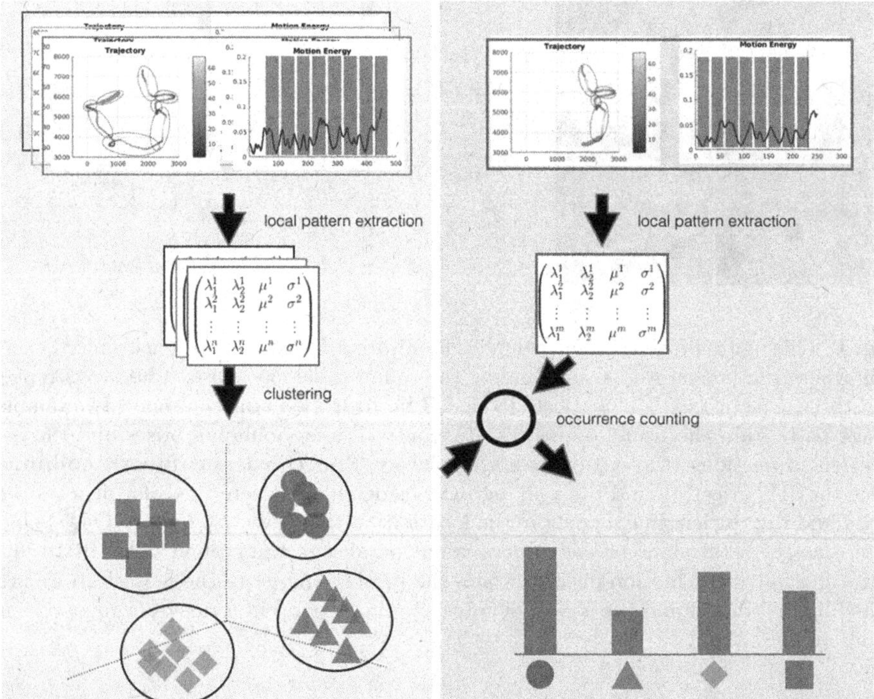

Fig. 2. Illustration of the *Bag-of-Words* pipeline. The left column represents the process of *dictionary learning*, generating a set of characteristic local behavior patterns. The right column represents the process of *encoding*. In the plots of walking paths the ellipsoids denote the covariance matrix of the path segment. In the plots of motion energy the red stripes denote the local time window from which the statistics of the motion energy are calculated. (Color figure online)

Local Movement Pattern. The local movement pattern is a mixture of the walking path structure and the motion energy statistics. Within a local time window $t \in W$, the covariance matrix of the walking path segment is given by

$$\boldsymbol{C} := \frac{1}{|W|} \cdot \sum_{t \in W} (\boldsymbol{x}_t - \bar{\boldsymbol{x}})(\boldsymbol{x}_t - \bar{\boldsymbol{x}})^T + \epsilon \boldsymbol{I}, \quad (2)$$

where $\boldsymbol{x}_t := (x_t, y_t)^T$ is the 2D location on the ground plane at time t, $\bar{\boldsymbol{x}}$ is the mean location in W, ϵ is a small positive constant and $\boldsymbol{I}$ is the identity matrix. The second term is used to guarantee the matrix $\boldsymbol{C}$ is always positive definite. We calculate the two eigenvalues λ_1 and λ_2 with $\lambda_1 \geq \lambda_2 > 0$. These are illustrated in Fig. 2 (the red ellipsoids). Table 1 demonstrates some examples of how the two eigenvalues represent behaviors.

Table 1. Some behavior exemplars indicated by the local walking path structure.

Eigenvalues	Behavior exemplars
$\lambda_1 \approx \lambda_2 \gg 0$	Fast multi-directional movements
$\lambda_1 \approx \lambda_2 \approx 0$	Standing still or doing tasks at some location
$\lambda_1 \gg \lambda_2 \approx 0$	Walking forward

The motion energy statistics within $t \in W$ is described by the mean μ and the standard deviation σ of the motion response magnitudes, again represented as a 2D pair. The relation between motion energy and behaviors is demonstrated by Table 2.

Table 2. Some behavior exemplars indicated by the local motion energy statistics.

Local motion statistics	Behavior exemplars
$\mu \approx 0$ and $\sigma \approx 0$	Standing still
$\mu \gg 0$ and $\sigma \approx 0$	Consistent action such as walking
$\mu > 0$ and $\sigma \gg 0$	Inconsistent action like manipulating objects

The local movement pattern is a mixture of these two pairs of features

$$\boldsymbol{\phi} := (\alpha\lambda_1, \alpha\lambda_2, (1-\alpha)\,\mu, (1-\alpha)\,\sigma)^T, \quad (3)$$

where $0 \leq \alpha \leq 1$ is a hyper-parameter to tune the weight between walking path structures and motion energy statistics.

Bag-of-Words Pipeline. By shifting the time window W with a stride S, one can obtain a large number of local movement patterns from all the training samples. To remove the influence of scaling, the patterns are first standardized by subtracting the mean and dividing by the standard deviation in each dimension. Then these pre-processed movement patterns are grouped into N_c clusters via an optimized *k-means* algorithm [4] initialized by the *k-means++* seeding approach [3]. The cluster centroids are regarded as the characteristic local movement patterns. These procedures are also referred to *dictionary learning.*

With these characteristic local movement patterns, we can convert each sample to the occurrence histogram. In this process, each local pattern is first standardized using the same mean and standard deviation in the dictionary learning step and then compared with all the characteristic patterns in terms of euclidean distance.

Behavior Classification. As a final step of movement pattern analysis, a multi-class linear SVM model is used to label the samples. The number of classes to differentiate depends on the annotated labels. Before training the classifier the occurrence histograms are first normalized so that the sum of elements is equal to one. The only hyper-parameter in the linear SVM model is the regularization weight, which is optimized via cross-validation and grid search. In our work, we used the SVM implementation in [8].

5 Experiments and Results

The Search Experiment.[2] This experiment had 24 subjects (12 males and 12 females) under the age of 50 year-old. During this experiment, the physical constraints of elderly people were simulated by using a special aging suit, which is composed of weights attached to torso and limbs and uses other fabric components to limit the movement of joints. The activity area contained different furnitures and cluttered by a number of irrelevant items such books and desktops. The degree of cluttering was well designed in order to introduce cognitive bias [13], causing subjects tending to believe targets were hidden in more cluttered places. However, we actually concealed them in a roughly uniform manner.

The subjects were required to find a cellphone, a credit card, a wallet and a keychain within five minutes. We performed cognitive interventions along three dimensions according to studies reporting that making decision under conditions of loss of information and chronic pain can distract attention and cause confusion [6, 7]. Figure 3(a) illustrates our categorization. In the case of *baseline*, the subjects were directly told where the targets were. In case of *route constraint*, the subjects could only walk anti-clockwise and were not allowed to turn back. In case of *task load*, the subjects were not aware of where the targets were hidden. In case of *disorientation*, besides the aging suit the subjects also wore special glasses to simulate retinitis pigmentosa, a headset to simulate tinnitus and a plastic panel to simulate back pain. On the other hand, they got imprecise hints.

[2] The study was conducted according to the ethical guidelines set out in the WMA Declaration of Helsinki (ethical committee approval was granted: 196/10-UBB/bal). The study protocol was approved by the ethics committee of University of Ulm, Germany.

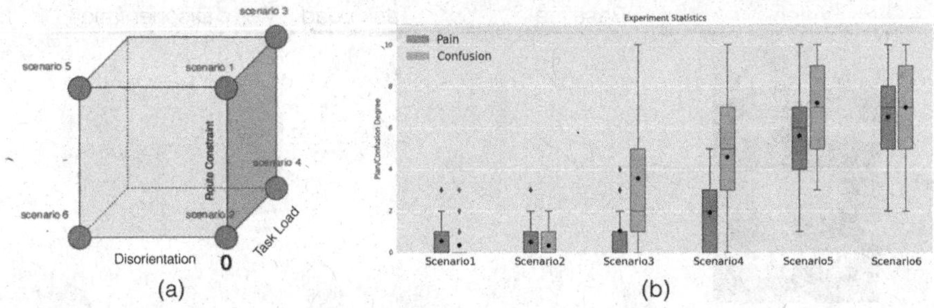

Fig. 3. Illustration of the searching experiment. (a) illustrates the three dimensions of cognitive interventions, where the origin denotes the *baseline* scenario. (b) shows the statistics from the questionnaire.

After each scenario, the subject were required to fill out a questionnaire for evaluating the effectiveness of our cognition intervention approaches. The statistical results shown in Fig. 3(b) indicate its success. Since combining Task Load and Disorientation made the experiment extremely difficult, we proposed six scenarios in the end.

To record visual sequences, we used two frame-based *IDS UEye-306x* cameras with the resolution 1280×960 by pixels and the frame rate 30 *fps*. To convert the video raw data to accessible files, we used the codec *H.264* and implemented the converter using *OpenCV* and *ffmpeg*. All sensors were synchronized.

From this experiment we created a dataset which incorporates samples from 24 participants, where 4 participants were recorded in a darker environment. When evaluating our methods, we only considered Scenario 2, Scenario 4 and Scenario 6 since they include more complex dynamics, and labeled them as *baseline*, *task load* and *disorientation*. For faster computation, we resized the frames to 320×240 pixels resolution.

Method Evaluation. We first partitioned the data into two groups. The *trainval* group contains recordings from 18 subjects and the *test* group contains the remaining 6 recordings which include all the recordings in the dark environment. Figure 4 shows some samples. From the data we extracted the local movement patterns, converted them to occurrence histograms and classified them into three categories corresponding to *baseline*, *task load* and *disorientation*. The results were evaluated based on the confusion matrix and the recognition rate (averaged recall).

We evaluated the influence of the time window size W and the number of clusters N_c in the dictionary using the *trainval* set. For a specific combination of W and N_c, we permutated the subjects 30 times and split the data for training and validating according to a $70:30$ ratio. We then used the training data to learn the dictionary and train the 3-class linear SVM, whose regularization weight was selected based on 5-fold cross-validation and grid search. The recognition rate was evaluated using the validation data. We varied the value of W from $\{10, 20, 30, 60, 120, 180, 240, 300\}$ in terms of number of frames and varied

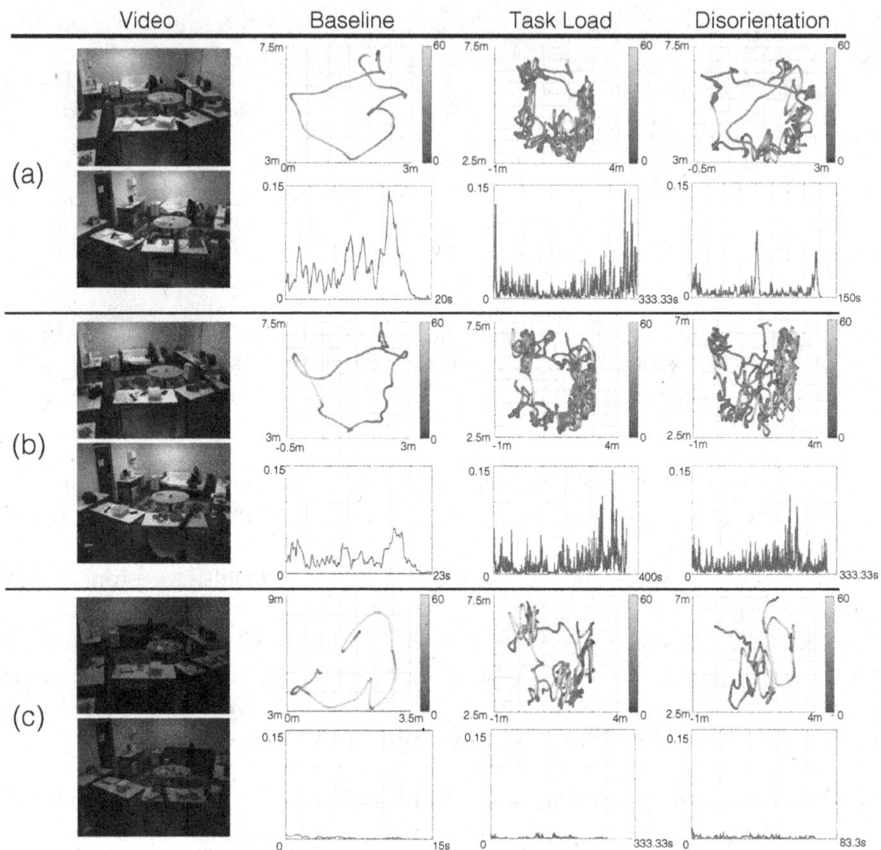

Fig. 4. Some results of walking path extraction and motion energy estimation from three subjects are present, where (a) and (b) were recorded under the normal lighting condition and (c) was recorded under the dark lighting condition. Associated with each subject, the *Video* column shows the stereo pair and the following three columns show the bird's eye view of walking paths and the motion energy respectively. The spatial domain of the walking path is scaled by meters and the temporal domain of the motion energy is measured by seconds. The color indicates the walking speed, which was computed as the movement along the walking path between two successive frames. (Color figure online)

the value of N_c from $\{10, 20, 30, ..., 1000\}$. The stride was fixed to $S = 15$ in all cases, indicating that local patterns were extracted by every 0.5 s.

In addition, we evaluated the influence of features in the local movement pattern. In Eq. (3) we set $\alpha = 0$, $\alpha = 1$ and $\alpha = 0.5$ and made the movement pattern described by only motion energy, only path structure and their mixture, respectively. After selecting the optimal (W, N_c) pairs with respect to the cross-validated recognition rate, we used all data in the *trainval* set to train and

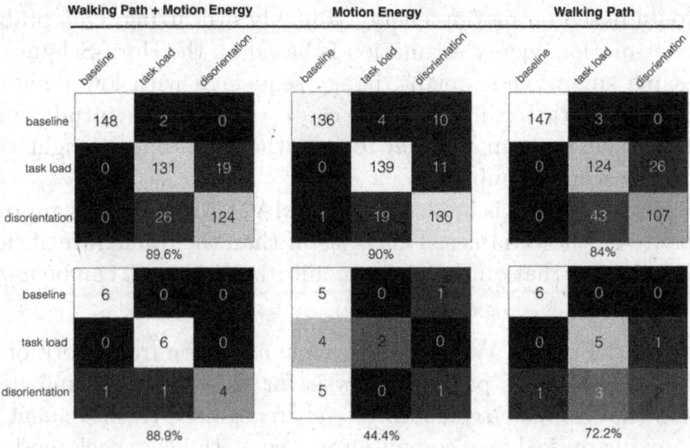

Fig. 5. Evaluation results in terms of confusion matrices and recognition rates. The first row shows the results of cross-validation with the optimal hyper-parameters (W, N_c) which are $(240, 10)$, $(180, 50)$ and $(300, 30)$ respectively. The second row shows the results of testing. In each confusion matrix, rows denote the ground truth and columns denote the predictions.

classified all samples in the *test* set. The cross-validation and test results are shown in Fig. 5.

6 Discussion and Conclusion

The confusion matrices from cross-validation indicate that the walking path feature performs best to differentiate normal and abnormal behaviors. This fact is also shown in Fig. 4, where the walking paths in *baseline* are highly different from other scenarios. However, the walking path feature performs worse to differentiate *task load* and *disorientation*. This ineffectiveness causes its overall performance lower than other features. On the other hand, the motion energy performs best to differentiate the two abnormal scenarios. A probable reason is that in *disorientation* the movements of the subjects were consistently slow, leading to smaller mean and smaller variance than *task load* where the movements were highly inconsistent. In *baseline* the movements were consistently high and hence differ from *disorientation* mainly in terms of motion energy mean rather than variance. This fact is also indicated in the second confusion matrix in the first row. The mixture of motion energy and walking path features performs best to differentiate *baseline* and other scenarios, while the performance of differentiating abnormalities seems to be their average. This fact indicates that walking path and motion energy provides complementary information for identifying whether the person is normal or abnormal. When considering identifying the type of abnormality, only using motion energy seems to be a better solution. However, according to the recognition performance on *test* data one can see that the model only based on motion energy is highly overfitting. One probable reason is that our motion energy estimation is based on the Horn-Schunck method. Using the same smoothness weight, image sequences with lower intensity will lead to a smaller data term and hence cause the flow magnitude smaller. To overcome this issue, one can consider to tune the smoothness weight adaptively according to the scene illumination.

Our tracking algorithm is implemented in MATLAB and takes approximately 0.02 s to update all the variables. This is faster than the frame rate of the camera (30 *fps*) and indicates that our behavior monitoring approach can be used in real-time.

Conclusion and Future Work. We provide a generic framework of behavior monitoring and movement pattern analysis for elderly people and use experiments to show that confusion can be effectively recognized via movement patterns. Besides improving optical flow computation, the methods in each module can be replaced by state-of-the-art versions as well. For example, the bounding boxes in each visual sequence can be generated by deep neural networks such as Fast R-CNN [18]. The clustering and feature encoding in the BoW pipeline can be replaced by Fisher kernel embedding [15]. Besides long-term behavior analysis, we are also interested in confusion event detection and suspicious action prediction. We expect that our investigations in this paper paves the way for future studies of confusion analysis for elderly people in ambient living environments.

Acknowledgments. This study is funded by the SenseEmotion project of German Federal Ministry of Education and Research (BMBF).

References

1. Aggarwal, J., Ryoo, M.: Human activity analysis: a review. ACM Comput. Surv. **43**(3), 16:1–16:143 (2011). http://doi.acm.org/10.1145/1922649.1922653
2. Alahi, A., Ortiz, R., Vandergheynst, P.: Freak: fast retina keypoint. In: 2012 IEEE Conference on Computer Vision and Pattern Recognition, pp. 510–517, June 2012
3. Arthur, D., Vassilvitskii, S.: k-means++: the advantages of careful seeding. In: Proceedings of the Eighteenth Annual ACM-SIAM Symposium on Discrete Algorithms, pp. 1027–1035. Society for Industrial and Applied Mathematics (2007)
4. Bottesch, T., Bühler, T., Kächele, M.: Speeding up k-means by approximating Euclidean distances via block vectors. In: Proceedings of the 33rd International Conference on Machine Learning, pp. 2578–2586 (2016)
5. Devernay, F., Mateus, D., Guilbert, M.: Multi-camera scene flow by tracking 3-D points and surfels. In: 2006 IEEE Computer Society Conference on Computer Vision and Pattern Recognition (CVPR 2006), vol. 2, pp. 2203–2212 (2006)
6. Eccleston, C.: Chronic pain and distraction: an experimental investigation into the role of sustained and shifting attention in the processing of chronic persistent pain. Behav. Res. Ther. **33**(4), 391–405 (1995)
7. Frisch, D., Baron, J.: Ambiguity and rationality. J. Behav. Dec. Mak. **1**(3), 149–157 (1988)
8. Fu, Y., Hospedales, T.M., Xiang, T., Gong, S.: Learning multimodal latent attributes. IEEE Trans. Pattern Anal. Mach. Intell. **36**(2), 303–316 (2014)

9. Horn, B.K., Schunck, B.G.: Determining optical flow. Artif. Intell. **17**(1–3), 185–203 (1981)
10. Laptev, I., Marszalek, M., Schmid, C., Rozenfeld, B.: Learning realistic human actions from movies. In: 2008 IEEE Conference on Computer Vision and Pattern Recognition, pp. 1–8, June 2008
11. Layher, G., Giese, M.A., Neumann, H.: Learning representations of animated motion sequences–a neural model. Top. Cogn. Sci. **6**(1), 170–182 (2014)
12. Mihailidis, A., Carmichael, B., Boger, J.: The use of computer vision in an intelligent environment to support aging-in-place, safety, and independence in the home. IEEE Trans. Inf. Technol. Biomed. **8**(3), 238–247 (2004)
13. Morewedge, C.K., Kahneman, D.: Associative processes in intuitive judgment. Trends Cogn. Sci. **14**(10), 435–440 (2010)
14. Morris, B.T., Trivedi, M.M.: Trajectory learning for activity understanding: unsupervised, multilevel, and long-term adaptive approach. IEEE Trans. Pattern Anal. Mach. Intell. **33**(11), 2287–2301 (2011)
15. Oneata, D., Verbeek, J., Schmid, C.: Action and event recognition with fisher vectors on a compact feature set. In: 2013 IEEE International Conference on Computer Vision, pp. 1817–1824, December 2013
16. Poppe, R.: A survey on vision-based human action recognition. Image Vis. Comput. **28**(6), 976–990 (2010)
17. Rashidi, P., Mihailidis, A.: A survey on ambient-assisted living tools for older adults. IEEE J. Biomed. Health Inform. **17**(3), 579–590 (2013)
18. Ren, S., He, K., Girshick, R., Sun, J.: Faster R-CNN: towards real-time object detection with region proposal networks. In: Advances in Neural Information Processing Systems, pp. 91–99 (2015)
19. Rosten, E., Drummond, T.: Machine learning for high-speed corner detection. In: Leonardis, A., Bischof, H., Pinz, A. (eds.) ECCV 2006. LNCS, vol. 3951, pp. 430–443. Springer, Heidelberg (2006). doi:10.1007/11744023_34
20. Tian, Y., Sukthankar, R., Shah, M.: Spatiotemporal deformable part models for action detection. In: Proceedings of the IEEE Conference on Computer Vision and Pattern Recognition, pp. 2642–2649 (2013)
21. Tsai, C.F.: Bag-of-words representation in image annotation: a review. ISRN Artif. Intell. (2012)
22. Tyagi, A., Potamianos, G., Davis, J.W., Chu, S.M.: Fusion of multiple camera views for kernel-based 3D tracking. In: IEEE Workshop on Motion and Video Computing (WMVC 2007), p. 1, February 2007

High Fidelity Simulation and Visualization of Activities of Daily Living in Persim 3D

Sirui Liu[1], Sumi Helal[2], and Jae Woong Lee[3](✉)

[1] Atypon Systems, Santa Clara, CA, USA
longlongquincy@gmail.com

[2] School of Computing and Communication, Lancaster University, Lancaster, UK
s.helal@lancaster.ac.uk

[3] School of Computer Science and Mathematics, University of Central Missouri, Warrensburg, MO, USA
jwlee@ucmo.edu

Abstract. A smart space simulation is cost-effective means to analyze human activities and design and test human-centered intelligence in real smart spaces. A powerful smart space simulator not only synthesizes sensor data, but also generates highly realistic activity visualizations that serve as immediate visual feedback for the simulation user to validate her/his simulation design. In this paper, we present our approach for creating highly realistic simulation and visualization of activities of daily living (ADL) in smart homes within our Persim 3D simulator. We design and compile a set of ADLs into Persim3D activity library. We present three simulation models for human actions and space objects (necessary for performing and visualizing the activities), and sensors (necessary for sensing the effect of interactions between the virtual character performing the activity and the virtual space). We evaluate Persim 3D's simulation fidelity through use study, by gauging users' perception of the realism of activity visualization.

Keywords: Simulation · Human activities · Smart homes

1 Introduction

Smart homes and ambient assisted living technology is of increasing importance in the context of designing assistive environments, such as smart homes, for the elderly and individuals with special needs. However, researchers often find their work progress hindered by the scarcity of available data collected from smart spaces. Significant cost and elaborate groundwork are often required to build a reliable smart living space. Even if there is a smart home available, it is difficult to recruit participants who are willing to live in such a relatively experimental environment where the residents' activities will be monitored for too long. Furthermore, in order to obtain sufficient activity data, the experiment must last for a very long period of time, which aggravates the cost issue even more. Therefore, powerful human activity simulators that are capable of generating accurate activity datasets are on demand and have rapidly grown in importance.

M. Mokhtari et al. (Eds.): ICOST 2017, LNCS 10461, pp. 136–148, 2017.
DOI: 10.1007/978-3-319-66188-9_12

Of course, the major challenge activity simulators need to address is efficacy, namely how similar the simulation outputs are to the real-world scenarios. But with an effective simulator at hand, it is possible to test ground theories and system design plans at relatively low cost, especially in abnormal situations, which is virtually impossible in experiments with human subjects due to regulatory limitations. It requires breakthrough in three different aspects to achieve simulation of high level of realism: (1) modeling of human activities specifically for simulation, (2) high fidelity visualization and playback of the activity, and (3) reflective simulation supported by accurate sentience capability of the virtual environment. Liu et al. presented Activity Playback Modeling, an approach to specifying and simulating human activities in a simulated pervasive environment, alleviating issue 1 [1]. It supports a limited set of activities and renders activity animation at an acceptable quality level, but lacks the ability to simulate a wider variety of common activities with smooth and realistic animations of low-level subtle actions and body movements.

In this paper, we describe our simulation methodology and the reflective activity visualization design to address issue 2 and 3 above. The virtual character's (VC) actions are modeled with realistic animations and are linked by activity simulation algorithms seamlessly, producing continuous and smooth animation throughout the activity. The modeling of objects and sensors and the interaction mechanism between objects, sensors and the VC enable the sentience of the virtual space.

2 Related Work

Our activities of daily living (ADLs) simulation approach is a framework to simulate a VC performing a wide range of common human activities in a 3D virtual living space. On one hand, this approach is capable of generating realistic animations of the VC's actions and body movements (e.g., walking, using objects to complete a certain task). On the other hand, the VC, his actions, home objects and sensors are modeled and programmed in a way that makes the smart space sentient to the VC's actions and interactions or "collisions" with these objects, thus reflecting their effects. Due to the limitations on the quantity of supported animations of VC's actions and body movements, the original Persim 3D action visualization module only provided acceptable visual realism. The proposed approach models a much larger number of human actions to cover common ADLs that could be of interest to a variety of interdisciplinary research teams. The activity simulation algorithm connects the animations of different actions seamlessly to render smooth activity animations. In addition, four types of sensors that are needed to detect the VC's actions are modeled and simulated in a similar way they work in real smart homes. Persim 3D provides a GUI that allows the user to select activities to simulate and control the simulation speed and displays simulation status.

Many activity simulators also have a GUI for the user to create simulation projects and/or see the simulated activity. IE Sim [2] is an intelligent environment simulator with a 2D GUI that allows the user to configure specific and exact parameters for objects, sensors and their relationships. SHSim [3] is another smart home simulator that shows the floor plan of the simulated space in a 2D bird's-eye view. It simulates various living scenarios and serves as a test platform for smart home applications. Kaldeli et al. introduced an software architecture for smart home device services that supports assisted living [4]. It visualizes the simulation scene at the center of the screen and shows the status of home appliances in separate windows, using the self-developed RuG ViSi tool, which is based on Google SketchUp.

SIMACT [5] provides a 3D simulation environment for users to design and simulate activities, which increases realism of the simulated space, objects and activities. However, it is limited by the lack of inter-model interference modeling for it requires the use of laborious "hand-made" techniques to specify the activity effects on sensors. Shen et al. developed a system to simulate human activities in a building to improve designer-user communications [6]. This simulator, based on 3DVIA Virtools, provides a GUI for the user to schedule activities at different locations and simulates the activities in the 3D building model. They used Autodesk 3ds Max to create VCs' action animations and then imported them to the simulator. The SHC system [7] was a 3D simulation framework for telehealth services. Implemented based on the OpenSim open source platform, it renders an interactive 3D virtual environment to demonstrate the VC's activities. In the simulation, scripts were developed and attached to simulation entities to control their behavior, enabling the interaction between the VC and home objects.

3 High Fidelity Simulation Modeling

3.1 Action-Oriented Model of Activities of Daily Living

The concept of ADLs was originally introduced in an elder care study by Katz et al. [8]. ADLs generally refer to an individual's daily fundamental functioning activities such as eating, bathing and toileting. Additionally, instrumental activities of daily living (IADLs) are activities that can let people live independently in a community [9]. Because of the uncertainty and flexibility of human behavior, there are countless of activities people can do at home and there are almost an infinite number of ways of performing them. It is beyond our ability to account for all these activities. Therefore, our approach is to focus on the most common and most frequently conducted ADLs and IADLs. Based on studies in [10] and the ADL checklists provided by [11], we finalized eight ADLs and three IADLs. In addition, we added Falling, an abnormal activity (AA) that is not rare on older adults and could cause severe injuries [12], to our activity library. Falls could result from vision problems, lower body weakness or acute medical conditions.

The ADLs/IADLs are analyzed and decomposed them into actions by the following modeling approach. In Persim 3D, an activity is decomposed into a sequence of actions, where an action is an operation at which the VC may or may not interact with an object and possibly changes the object's status [1]. We analyzed the typical human behavior in each activity and broke it down into a series of major steps, with each step being a simple action. An action doesn't necessarily belong to only one activity; it could occur in multiple activities. For example, the action "turn on TV" only belongs to activity Watching TV, while the action "turn off light" may occur in multiple activities, such as Leaving Home, Washing Hands, Sleeping, etc.

Generally, an individual performs a series of actions at different locations with various postures within an activity. From the animation's perspective, the VC is at a location in a certain posture in the last frame of the current action's animation and will possibly be at another location in a different posture in the first frame of the next action's animation. To ensure continuous and realistic activity animation, Persim 3D's Visualization Engine inserts transitioning movements to fill the gap between successive animations. Details of the activity simulation process are discussed in Sect. 4. An action's animation is independent on its location and objects. For example, activity Shaving involves the action "picking up" a razor from the bathroom counter and activity Taking Medication involves "picking up" a pill bottle from the table. They are essentially the same action and can use the same animation, only at different locations with different objects.

As actions are the key building blocks of the activity simulation, an explicit action model is designed and used featuring seven activity attributes: (1) Name, which is a unique identifier, (2) Object, an optional entity that the VC may be using in an action, (3) Animation, which defines the VC's behavior and movements while preforming the action, (4) Effect, which is the desired visual and digital change on the involved object's status, including on/off status, position, and other physical property, (5) Importance, signaling whether the action is optional or necessary, (6) Max-Occurrence, which defines the maximum number of times an action could occur in a given activity, and finally (7) Prerequisites, describing pre-conditions for an action to occur. If an action's prerequisite action occurs in a given activity, its number of occurrence would depend on its importance and max-occurrence attributes. But if the prerequisite action doesn't occur, the impending action won't occur either. For example, in the Washing Hands activity, the action "turn on light" is a prerequisite of action "turn off light". If the VC turns on the bathroom light before washing hands, he may or may not turn off the light when leaving the bathroom. But if the VC doesn't turn on the light, he will certainly not turn off the light after washing.

We applied this modeling approach to all actions, which serve as a basic action library to construct activities. Proper combination and permutation of these actions will result in desired activity simulation. Persim 3D also allows the user to model new actions using the same methodology and add them to the action library.

3.2 Reflective Simulation Model of Sensors

In order to track the status of the smart space and all objects used in the activities, we model smart house sensors and attach them to relevant objects. Additionally, we track the VC's motion, simplifying the process of tracking the VC's location by analyzing smartphone sensors. We analyze the modeling of these two categories below.

Smart home sensors. The VC's actions may cause interferences with objects and/or the environment. Smart home sensors are modeled to capture such interference by repeatedly scanning the environment within its working range. In case of interference, the sensor detects the status change of the object to which it is attached and reflects this impact on its sensor reading value. The sensor value could be discrete (e.g., faucet on/off) or continuous (e.g., pressure imposed on a couch).

We finalized four proper kinds of sensors to simulate based on the objects used in the virtual smart house. The contact sensor checks if two objects are in contact and can be attached to doors, windows, and drawers to detect opening or closing events. The motion sensor detects the motion of and around the object. For example, when the VC is standing on the floor, the motion sensor grid installed under the floor could sense VC's presence. A useful application is that the VC's movement path could be identified by analyzing the series of reading value changes of all sensors. IR sensors detect the presence of objects and thus can be installed on faucets and toilets to enable touchless operations. For example, when the IR sensor senses that VC's hands are within its range, it will send a signal to open the water valve. And when the hands move out of its range, it closes the valve. An RFID tag can be attached to an object, and an RFID reader can be attached to the VC so that it can be used to identify the VC's action by checking if he is holding or near an object with a RFID tag.

Smartphone sensors. Persim 3D's sensor simulation framework also supports the modeling and simulation of smartphones to record the VC's activity data. Human activity monitoring and analysis using accelerometers has long been researched [13]. Various data clustering techniques that use smartphones equipped with accelerator and gyroscope sensors to track the user's motion for activity recognition have been proposed [14, 15]. Persim 3D keeps track of the VC's movement, equivalent to obtaining the VC's position by processing the smartphone's sensor data. They are not implemented in the current version of Persim 3D, but can be added if they are properly modeled and fit the simulation purpose.

A sensor, regardless of its kind, is modeled to have five attributes: (1) ID, a unique reference, (2) Kind, which is id of the sensor type, (3) Attaching Entity, a sensor must be attached to a physical entity such as an object, home appliance, furniture, or the VC, (4) Value, reflecting the sensor's current reading, and finally (5) Sensing Function, which links the sensor reading to the attaching entity's attribute. When the entity status changes, the sensor's reading should be updated in response according to the sensing function.

4 Persim 3D Implementation

Persim 3D is implemented in the Unity 5 game engine and relies on Unity's animation system and physics engine to enable high quality activity animation and interactions between the VC and the virtual environment. Figure 1 is a screenshot of the running simulation where the VC is walking in the living room. On the right of the screen is a list of activity buttons, each representing one activity. When an activity button is clicked, the activity will be added to the activity playlist on the left side of the screen. The label above the playlist shows the number of upcoming activities. The user can add any number of activities to the playlist any time and the added activities will be simulated in order. When hovering over the activity name in the playlist, a delete button will show up next to the text and the activity will be removed from the list if the button is clicked. The user can also clear the playlist by clicking the Clear button on the label. In the top

Fig. 1. Screenshot of Persim 3D

right corner of the screen is the simulation control panel that shows the current time and activity, and allows the user to control the gameplay like a media player.

This section overviews Persim 3D's architecture and presents the implementation of the Visualization Engine, Sensor Simulation Engine and Context-driven Simulation Engine, which drives the simulation forward by scheduling activities for the VC to perform.

4.1 Persim 3D Architecture

Helal et al. made an early effort to simulate human activities in smart home by developing Persim [16]. It is an event-driven simulator in the sense that the user needs to design the simulated smart home, the resident's actions and the way actions would trigger sensor events in order to produce a sensor dataset resulted from the simulated human activities. It showed promising results that the synthesized data from Persim was fairly statistically similar to the data acquired from activities conducted by human subjects in a real smart house. It also presented three key challenges that needed to be overcome in its future generations: scalability, realism and accuracy.

Persim 3D, as Persim's successor incarnation, was developed to alleviate these issues [1]. Persim 3D improves simulation scalability greatly by using a context-driven approach instead of event-driven. A context is a high-level simulation state that contains all information of entities of interest in the simulation, such as the simulated space, objects, sensors and virtual characters. Under this approach, the simulation advances by moving from context to context, in which human activities are scheduled and simulated. The high fidelity activity simulation design proposed in this paper attempts to address the simulation realism and accuracy issues.

From an architectural perspective, Persim 3D comprises three major components: Simulation GUI, Sensor/Action Simulation Module and Activity/Context Simulation Module, with the Simulation Interface coordinating in between, as shown in Fig. 2. The Simulation GUI is the main user interface in which the user can configure different components of the simulation, such as the virtual space, the VC's actions and activities, and control the simulation process like playing music in a media player. The Activity/ Context Simulation Module has two major components: Context-driven Simulation Engine and Activity Playback Engine. The Context-driven Simulation Engine drives the simulation on the context level using the context graph defined by the user as well as selects, schedules and simulates activities in each context. For each simulated activity, Persim 3D leverages the Activity Playback Engine to construct its action sequence with the modeled actions and objects [1]. The action sequence is then provided to the Activity Visualization Engine to render its animations. Activity Visualization Engine's enclosing component, the Sensor/Action Simulation Module, utilizes the abovementioned modeling of sensors, objects and actions to create realistic activity animations and physical interactions between the VC and the simulated space. Implementation details will be discussed in the next sub-section.

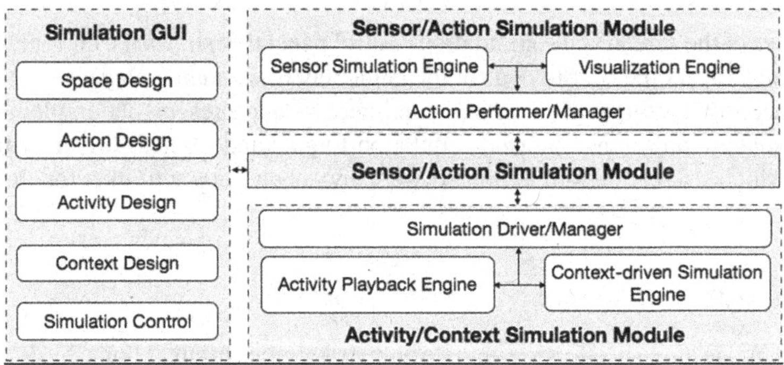

Fig. 2. Persim 3D system architecture.

4.2 Visualization Engine

Figure 3 illustrates the AVS workflow and its communication mechanism with the activity simulation module in Persim 3D. For a given activity, the Activity Playback Engine constructs an action queue and then outsources it to the Activity Visualization Engine to render the animations. Take the Washing Hands activity as an example. Suppose the first action is turning on the bathroom light. The VC could be anywhere in the house when the activity starts. If the VC needs to walk to the light switch, AVS prepares the transitioning movement "walking to bathroom light" so that the virtual character moves to the location of the first action. This transitioning movement is not predefined in the activity, but computed by AVS in real time based on virtual character's current status. If the virtual character happens to be at the bathroom light, then this transitioning movement won't happen at all. After the virtual character moves to the bathroom light switch, he raises the right arm to switch on the light. This action changes the status of the light from off to on, and the motion sensor installed with the switch will detect this action. As the action takes effect, the bathroom will be brighter when the light is turned on. AVS then starts to prepare the next action. Throughout the activity, transitioning movements are computed when an action finishes and are inserted before the next action when necessary.

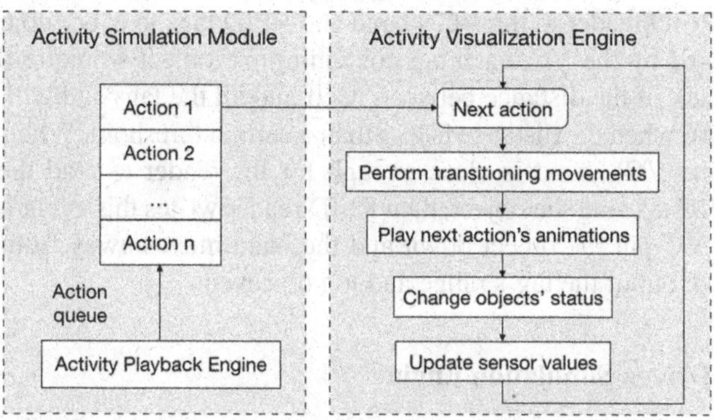

Fig. 3. Activity visualization streamline's workflow.

4.3 Sensor Simulation Engine

As discussed in the last section, Persim 3D simulates four types of sensors that are essential for detecting the VC's actions and interactions with home objects. All sensors are modeled to mimic the functionality of actual sensors, and log the sensor event in the sensor dataset when there is a value change. In this version of the simulator, sensor noise signals or occurrences of sensing errors are not simulated or accounted for. We focus only on the fundamental operations of sensors in this paper.

In the current implementation, the contact sensor is used to detect if a door is open or closed. A contact sensor actually consists of two parts, and when installed on a door, one part is attached to the door frame and the other part is attached to the door near the edge at the same height. When the door is being closed, the two parts come in contact triggering a collision event. The contact sensor detects this collision, changes its status to "closed" and records this event in the sensor data log. When the door is being opened, the two parts lose contact with each other and the sensor changes its status to "open" and records this event when the collision is finished.

Motion sensor is also a binary-valued sensor. It detects the collision between an object and the VC's body parts and changes its value when the collision begins or ends indicating the VC is using the object in a certain way. For example, the VC sitting down on the chair will trigger a collision event between the sensor and the VC's butt. The motion sensor installed on the chair will change its value to "on" when this collision occurs. Similarly, when the VC stands up, the motion sensor would lose contact with the VC's body and change its value to "off".

An IR sensor calculates the distance between itself and the VC, and is activated when the VC is within a certain range. In the Washing Hands activity, when the VC stands by the sink and moves his hands towards the faucet, the IR sensor on the faucet will be activated and set the faucet's status to "on" when the distance between the VC's hands and the faucet is less than the threshold. The IR sensor will be deactivated and set the faucet's status to "off" as the hands move away from the sensor.

In order to track how the VC uses small objects (e.g., cup, pill bottle, comb, etc.), we attached a RFID reader to the VC's hand and RFID tags to every object that can be picked up or used by the VC, each tag containing the object's unique ID. The RFID reader keeps track of the distance between itself and all the tags and will only read the tag's information when the distance is less than a certain threshold. When the VC picks up an object, the VC's hand is close enough for the reader to read the object's ID, indicating the VC is using the object, then RFID reader writes this event into the sensor log. When the VC put the object down and the hand moves away from it, the RFID reader will move out of the tag's range and log this event.

4.4 Context-Driven Simulation Engine

Persim 3D is a context-driven activity simulator where the simulation is driven and guided by the context graph, which consists of contexts [17]. A context represents special states of interest of the simulated space. A context is defined by pre-conditions and a set of activities that are allowed to take place in it. When an activity is scheduled to be simulated in a given context, Persim 3D invokes the Activity Playback Engine to play the activity, which will change the state space in this context.

The Context-driven Simulation Engine oversees two simulation loops, as illustrated in Fig. 4. The outer loop is an inter-context loop that drives simulation at the context graph level and focuses on simulating scenarios through transitioning from one context to another. The inner loop is an intra-context loop that takes place within a newly entered context in which one or more activities are selected, scheduled, ordered and performed. The state space of the simulated environment is changed by the simulated activities, and given the same set of activities, the state space can be changed in different ways with differently scheduled activity sequence within a context. Therefore, the selection and scheduling of activities is essential for context-driven simulation. Algorithms for proper activity selection and scheduling have been proposed in [19]. The algorithms calculate Euclidean distance measures obtained from the evaluation of context and activity pre-conditions with respect to state space variables at the time of evaluation. Planning methods are applied accordingly to find and select the activity that is the most likely to occur next.

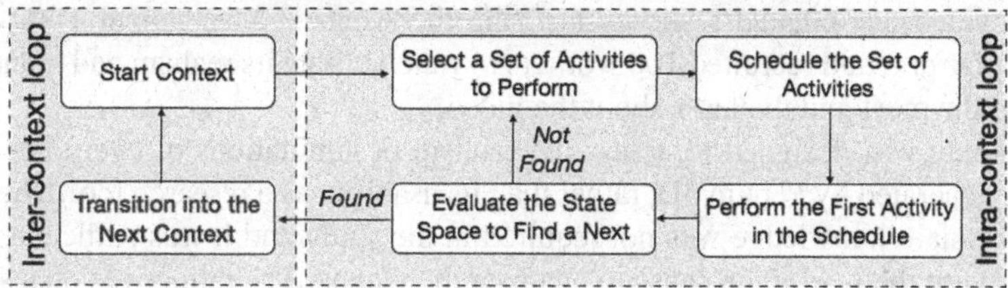

Fig. 4. Context-driven simulation engine's workflow.

Once an activity is performed within a context, the changed state space is "reflected" and all possible next contexts are checked by evaluating their pre-conditions for possible transitioning within the context graph. Similar to selecting and scheduling activities, Euclidean distance is used to evaluate comparative measures to select the next context. Dependent on the evaluation result, the simulation could stay in the current context or advance to a new context.

5 Experimental Evaluation

To evaluate the visualism and realism of Persim 3D, we conducted user studies online where we asked users to watch the screen recording of the generated visualizations of activity simulation and rate on how realistic they thought the videos were. For the user study, we modeled the smart house and activities using Persim 3D, and recorded each activity. The smart house is embodied from out Gator Tech Smart House (GTSH) [18], and we modeled the following seven activities: Washing Face, Washing Hands, Drinking Water, Combing Hair, Shaving, Using Cellphone and Falling. For each activity, we screen-recorded the simulation to generate 3 different videos, which were labeled with the same name, but varied in the VC's actions, yielding 21 videos in total.

Table 1. Ratings on Realism of Activity Simulation

Activity	Video 1		Video 2		Video 3	
	Rating	SD	Rating	SD	Rating	SD
Washing Face	7.05	2.04	7.01	1.97	7.01	1.82
Washing Hands	7.48	1.90	7.51	1.73	7.39	1.62
Drinking Water	7.60	1.59	7.84	1.80	7.74	1.68
Combing Hair	7.64	1.75	7.27	1.75	7.35	1.62
Shaving	6.56	2.11	7.00	1.60	6.86	1.91
Using Cellphone	7.43	1.73	7.53	1.76	7.68	1.73
Falling	6.81	2.10	6.84	2.03	7.01	1.94

For each video, we created a survey utilizing the Amazon Mechanical Turk crowdsourcing platform and recruited 100 workers to watch it, rate its realism and tell us what they liked the most and the least about the video.

This study was designed to assess the realism of simulations of everyday human activities generated by Persim 3D, rather than its usability as a research tool. Therefore, research domain knowledge was not required in the study and it was sufficient for the workers to use their common sense to evaluate the videos. The rating was on a scale of 1 to 10, 1 being very unrealistic and 10 being very realistic. There were a total of 952 workers who actually participated in our online survey, and many of them watched and rated more than one video. Their ages ranged from 15 to 77 ($avg = 33.96$, $SD = 10.85$). Table 1 summaries the users' ratings on the realism of the visualizations generated by activity simulations on Persim 3D.

Most workers gave helpful and constructive criticism after watching the video. Drinking Water got 7.73 average rating with three videos, which was the highest rating among all the seven activities. There was a consensus that the activity was demonstrated clearly and realistically in a nice kitchen setting. Even though the videos lacked variety of actions that some people would do when drinking, such as taking ice from the fridge and washing the cup before or after use, it represented acceptably high realism of simulation. Washing Face, Washing Hands, Combing Hair, and Using Cellphone also demonstrated the key actions in an adequately realistic way with good details, and therefore showed high rating score. Shaving and Falling did receive less rating scores (less than 7.0). The models of the activities had sufficient and realistic details, however, they were difficult to animate,

In the survey we asked the workers if they had experience in computer graphics or game development. We found out that those who had experience in relevant fields tended to give more professional feedback. Some gave suggestions on camera positions and close-up shots in order to better show the VC's actions. Overall, the users thought the simulations were of high fidelity with mixed opinions towards the VC's action details. There are a number of factors that could affect simulation's visual effect, such as the quality of object models used, the VC's rig, animation details, lighting in the scene, camera position, etc. All the feedback and comments the users left are helpful for us to improve the realism of the simulation.

The simulation visualization generated by Persim 3D is not only a means for its creator to access the simulation methodology, but also an immediate visual feedback provided to the simulation user to validate the simulation model on the fly. It creates a closed loop system in which users are enabled to rapidly run the simulation and obtain visual results, fix things that went wrong and re-run the simulation on updated models.

6 Conclusion

In this paper, we presented a novel approach to creating high fidelity simulation and visualization of ADLs. We discussed the rationale of the selection of simulated activities and the analysis and modeling of actions, objects and sensors. We presented the implementation of the Activity Visualization Engine, Sensor Simulation Engine, the supporting Context-driven Simulation Engine and how these engines work together within the Persim 3D framework. We validated 7 activities by conducting online user studies. With a powerful human activity simulator, it is possible to develop and test smart spaces preliminarily without costly built environments. We believe that better smart home simulators could empower the development of a broad range of ambient intelligence applications. In the next version of the simulator, we will extend the sensor simulation engine to account for sensor noise and errors which will enable us to simulate uncertain situations and scenarios.

References

1. Liu, S., Helal, S., Lee, J.W.: Activity playback modeling for smart home simulation. In: Geissbühler, A., Demongeot, J., Mokhtari, M., Abdulrazak, B., Aloulou, H. (eds.) ICOST 2015. LNCS, vol. 9102, pp. 92–102. Springer, Cham (2015). doi:10.1007/978-3-319-19312-0_8
2. Synnott, J., Chen, L., Nugent, C., Moore, G.: The creation of simulated activity datasets using a graphical intelligent environment simulation tool. In: Annual International Conference of the IEEE Engineering in Medicine and Biology Society, pp. 4143–4146 (2014)
3. Lei, Z., Yue, S., Yu, C., Yuanchun, S.: SHSim: An OSGI-based smart home simulator. In: IEEE International Conference on Ubi-Media Computing, pp. 87–90 (2010)
4. Kaldeli, E., Warriach, E.U., Bresser, J., Lazovik, A., Aiello, M.: Interoperation, composition and simulation of services at home. In: Maglio, P.P., Weske, M., Yang, J., Fantinato, M. (eds.) ICSOC 2010. LNCS, vol. 6470, pp. 167–181. Springer, Heidelberg (2010). doi: 10.1007/978-3-642-17358-5_12
5. Bouchard, K., Ajroud, A., Bouchard, B., Bouzouane, A.: SIMACT: a 3D open source smart home simulator for activity recognition. In: Kim, T., Adeli, H. (eds.) ACN/AST/ISA/UCMA -2010. LNCS, vol. 6059, pp. 524–533. Springer, Heidelberg (2010). doi: 10.1007/978-3-642-13577-4_47
6. Shen, W., Shen, Q., Sun, Q.: Building information modeling-based user activity simulation and evaluation method for improving designer–user communications. Autom. Constr. **21**, 148–160 (2012)
7. Velasquez, C., Soares, C., Morla, R., Moreira, R.S., Torres, J., Sobral, P.: A 3D simulation framework for safe ambient-assisted home care. In: International Conference on Mobile Ubiquitous Computing, Systems, Services and Technologies, pp. 61–66 (2011)
8. Katz, S., Ford, A.B., Moskowitz, R.W., Jackson, B.A., Jaffe, M.W.: Studies of illness in the aged: The index of ADL: A standardized measure of biological and psychosocial function. JAMA **185**(12), 914–919 (1963)
9. Bookman, A., Harrington, M., Pass, L., Reisner, E.: Family Caregiver Handbook. MIT, Cambridge (2007)
10. Lawton, M., Brody, E.M.: Assessment of older people: Self-maintaining and instrumental activities of daily living. Nurs. Res. **19**(3), 278 (1970)
11. Checklist of Activities of Daily Living. http://www-tc.pbs.org/wgbh/caringforyourparents/caregiver/pdf/cfyp_adl_checklist.pdf
12. Stevens, J.A., Mahoney, J.E., Ehrenreich, H.: Circumstances and outcomes of falls among high risk community-dwelling older adults. Injur. Epidem. **1**(1), 1–9 (2014)
13. Veltink, P.H., Bussmann, H.B., de Vries, W., Martens, W.L., Van Lummel, R.C.: Detection of static and dynamic activities using uniaxial accelerometers. IEEE T. Rehabil. Engin. **4**(4), 375–385 (1996)

14. Kwon, Y., Kang, K., Bae, C.: Unsupervised learning for human activity recognition using smartphone sensors. Expert Syst. Appl. **41**(14), 6067–6074 (2014)
15. Anguita, D., Ghio, A., Oneto, L., Parra, X., Reyes-Ortiz, J.L.: Human activity recognition on smartphones using a multiclass hardware-friendly support vector machine. In: Ambient Assisted Living and Home Care, pp. 216–223 (2012)
16. Helal, S., Lee, J.W., Hossain, S., Kim, E., Hagras, H., Cook, D.: Persim-simulator for human activities in pervasive spaces. In: International Conference on Intelligent Environments, pp. 192–199 (2011)
17. Lee, J.W., Cho, S., Liu, S., Cho, K., Helal, S.: Persim 3D: Context-driven simulation and modeling of human activities in smart spaces. IEEE Trans. Autom. Sci. Eng. **12**(4), 1243–1256 (2015)
18. Helal, S., Mann, W., King, J., Kaddoura, Y., Jansen, E.: The gator tech smart house: A programmable pervasive space. Computer **38**(3), 50–60 (2005)
19. Lee, J.W., Helal, S., Sung, Y., Cho, K.: Context activity selection and scheduling in context-driven simulation. In: Symposium on Theory of Modeling and Simulation, pp. 60–67 (2014)

Independent Living Technology

Exploring Opportunistic Ambient Notifications in the Smart Home to Enhance Quality of Live

Andreas Seiderer(✉), Chi Tai Dang(✉), and Elisabeth André(✉)

Augsburg University, Universitätsstr. 6a, 86159 Augsburg, Germany
seiderer@hcm-lab.de, {dang,andre}@informatik.uni-augsburg.de

Abstract. Smart home technology became more and more widespread within recent years. They aim to make life easier and taking over unwanted tasks. In traditional homes, it is often not clear whether all windows and doors of a house are closed before inhabitants leave the home or go to sleep. However, this can be easily addressed by smart homes. We present a system based on opportunistically located ambient lights that assist inhabitants of a smart home in answering this question. In this paper, we show the concept of our system and the inhabitant-centered design process behind the development. The system was installed in a one-family smart home. We report on insights gained through data collected from this deployment over a period of six months. Within interviews, we found that the ambient light system gave inhabitants a more confident feeling about open doors/windows.

Keywords: Ambient notifications · Ambient light · Smart home

1 Introduction

"Did you close the window in the bathroom?" Many of us had this situation after just having locked the front door before leaving. Without a smart home, inhabitants of a house would have to unlock the front door again and check the window state. In particular, the chances to oversee opened windows or doors rise with increasing number of windows, doors, and inhabitants of a house. Inadvertently leaving windows or doors open encourages burglars to break in as such houses represent easy targets. Windows or doors that were left opened may also lead to severe damage to the interior of a house caused by water from heavy rain or wind of a strong storm. Smart homes, however, usually have the capability to gather such information through motion detectors and door/window contact sensors and inform their inhabitants before they leave the home or go to bed, thus help avoid windows and doors that were inadvertently left open. Such a functionality exactly fulfills some of the expectations that people have on smart homes, that is, "make life easy" and "taking over the unwanted tasks" [1].

In this paper, we present a system that addresses this circumstance and informs inhabitants about such security risks through ambient notifications in the form of opportunistically located ambient lights. In contrast to LCD displays

M. Mokhtari et al. (Eds.): ICOST 2017, LNCS 10461, pp. 151–160, 2017.
DOI: 10.1007/978-3-319-66188-9_13

or smartphones that have the capability to show arbitrary textual or graphical content, lights have a limited information channel. Hence, ambient lights are not suitable to directly tell users which of the relevant windows or doors is still open. However, they can be placed unobtrusively in users' periphery and perceived easily [3,9] while having the potential to quickly conveying information of different urgency levels through color, brightness, or effects (e.g. dim loops) [11]. The ambient lights in our system act as a reminder and seek to increase the subjective safety feeling of inhabitants. For example, by glowing with a "good" color (e.g. green) to indicate that all windows and doors are closed, inhabitants receive the signal that it is safe now to leave the home. For the development of our system, we applied an inhabitant-centered design process as every (smart) home is different and habits, as well as suitable opportunistic places for ambient lights, may vary largely. Based on the implemented and deployed system, we collected data from the lights and sensors in a smart home with two inhabitants of a one-family house. We report on insights from the data for a period of six months. In the discussion section, we will report on quantitative insights from the collected data as well as experiences of the inhabitants with the system.

2 Related Work

Ambient notifications in the form of light colors or light effects received increasing research interest distributed across recent years (e.g., [2,3,5–7,10]). For example, Hazlewood et al. [3] studied a small spherical object made of frosted glass, which illuminated with different colors in order to reflect the confidence level of students during university courses. Occhialini et al. [8] explored how ambient lights that showed dynamic patterns on the walls of a meeting room help in time management of meetings. Another example for time management was investigated in a lab study by Mueller et al. [7]. Their "Ambient Timer" unobtrusively notified users of upcoming events through ambient light that was emitted by RGB-LEDs mounted behind a monitor. In terms of energy awareness, Gustafsson et al. [2] demonstrated the intuitiveness of their "Power-aware Cord" within a Wizard-of-Oz experiment. Their intention was to increase the awareness of energy consumption of electronic devices by means of glowing light patterns expressed by electrical cords. However, none of the previous works addressed ambient light notifications to opportunistically inform inhabitants of a domestic environment about a "home state".

Domestic environments, such as smart homes, are different from public or work places as domestic environments are private spaces in which acceptance of technology and techniques may not be the same as for public/work spaces. Vastenburg et al. [11] explored the acceptability of notifications in the home and found that acceptability depends on urgency levels of notifications and their intrusiveness in presentation. Acceptance of urgent notifications was high if presented intrusively and acceptance of non-urgent notifications can be increased if presented non-intrusively.

Pousman et al. [9] presented a taxonomy for 19 existing ambient information systems consisting of four archetypes which they described as symbolic sculptural display, multiple-information consolidators, information monitor display, and high throughput textual display. Our system falls into the category symbolic sculptural display as we display only few information in an abstract sculptural way. Matviienko et al. [6] studied a variety of ambient light patterns and presented design guidelines to help in designing ambient light systems. In particular, their guidelines suggest that colors known from traffic lights (which our system is based on) are most suitable for assessment of everyday situations.

2.1 Concept of Opportunistic Ambient Notifications

The concept of our ambient notifications was kept as unobtrusive and simple as possible in order to avoid disturbing inhabitants while enabling them to quickly understand the notification at the first glance. Hence, it is based on opportunistically placed ambient lights, that is, lights embedded into daily routines of inhabitants or daily objects of the household which are part of daily routines as proposed in [9,10]. Ambient lights combined with such a placement aim to be placed unobtrusively in users' periphery while at the same time allow inhabitants to quickly perceive and understand notifications in order to support their daily activities. The lights serve to indicate the states of door and window contacts installed in a home. Due to the limited information channel of lights and a potentially high number of door and window contacts, we chose not to encode particular contacts into the notifications in favor of a quickly perceivable accumulated state, which is reflected by three colors known from traffic lights in western countries, that is, green, orange, and red.

Table 1. Color encoding of ambient lights.

Color	Meaning
Green	All critical and non-critical contacts are closed
Orange	At least one non-critical needs to be closed
Red	At least one critical contact must be closed

Table 1 shows our concept's encoding of colors in which we mapped the three colors to an accumulated state that reflects the door/window contact categories critical and non-critical. The critical category represents doors/windows that allow burglars to easily get into a house such as the main door or a window on the first floor. The non-critical category represents, for example, windows on the second floor, which should be closed but would not allow burglars to quickly break into a house (e.g., as there is no direct access from outside). Such windows are often left open in bedrooms for air exchange overnight or to lower humidity in bathrooms.

3 Inhabitant-Centered Design Process

Every building is different (e.g., in terms of architecture, construction, or number of floors, windows, or doors), and every home/household together with its inhabitants has different habits and daily routines. Usually, technology within households is configured to appropriately support such routines as ascertained by Hughes et al. [4]. Inhabitant-centered design denotes the focus of design processes on such daily routines and accompanying experiences instead of addressing tasks and performance/efficiency of tasks known from user-centered considerations. Therefore, an ambient notification system as proposed in this paper must be designed with respect to the particular house as well as an understanding of the daily practices of occupants [11] in order to provide real benefit to inhabitants. Hence, the development of our system followed a design process in which the inhabitants were highly involved during design, implementation, and installation phases.

3.1 Inhabitants

For the development of our system, we recruited a household that already had installed home automation technology consisting of motion detectors and contact sensors on all windows and doors as preparation for an alarm system. The one-family house had three floors including a garden and a garage. The household consisted of two inhabitants aged between 60 and 70. The inhabitants were not given any fees for their participation but the developed system.

3.2 Design Process

Within an initial meeting, we discussed the concept with the inhabitants and made sure that they fully understood the color encodings. Afterwards, we determined situations and daily routines in which the inhabitants particularly have an interest in knowing the state of their windows and doors. We quickly came across daily routines when they are about to leave their home, go to bed, or linger in the living room.

Ambient Light Locations. Depending on the determined routines, we identified locations in the building for placement of ambient lights, which opportunistically support their daily routines, for example, locations where the inhabitants often pass by during the routines. Those locations are the front door, the living room, and the bedroom. If inhabitants are located near the front door, they might leave the house and want to make sure that all windows/doors are closed and locked. The ambient light for this routine was installed in the corridor near the front door as there was already a lamp mounted on the wall, c.f. Fig. 1a. This lamp was used as an automatic light source at night and also partly enlightened the stairs down to the cellar and up to the second floor. By reusing the placement and enhancing the lamp to display ambient notifications (i.e., replacing

Fig. 1. (a) is showing the RGBW bulb near the front door. The lamp in (b) is placed in the living room. Lamp (c) is located near the bedroom. In this case, the wireless motion detector is placed upon the lamp. (Color figure online)

the bulb), the ambient light got an unobtrusive location (as inhabitants were already used to the lamp) and opportunistically support inhabitants in their daily routines.

When the inhabitants linger in the living room for a longer period (e.g. watching TV), they wanted to get notified in case they forgot to close the front door or a window on the first floor. Instead of reusing the main lights on the ceiling for ambient notifications, the inhabitants chose a more unobtrusive location near the terrace, c.f. Fig. 1b. Even though this location is in the inhabitants' periphery, the ambient light can still be quickly perceived. Because one of the daily routines in this room is to watch TV, the brightness of the ambient light had to be dimmed down. Otherwise, the ambient light would disturb the daily routines too much.

One of the critical moments when the inhabitants want to make sure that no doors or windows remain open was before they go to sleep. Therefore, the last ambient light was placed near the stairs on the second floor where the inhabitants have their bedroom (c.f. Fig. 1c). This ambient light is dimmed down so that not too much light falls into the bedroom but still being bright enough to act as an automatic light for the night, which slightly enlightens the stairs.

Inhabitant-Adapted Color Encodings. The final step in the design process was to assign door/window contacts to the categories in Table 1. Depending on the location (and context) of an ambient light, door/window contacts had to be treated slightly different, which must be logical and clear to the inhabitants. The color Green always indicates that all doors and windows are closed and there are no security concerns.

Windows on the second floor are generally assigned to the non-critical category as they do not provide direct access into the building from outside. Their state is indicated through the color Orange if at least one window is open. Inhabitants should get an indication of this state, for example, to prevent damages due to upcoming weather conditions (e.g. rain, wind). There is one exception regarding this category. The inhabitants were used to sleep with one window tilted, which should not result in an orange colored warning notifier. Otherwise, the inhabitants would ignore this indication before they go to sleep and probably miss another opened window of the non-critical category. Therefore, the ambient light near the bedroom shows Green if only the window in the bedroom is open.

Red color indicates that a door/window of the critical category is open, for example, the front door or the garage door. Regarding this category, there is an exception for the ambient light near the front door. The state of the front and garage door is not used to adapt the color of this ambient light. Usually, before leaving the house, the garage door is always open and the front door is in direct view, thus, do not need to be indicated by the system. This ambient light is switched to Green if just the garage and/or front door is still open.

The ambient light in the living room behaves like the ambient light near the bedroom with one exception, which was an explicit request expressed by the inhabitants. If only the garage and/or front door is still open, the ambient light in the living room is colored blue as the inhabitants regularly forgot to close this door. In such a case, they wanted a clear and distinct indication of that situation.

4 System Design

The existing home automation technology in the smart home of our volunteers employed wireless sensors (door/window contacts, PIR motion detectors) of the home automation system Homematic[1], which is a widespread technology in Germany. In each room of the chosen ambient light locations, the home had already motion sensors installed. In order to enhance the system with ambient lights as proposed in our concept, we extended the system with radio controlled (2.4 GHz) RGBW LED bulbs, which are part of the Milight[2] system. They represent a low-cost alternative to the Philips Hue system. Although these bulbs are less expensive, they work quite reliably and produce colored light that has a higher saturation for some colors (especially green) than the Hue bulbs. Nevertheless, the brightness of the Milight bulbs seems to depend more on the color than the Hue bulbs. In our case, the saturation of the color was more important than a stable brightness as the bulbs were just used in addition to existing regular lighting. In order to control the homematic devices as well as the ambient light bulbs, the system made use of so-called bridges as outlined in Fig. 2. The existing home automation technology was based on the open source home automation software FHEM[3] running on an always-on Linux system powered by a low power Intel NUC-Kit DN2820FYKH with 4 GB RAM and a 120 GB SSD. Hence, we implemented and integrated the ambient light notification logic as an extension of the FHEM installation.

[1] http://www.homematic.com/.
[2] http://www.milight.com/.
[3] http://fhem.de/fhem.html.

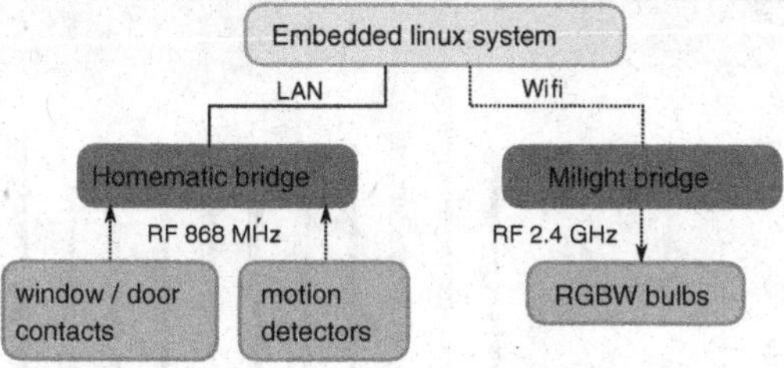

Fig. 2. Overview of the relevant system hardware. (Color figure online)

5 Insights and Discussion

After designing, implementing, and installing the ambient light system, we collected log data from the home automation system, which included data from all motion sensors and ambient lights. In the following, we analyzed data from a period of six months. Additionally, we did first interviews with the participants.

The system ran quite stable for most of the time and functionality was maintained by an experimenter at least twice a month. Rarely, higher latencies between the detection of an inhabitant and the system output by the ambient lights occurred due to delayed sensor data transmission or higher response time of the LED bulbs. Sometimes, it also happened that signals of the sensors were not received by the home automation, thus an old state was used by the system. If FHEM did not receive the state of sensors for a longer time, the sensor was considered to be "dead", which was identifiable in the logs. For example, this sometimes happened to the contact sensor at the garage door during the winter months. The low temperature condition most probably had a negative (but temporary) influence on the sensor's battery. In order to account for possible transmission errors of the home automation system to the ambient lights, commands (i.e. the accumulated state) to the lights were sent every time motion was detected or the state of a door/window changed.

An important question is how often and when the bulbs were visible to inhabitants and whether the chosen positions for the ambient lights were adequate and actually frequently passed. Information about this can be obtained by analyzing the sensor data from the motion detectors that were placed near the ambient lights. Activity detected through motion sensors resulted in light activity through the ambient lights. The aggregated sum of the detected motion events per hour of the three motion detectors are given in Fig. 3. During 8 to 0 o'clock, most of the detected motions occurred in the living room. The second highest event count occurred near the front door. During the night and in the morning from 1 to 7 o'clock, the inhabitants usually passed the bulb near the bedroom. The ambient light in the living room and near the front door are more visible to the inhabitants during the day than the ambient light near the bedroom. In the evening when the inhabitants go to bed and in the morning when they get up the ambient light near the bedroom is more likely to be noticed.

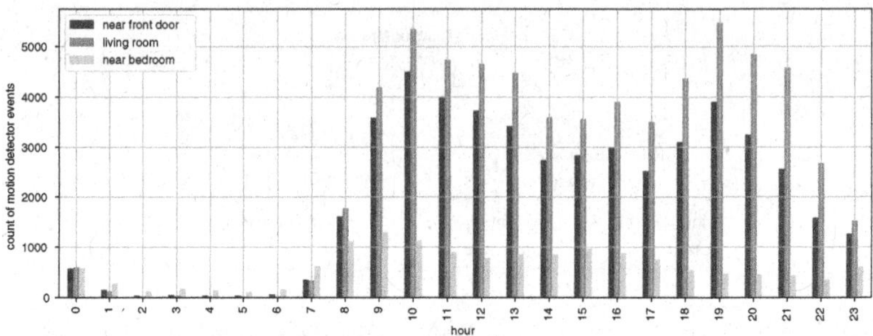

Fig. 3. Count of motion events per hour for each motion detector summed up over six months. (Color figure online)

The question whether the system had an influence on the inhabitants cannot be reliably answered by solely interpreting the recorded sensor data. From the collected data, at least two requirements to answer this question can be derived. First, it is possible to detect when the participants left the house by considering a specific time duration without motion during the day as absent. Second, the color of the ambient light that was shown to them before leaving can be identified. However, it is sometimes not clear whether they left specific non-critical windows or doors open by intention or by accident. Furthermore, it would also be possible to detect whether the inhabitants closed doors or windows before they left so that the system would show a green colored light. Still, it is hard to tell if they did this because of the ambient light. In addition, several external influences may occur that change the usual behavior of the inhabitants and are partly visible in the sensor data. This could be a visit from a family member or in case of bad weather for several days.

Thus, we additionally questioned the inhabitants whether the system helped them remember opened doors/windows. One of the inhabitants answered that they usually still know which windows/doors are open but the system gave them a better feeling as the system also confirmed their assumption. Although the lamps cannot show which door/window was open, it was usually sufficient for reminding the inhabitants. In rare cases, it happened that they had to search the open door/window. The inhabitants also confirmed that they were sometimes leaving a (non-critical) window on the second floor open during the day if they were leaving just for a short time or for garden work.

6 Conclusion

We have presented the inhabitant-centered design process for an ambient light notification system that addresses smart homes and reported on an ongoing longitudinal deployment of the system. Opportunistic locations for placement of the lights were chosen in tandem with the daily routines of inhabitants. According to interviews with the participants, the system seemed to reduce the amount of forgotten doors/windows but more importantly, an improved certainty about the state of the doors/windows was expressed by the inhabitants. Since this system was tested with two inhabitants living in the same home, they also reminded each other. Thus, it would be interesting to test such a system in an additional study with elderly people that live on their own in their own house or apartment.

References

1. Eggen, B., Hollemans, G., van de Sluis, R.: Exploring and enhancing the home experience. Cognit. Technol. Work **5**(1), 44–54 (2003). http://dx.doi.org/10.1007/s10111-002-0114-7
2. Gustafsson, A., Gyllenswärd, M.: The power-aware cord: energy awareness through ambient information display. In: CHI 2005 Extended Abstracts on Human Factors in Computing Systems (CHI EA 2005), pp. 1423–1426, NY, USA (2005). http://doi.acm.org/10.1145/1056808.1056932
3. Hazlewood, W.R., Stolterman, E., Connelly, K.: Issues in evaluating ambient displays in the wild: two case studies. In: Proceedings of the SIGCHI Conference on Human Factors in Computing Systems (CHI 2011), pp. 877–886, NY, USA (2011). http://doi.acm.org/10.1145/1978942.1979071
4. Hughes, J., O'Brien, J., Rodden, T., Rouncefield, M., Viller, S.: Patterns of home life: informing design for domestic environments. Personal Technol. **4**(1), 25–38 (2000). http://dx.doi.org/10.1007/BF01613596
5. Mateevitsi, V., Reda, K., Leigh, J., Johnson, A.: The health bar: a persuasive ambient display to improve the office worker's well being. In: Proceedings of the 5th Augmented Human International Conference (AH 2014), pp. 21: 1–21: 2, NY, USA (2014). http://doi.acm.org/10.1145/2582051.2582072
6. Matviienko, A., Cobus, V., Müller, H., Fortmann, J., Löcken, A., Boll, S., Rauschenberger, M., Timmermann, J., Trappe, C., Heuten, W.: Deriving design guidelines for ambient light systems. In: Proceedings of the 14th International Conference on Mobile and Ubiquitous Multimedia (MUM 2015), pp. 267–277, NY, USA (2015). http://doi.acm.org/10.1145/2836041.2836069
7. Müller, H., Kazakova, A., Pielot, M., Heuten, W., Boll, S.: Ambient timer – unobtrusively reminding users of upcoming tasks with ambient light. In: Kotzé, P., Marsden, G., Lindgaard, G., Wesson, J., Winckler, M. (eds.) INTERACT 2013. LNCS, vol. 8117, pp. 211–228. Springer, Heidelberg (2013). doi:10.1007/978-3-642-40483-2_15
8. Occhialini, V., van Essen, H., Eggen, B.: Design and evaluation of an ambient display to support time management during meetings. In: Campos, P., Graham, N., Jorge, J., Nunes, N., Palanque, P., Winckler, M. (eds.) INTERACT 2011. LNCS, vol. 6947, pp. 263–280. Springer, Heidelberg (2011). doi:10.1007/978-3-642-23771-3_20
9. Pousman, Z., Stasko, J.: A taxonomy of ambient information systems: four patterns of design. In: Proceedings of the Working Conference on Advanced Visual Interfaces (AVI 2006), pp. 67–74, NY, USA (2006). http://doi.acm.org/10.1145/1133265.1133277

10. Ramos, L., van den Hoven, E., Miller, L.: Designing for the other 'hereafter': when older adults remember about forgetting. In: Proceedings of the 2016 CHI Conference on Human Factors in Computing Systems (CHI 2016), pp. 721–732, NY, USA (2016). http://doi.acm.org/10.1145/2858036.2858162
11. Vastenburg, M.H., Keyson, D.V., de Ridder, H.: Considerate home notification systems: a user study of acceptability of notifications in a living-room laboratory. Int. J. Hum. Comput. Stud. **67**(9), 814–826 (2009). http://dx.doi.org/10.1016/j.ijhcs.2009.06.002

Proof of Concept Evaluation for an Intelligent Oven

Susan E. Reid[1], Bessam Abdulrazak[2(✉)], and Monica Alas[2]

[1] Bishop's University, Lennoxville, QC, Canada
sreid@ubishops.ca
[2] Université de Sherbrooke, Sherbrooke, QC, Canada
{bessam.abdulrazak,monica.alas}@usherbrooke.ca

Abstract. As the senior portion of the population continues to rise considerably, age-related deterioration of the human body has become an increasing challenge and concern in the fields of health, economics and sociology. Related to these concerns, many technologies are being designed to provide cognitive and physical assistance to enable seniors living independently in their homes, to do so in more safe environments. To this end, we propose a new kitchen solution, 'InOvUS', which focuses on safety and reducing the risks of fire, burn and smoke inhalation. Interestingly, most evaluation works focus on technical mechanisms and algorithms validation. Our study, instead, evaluates the adoption intention and interest in InOvUS from a senior user perspective. Our method is based on the Willingness-to-Adopt concept and was tested among seniors aged 65+. The evaluation results show clear buying and use intentions for InOvUS by seniors.

Keywords: Aging-in-place · Willingness-to-adopt · Safety · Seniors

1 Introduction

The aging process triggers deterioration in distinct physiological functionalities of the human body. This phenomenon translates, for seniors, into higher levels of vulnerability and susceptibility to various risks associated with indoor and outdoor activities of daily life [19]. Ensuring safety becomes a vital element in helping seniors remain independent and even more particularly while performing what can potentially become high-risk activities, such as cooking, which are conducted frequently. Cooking is a high-risk activity for seniors because there is an increasing likelihood of both physiological deterioration and memory impairments, which have the potential to impact people's capabilities in performing cooking-related tasks in a safe manner. For example, while watching television, a senior might want a cup of tea and start boiling water on a pot over an oven burner. The phone may ring causing the senior to forget about the pot and the tea. Indeed, physiological deterioration such as attention and memory problems can easily lead to fire and inhaling [1]. Hence, when seniors are cooking they become exposed to three major risks: fire, burn (contact or splash) and inhaling (gas or smoke) [1].

M. Mokhtari et al. (Eds.): ICOST 2017, LNCS 10461, pp. 161–172, 2017.
DOI: 10.1007/978-3-319-66188-9_14

The rising number of seniors 65+ globally is expected to jump from 390 to 800 million by 2025 [18] and these statistics accentuate the urgency to reduce the safety issues associated with their indoor and outdoor Activities of Daily Living (ADL). To this end, we propose a sensor-based cooking safe system, or intelligent oven, called InOvUS. The system aims at discerning hazardous situations by monitoring and measuring pertinent parameters around the oven. These parameters include concentrations of Volatile Organic Compound (VOC) and Alcohol gases in the cooking environment. Burn parameters include relative humidity, utensil temperatures, burner temperature and presence of utensils on the burner for burn by splash and contact. Lastly, for intoxication by gas/smoke, the concentration of Carbon monoxide (CO) gas in the cooking smoke is observed. These parameters are extracted based on the extensive risk analysis and assessment experimental results conducted by our extended team [1].

In this paper, we focus on presenting the evaluation of systems for seniors designed to provide a safe environment while cooking. This research study has three broad aims: (1) to survey the literature to establish the risks posed for seniors when cooking in the kitchen; (2) to perform a qualitative analysis aimed at elaborating how, where and when these risks typically occur and (3) to perform an early assessment of potential interest by seniors in an intelligent oven, such as InOvUS, designed to help reduce and/or better manage such risks.

2 Literature Review and Related Work/Systems

In all related work, it is noted that there are two main categories of interventions to reduce the consequences of cooking-related risks affecting seniors: human and technological [19]. Our goal is to provide a proper evaluation method for an assistive technology, such as InOvUS, from the senior user's perspective. As such, the related literature and systems that we examined focused on the evaluation of technological interventions to help seniors age-in-place. The fact that most seniors prefer to remain independent and age in their home for as long as possible, reinforces (a) the importance to develop and use an accurate approach for assessing the willingness to use InOvUS, (b) the importance of evaluating their perceptions surrounding oven safety features and (c) the importance to ensure that InOvUS meets the needs of seniors.

Much of the related work and literature in this field is specific to the development and evaluation of intelligent awareness systems (i.e., pervasive technology solutions). These systems involve activity monitoring by using sensors. They have been designed to serve three user groups (i.e., seniors, family/friends, and caregivers) by monitoring seniors' activity, interpreting sensor data, and providing feedback [8]. These intelligent awareness systems were developed after studying ADL (such as cooking, cleaning, etc.) through behavioral studies and give peace of mind to seniors and their family and friends. However, for caregivers this type of system is perceived as a remote monitoring system for operating more efficiently and cost effectively [8].

Moreover, these systems depend on high-level interpretation of sensor data. For example, these sensors will monitor, detect and signal unsafe situations (through raw sensor data like raw numerical computation) by tracking the presence of a senior at a specific location, like the kitchen. A signal will be emitted to the caregiver, if the senior is rarely visiting the kitchen, as it could mean that the senior is not eating or drinking enough liquid. The overall goal of these systems is to help seniors with aging-in-place with safety. That said, the focus of a great number of papers, such as [5, 8, 10, 11, 14, 17], is on the evaluation of the technical development and algorithms of these systems and not on the user's evaluation or satisfaction with such systems. As an example, Nef et al. [11] focused on the evaluation of the performance of three machines which used learning algorithms related to their sensitivity and specificity in recognizing ADL like cooking. Indeed, a limited number of papers focus on evaluation from the perspective of the user.

As one example, Horst and Sinitsyn [8] developed a laboratory evaluation which used an experimental simulation approach to understanding a senior's living environment. Their safety system was composed of two separate systems: a demonstrator and a monitoring system. The demonstrator was created to track the presence of one senior, aged 82, in specific locations in the senior's living environment. The monitoring system was evaluated through the deployment into the homes of seven seniors living alone and their caregivers. Their evaluation interest was on the sensing infrastructure [8]. Horst & Sinitsyn acknowledge that the user evaluation was not the focus of their work.

Another work relates to the design, deployment and testing of integrated home-based ambient assisted-living systems for seniors involving a combination of sensor and interactive support technology [4]. The system aims at providing senior home security through ambient monitoring, behavior recognition and providing interventional feedback to support the maintenance of independent living and quality of life of seniors. The evaluation was done on how effective seniors perceived the system's feedback to be and how they found living and using such technology. The system was deployed in 16 seniors' homes. While part of the feedback included how the seniors felt about the experience of living in a smart home, there was a greater emphasis on the methodology used to evaluate the technical components of the sensor network, sensor data validation, system data loss, sensor failure, and external driven system downtime.

Another work by Sarni [13] focused on the evaluation of a smart kitchen concept to provide seniors remote cooking guidance. This smart kitchen enables formal and informal caregivers to remotely monitor and guide all activities in the kitchen environment to ensure security of seniors suffering from dementia. A pilot test was used to evaluate the system with 2 participants, 1 student and 1 university employee, performing a role-play situation where the focus was on a coffee-making process and workflow model, including video clips, textual instructions, camera information and utensil images. The focus, again, was not on the use experience, but rather the technical evaluation.

Related to this, another relevant work by Ficocelli and Nejat [6], was an assistive kitchen system designed for promoting aging-in-place and consisting of a user-interface with two-way speech communication and automated cabinet system that provides the location of an item to a user. Its cognitive assistance feature is designed to help seniors overcome initiation, planning, attention and memory deficits while performing cooking activities. Two separate evaluations were conducted. The first one was a technical evaluation involving performance testing of the initial prototype of the assistive kitchen system. The second evaluation consisted of a small-scale study to measure the acceptance and use of the assistive kitchen by 15 participants. Although, this kitchen system is designed for seniors it was evaluated among a younger population. 10 participants were within the ages of 20–35 and 5 within the ages of 56–68.

Closer to the user evaluations of interest for our research was the work of Portet et al. [12], where the focus was on assessing the acceptance and fear of seniors with general ambient home technology, based on voice commands. The user evaluation was conducted with 8 healthy seniors, 7 relatives and 3 professionals. Portet et al. highlight in their work that there is no standard procedure that has emerged in the literature for conducting evaluations of systems on senior users. As such, the interview focused on aspects to guide the development of the system in terms of usefulness, usability, personalization, interactiveness, proactiveness, intrusiveness, social interaction and security.

Ficocelli and Nejat [6] used a modified version of the Unified Theory of Acceptance and Use of Technology (UTAUT) scale by Venkatesh, Morris, Davis, and Davis [16] to evaluate the acceptance and use of their assistive kitchen system. UTAUT combines 8 models of technology acceptance into one model and integrates factors such as Behavioral Intention, Anxiety, and Attitude. UTAUT was originally designed to be adapted to any technology of interest. Nevertheless, Heerink, Krosë, Wielinga, and Ever [7] revised the UTAUT scale in order to measure users' acceptance of assistive robots by adding 4 constructs from the Technology Acceptance Model (TAM): Trust, Perceived Adaptability, Perceived Ease of Use and Perceived Usefulness. The revised UTAUT model was tested with seniors using an assistive robot in a long-term care facility and this is the instrument that is the foundation of Ficocelli & Nejat evaluation. Ficocelli & Nejat included 8 of the revised UTAUT constructs, for a total of 24 questions, to measure the acceptance and use of the assistive kitchen system. These were measured on a 5-point Likert scale ranging from 1 (not at all) to 5 (very much). Only the 5 participants within the ages of 56–68 were asked to complete the modified UTAUT questionnaire. All constructs in the modified UTAUT satisfied the Cronbach's alpha test of reliability except for Trust (TU) (0.63) likely as a result of the small number of questions (i.e., 2) used to measure TU.

To summarize, to the best of our knowledge, to date, only a handful of assistive technologies has been developed to assist seniors either as part of smart-home technology solutions or in assistive kitchens. These technologies can be categorized as providing cognitive assistance or physical assistance [6], but none focuses specifically on safety and reducing the risk of fire, burn and inhaling and/or addressing these issues from the senior perspective. As such, the following methodology seeks to address this purpose.

3 Methodology

The closest related work for us to build on was the evaluation work done by Ficocelli and Nejat [6]. Key to their evaluation method, for measuring the acceptance and use of their assistive kitchen system, is the modified UTAUT model that includes the Perceived Ease of Use and Perceived Usefulness from the TAM model. But the modified

UTAUT was tested on only 5 participants within the ages of 56–68 and their system was not designed to address kitchen safety issues (fires, burns, and inhaling).

The limited publication in this area and based on our interest in how usability (as measured by UTAUT/TAM) affects willingness to buy and use a product, this led us to ask an open question to a group of marketing experts: "What are the best measures of 'Willingness-to-adopt' and/or 'Consumer Innovativeness' for use with electronic devices?" Fifteen answers were received during a one-week period. The most popular response was the one, which seemed to best respond to our needs with seniors, and lead us to the Alexander et al. [2] metric on Consumer Adoption Intention (CAI), a 4-item scale. These authors measured the adoption intention of 22 telecom and electronic products with CAI, asking participants to rate their agreement with 4 statements on a 5-point scale from "strongly disagree" to "strongly agree":

1. "I feel quite certain of the benefits I could expect to get if I bought (adopted) this product/service." (reverse coded)
2. "I'm quite sure of what the relevant trade-offs are among the costs and benefits of buying and using this product/service." (reverse coded)
3. "I'll have to change my behavior significantly to attain the potential benefits of this new product/service."
4. "Using this new product/service would allow me to do things that I can't easily do now."

Based on the expert feedback, it appeared to be the best metric to use as a base to measure 'Willingness-To-Adopt'. In addition, Alexander et al. [2] posited a positive directional (antecedent) relationship from Consumer Innovativeness (CI), a single item measure: "I am always the first in my circle of friends to adopt a new product or service" to Consumer Adoption Intention (CAI).

We examined other suggested metrics related to CAI such as the Technology Acceptance Model (TAM) of Venkatash and Bala [15]. Given from [6] that TAM is related to 'ease of use' and 'usefulness', and given that that in the Venkatesh and Bala TAM3 model the output variable is 'buying intention' (BI), it would seem that CAI and BI are potentially related and that therefore the perceived ease of use (PEOU) and perceived usefulness (PU) would be potential precursors to these intention constructs, along with Consumer Innovativeness (CI).

Additionally, a meta-analysis on the drivers of consumer intentions and criteria used in the innovation adoption process has shown that 'opinion leaders' can be key drivers in the decision to adopt an innovation [3]. Indeed, opinion leaders trigger a positive main effect on consumer innovation adoption [3] and in a more recent work; group decisions were demonstrated to moderate motivation to adopt new technologies and their perceived usefulness [9]. For these reasons, we believed it appropriate to include key questions on Impact on Consumer Adoption Intention (IOCAI) and Usefulness for Family Influencers (UFI) as moderators. For the purpose of our work, we consider family members and caregivers as opinion leaders regarding decisions made by seniors.

Our model and questionnaire, with the 7 metrics of interest adopted to analysis related to the InOvUs solution - CAI, PEOU, PU, CI, IOCAI, UFI, BI - are presented in Fig. 1 and Table 1. We used a 7-person pre-test focus group (65+) to verify the

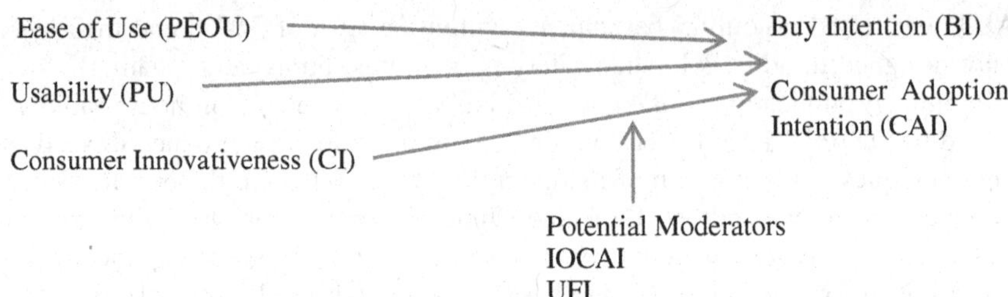

Fig. 1. Model Used: CAI: Consumer Adoption Intention; PEOU: Perceived Ease of Use; PU: Perceived Usefulness; CI: Consumer Innovativeness; IOCAI: Impact on Consumer Adoption Intention (by family members, caregivers); UFI: Usefulness for Family Influencers; BI: Buying Intention.

Table 1. Construct and Statement Used

#	Items
CAI – 4101	I feel quite certain of the benefits I could expect to get if I bought (adopted) this product
CAI – 4102	I'm quite sure of what the relevant trade-offs are among the costs and benefits of buying and using this product
CAI – 4103	I'll have to change my behavior significantly to attain the potential benefits of this new product
CAI – 4104	Using this new product would allow me to do things that I can't easily do now
PEOU – 4105	Use of such a product is clear and understandable
PEOU – 4106	Using such a product would not require a lot of my mental effort
PEOU – 4107	I would find the product to be easy to use
PEOU – 4108	I would find it easy to get the product to do what I want it to do
PU – 4109	Using such a product would improve my cooking performance
PU – 4110	Using such a product would enhance my cooking effectiveness
PU – 4111	Using such a product would increase my cooking productivity
CI – 4112	I am always the first in my circle of friends to adopt a new product or service
IOCAI – 4113	My family members/caregivers would understand the benefits of buying such a product
IOCAI – 4114	My family members/caregivers would understand the costs of buying such a product
IOCAI – 4115	My family members/caregivers could facilitate collecting information about such a product
IOCAI – 4116	My family members/caregivers could facilitate buying such a product
UFI – 4117	Such a product would give my family members/caregivers peace of mind
UFI – 4118	Such a product would make things easier for my family members/caregivers
UFI – 4119	Such a product would enable me to continue cooking on my own
BI – 4120	If I had access to such a product, my intention would be to use it
BI – 4121	If I had access to such a product, I predict that I would use it
B1 – 4122	I would use such a product

wording and understanding of our questionnaire. Based on the focus group comments, limited changes were made to the questionnaire.

4 Results and Discussion

Table 2. Demographics of the sample

Gender	Male	46	Female	14			
Driver's Licence	Yes	52	No	8			
Age	65 - < 70	70 - < 75	75 - < 80	80 - < 85	85 - < 90	90 - < 95	95+
	20 (33.3%)	18 (30.0%)	14 (23.3%)	3 (5.0%)	4 (6.7%)	1 (1.7%)	0 (0%)
General Health	Excellent	Very Good	Good	Fair	Poor		
	19	22	17	1			
Physical Health or Emotional Problems Interference with Social Activities	None of the time	A little bit of the time	Some of the time	Most of the time	All of the time		
	45	12	1	1			
Marital Status	Single	In couple	Married	Divorced	Separated	Widow	
	5	9	22	10	1	13	
Income	0 –10,000	10,001 – 15,000	15,001 – 20,000	20,001 – 25,000	25,001 – 40,000	> 40,001	not disclose
	1 (1,7%)		14 (23.3%)	4 (6,7%)	10 (16,7%)	30 (50,0%)	1

Our evaluation model on seniors' adoption intention and interest on InOvUS, as an innovativeness safety kitchen system, was randomly tested among 60 participants. The key demographics of our sample are provided in Table 2.

In a preliminary phase, we asked 8 senior participants via a focus group session what were the challenges that they felt they faced or other seniors faced when using the stove. The problems that they reported are all related to the risk of fires and safety issues (4/8), design of the stove (4/8), lack of attention risks (1/8) and maintenance or ease of use (1/8). The problems related to risks of fire, safety, user-friendly design, lack of attention or cognitive decline and ease of use have all been studied in the conception and design of InOvUS. This was the foundation of our work in order to ensure our solution corresponds to the needs and requirements of seniors. Now that InOvUS has been developed, our next step was to evaluate the interest that exists from a Willingness-to-Adopt perspective based on quantitative data.

Our instrument was tested among seniors aged 65+. In this paper we present the evaluation results of InOvUS through the application of our model. Prior to presenting these results, it is important to note that the factorability and sampling adequacy of the data was done using the KMO measure. Results testing our 22 items produced a KMO value of 0.723 pointing to an adequate adequacy of our constructs. The internal consistency of our instrument was computed using Cronback's α. Results demonstrate that our scales hold satisfactory consistency (CAI: α = 0.717; PEOU: α = 0.830; PU:

$\alpha = 0.834$; IOCAI: $\alpha = 0.884$; UFI: $\alpha = 0.716$; Bi: $\alpha = 0.919$; CI no alpha for single item measure). A detailed examination of the Willingness-to-Adopt metrics and reliability tests are under preparation for a separate paper.

The results of the descriptive statistics for the individual questions forming our evaluation model on seniors' adoption intention and interest on InOvUS are presented in Table 3. In general, it can be seen that seniors' consumer adoption intention of InOvUS is good. The driving reason is primarily due to the benefits they would be getting if they bought InOvUS (Q# CAI 4101 & 4104). In parallel, the perceived ease of use of InOvUS is clear to them (Q# PEOU 4107, 4108 & 4106). Seniors find that InOvUS is easy to use, it's easy for them to get InOvUS to do what they want it to do and it doesn't require a lot of mental effort from them. However, it seems to be less clear to seniors how InOvUS could assist them to improve their cooking performance, effectiveness and productivity (Q# PU 4109, 4110 & 4111). In other words, the perceived usefulness is less evident to them, yet this group of seniors is not among the first ones to adopt new products (Q# CI 4112). On the other hand, results show that seniors feel positive their family members/caregivers would understand InOvUS' benefits and costs and that it would be easier for them to collect its product's information (Q# IOCAI 4113, 4114, 4115 & 4116). It is important to mention that seniors believe

Table 3. Descriptive statistics for the individual questions

Question#	Min	Max	Mean	Std. dev	Question#	Min	Max	Mean	Std. dev
CAI 4101	1	7	4.91	1.740	CI – 4112	1	7	3.00	1.878
CAI – 4102	1	7	4.70	1.640	IOCAI – 4113	1	7	4.38	1.884
CAI – 4103	1	7	4.17	1.969	IOCAI – 4114	1	7	4.20	1.850
CAI – 4104	1	7	4.89	1.910	IOCAI – 4115	1	7	4.49	1.865
PEOU – 4105	1	7	4.80	1.870	IOCAI – 4116	1	7	4.16	1.883
PEOU – 4106	1	7	5.05	1.948	UFI – 4117	1	7	4.39	2.078
PEOU – 4107	1	7	5.33	1.735	UFI – 4118	1	7	4.07	1.942
PEOU – 4108	1	7	5.11	1.865	UFI – 4119	1	7	4.39	2.050
PU – 4109	1	7	2.95	1.850	BI – 4120	1	7	5.19	1.738
PU – 4110	1	7	3.44	1.991	BI – 4121	1	7	5.14	1.885
PU – 4111	1	7	3.23	1.809	B1 – 4122	1	7	5.02	1.904

InOvUS would enable them to continue cooking on their own (Q# UFI 4119) and that such system would give peace of mind to their family members and make things so much easier for them (Q# UFI 4117 & 4118).

Out of all 7 constructs examined, seniors' buying intention of InOvUS is the one that generated the highest scoring. Our results therefore affirm a high level of interest by seniors in planning to use InOvUS if they had access to it (Q# BI 4120, 4121 & 4122).

Results in Table 4 show the relevant correlations between the constructs constituting our evaluation model of seniors' adoption intention and interest with InOvUS. Some of the most important findings pertain to the positive relationship between

Table 4. Relevant correlations between the constructs

Independent variable	Dependent variable	Pearson correlation	Sig. (.05 2-tail)
CAI	BI	.303	.043
PEOU	BI	.439	.002
PU	UFI	.403	.006
CI	BI	.012	.932
IOCAI	BI	.309	.033
UFI	BI	.454	.001
BI	PEOU	.439	.002

seniors' behavioral intention to use InOvUS and the usefulness InOvUS would have for their family members. These results come to confirm that family members/caregivers have a positive key role in the adoption of InOvUS. This also is further evidenced through the strong relationship between seniors perceived usefulness of InOvUS and the usefulness of InOvUS for seniors' family members. Moreover, our results highlight a strong positive relationship between seniors' intention to use InOvUS and its perceived ease of use. This relationship brings forth the importance for seniors to be able to understand the benefits of InOvUS in terms of a safety kitchen system from the very beginning, in order for them to have the intention to use InOvUS in the future.

In order to assess the importance and relevance of a safety kitchen system for the senior population, we asked our participants, "Have you ever experienced an incident or an accident in the kitchen (e.g., use of the stove, fall, burn, fire starting)?" Slightly more than 1/3 (22/60) acknowledged they have experienced an incident/accident in the kitchen. As it can be seen in Table 5, men (17/22) have been more prone in having incidents/accidents in the kitchen, are aged between 65–80, and are in a good health condition (good 11/22, very good 5/22, excellent 6/22). Leaving the number of women having had incidents/accidents in the kitchen to be less (5/22). They are aged between 70–85 and also are in a good health condition (good 4/22, very good 1/22).

To validate the necessity of having a safety kitchen system, we also asked seniors how often and with which tools or appliances (e.g., stove-top burner, oven, deep fryer, microwave, coffee machine, knife) they use to prepare their breakfast, lunch and dinner. Table 6 shows the frequency results collected for the total senior population and for the ones who had experienced accidents/incidents, but the focus is on the stove-top burner and oven. Overall, it is demonstrated that both groups have corresponding frequencies when it comes to the use of their stove-top burner and oven to prepare their breakfast, lunch and dinner. This indicates that seniors who had an incident/accident in the kitchen continue to use their oven or stove-top burner as much as prior the accident/incident to prepare their meals.

An open question was asked to the 22 seniors who had an incident/accident to see what type of incident/accident they had. 14 seniors mentioned it was a burn, 6 said a fire, 1 explained it was an explosion of a pressure cooker, 3 seniors said they left a boiling pot boil dry, and 1 mentioned it was a cut. 12 seniors out of the 22 acknowledge that these incidents/accidents have occurred to them more than once.

Table 5. Experiences of incident/accident in the kitchen

Male (N = 17)						Female (N = 5)					
65–70	70–75	75–80	80–85	85–90	90–95	65–70	70–75	75–80	80–85	85–90	90–95
8	4	3		2			2	2	1		

Table 6. Frequency of use of tools or appliances to prepare meals

	All seniors							Seniors with incident						
	Frequency per week							Frequency per week						
	1	2	3	4	5	6	7	1	2	3	4	5	6	7
Breakfast – top burner use per week	1	2	1			3	28		1	1				11
Breakfast – oven use per week			1			1	16			1				5
Lunch – top burner use per week			2	4	6	1	30			1	2	2	1	9
Lunch – oven use per week			1	1	2	2	22			1	1		1	8
Dinner – top burner use per week	2	1		6	3	4	36				4		2	13
Dinner – oven use per week	2			5	3	6	34				4		3	13

Furthermore, still out of the 22 seniors who reported having had an incident/ accident, 12 believe that the main risk associated with the use of the stove/oven is the risk of burning themselves, 13 believe that it is burning the food, and 12 believe is the risk of fire and 4 said other. The other included distractions and forgetting the kettle/oven on (3) and smoke cloud (1). Participants could select multiple answers to this question. Lastly, when asked what they would find helpful to avoid these situations in the future, still with the option of selecting multiple answers to this question, 9 seniors selected an alarm reminder that they could control to notify themselves, 1 chose an auto sensor to buy separately from the oven which would be connected to a 911 number and 4 said an auto-sensor as an option when buying the oven.

The evaluation approach proposed in this paper shows a promising starting point in the measurement of seniors' willingness to adopt a safety kitchen system. Indeed, our findings not only captured seniors' buying intention of InOvUS but also that seniors predict using it. Additionally, another important finding in our evaluation is that seniors believe InOvUS would enable them to continue cooking on their own. Food, cooking, and eating are essential for survival and we know that most seniors, if not all, prefer to age in their home. We also saw that even after having experienced some incident(s)/ accident(s) in the kitchen, the frequency usage of the kitchen top-burner/oven to prepare their breakfast, lunch and dinner did not diminish when compared with the total senior population. Lastly, our findings revealed that because seniors' intention to use InOvUS and its perceived ease of use are strongly correlated, it is highly important for seniors to be able to understand the safety benefits of InOvUS from the very beginning, to solidify their intention to use InOvUS in the future.

5 Conclusion

This study focused on the development of a model to evaluate seniors' adoption intention and interest related to a potential intelligent oven, InOvUS. To do so, we based our model on consumers' willingness-to-adopt. More specifically, this study focused on evaluating seniors' adoption intention and interest by means of the CAI, PEOU, PU, CI, IOCAI, UFI, and BI scales. The key highlight of our findings is that seniors have a positive buying intention for a safety kitchen system, like InOvUS. Seniors evaluated the product as one that would be relatively easy to adopt. The need to have access to such a safety system also became more evident with the rate of 22/60 senior participants having had incident(s)/accident(s) while cooking.

It is known that taking care of the senior population can generate significant burdens through stress and costs placed on seniors' family, friends and caregivers, as well as themselves [17]. Working and developing systems that meet the needs of senior users is essential. While the review of related works has shown that several technological systems have been created, we have found an important gap in the evaluation process.

The results obtained in our study provide a key insight, as to the importance of conducting evaluations with seniors to test their adoption interest of any system being developed. This can help generate a win-win situation. On the one hand, product engineers will know if seniors accept and intend to use their system. On the other hand, seniors will benefit from a system that matches their needs.

One limitation of this study was that almost every participant was in good health. Further studies should include a more balanced health condition with a wider range of physical and cognitive disabilities in order to see their respective impact on the willingness-to-adopt and interest on InOvUS. Further, we will continue to evaluate the model and metrics developed in this study with other technologies aimed at senior in-home safety assistance.

Acknowledgments. The authors would like to acknowledge the generous financial support of the Fonds de recherche du Quebec nature et technologie, awarded through the INTER research team, the University of Sherbrooke and Bishop's University, as well as the volunteer assistance of Lizzy Fontana and Mary Jean Reid.

References

1. Abdulrazak, B., Yared, R.: Prevent cooking risks in kitchen of elderly people: adaptable reasoning engine based on fuzzy logic for smart oven. In: IEEE International Conference on Computer and Information Technology, pp. 2165–2172. IEEE Computer Society (2015)
2. Alexander, D.L., Lynch, J.G., Wang, Q.: As time goes by: do cold feet follow warm intentions for really new versus incrementally new products? J. Mark. Res. **45**(3), 307–319 (2008)
3. Arts, J.W.C., Frambach, R.T., Bijmolt, T.H.A.: Generalizations on consumer innovation adoption: a meta-analysis on drivers of intention and behavior. Int. J. Res. Mark. **28**(2), 134–144 (2011)

4. Doyle, J., Kealy, A., Loane, J., Walsh, L., O'Mullane, B., Flynn, C., et al.: An integrated home-based self-management system to support the wellbeing of older adults. J. Ambient Intell. Smart Environ. **6**, 359–383 (2014)
5. Eldib, M., Deboeverie, F., Philips, W., Aghajan, H.: Behavior analysis for elderly care using a network of low-resolution visual sensors. J. Electron. Imaging **25**(4), 041003 (2016)
6. Ficocelli, M., Nejat, G.: The design of an interactive assistive kitchen system. Assist. Technol. **24**(4), 246–258 (2012)
7. Heerink, M., Krosë, B.J.A., Wielinga, B.J., Evers, V.: Measuring acceptance of an assistive social robot: a suggested toolkit. In: Proceedings of IEEE International Symposium on Robot and Human Interactive Communication, pp. 528–533, Toyama, Japan (2009)
8. Horst, H.J., Sinitsyn, A.: Structuring reasoning for interpretation of sensor data in home-based health and well-being monitoring applications. J. Ambient Intell. Smart Environ. **4**, 461–476 (2012)
9. Koo, C., Chung, N., Nam, K.: Assessing the impact of intrinsic and extrinsic motivators on smart green IT device use: reference group perspectives. Int. J. Inf. Manage. **35**(1), 64–79 (2015)
10. Machado, A., Maran, V., Augustin, I., Wives, L., de Oliveira, J.: Reactive, proactive, and extensible situation-awareness in ambient assisted living. Expert Syst. Appl. **76**, 21–35 (2017)
11. Nef, T., Urwyler, P., Büchler, M., Tarnanas, I., Stucki, R., Cazzoli, D., et al.: Evaluation of three state-of-the-art classifiers for recognition of activities of daily living from smart home ambient data. Sensors **15**(5), 11725–11740 (2015)
12. Portet, F., Vacher, M., Golanski, C., Roux, C., Meillon, B.: Design and evaluation of a smart home voice interface for the elderly: acceptability and objection aspects. Pers. Ubiquit. Comput. **17**(1), 127–144 (2011)
13. Sarni, T.: Remote care for elderly people suffering from dementia: a novel information system design. IADIS Int. J. **11**(3), 126–139 (2017)
14. Vanus, J., Koziorek, J., Hercik, R.: Design of a smart building control with view to the senior citizens' needs. IFAC Proc. Vol. **46**(28), 422–427 (2013)
15. Venkatesh, V., Bala, H.: Technology acceptance model 3 and a research agenda on interventions. Decis. Sci. **39**(2), 273–315 (2008)
16. Venkatesh, V., Morris, M., Davis, F., Davis, G.: User acceptance of information technology: toward a unified view. MIS Q. **27**, 425–478 (2003)
17. Wong, J., Leung, J., Skitmore, M., Buys, L.: Technical requirements of age-friendly smart home technologies in high-rise residential buildings: a system intelligence analytical approach. Autom. Constr. **73**, 12–19 (2017)
18. World Health Organization: World Health Report 2013: Research for Universal Health Coverage. Switzerland, Geneva (2013)
19. Yared, R., Abdulrazak, B.: Ambient technology to assist elderly people in indoor risks. Computers **5**(4), 22 (2016)

Life-Support System for Elderly as Assistance in Independent Living

Denis Žele(✉), Nadja Jurančič, Ines Kožuh, and Matjaž Debevc

Faculty of Electrical Engineering and Computer Science, University of Maribor, Smetanova ulica 17, 2000 Maribor, Slovenia
denis.zele@gmail.com, nadja.jurancic@gmail.com, {ines.kozuh,matjaz.debevc}@um.si

Abstract. As the segment of the population aged 65 years and over continues to grow, solutions/interventions are needed to ensure quality ageing. Although several solutions have been developed, there is a lack of sufficient tools designed intentionally for informal caregivers which would allow elderly people to remain independent in their own homes as long as possible. The aim of this study was to design the prototype of the mobile application which allows informal caregivers monitoring daily activities of elderly where data is received from remote sensors installed in elderly homes. The study comprises three phases: (i) review of related solutions; (ii) development of a prototype app for active ageing; and (iii) evaluation. The last phase consisted the evaluation procedure, where the User Experience Questionnaire has been used. Results revealed that the prototype of the application falls in the range of 10% of the best results when perspicuity, efficiency, dependability and novelty are considered.

Keywords: Elderly · Health monitoring · Active ageing · Information and Communications Technology · User interface · User experience evaluation

1 Introduction

1.1 Ageing of the Population

The process of ageing has changed dramatically in the past few decades. United Nations Population Fund (UNFPA) estimates that in 1950, there were 205 million people aged 60 years and over, by 2012 the number had increased to 810 million and by 2050, there are expected to be 2 billion older people [1].

This information leads us to the conclusion, that the older population is growing at the fastest rate in the entire population. It is extremely difficult to use a line to divide younger and older cohorts of a population, as the evaluation of ageing is relative. The United Nations (UN) uses the population, aged 60 years to refer as older people [2]. On the other hand, United Nations Population Fund stresses out, that many developed countries use the line at the age of 65 as a reference point for older persons [1]. Furthermore, they mention that at this age most persons become eligible for old-age social security benefits.

M. Mokhtari et al. (Eds.): ICOST 2017, LNCS 10461, pp. 173–182, 2017.
DOI: 10.1007/978-3-319-66188-9_15

People over 65 years expect to live longer, healthier and be more educated than they were previously, at least in developed countries [3]. Current eldercare system is already operating at the limits of the human resources and accommodations. Therefore, terms like active ageing and information and communications technology (ICT) became important to the elderly, because they can make their lifes easier. United Nations define active ageing as a "Process of optimizing opportunities for health, participation and security in order to enhance quality of life as people age" [2]. From this we can sum up, that active ageing enables elderly to realize and participate in social life and provide them with security and assistance. We assume, that for active or quality ageing use of ICT is of importance. ICT, however, does not exist without its financial costs, relationships, physical environment and ethical thinking [4].

1.2 ICT and Elderly

United Nations Educational, Scientific and Cultural Organisation [5] names such a society a knowledge society, that is strengthened by its dissimilarity and its efficiency. Dzidonu [6] reminds us that without ICT development is not possible. The term ICT refers to all the technology used to "Handle telecommunications, broadcast media, intelligent building management systems, audiovisual processing and transmission systems, and network-based control and monitoring functions" [7].

Casado-Munoz [8] believe that we can talk about technologies and the health of elderly, knowing that their needs and concerns differ from the younger population. Dinet [9] identify that the most searched topic on the Web by elderly users, aged 68–73 years, was about health, and the second was about recreation and travel.

Although ICT can be useful for the elderly, they sometimes react to them with enthusiasm and sometimes with negativism. The reason for this is mainly the attitude that technology is "no good" for the elderly and that it might cause them confusion [10] or that people with accessibility needs through ageing do not want to identify themselves as "disabled" [11].

On the basis from above mentioned facts we can conclude that the elderly is actually afraid of using new technologies, because of the lack of information. On the other hand, we should not observe the elderly stereotypically. Weinschenk [12] warns designers against stereotyping older people as inexperienced users of new technologies.

2 Related Works

Global demographic changes have led us to an expanding market of technology meant for the elderly. Gaßner and Conrad [13] discover that the term ICT will mainly contribute to keep care related costs manageable and will also influence the economy through the creation of new market occasions. Jännes [14] believes that elderly people are, however, not a homogeneous group and that their wants, needs and limitations differ and they could change. This change should always be considered when selecting technology for older people. It is important to define the sensory injuries that develop with age, such as impaired vision, dexterity and hearing [15].

On the topic, related to elderly and the use of new technologies several studies were made. Marshall McLuhan [16] had already predicted forty years ago, that in the 21st century the world will become a global village, networked with instant communication. According to him, consumers' expectations are constantly changing, therefore it is necessary to provide a more focused and oriented attitude towards today's consumers. Redish and Chisnell [17] discover that for elderly the most important thing on the Web is excellent design, which e.g. includes clear writing and active voice. Theofanos and Redish [18] defend introduction of highly brief text, e.g. setting up the most important keywords at the beginning of each item in the list. A study by Johnson and Kent [19] shows some of the design aspects aiming to the elderly, which were larger text size, intelligibly link text, simple background and detailed instructions. Wilkowska, Ziefle and Himmel [20] have studied the privacy of the information and communication technologies, which included a focus on smart home technologies that are meant to support inhabitants by their health obligations and daily activities by using the measurement of vital parameters. Studies have shown that it is consumers' decision how much they will tolerate encroachment of privacy. In fact, this is closely connected with feelings, like for example being old, sick or dependent on other people.

It may therefore be appropriate to, for example, use the technology of remotely accessing information about elderly, simplified information and communication technology. In addition to ICT, Peruzzini and Germani [21] mention the concept of Smart Objects (SO), which describe everyday technology-enhanced objects with sensors and memory, with the aim to communicate and exchange data.

One of the existing solutions is MiMov, that provides emergency location and communication service optimizing contact between loved ones and family members [22]. Users, carers and family members can accompany and configure the MiMov device anywhere via the Web Platform and Caregiver App. The device can be monitored and tracked by GPS as well. Users can use the proposed telecare service via terminal, smartphone or application for an existing phone. On the other hand, there is a similar existing solution, named Secure Active Aging: Participátion and Health for the Old [23]. Users carry out the scoreboard through a special SAAPHO tablet, which offers adapted user interface and experience of direct interaction. The application based on the sensors, analyses the habits and needs of the individual and offers him appropriate lifestyle advices [23]. The third existing example is a mobile application Sensara, which is available on Android and iOS. Users can download it through the Google Play store or Appstore. Sensara is a remote monitoring system that uses small, unobtrusive sensors to help relatives and loved ones to keep a caring eye on elderly family members and friends who live alone in their homes [24]. Fourth existing example is the service CareSignal, which represents a slightly upgraded classic shape of the buffer of the alarm system via the telephone line. It is important to mention that this service is primarily targeted on relatives and loved ones who care for the elderly. Sensors consist of buttons for emergency calls, different contact sensors for doors and windows, motion and ambient sensors that detect carbon monoxide (CO), smoke or eventual water spillage [25].

We discover that SAAPHO project is the only one from the above mentioned existing examples, which targets the elderly and not just their relatives or loved ones. Their service, however, essentially requires older people, who are technically knowledgeable. MiMov, which was one of the first family telecare services on the market, no longer works under that name. The main problem of the CareSignal Platform is that a relative does not know what exactly is happening with the elderly. If there is an alarm, the relative knows that something is wrong with the elderly, but if the system does not detect any problems, the relative does not know whether this is true or not. Sensara is focused on the solution of the same problem, but is oppositely to CareSignal Platform not centralized. The best solution would be to offer a mobile application, which would be able to track the current situation of the elderly and, if necessary, in combination with the experts of the secure system, react and help the elderly.

3 Methods

3.1 Prototyping the User Interface

As we mentioned in the previous section, there were made several studies on this topic. What guidelines we follow, depends on the target group and their goals in relation to the product [26]. In our case the target group are families and loved ones of older people, and not the elderly itself. Hurst [27] warns us that we cannot repeat the same mistakes as previous generations and that the major new products are actually new realizations and combinations of existing technologies.

Leventhal and Barnes [28] mentioned that in the early 1980s there were studies carried out by Boehm, Gray and Seewaldt, where they discover that products which were prototyped needed 40% less programming than those, which were not. Therefore, we see a great advantage in prototyping, since it offers us the opportunity to immediately eliminate mistakes and change the user interface when needed. This gains us time, which we otherwise might have spent with programming of the application. Leventhal and Barnes [28] think that we need to be careful and remind users that despite everything the prototype is still a non-functional system. There are several types of prototype tools on the market, which differ from one another mainly by making testing the design on real devices possible.

User interface design (UI design) is an important component in the development of prototypes, because it visually represents the entire event. Marcus [29] said that the user interface includes physical and communicative aspects of input and output, or interactive activity. Or as determined by Leventhal and Barnes [28] the UI is a boundary between the user and the functional parts of the system.

While designing the user interface for our prototype, we were particularly careful on the user interface components by Marcus [29]: metaphors, interaction, mental models, navigation and appearance. In his opinion, metaphors are substitutes for elements, which help users to understand activities, carried out with the system. In our case, we used metaphors that are generally known and simple and could be found in the real world. Furthermore, Marcus [29] mentions interaction, which includes all input and output techniques, status display and other feedback.

We later considered the use of contact sensors, which would allow relatives of the elderly, to discover where the elderly is currently located and if there are any deviations on a screen of a smartphone. Mental models are structures of data, tasks, roles and people in groups at work or play [29].

Modern versions include use case scenarios where we identify an actor or a person to perform a specific task, use case or a task, which has to be achieved by the use of the system and the relationship, which is a link between the actor and the use case [28].

One of our use case scenarios is an actor (an elderly) in the kitchen, who opens the refrigerator and consumes a daily ration. The next component of the user interface is the navigation, which involves moving, through a mental model or through content and tools [29].

In our case this concerns menus and panes, which are further divided into events, the current status and review (where the activities are recorded every hour), and the correct selection of icons (for example, the toilet bowl, which symbolizes the toilet room). The last user interface component is appearance, which, according to Marcus [29] includes all the essential perceptual properties. This includes, for example, the right choice of colours and fonts. We have chosen the blue colour, because it works calming and because it associates us on the sea, streams and furthermore on the hospital. We have also considered Google's guidelines for the so-called Material design, which is mainly used in execution of mobile applications for the Android operating system. Figure 1 represents the final prototype of the user interface.

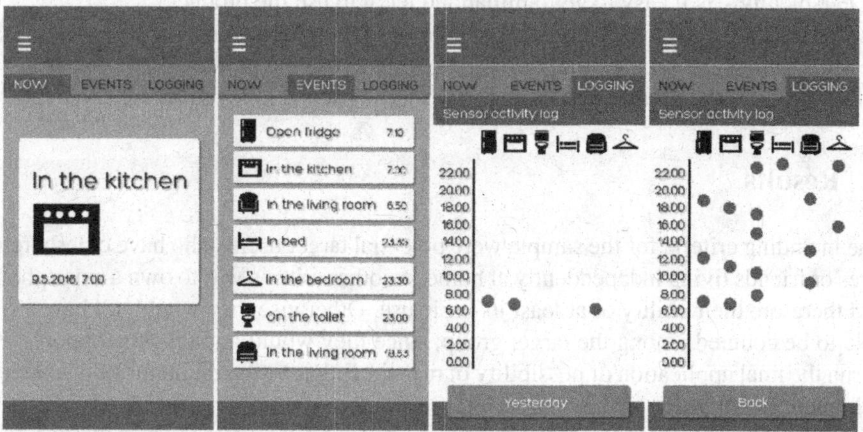

Fig. 1. Prototype of the user interface for distance monitoring [30] (Color figure online)

3.2 Evaluation

Leventhal and Barnes [28] identified that the evaluation of the usefulness is a critical step, which can take different forms. It can be in the form of user analysis or in form of evaluation by trusted professionals. This applies particularly in the case where access to the evaluation is limited or expensive. It can be done with controlled experiments, various questionnaires, interviews and focus groups, cognitive models, gaze tracking, a variety of formal analysis, statistical methods, qualitative approach, real-time observation and methodological development [31].

We finished the evaluation of prototype but not the final version of the application, so we decided to choose the form of questionnaire, which is effective for the analysis of the results from both cost and time perspectives, while offering us enough answers to correct our user interface as optimally as possible. In our case, we focused on the primary users, i.e. relatives to the elderly who will use the application as an aid in monitoring the situation at elder's home. Elderly living alone at home represents a secondary user, but was not included in the evaluation of the prototype because the app itself will not have anything to do with them. They will not be able to see it, but it will of course affect them, as there will be sensors in their homes to send data that the application will display.

We chose User Experience Questionnaire (UEQ) since it allows a quick assessment of the user experience of interactive products [32]. The UEQ presents an analytical tool to precisely interpret the results easily [33]. Santoso [33] shows that the UEQ has already been used in several research contexts, for example for the evaluation of development tools, web sites and web services or social networks. The original UEQ was created in 2005 with help of the brainstorming sessions with various usability experts. They created a list of 229 potential items related to user experience [34].

UEQ test contains six scales with 26 items [33, 34]:

- Attractiveness – do users like the product - overall impression
- Efficiency – can users use the product fast without unnecessary effort
- Perspicuity – is it easy to get familiar and learn to use the product
- Dependability – does the user feel in control of the interaction
- Stimulation – is it motivating or even exciting to use the product
- Novelty – is the product something new for the users – innovative, creative.

4 Results

The including criteria for the sample were potential target users, who have elderly relatives or friends living independently at home. Another criteria was to own a smartphone and therefore their ability of at least its basic use. Otherwise they would not have been able to be counted among the target group, since they would not have the opportunity to run the final application or possibility of real-time monitoring the status of the elderly at home.

Given, that between 20 to 30 participants is enough for stable results, testing was performed on 32 test participants. The selected test group was slightly heterogeneous, because we wanted to test users that simulate the actual target group of potential final version of application. The service related to the application, the purpose of which is to provide independent active ageing for older people is intended for elderly people, who will not have any contact with the app itself. App will be used by their relatives, who are usually in different age groups and have different levels of knowledge (but all of them have possession of smartphone in common).

In relation to individual categories, our average values are ranging from negative (−3) over neutral (0) to positive (3). Test users have evaluated our application as good, because the values of attractiveness (2.13), perspicuity (2.13), efficiency (2.34) and dependability (1.99) are hanging close to 2 or even over it. The last two categories, stimulation (1.46) and novelty (1.73) are slightly worse. The smallest interval error or the most homogeneous and accurate result is at attractiveness, which represents a measure of agreeableness or disagreeableness of a product. Other categories may have slightly larger interval errors, because of various prior knowledge and the age of test users. User Experience Test - UEQ distinguishes between evaluating the attractiveness, pragmatic quality and hedonic quality (Table 1). According to Hassenzahl [33] perspicuity, efficiency and dependability are goal-oriented, pragmatic quality aspects, whereas stimulation and novelty are non-goal oriented hedonic quality aspects.

Table 1. Average evaluations per attractiveness, pragmatic and hedonic quality

Pragmatic and hedonic quality	
Attractiveness	2,13
Pragmatic quality	2,15
Hedonic quality	1,59

Given estimates suggest that the prototype application is perfect from the point of view of the effective implementation of tasks, but is on the other hand only slightly inferior in achieving originality of design and aesthetics of the user interface. At the end of the test, UEQ offers us a final assessment of the product (Fig. 2) for each category.

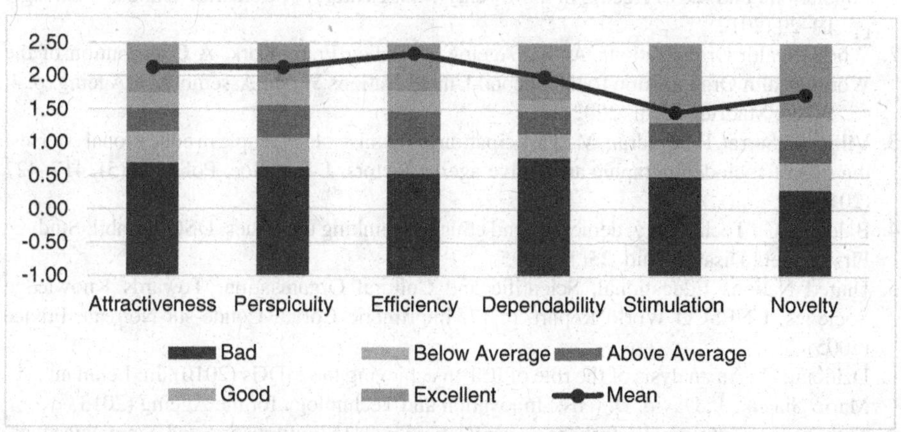

Fig. 2. Final evaluation of the prototype

In term of attractiveness, as well as in terms of perspicuity, efficiency, dependability and novelty, our prototype of app falls in the range of 10% of the best results. Only stimulation is in the interval where 10% of the results are better and 75% of the results are worse. As previously stated, the reason is probably in slightly heterogeneous test users who are differently aged and have different interpretations of how the application entertains them.

5 Conclusion

Due to demographic changes and growing number of the elderly, it is necessary to develop solutions that would without much effort enable them to independently live at home. There are already some solutions, but none of them completely relieves the elderly and remotely gives their relatives the feeling that the elderly is all right.

This paper presents the development of a prototype mobile application for active ageing and its evaluation with the help of the User Experience Questionnaire (UEQ), which is presented as a cheap and easy way to measure user experience. Furthermore, it presents the potential of information and communication technologies with the purpose of active ageing and independent ageing in own homes.

We have also identified that it is necessary to know who our users and target group are, get to know them and in relation to the product, what their goals and desires are. Consequently, the visualization and functionality of the user interface is important, because it can reduce the decoding and save us a lot of time and money.

References

1. United Nations Population Fund, HelpAge International: Setting the scene. In: United Nations Population Fund (eds.) Ageing in the Twenty-First Century: A Celebration and a Challenge, pp. 19–20 (2012)
2. World Health Organization.: Active Ageing: A Policy Framework. A Contribution of the World Health Organization to the Second United Nations World Assembly on Ageing. p. 4, 12. WHO, Madrid, Spain (2002)
3. Villar, F., Serrat, R., Celdrán, M.: Participation of Spanish older people in educational courses: the role of sociodemographic and active ageing factors. J. Eur. Soc. Policy **26**(5), 417–427 (2016)
4. Baldwin, C.: Technology, dementia, and ethics: rethinking the issues. DSQ-Disabil. Stud. Q. First J. Field Disabil. Stud. **25**(3) (2005)
5. United Nations Educational, Scientific and Cultural Organisation: Towards Knowledge Societies: UNESCO World Report, p. 17. Imprimerie Corlet, Condé-sur-Noireau, France (2005)
6. Dzidonu, C.: An analysis of the role of ICT in achieving the MDGs (2010). In: Lehmann, A., Marie Giacini, J., David, D. (eds.) Innovation and Technology for the Ageing (2013)
7. Techopedia. https://www.techopedia.com/definition/24152/information-and-communications-technology-ict
8. Casado-Muñoz, R., Lezcano, F., José Rodríguez-Conde, M.: Active ageing and access to technology: an evolving empirical study. Comunicar J. **XXIII**(45), 38 (2015)
9. Dinet, J., Brangier, E., Michel, G., Vivian, R., Battisti, S., Doller, R.: Older people as information seekers: exploratory studies about their needs and strategies. In: Stephanidis, C. (ed.) UAHCI 2007. LNCS, vol. 4554, pp. 877–886. Springer, Heidelberg (2007). doi: 10.1007/978-3-540-73279-2_98
10. Bjørneby, S., Topo, P., Cahill, S., Begley, E., Jones, K., Hagen, I., Macijauskiene, J., Holthe, T.: Ethical considerations in the ENABLE project. Dementia **3**(3), 297–312 (2004). Sage publications
11. Bjørneby, S.: The Seniornett Project. ERCIM News No. 27, April 1999

12. Weinschenk, S.: Selling Older User Short. UI Design Newsletter, Human Factors International (2006)
13. Conrad, M., Gaßner, K.: ICT enabled independent living for elderly: a status-quo analysis on products and the research landscape in the field of Ambient Assisted Living (AAL) in EU-27, p. 5. Institute for Innovation and Technology (2010)
14. Jännes, J., Hämäläinen, P., Hanski, J., Lanne, M.: Homelike living for elderly people: a needs-based selection of technological solutions. Home Health Care Manage. Pract. **27**(2), 64–65 (2015)
15. W3C, Web Accessibility for Older Users: A Literature Review. W3C Working Draft, 7 May 2008 (2008)
16. Seitel Fraser, P.: The Practice of Public Relations, 7th edn, pp. 225–226. Prentice Hall Inc., New Jersey (1998)
17. Redish, J., Chisnell, D.: Designing Web Sites for Older Adults: A Review of Recent Literature, p. 4. Prepared for AAR, Washington, DC (2004)
18. Theofanos, M., Redish, J.: Helping low-vision and other users with web sites that meet their needs: is one site for all feasible. Tech. Commun. **52**, 1 (2005)
19. Johnson, R., Kent, S.: Designing universal access: web-applications for the elderly and disabled. Cognit. Technol. Work **9**(4), 209–218 (2007)
20. Wilkowska, W., Ziefle, M., Himmel, S.: Perceptions of personal privacy in smart home technologies: do user assessments vary depending on the research method? In: Tryfonas, T., Askoxylakis, I. (eds.) HAS 2015. LNCS, vol. 9190, pp. 592–603. Springer, Cham (2015). doi: 10.1007/978-3-319-20376-8_53
21. Peruzzini, M., Germani, M.: Designing a user-centred ICT platform for active aging. In: Conference Paper for the IEEE/ASME International Conference on Mechatronic and Embedded Systems and Applications, p. 3, September 2014
22. MiMov – Family telecare service. http://www.mimov-telecare.com/
23. SAAPHO, Secure Active Aging: Participation and Health for the Old. https://goo.gl/0ePoJm
24. Google Play – Sensara. https://goo.gl/nzODOk
25. Platform, C.: Internal promotional brochure, p. 2. Smart Com, Ljubljana (2016)
26. Jokela, T., Koivumaa, T., Pirkula, J., Salminen, P., Kantola, N.: Methods for quantitative usability requirements: a case study on the development of the user interface of a mobile phone. Pers. Ubiquit. Comput. **10**, 345–355 (2005). Springer - Verlag London Limited, London
27. Hurst, K.: Engineering Design Principles, p. 1. Wiley, New York (1999)
28. Leventhal, L., Barnes, J.: Usability Engineering: Process, Products and Examples, p. 4, 75, 197, 199, 207. Pearson Education, Inc., New Jersey (2008)
29. Marcus, A.: Dare We Define User – Interface Design, pp. 22–24. Association for Computing Machinery, New York (2002)
30. Žele, D.: Development and evaluation of mobile application prototype for active ageing (master's thesis), p. 32. University of Maribor, Faculty of Electrical Engineering and Computer Science (2016)
31. Cairns, P., Cox, A.L.: Research Methods for Human-Computer Interaction, p. 1. Cambridge University Press, New York (2008)

32. Laugwitz, B., Held, T., Schrepp, M.: Construction and evaluation of a user experience questionnaire. In: Holzinger, A. (ed.) USAB 2008. LNCS, vol. 5298, pp. 63–76. Springer, Heidelberg (2008). doi:10.1007/978-3-540-89350-9_6
33. Santoso, H.B., Schrepp, M., Isal, R.Y.K., Utomo, A.Y., Priyogi, B.: Measuring user experience of the student-centered e-learning environment. J. Educ. Online JEO **13**(1), 60–63 (2016). ISSN 1547-500X
34. Schrepp, M., Hinderks, A., Thomaschewski, J.: Applying the user experience questionnaire (UEQ) in different evaluation scenarios. In: Marcus, A. (ed.) DUXU 2014. LNCS, vol. 8517, pp. 383–392. Springer, Cham (2014). doi:10.1007/978-3-319-07668-3_37

Smart Home Technology

Attribute-Based Encryption for Preserving Smart Home Data Privacy

Rasel Chowdhury(✉), Hakima Ould-Slimane, Chamseddine Talhi, and Mohamed Cheriet

Department of Software Engineering and Information Technology, École de technologie supérieure, Montreal, Canada
rasel.chowdhury.1@ens.etsmtl.ca,
{cc-Hakima.OULD-SLIMANE,chamseddine.talhi,mohamed.cheriet}@etsmtl.ca

Abstract. Cloud Computing is emerging as the new trending technology for storing, sharing and processing data. Smart home is one of the Internet of Things (IoT) applications that is following this trend. However, sensors and smart devices are generating data that may reveal personal information about home inhabitants. Therefore, outsourcing sensed data from smart home to the cloud is raising serious privacy concerns. In particular, when untrusted third party cloud services are accessing personal identifiable information (PII) beyond their collection purpose. One privacy preserving approach consists of encrypting the data, before it is outsourced to the cloud, according to user settings. In this paper, we target preserving data privacy of smart home inhabitants. For this purpose, we proposed an architecture integrating attribute based encryption (ABE) schemes to the Smart Home Middleware 'Openhab'. To evaluate our framework, we conducted experiments to measure the performances and the overheads introduced by the proposed privacy preserving solution.

Keywords: Data privacy preserving · Attribute-based encryption · Applied cryptography · Smart home

1 Introduction

During the last decade, we are attending to the rise of Cloud Computing as the ubiquitous computing paradigm. Thanks to its powerful processing and storage capabilities, Cloud Computing can easily satisfy the changing and massive demand on different resources. Smart home is one of the IoT applications that are taking full advantage of the Cloud. Indeed, since sensors and smart devices are resource-constrained, outsourcing sensed data to the Cloud is definitely the best solution to overcome these barriers. In addition, interconnecting smart home (see Fig. 1) to the Cloud enables analytics for enhancing many appealing cloud-based smart services such as: healthcare and energy efficiency. However, sensors and smart devices are pervasively generating data that may reveal personal identifiable information (PII) [1] about home inhabitants. Therefore, outsourcing sensed

M. Mokhtari et al. (Eds.): ICOST 2017, LNCS 10461, pp. 185–197, 2017.
DOI: 10.1007/978-3-319-66188-9_16

data from smart home to the cloud is raising serious privacy concerns [2]. Indeed, many threats are targeting sensed data from their generation to their destruction. A common privacy issue is encountered when untrusted third party cloud services are accessing and using PII beyond their collection purpose. One privacy preserving approach addressing this specific problem consists to encrypt data, before its outsourcing to the cloud, according to smart home owner preferences.

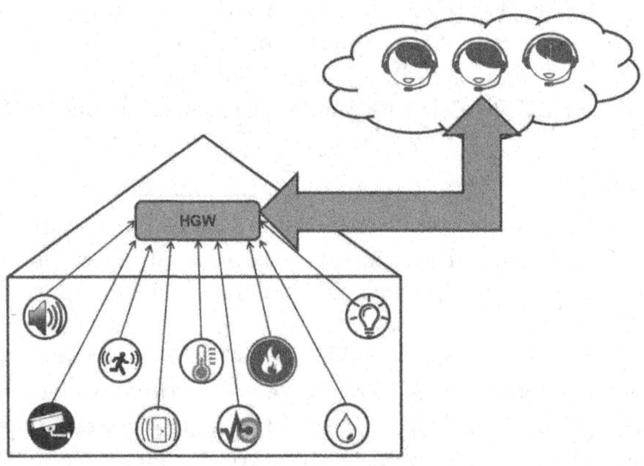

Fig. 1. Generic smart home

In this paper, we are adopting an encryption approach where only privacy-compliant accesses can be granted. For this purpose, we propose an architecture integrating attribute based encryption (ABE) [3] schemes in the Smart home Middleware 'Openhab' [4]. In ABE, data is encrypted and decrypted according to some attributes (e.g., zipcode, sensor category, etc.). The attributes can be attached to the encrypted message or to the asymmetric keys of the users. The data owner can limit the access to a subset of data by specifying an access policy over attributes. Only users owning the required attributes needed to satisfy this policy can decrypt the ciphertext and hence access the protected data. The main asymmetric encryption schemes belonging to ABE class are: Key-Policy Attribute-Based Encryption (KP-ABE) [3] and Ciphertext-Policy Attribute-Based Encryption (CP-ABE) [5]. The main advantage provided by ABE is the possibility of specifying flexible and expressive fine-grained access control policies over encrypted data. This feature satisfies the data minimization principle, a very important privacy requirement. In addition, this encryption system does not put any restriction on neither the number of authorized entities nor their identities. This feature enables a reliable anonymous access control.

The main contribution of this paper is proposing the integration of privacy preserving mechanisms to a well-known smart home framework "openHAB". The integrated mechanisms allow the accurate specification of attribute based access control policies and their enforcement based on ABE schemes. The proposed solution is defined in the context of Cloud-based smart home services where data is collected from houses using sensors and stored in centralized databases hosted on the Cloud. The various encryption policies allow restricting the access of third party users and services to the collected data. Moreover, our study targets the usability of ABE schemes on smart home by adopting a popular IoT device and experimenting a realistic environment.

The rest of the paper is organized as follows. Section 2 reviews the related work. In Sect. 3, we present the background introducing ABE schemes. In Sect. 4, we describe our privacy preserving architecture. In Sect. 5, we present our case study and our integration of KP-ABE and CP-ABE schemes to openHAB and their performance evaluation. Finally, the conclusion of this paper is drawn in Sect. 6.

2 Related Work

There are lot of research that have been conducted in the field of IoT and Smart-Home security and privacy. In [6] the authors discussed different issues like functional, non-functional, and architectural requirements regarding IoT middlewares, they also indicated the research challenges, advantages and disadvantages of IoT middlewares. Razzaque et al. [7] categorized various smart home middlewares and discussed their advantages and disadvantages according to the middleware requirements. The authors also pointed the different issues regarding these middlewares like resource management, code management, security and privacy etc. In [8], a security analysis of the SmartThings platform (owned by Samsung) is presented. SmartThings is the most adopted smart home platform and it supports a wide range of devices including motion sensors, fire alarms, door locks, etc. Based on the static source code analysis of 499 SmartThings apps and 132 device handlers, the study revealed two intrinsic design flaws that lead to significant over privileges. The authors exploited the uncovered design flaws to construct four proof-of-concept attacks [8].

Marlin et al. [9] introduced an architecture using Trust Manager and Credential Manager for authenticating the users of the smart home. Moncrieff et al. [10] used rule based privacy for accessing the sensor data which changes based on the activity of the user. Jung et al. [11] used the Security Assertion Markup Language (SAML) and the eXtensible Access Control Markup Language (XACML) for enforcing privacy in the smart home gateway. The main idea of [12] is discussing a way to give full access control to the data owners before outsourcing the data to the unsecured cloud. This was achieved using trust point and security enhanced smart home gateway. Henze et al. [13] explained a user-driven enforcement for cloud based services in the IoT by adopting the idea of trust point introduced by [12] for fine-grained privacy enforcement. Along with the research on privacy, researches are also focusing on the data security of IoT. In [14], Liu et al. use signcryption for encrypting health care data. In [15], the authors presented a security and privacy-aware mechanism of energy consumption management for smart houses. The proposed approach is based on local ad-hoc Mobile Cloud Computing (MCC) taking advantage of the computing power of the mobiles of each resident. The MCC is isolated from the Internet which reinforces the security and privacy of data collected by the sensors inside the smart house. In [16], a lightweight and secure session key establishment scheme was introduced for smart home environments where each sensor and control unit uses a short authentication token. This scheme was proposed to provide protection mainly against denial-of-service and eavesdropping attacks.

3 Background on Attribute-Based Encryption

In order to achieve a flexible and expressive fine-grained data access control, we adopted an attribute-based access control model. Indeed, thanks to this model, we can easily specify access control policies over attributes with a high level of accuracy regarding who will access which piece of data. Attributes are objects descriptors like: zipcode, gender, age, etc. Figure 2 depicts the expressiveness of attribute-based specification compared to name-based model. For example, Alice and Bob are living in a smart home which is offering two main classes of cloud-based smart services: 'S_{ee}' for energy efficiency and 'S_{hc}' for remote health care. To provides these services like humidity, temperature, light, blood pressure and heart rate values, are collected from fixed and mobile sensors. The service 'SR3' needs to collect all the humidity values of the second floor since 2014. In the attribute-based model, only these data are collected while in the name-based model, a super set is collected with no constraint on the collected data.

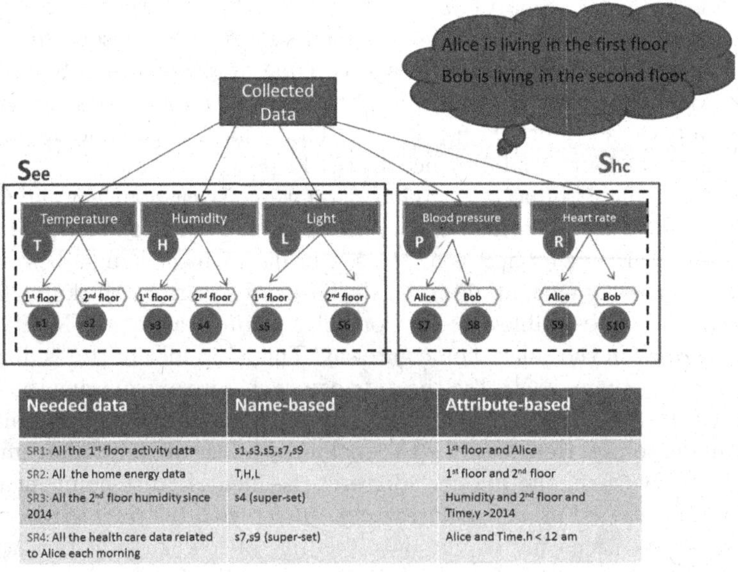

Needed data	Name-based	Attribute-based
SR1: All the 1st floor activity data	s1,s3,s5,s7,s9	1st floor and Alice
SR2: All the home energy data	T,H,L	1st floor and 2nd floor
SR3: All the 2nd floor humidity since 2014	s4 (super-set)	Humidity and 2nd floor and Time.y >2014
SR4: All the health care data related to Alice each morning	s7,s9 (super-set)	Alice and Time.h < 12 am

Fig. 2. Attribute based specification expressiveness

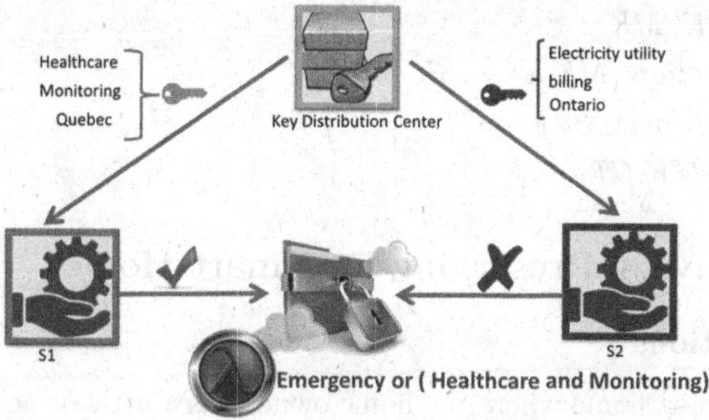

Fig. 3. ABE principles

To implement this access control model, we adopt Attribute-based Encryption (ABE), a form of public key encryption system. Instead of encrypting a message for each entity owning a certain key, the message can be encrypted for many entities. Moreover, ABE enables a reliable anonymous access control. Hence, the data owner does not need to know the identity of the requesters to define his authorization. The data owner has just to specify an access policy which is a boolean formula over a set of attributes. Only entities owning private keys generated according to a set of attributes satisfying the access policy, will be able to decrypt the ciphertext.

Example: 'P = Emergency or (Healthcare and Monitoring)', is an access policy stating that the data collected from the smart home can be only accessed by Emergency services or Healthcare and Monitoring services (see Fig. 3).

There are two main classes of ABE schemes, the first one is Ciphertext-Policy Attribute-based encryption (CP-ABE) scheme and the second one is Key-Policy Attribute-Based Encryption (KP-ABE) scheme. In CP-ABE, the access policy is embedded in the ciphertext (i.e., the encrypted data) and private keys are generated according to a set of attributes. To decrypt the ciphertext, the user should own the private key related to a set of attributes satisfying the access policy. There are four functions defining CP-ABE:

$Setup \rightarrow PK, MK$ //PK:Public Key, MK:Master Key

$Key\ Generation(MK, S_A) \rightarrow SK$ //S_A:Set of Attributes, SK:Secret Key

$Encryption(PK, M, \mathbb{A}) \rightarrow CT$ //M:Message, $\mathbb{A}$:Access Policy, CT:Ciphertext

$Decryption(SK, CT) \rightarrow M$

In KP-ABE, the access policy is saved in a private key and the ciphertext is described by a set of attributes. This scheme is the dual of CP-ABE. Decryption is possible, if the access policy embedded in the private key is satisfied by the set of attributes defining the ciphertext. KP-ABE is defined according to the following primitives:

Setup $\rightarrow$ *PK, MK*
Key Generation (MK,$\mathbb{A}$*)* $\rightarrow$ *SK*
Encryption(PK,M,S_A*)* $\rightarrow$ *CT*
Decryption(SK,CT) $\rightarrow$ *M*

4 Data Privacy Preserving for Smart Home

4.1 Assumptions

We assume a smart home where the home owner has a little or no control on the data sent to the cloud and third party users or service providers. The collected data is usually not encrypted before being uploaded to the cloud and if third parties have access to the data sensed in the house, they can easily see all the data collected from devices without restrictions. In this context, we are proposing the integration of privacy preserving mechanisms in order to restrict the access of third party users and services to the data collected by sensors inside the smart home.

Middleware plays an important role in the IoT infrastructure. Middleware is a collaboration of hardware and software which is responsible for receiving or sending the data from and to the sensors on behalf of the users. It serves as an intermediary for the embedded systems and the application to communicate with each other. They provide a platform for the users to communicate with the sensors and actuators.

We consider a cloud-based smart home including a set of sensors and smart devices. We are assuming that the data coming from the sensors to the middleware is protected using private key cryptography and Transport Layer Security (TCP/IP with TLS and 128 bit AES pre-shared-key). The user key is generated by the owner of the house which is transferred to the end-users securely. Hence, we assume that confidentiality and integrity requirements are satisfied inside the house.

We have used BeagleBone Black Single-Board computer as the hardware hosting the privacy solution. The hardware and the software specification are illustrated in Table 1. To conduct our experiments, we adopted three ABE schemes: KP-ABE, CP-ABE and an enhanced version of KP-ABE [17].

Table 1. Hardware and software specification

Processor	M335X 1 GHz ARM Cortex-A8
RAM	512 MB DDR3
Storage	2 GB eMMC flash storage
Operating system	Ubuntu minimal
Program	OpenHAB

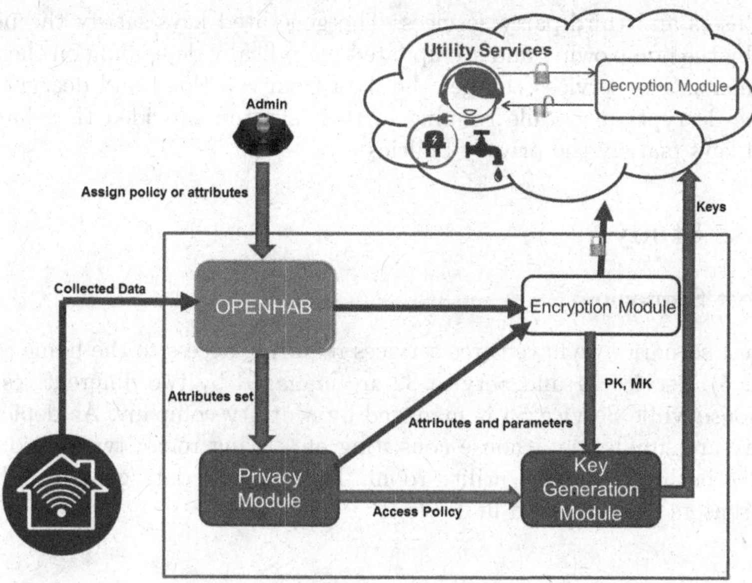

Fig. 4. Architecture overview

4.2 Design and Implementation

Figure 4 shows an architecture overview of the proposed solution. Our system is divided into three modules:

- Encryption Module (EM): responsible for encrypting and generating public keys (PK) and master secret keys (MK).
- KeyGen Module (KG): responsible for generating the user secret keys (SK).
- Privacy Module (PM): providing the necessary pre-computations of cryptographic primitive required for EM and KG.

The modules EM and KG are implemented using python while PM is implemented using JavaScript. Thanks to openHAB's rules features, we defined the pipeline allowing the transmission of the data collected by the sensors to the EM module. This ensures the confidentiality of the collected data through the application of the ABE encryption functionalities provided by EM module. Thus, all the collected data uploaded to the cloud is encrypted. To define the privacy settings (the ABE policies), we have used a form as user interface for the PM module which interacts with the home owner allowing him to specify the access policies. In addition, the PM module interacts with openHAB to get the up to date list of active sensors, their types and their organization inside the smart home. Thanks to the PM interface, the home owner can set up the parameters required for the EM and KG. Furthermore, he is responsible for adding users and third-party services as well as assigning attributes to sensors. The KG module is responsible for generating cryptographic keys and transmitting them to the allowed users and third-party services. The generated keys satisfy the policies defined by the home owner and are updated periodically depending on the owner requirements. The services can get the data from the cloud and decrypt them using the decryption module running in their system, provided they have the required keys (satisfy the privacy policies).

5 Case Study

5.1 Test Scenario

In our test scenario, we have three services requiring access to the home sensors (See Fig. 5). Service S1 and Service S2 are managed by two different residents of the house while Service S3 is managed by a utility company. As depicted in Fig. 5, we are simulating a house consisting of a living room, two bedrooms, a kitchen, a bathroom, and a utility room. The types of data generated by the various sensors are presented in Table 4.

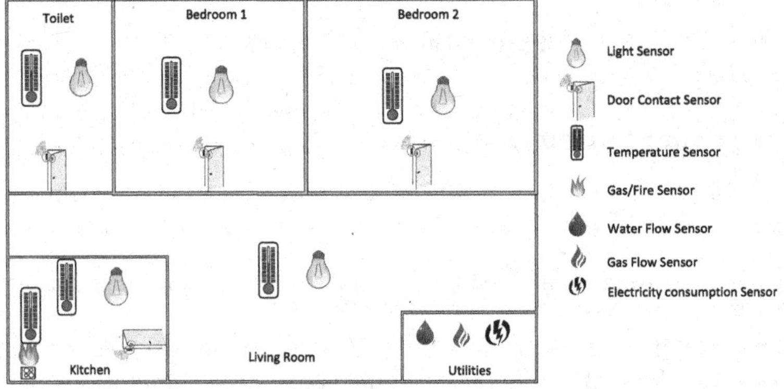

Fig. 5. Test schematics and sensors locations

Figure 6 shows the GUI provided by the PM module to set up the access policies. Here, we show the settings when the KP-ABE scheme is applied. Indeed, the GUI allows assigning attributes to sensors and specifying policies overs attributes for services. The PM module provides also a dual GUI for the CP-ABE settings where policies are specified for sensors and attribute sets are assigned to services. The attributes set used for this example is: A1, A2, A3, A4, A5, A6. An example of possible KP-ABE settings is presented in Table 2 (assigning attributes to sensors) and Table 3 (policies specification for the involved services).

The services use a web interface to get the data for all the sensors but they can only view the sensed data for which they have access right. For those sensed data for which a service does not have the right to access, the message 'denied' is displayed. From Fig. 7, we can see that Service S1 is denied from accessing the

Table 2. Services access and policy

Service	Sensors access	Access policy
S1	Bedroom 1, living room, bathroom, kitchen	A1 or A2
S2	Living room, bedroom 2, bathroom	A3 or A4
S3	Utility room	A5 or A6

Table 3. Attribute set for sensors

Sensor location	Attribute set
Living room	A1, A2, A3, A4
Bedroom 1	A1, A2
Bedroom 2	A3, A4
Kitchen	A1, A2
Bathroom	A1, A2, A3, A4
Utility room	A5, A6

Table 4. Sensor details and locations

Sensor type	Locations	Data type
Light	Bedroom1, bedroom 2, living room, bathroom, kitchen	String [dim, bright, very bright]
Temperature	Bedroom1, bedroom 2, living room, bathroom, kitchen	Float [2 decimal places]
Contact [Door]	Bedroom1, Bedroom 2, living room, bathroom, kitchen	Binary [open/close]
Gas detection	Kitchen	String [low, medium, heavy]
Water flow	Utility room	Integer
Electricity consumption	Utility room	Integer
Gas flow	Utility room	Integer

data collected from Bedroom 2 and Utility room. For the sake of demonstration, we added two other services:

- The 'Smart House' service granted access to all the sensors (holding all the required decryption keys). As shown in the first column of Fig. 7, all the sensed data values are displayed in plaintext (successfully decrypted by the service).
- The 'Encrypted' service being denied access to all the sensors (having no valid decryption key). As shown in the second column of Fig. 7, all the sensed data is displayed as ciphertext (unintelligible because the service failed to decrypt them).

5.2 Evaluation

In order to evaluate our implementation, we have measured the encryption overhead of three different ABE schemes: the CP-ABE and the KP-ABE

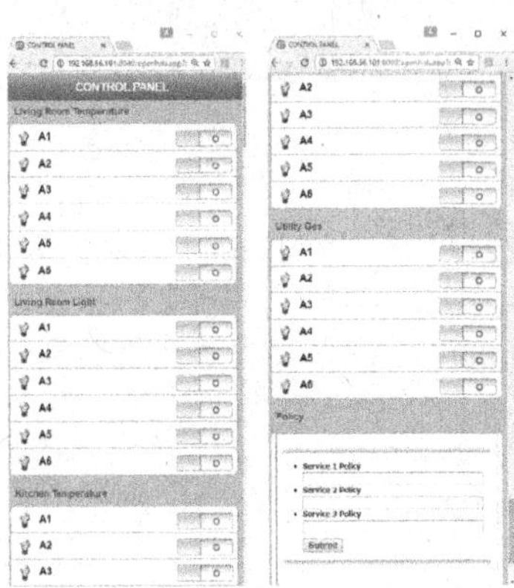

Fig. 6. Assignment of attribute sets and privacy setting

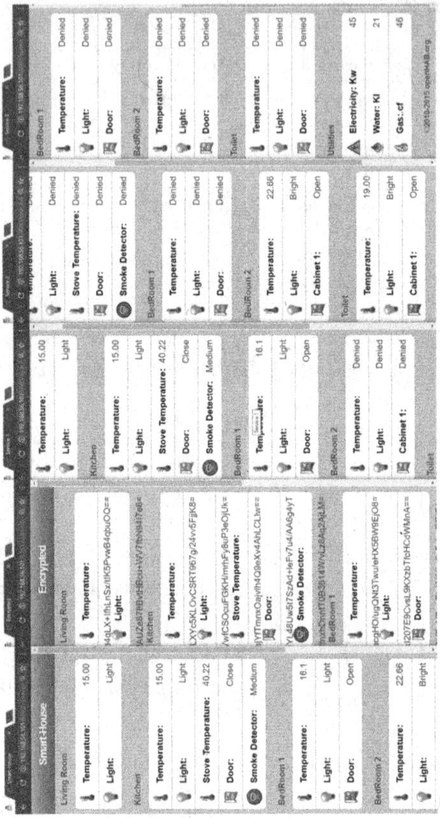

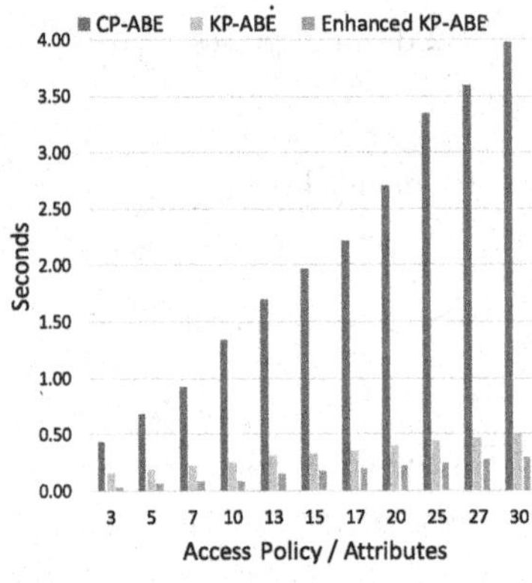

Fig. 8. Time overhead of ABE encryption schemes

Fig. 7. Screen shot of different users

implementations provided by [18] and an enhanced implementation of KP-ABE [17]. We have used all the nineteen sensors presented in the test scenario. Each sensor sends periodically a new data value every twenty seconds. In addition, we have varied the number of used attributes or policy from five to thirty. We have measured the overall execution time required to encrypt the data received by the EM module from openHAB (Fig. 8). More detailed results are presented in Figs. 9, 10, 11, 12, 13, 14, 15, 16 and 17, they depict the resources utilization and the latency of the overall process, in term of data frequency, number of sensors and keeping the attribute or policy fixed at thirty.

As shown by all the experimental results, resources consumption and system latency are negatively impacted by increasing the number of connected sensors

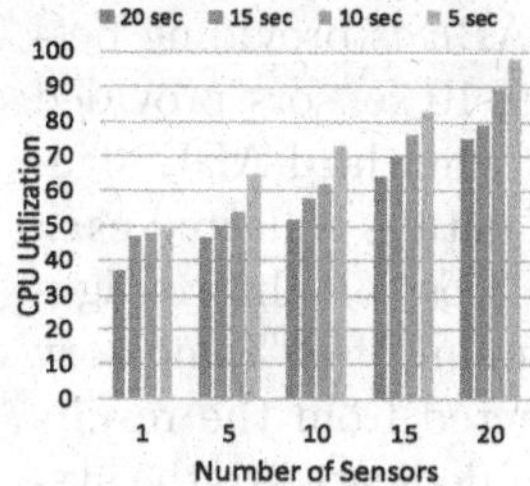

Fig. 9. CP-ABE CPU utilization

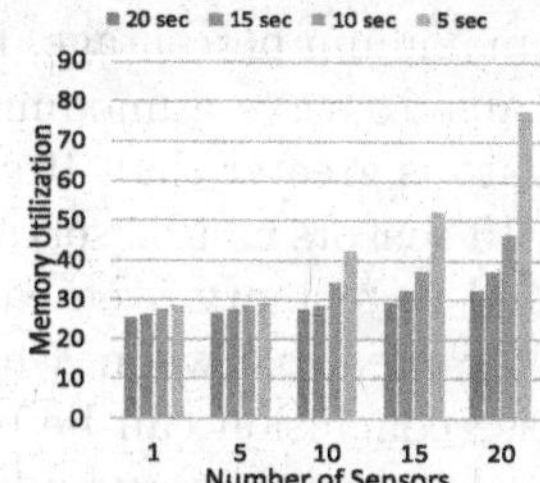

Fig. 10. CP-ABE memory utilization

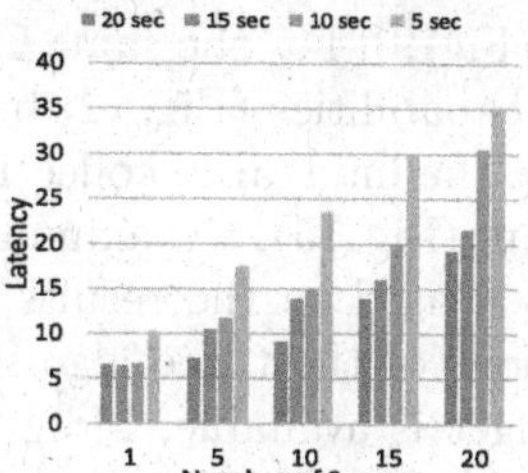

Fig. 11. CP-ABE latency

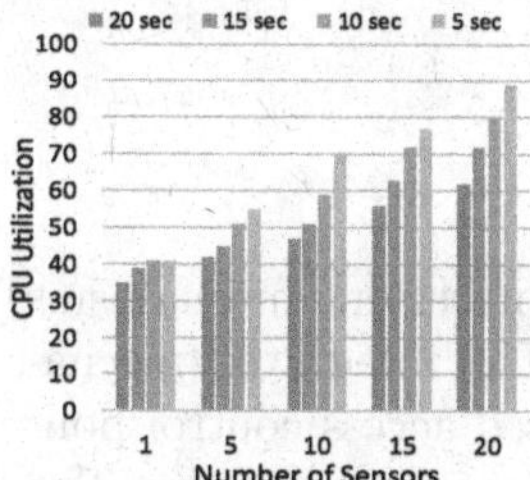

Fig. 12. KP-ABE CPU utilization

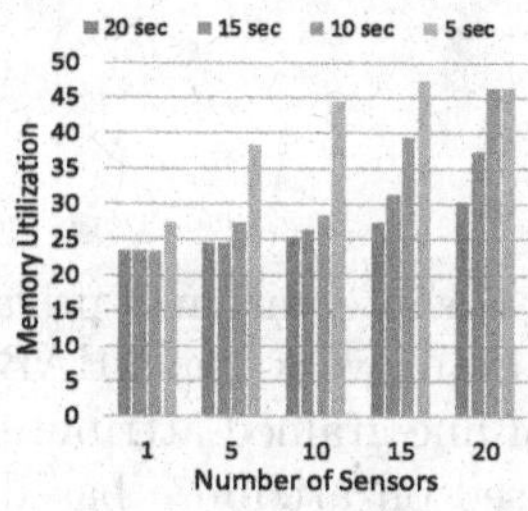

Fig. 13. KP-ABE memory utilization

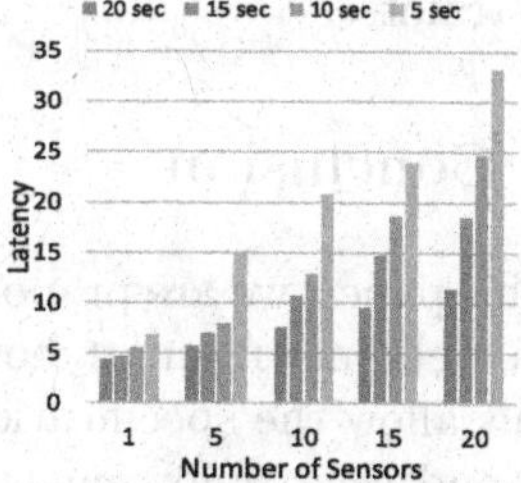

Fig. 14. KP-ABE latency

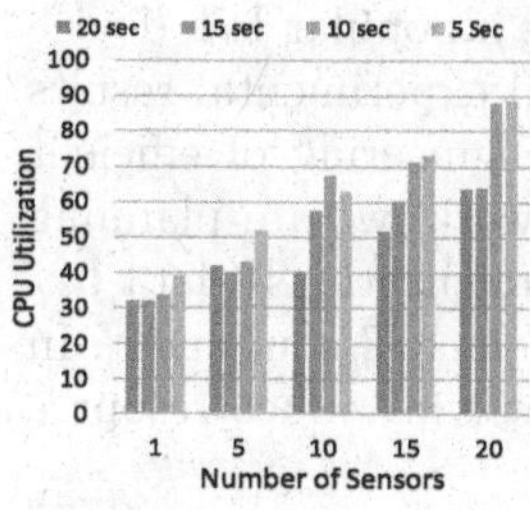

Fig. 15. Enhanced KP-ABE CPU utilization

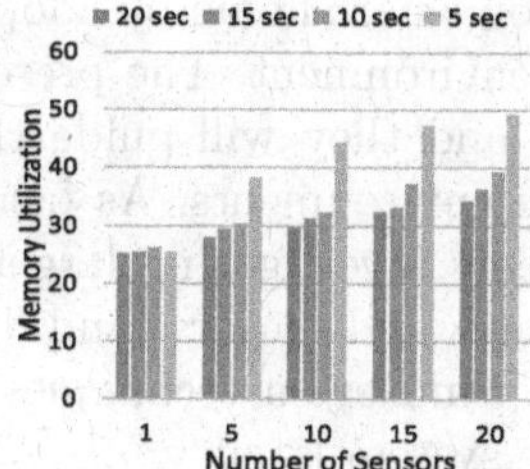

Fig. 16. Enhanced KP-ABE memory utilization

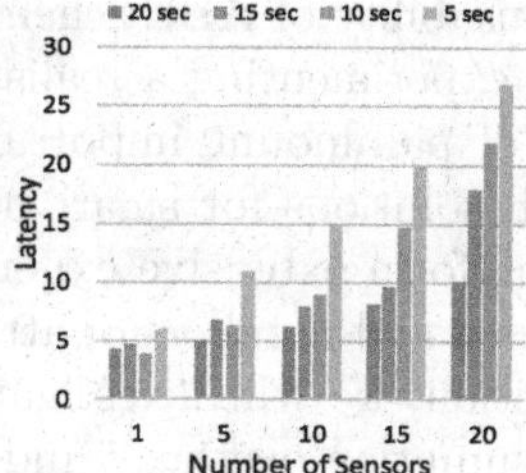

Fig. 17. Enhanced KP-ABE latency

and the frequency of the data they are generating. However, more valuable conclusions can be extracted from careful investigation of the results shown by each figure. Let us start with the results related to CPU consumption. Depending on the maximum CPU% that can be granted to the system, some configurations become infeasible. For example, if the maximum CPU percentage is 50%, then the system equipped by CP-ABE cannot serve more than 5 sensors and the interval of collecting data for this maximum should be strictly greater than

5 s (Fig. 9). For the same CPU maximum percentage, KP-ABE is providing better capabilities (Fig. 12) being able to serve a maximum of 10 sensors provided that the interval of collecting data is greater than 10 s. For the third ABE algorithm (Fig. 15), a maximum of 15 sensors can be served if data is collected each 20 s. Based on the results related to memory overhead, almost all the configurations of the three algorithms are feasible when a maximum of 50% memory budget is available. More precise conclusion can be extracted from the results provided by Figs. 10, 13 and 16 when less memory budget is dedicated to the system. The results related to latency are of paramount importance especially for environments where the most up to date data is required. In fact, if the remote services should be aware of any update within a maximum of 5 s, then CP-ABE should be discarded. More precise conclusions can be extracted for other latency constraints.

6 Conclusion

In this paper, we are proposing the integration of privacy preserving mechanisms to a well-known smart home Framework "openHAB". The integrated mechanisms allow the specification of fine grained attribute based access control policies and their enforcement based on attribute based encryption schemes. The proposed solution is defined in the context of Cloud-based smart home services where data is gathered from houses using sensors and stored in centralized databases hosted on the Cloud. The various encryption policies allow restricting the access of third party users and services to the collected data. Our study showed the usability of ABE schemes on smart home by adopting a popular IoT device and experimenting a realistic environment. The presented experimental results are of paramount importance and they will guide the engineering of efficient ABE solutions for smart home environments. As future work, we are planning to perform extensive experiments investigating larger configurations (data frequency and numbers of attributes and sensors) and different IoT equipment. In addition, we will investigate optimization techniques that will reduce resource consumption overhead and the system latency.

References

1. Wilbanks, L.: The impact of personally identifiable information. IT Prof. **9**, 62–64 (2007)
2. Gartner: Seven cloud-computing security risks. http://www.infoworld.com/article/2652198/security/gartner-seven-cloud-computing-security-risks.html. Accessed 20 Mar 2017
3. Goyal, V., Pandey, O., Sahai, A., Waters, B.: Attribute-based encryption for fine-grained access control of encrypted data. In: Proceedings of the 13th ACM Conference on Computer and Communications Security (CCS 2006), pp. 89–98. ACM, New York (2006)
4. The open home automation bus (openhab). http://www.openhab.org/. Accessed 20 Mar 2017

5. Bethencourt, J., Sahai, A., Waters, B.: Ciphertext-policy attribute-based encryption. In: Proceedings of the 2007 IEEE Symposium on Security and Privacy (SP 2007). IEEE Computer Society, Washington, DC (2007)
6. Stankovic, J.A.: Research directions for the Internet of Things. IEEE Internet Things J. **1**, 3–9 (2014)
7. Razzaque, M.A., Milojevic-Jevric, M., Palade, A., Clarke, S.: Middleware for Internet of Things: a survey. IEEE Internet Things J. **3**, 70–95 (2016)
8. Fernandes, E., Jung, J., Prakash, A.: Security analysis of emerging smart home applications. In: 2016 IEEE Symposium on Security and Privacy (SP), pp. 636–654, May 2016
9. Marin, A., Mueller, W., Schaefer, R., Almenarez, F., Diaz, D., Ziegler, M.: Middleware for secure home access and control. In: Fifth Annual IEEE International Conference on Pervasive Computing and Communications Workshops (PerCom Workshops 2007), pp. 489–494, March 2007
10. Moncrieff, S., Venkatesh, S., West, G.: Dynamic privacy in a smart house environment. In: 2007 IEEE International Conference on Multimedia and Expo, pp. 2034–2037, July 2007
11. Jung, M., Kienesberger, G., Granzer, W., Unger, M., Kastner, W.: Privacy enabled web service access control using SAML and XACML for home automation gateways. In: 2011 International Conference for Internet Technology and Secured Transactions, pp. 584–591, December 2011
12. Henze, M., Hummen, R., Matzutt, R., Wehrle, K.: A trust point-based security architecture for sensor data in the cloud. In: Krcmar, H., Reussner, R., Rumpe, B. (eds.) Trusted Cloud Computing, pp. 77–106. Springer, Cham (2014). doi:10.1007/978-3-319-12718-7_6
13. Henze, M., Hermerschmidt, L., Kerpen, D., Häußling, R., Rumpe, B., Wehrle, K.: A comprehensive approach to privacy in the cloud-based Internet of Things. Futur. Gener. Comput. Syst. **56**, 701–718 (2016)
14. Liu, J., Huang, X., Liu, J.K.: Secure sharing of personal health records in cloud computing: ciphertext-policy attribute-based signcryption. Futur. Gener. Comput. Syst. **52**, 67–76 (2015). Special Section: Cloud Computing: Security, Privacy and Practice
15. Ribeiro, R., Santin, A., Abreu, V., Marynowski, J., Viegas, E.: Providing security and privacy in smart house through mobile cloud computing. In: 2016 8th IEEE Latin-American Conference on Communications (LATINCOM), pp. 1–6, November 2016
16. Kumar, P., Gurtov, A., Iinatti, J., Ylianttila, M., Sain, M.: Lightweight and secure session-key establishment scheme in smart home environments. IEEE Sens. J. **16**, 254–264 (2016)
17. Yao, X., Chen, Z., Tian, Y.: A lightweight attribute-based encryption scheme for the Internet of Things. Futur. Gener. Comput. Syst. **49**, 104–112 (2015)
18. Charm: A tool for rapid cryptographic prototyping. http://charm-crypto.com/. Accessed 20 Mar 2017

Generating Bayesian Network Structures for Self-diagnosis of Sensor Networks in the Context of Ambient Assisted Living for Aging Well

Camila Helena Souza Oliveira(✉), Sylvain Giroux, Hubert Ngankam, and Hélène Pigot

Domus Lab, Université de Sherbrooke,
2500 Boulevard de l'Université, Sherbrooke, QC, Canada
{camila.oliveira,sylvain.giroux,
hubert.ngankam,helene.pigot}@usherbrooke.ca

Abstract. The aging of the population makes it compulsory to develop innovative solutions to foster aging in place. Aiming to offer a solution to this problem, our team works on the development of an autonomic Do-it-Yourself Adaptable Intelligent Domestic Environment (DIY-AIDE) system. In this paper, we propose a self-diagnosis framework that allows the DIY-AIDE system to detect and diagnose its faults. The framework is built based on the Bayesian Network modeling approach. Although powerful, when using BN we have to deal with the construction of the BN structure which happens to be a complex task because of the customized service offered by the DIY-AIDE system. To overcome this challenge, we developed the AAL-based Bayesian Network Construction Algorithm (AAL-BNCA). Through a case study, we show the operation mode of our framework and the performance of AAL-BNCA in diagnosing a system fault in a given assistance scenario.

1 Introduction

The growth of the elderly population in many countries brings a great concern to governmental authorities that seek solutions to allow the elderly and people with cognitive deficits remain autonomous and stay longer at home. Today, the support to those people is provided by caregivers that quickly become overwhelmed with the heavy burden of ensuring their safety. In the context of assisting the elderly or people with cognitive deficits, Ambient Assisted Living (AAL) provides ubiquitous assistive technologies to help with their common life activities while relieving the caregiver's responsibilities [10]. Aiming to create a product that offers the benefits of the AAL technologies and can be installed in a plug and play way, our team works on the development of an autonomic Do-it-Yourself Adaptable Intelligent Domestic Environment (DIY-AIDE) system.

As the people receiving the assistance offered by the DIY-AIDE system represent a fragile population, the system ability to detect and diagnose dysfunctions in its sensor and actuator network is an aspect of utmost importance in

M. Mokhtari et al. (Eds.): ICOST 2017, LNCS 10461, pp. 198–210, 2017.
DOI: 10.1007/978-3-319-66188-9_17

its development. In this paper, we propose a self-diagnosis framework (SDF) responsible for ensuring the system operation, and as a result the assistance service it provides. The SDF models a DIY-AIDE instance (network devices and context information) using the Bayesian Network strategy. The step of modeling a system into a BN has significant impact on the diagnostic performance. However, identifying the nodes and their causality relation from a given system in a specific situation is not a trivial work. There are some algorithms used to learn a BN structure from a dataset. Nonetheless, these solutions are computationally expensive, depend on the existence of datasets, and require a specific parameterization.

In the context of the DIY-AIDE system, a personalized network is proposed to users according to their profile, needs, and house plan. So that, for a given DIY-AIDE instance, different elements and relations will be established. In order to ensure the resilience of such a personalized system, SDF implements the AAL-based Bayesian Network Construction Algorithm (AAL-BNCA). AAL-BNCA allows a modeling approach based on the identification and position of the devices composing the network. The flow of information in the SDF, illustrated in Fig. 1, is defined by three main components: two input files that represent all the necessary information to model a DIY-AIDE instance (Scenario description and Rules); AAL-BNCA, the algorithm used to build the BN structure; and the data sent by the devices that make up the DIY-AIDE instance. The data generated by the sensors feed the Bayesian network and define the evidence nodes that are used by the inference engine. The inference results in the probabilities that allow the system to diagnose the dysfunctions of its devices.

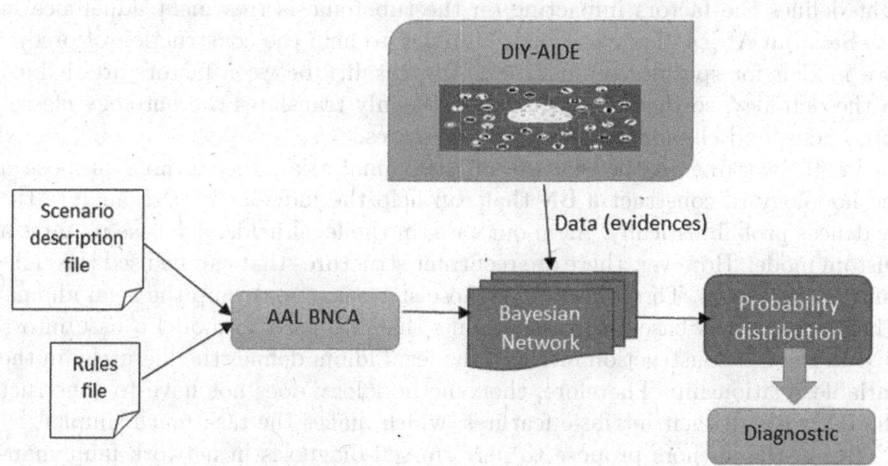

Fig. 1. Flow of information in the self-diagnosis framework.

In addition to providing a self-diagnosis solution, SDF approaches the system robustness by checking the network redundancy. In this case, SDF hypothetically adds new devices to the DIY-AIDE kit, updates the BN, and infers over the new structure to verify if with the new devices it gives more accurate results. The contributions of this paper are then twofold: (1) we design a framework that allows the use of BN in two different levels of abstraction, the fault diagnosis, and the network redundancy verification; and (2) we propose a case-based BN construction algorithm that is able to capture the finesse of the hierarchical relations between devices present in the assistance scenarios offered by the system.

The rest of the paper is organized as follows. In Sect. 2, we discuss the related works and their drawbacks. Section 3 provides an overview of the DIY-AIDE system. The description of the self-diagnosis framework is presented in Sect. 4. In Sect. 5, we validate our contribution by illustrating the operation mode of AAL-BNCA over a case study scenario. Section 6 concludes this paper and sketches future works.

2 Related Works

Bayesian Network is a powerful model-based strategy to model uncertain situations about which one's knowledge is incomplete. However it can be complex to work with. Its complexity lies on the construction of a network structure that models a given situation. Most works that use BN do not approach the structure construction issue, [2,4]. In these cases, large datasets are created to be used by learning structure algorithms. However, in the context of personalized assistance offered by the DIY-AIDE system, such approach is not suitable. As in our case, few other works faced similar problems. In [7], the authors propose an ontology that defines the factors impacting on the tuberculosis treatment adherence in sub-Saharan Africa. They use their ontology to help the construction of predictive models for specific communities. All causality between factors are defined in the ontology, so the algorithm proposed only translates the ontology classes into nodes, and class instances into node states.

In [9], working in the context of a criminal trial, the authors propose a methodology to construct a BN that can help the judge or jury to analyze the evidences probabilistically. As in our case, in the legal field, each case requires a custom model. However, there are recurrent structures that can be used throughout different cases. The collection of those structures makes up the legal idioms. Their approach is based on these idioms that are used to model a case into a BN. In the BN construction method, the legal idiom defines the hierarchy in the variable relationship. Therefore, their methodology does not have to construct the BN with all their intrinsic features, which makes the task much simpler.

In [3], the authors propose to perform self-diagnosis in network fault management using Bayesian network. Their idea is to identify different families of network resources and generalize their relations. Once a generalized structure is defined, the diagnostic is performed over an instance created from the general pattern. In our case, however, the BN network cannot be instantiated from a general model. Although there are in common entities, a specific BN has different variables that are created depending on the context and on the assistance our system is providing. Hence, we propose a BN construction algorithm based on a set of AAL-based Guidelines (AAL-G) that we defined for assistance scenarios in the context of AAL technologies.

3 The DIY-AIDE System

The DIY-AIDE system is one solution developed to be easily installed at the elders home with the aim of assisting elders in aging in place and relieving the caregivers' burden. In order to address the custom requirements of the users, the composition of what we call a DIY-AIDE kit differs from case to case. A DIY-AIDE kit defines the sensor and actuator network that will be used for providing the users assistance. Although operating with different kits, the architecture of the DIY-AIDE system, designed as shown in Fig. 2, is the same for all the DIY-AIDE instances. At the physical layer there is a sensor and actuator network responsible for gathering information on the users behaviors, and a physical interface that allows the access by the components in the upper layers to the collected information.

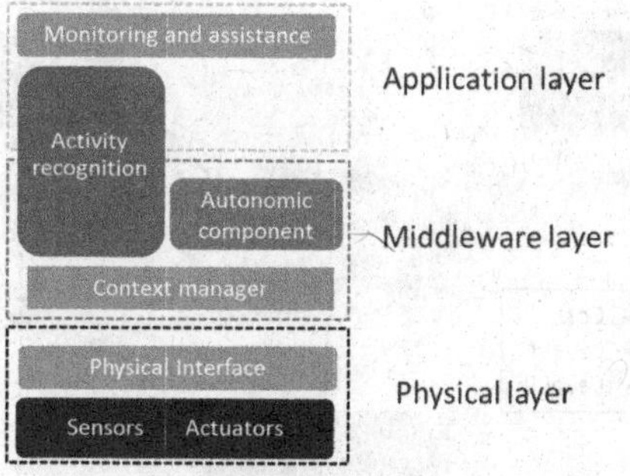

Fig. 2. Layer architecture of DIY-AIDE system.

In the middleware layer, we have the core of the DIY-AIDE system that is made up of three entities: the activity recognition, the context manager and the autonomic component. The activity recognition component analyzes the context information to recognize specific patterns of daily living activities, problematic behaviors, or hazardous situations. The context manager deals with all aspects concerning the context where the DIY-AIDE system will be employed (such as environmental information and user requirements). The autonomic component implements the self-healing property. Self-healing defines the capacity of the system to detect, diagnose and recover from failures, [1]. Finally, in the third layer, there is the monitoring and assistance interface that allows the system to capture the user needs and personal information (habits, house plan, etc.) necessary to compose the DIY-AIDE kit. In this paper, we focus specifically on the self-healing property of the DIY-AIDE system.

4 The Self-diagnosis Framework

In this work, we propose a framework that enables the diagnostic of failures that could jeopardize the user assistance provided by the DIY-AIDE kit. In the self-diagnosis framework, we use the Bayesian Network strategy to model the DIY-AIDE system using information about the user needs and his environment. The Bayesian Network is a graph structure called Directed Acyclic Graph (DAG), which means that it must not have a direct path from a node to itself by following the directed arcs. In this graph, the nodes represent the random variables (X = $X_1, ..., X_i, ..., X_n$) from the domain being modeled, and the arcs ($X_i \rightarrow X_n$) define the relations of cause-effect between variables. The strength of these relationships is defined by a conditional probability distribution assigned to each node in the BN. Once the BN is built, an inference engine is used to reason about the domain modeled in order to diagnose the root cause of a problem and/or predict the possible effects from known causes. The inference engine uses a set of evidence nodes (data collected from the sensors) to calculate the posterior probability distribution for a particular set of query nodes [5].

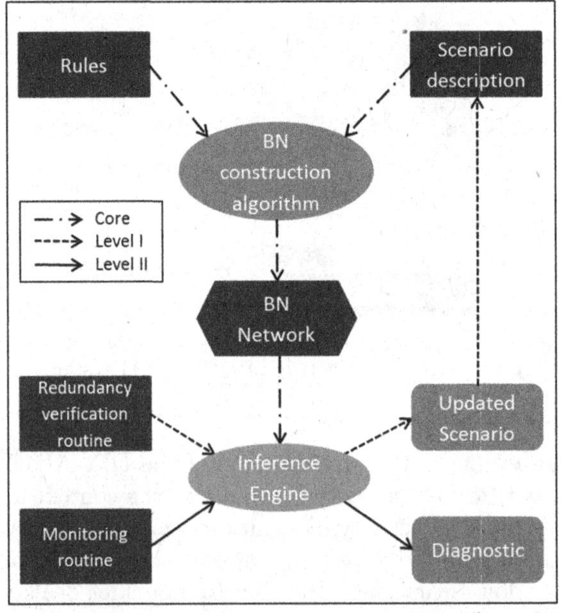

Fig. 3. Self-diagnosis framework.

The design of the framework (shown in Fig. 3) is mainly based on the AAL-based Bayesian Network Construction Algorithm (AAL-BNCA). The AAL-BNCA and the two input files, *Rules* and *Scenario description*, make up the framework core.

The *Rules* file defines the causal relations between variables that are generally found in the assistance scenarios created to help elderly people with cognitive disorders. On the other hand, the *Scenario description*, which is created according to a given application scenario, is defined based on two elements: (1) the required assistance; and (2) the context information (house description). From these two elements, the list of devices needed by a DIY-AIDE kit to provide the required assistance is generated. The *Scenario description* file puts all that information together and describes for every device in the DIY-AIDE kit the following information: the room where the device should be placed, the room features, the type of device, the values the devices can return or be assigned, the device identification, the functionality linked to the device (its expected action), and the power source used by the device.

The output of the framework core operation is a BN structure produced by the AAL-BNCA over which two different levels of operations may be performed:

Level I - In this level the framework might operate with two different objectives. The first one is the adaptation of the model according to the changes in the context, such as new devices added to the DIY-AIDE system or physical modification in the user's environment. And the second one is the execution of a redundancy verification routine in order to find a DIY-AIDE kit able to ensure the system reliability.

Level II - This level carries out the diagnosis of the failures in the DIY-AIDE system regarding the operation of the sensors and actuators devices.

The *monitoring* and *redundancy verification* routines define the diagnosis queries that will be used by the inference engine to find the diagnosis and an updated scenario, respectively. The updated scenario may continue into the loop until a scenario deemed reliable is found.

4.1 AAL-Based Bayesian Network Construction Algorithm

The model we want to build needs to capture the application scenario for which a DIY-AIDE instance is employed. The logic behind the AAL-BNCA is based on the set of the AAL-based guidelines (AAL-G) that we defined through a study of different assistance application scenarios. In this study, we determined the role of the sensor and actuator devices in providing the required assistance. AAL-G specifies, for instance, that a movement sensor relates with two requested functionalities in elderly assistance: presence detection and shifting detection.

In the BN construction process, we use a graph nomenclature where a variable is called node, and the relation from a node A to a node B means a parent-child relation in which the value of the parent node affects the value of the child node. The construction of a BN involves three stages:

I. The creation of the nodes;
II. The identification of the parent-child relations;
III. The assignment of the conditional probability tables (CPTs) for each created node.

Table 1. Line example (*scenario description* file).

Room	nb_room	room_feature	sensor_type	sensor_value	sensor_id	Action	source_en
bedroom	hall	door_hall	movement	0, 1, none	movement1	detect_bedroom_person	battery

In the stage I, AAL-BNCA creates a node in the BN structure for every line in the *Scenario description* file (Table 1). Then, according to the type of device described in the line and the conditions defined in AAL-G, AAL-BNCA creates new nodes. For example, suppose the following line:

Reading this line, AAL-BNCA creates an observable node *movement* (an observable node means that its value can be directly consulted by the system). Then, as there is a movement sensor in the bedroom, AAL-BNCA knows from AAL-G that an unobserved node *movementdetected* should be created. The unobserved nodes are created to establish indirect relations between device nodes that have different functionalities but are affected by in common variables.

In the stage II, for every line in the *Rules* files, AAL-BNCA verifies among the nodes created in Stage 1 those that fit the parent-child relation defined in the line. Taking the movement sensor as an example, the *Rules* file defines: **movement = movementdetected, listen, detect**. This line claims that a causality relation exists between the observable node that represents the movement sensor (child node) and the variables movementdetected, listen and detect (parent nodes). So that, whenever the variables described in the line are present in the scenario being modeled, the relation is created in the BN structure. The implementation of stages 1 and 2 is shown in Algorithm 1. The AAL-BNCA goes through stages 1 and 2, and generates automatically a BN structure that accurately matches the personalized DIY-AIDE kit.

The stage III is of utmost importance for the accuracy of the results returned by the inference engine. The CPTs define the strength of each relation and they are calculated based on the node Parents' CPTs. Except, for the CPTs of the parent nodes that represent the roots of the structure. Every line in the CPT of a child node represents a combination of the values that can be attributed to the child node's parents. So, the size of a CPT depends on the number of parents and the quantity of value that can be assigned to each parent. The AAL-BNCA calculates the CPTs by identifying the strength of some parents in affecting its child's value. Weights are associated to the parents conforming to their influence on the child's value. Then, for each line in the table, AAL-BNCA applies a function that calculates a child node's conditional probability distribution according to the weight and value of the node parents.

5 A Case Study

We define a case study to show the BN structure generated by the AAL-BNCA for a particular application scenario. We suppose the application scenario described below.

Algorithm 1. AAL-BNCA

```
Input:Scenarioinformation file and Rules file
Output:Bayesian Network
Stage I - Node definition
for line ∈ Scenarioinformation do
  device = type_of_device;
  Create_node_device();
  Create_derived_node(device, conditions);
end for
Stage II - Relation definition
for line ∈ Rules do
  Child = take_device_ left_ side(symbol);
  Parents = take_device_ right_ side(symbol);
  for parent ∈ Parents do
    for node created do
      if node = parent then
        for node created do
          if node = child then
            Create edge between Parent and child
          end if
        end for
      end if
    end for
  end for
end for
```

Application Scenario

> A 67-year-old man with Alzheimer's disease who presents nighttime wandering episodes. He lives with his daughter who wishes to be alerted when he leaves his room in the middle of the night, and also that he can be guided to the exit of the bedroom so that he will not hit the furniture and get hurt. His bedroom has a door to the hall and no window. Using a set of sensors and actuators, DIY-AIDE system must be able to offer the assistance *leaving the bedroom* that consists on guiding the man to the door and alerting his daughter by a text message.

Considering the user needs described in the scenario and the room description, the DIY-AIDE system proposes a kit to be installed in the user's house in order to provide the assistance required. A possible DIY-AIDE instance for this application scenario is shown in Fig. 4. In this case, the light paths (actuators) are used to guide the man to the bedroom exit while the sensor devices - such as a movement sensor, a pressure sensor placed under his bed, a pressure mat placed next to the bed, and a beam sensor placed at the door to detect that he left the bedroom - produce the data used by the system to recognize the man's activity and trigger the assistance procedure. The complexity behind the generation of a personalized DIY-AIDE kit involves the work of two components in the DIY-AIDE architecture, the context manager and the autonomic component. In this work, we do not approach the context manager implementation. We assume the flow of information defined in the self-diagnosis framework (Fig. 1), by which AAL-BNCA is supposed to receive a *Scenario description* file with all required information and created in accordance with the AAL-G (the set of

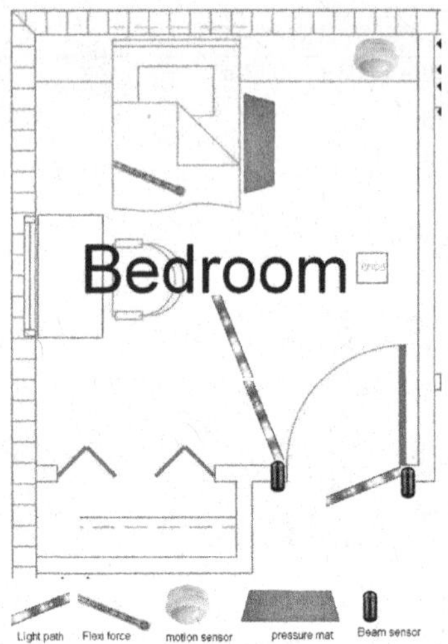

Fig. 4. An example of a DIY-AIDE kit.

Table 2. *Scenario description* file.

Room	nb_room	room_feature	sensor_type	sensor_value	sensor_id	Action	source_en
bedroom	hall	door_hall	movement	0, 1, 2	movement1	detect_bedroom_person	battery
bedroom	hall	door_hall	beam	0, 1, 2	door-bedroom-hall	detect_door-bedroom-hall_crossed	cable
bedroom	hall	door_hall	pressuremat	0, 1, 2	bed	detect_bed_person	cable
bedroom	hall	door_hall	pressure	0, 1, 2	bed	detect_bed_person	cable
bedroom	hall	door_hall	light	0, 1, 2	light1	illuminate_bedroom_person	battery
bedroom	hall	door_hall	lightpath	0, 1, 2	lightpath1	turnon_lightpath1_person	battery
bedroom	hall	door_hall	lightpath	0, 1, 2	lightpath2	turnon_lightpath2_person	battery

AAL-based guidelines). Table 2 illustrates the *Scenario description* for our case study scenario.

Using the *Rules* file and the *Scenario description* information shown in Table 2, AAL-BNCA generates the BN structure presented in Fig. 5. The BN created represents the variables identified in the application scenario and their cause- effect relationships. Regarding the nodes' CPTs, due to space constraints, we show only the beam sensor's CPT. At this point, according to the operation mode of SDF, the execution of the monitoring and/or the redundancy verification routines can take place.

Aiming to validate the performance of the BN created by AAL-BNCA, we suppose in this case study the fault scenario described next.

Fault scenario

The 67-year-old man gets up in the middle of the night and gets out of his bedroom. The assistance defines that since the man gets up at night the light paths, one in direction to the door and another used to identify the

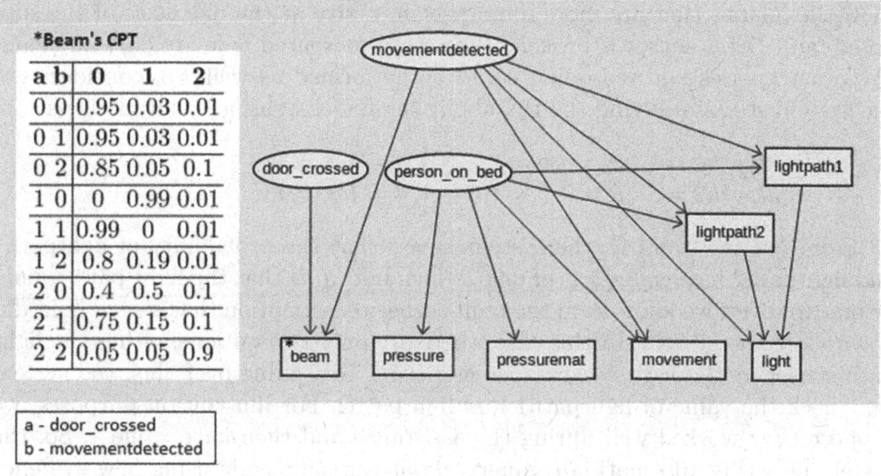

a	b	0	1	2
0	0	0.95	0.03	0.01
0	1	0.95	0.03	0.01
0	2	0.85	0.05	0.1
1	0	0	0.99	0.01
1	1	0.99	0	0.01
1	2	0.8	0.19	0.01
2	0	0.4	0.5	0.1
2	1	0.75	0.15	0.1
2	2	0.05	0.05	0.9

Fig. 5. BN structure.

localization of the door, should be turned on. So, suppose that the movement sensor captures the man's movement, the pressure sensor detects that the man got up from the bed (no pressure detected), the beam sensor detects that the man crossed the door, and the assistance takes place turning the light paths on. We assume that after detecting an event the sensors send their information to the system. As a matter of illustration, the problem in this scenario occurs in the light sensor that is broken and as a result does not capture the lightness from the light paths.

Henceforth, we present a possible set of steps that a monitoring routine could perform in order to find the diagnostic of the problem in the sensor and actuator network employed by the DIY-AIDE system.

According to Table 2 (sensor_value column), each sensor can have three values: 0, 1 and 2. The pressure sensor has value 1 when weight detected, the movement sensor has value 1 when movement detected, the beam sensor has value 1 when someone goes through the door, the light paths have value 1 when they are on, and the light sensor has value 1 when lightness is captured. For all nodes in the BN, the value 2 means that there is no information about the state of that node, and value 0 has the opposite meaning of that represented by 1. The fault scenario defines the following evidence nodes with their respective values: **a - pressure (0); b - movement (1)** and **c - beam (1)**. From these evidence nodes, the system derives other evidence nodes: **d - movementdetected (1)**, since movement node has value 1; and **e - door_crossed (1)**, since beam node has value 1.

Using these evidences, the system can get the probability distribution of all nodes in the BN. SDF uses the inference engine provided by JAYES, a java library for Bayesian networks available in [6]. As a matter of simplicity, we only show the queries that are more important to arrive at the diagnosis of the supposed fault (light sensor is broken). The steps presented here are only an example, other queries and reasoning could be performed as well. So, consider that the system starts querying the BN about the nodes lightpath1 and lightpath2:

I - $P(lightpath1 = 1 \mid a = 0, b = 1, c = 1, d = 1, e = 1)$
II - $P(lightpath2 = 1 \mid a = 0, b = 1, c = 1, d = 1, e = 1)$

From queries I and II, the system knows that the probability of lightpath1 and lightpath2 have value 1 is of 0.96, which indicates that the light path should be on. However, we know from the fault scenario description that sensor light did not update the system. In this case, there are only two options: either the light path sensor or the light sensor does not work. Reasoning over this, the system can check the value of lightpath1 and lightpath2. For illustration purposes, we suppose they worked well during the assistance and then have value 1. So, the system uses this information to query about the light node using new evidence nodes (**f - lightpath1 (1)** and **g - lightpath2 (1)**) in the diagnosis query III.

III - $P(light = 1 \mid a = 0, b = 1, c = 1, d = 1, e = 1, f = 1, g = 1)$

Here, the inference engine answers that the light node value should be 1 with probability 0.93, which means that it should have captured the light of the light paths devices. As the light sensor did not send any update, the system deduces its problem is in the light sensor. However, what is exactly the problem with the light sensor? From experiments performed in a smart apartment (as presented in [8]), we detected the existence of three main sources of problems, they are: (1) the device is out of batteries, (2) there is interference during communication and (3) the device is broken.

Using some conditional rules of the type *if then*, the system performs a few tests and arrives to a precise diagnostic. In our example, it would be as follows. First, the sensor battery level is verified. As the system does it frequently for all sensors, it can keep track on the state of the sensors regarding their energy level. In this case, we suppose the light sensor had enough battery. Then, the system verifies if it is an interference problem. It tries to reach the light sensor and some other sensor. If, after some attempts, it communicates with the other sensor but not with the light sensor, it assumes that this is not an interference problem. Finally, it deduces that the light sensor is broken.

We wish to show with this case study that the BN structure created by AAL-BNCA matches the application scenario, and as a result enables the system to find an accurate diagnosis. Indeed, we could see by supposing a hypothetically fault scenario that the results given by the inference engine managed to capture the relations of cause effect between the variables identified in the application scenario. We see that explicitly, when, for example, adding the evidences that lightpath1 and lightpath2 are on (value 1), the inference engine gives that the light value should be 1 with high probability. It means that the AAL-BNCA modeled with success the causality relation between light path and light devices.

6 Conclusion and Future Works

In this paper, we presented a self-diagnosis framework to ensure the reliability of the DIY-AIDE system. The framework has two functions: (1) to perform fault management and (2) to ensure the construction of a redundant network to be used by the system. The principal component in this framework is the AAL-BNCA, an algorithm that, thanks to a set of the AAL-based guidelines that we built over the development of this work, models the DIY-AIDE instances into BN structures. Our main contribution is the design and implementation of the AAL-BNCA. We validated the success of the AAL-BNCA performing a case study with an assistance scenario to nighttime wandering episodes. We saw that AAL-BNCA is able to build a BN structure that gives accurate probabilities distribution regarding the cause-effect relation modeled between variables in a given application scenario.

In this work, we presented the contributions obtained in the first phase of the DIY-AIDE system development, in particular with regard to its self-healing property. Since with our self-diagnosis framework, we are able to detect and diagnose the faults, the next step consists of designing a recover solution. The idea is to use the same BN structure to implement a decision-making algorithm. In addition, once the implementation of the self-healing framework is finished, we will perform experiments in a smart apartment kept by our Laboratory and at the user's houses.

References

1. An architectural blueprint for autonomic computing. Technical report, IBM, June 2005
2. Hannan, B., Zhang, X., Sethares, K.: iHANDS: intelligent health advising and decision-support agent. In: International Joint Conferences on Web Intelligence and Intelligent Agent Technologies, vol. 3, pp. 294–301, August 2014
3. Hounkonnou, C., Fabre, E.: Empowering self-diagnosis with self-modeling. In: 2012 8th International Conference on Network and Service Management (CNSM) and 2012 Workshop on Systems Virtualiztion Management (SVM), pp. 364–370, October 2012
4. Koh-Dzul, R., Vargas-Santiago, M., Diop, C., Exposito, E., Moo-Mena, F.: A smart diagnostic model for an autonomic service bus based on a probabilistic reasoning approach. In: IEEE 10th International Conference on Ubiquitous Intelligence and Computing, pp. 416–421, December 2013
5. Korb, K.B., Nicholson, A.E.: Bayesian Artificial Intelligence, 2nd edn. CRC Press Inc., Boca Raton (2010)
6. Kutschke, M.: An introduction to bayesian networks with jayes (2013). http://www.codetrails.com/blog/introduction-bayesian-networks-jayes
7. Ogundele, O.A., Moodley, D., Seebregts, C.J., Pillay, A.W.: An ontology for tuberculosis treatment adherence behaviour. In: 2015 Annual Research Conference on South African Institute of Computer Scientists and Information Technologists (SAICSIT 2015), pp. 30: 1–30: 10, NY, USA. ACM, New York (2015)

8. Radziszewski, R., Ngankam, H., Pigot, H., Grégoire, V., Lorrain, D., Giroux, S.: An ambient assisted living nighttime wandering system for elderly. In: Proceedings of the 18th International Conference on Information Integration and Web-based Applications and Services, pp. 368–374. ACM, New York (2016)
9. Vlek, C., Prakken, H., Renooij, S., Verheij, B.: Constructing and understanding bayesian networks for legal evidence with scenario schemes. In: 15th International Conference on Artificial Intelligence and Law, pp. 128–137. ACM, New York (2015)
10. Yachir, A., Amirat, Y., Chibani, A., Badache, N.: Event-aware framework for dynamic services discovery and selection in the context of ambient intelligence and internet of things. IEEE Trans. Autom. Sci. Eng. **13**(1), 85–102 (2016)

AR-Alarm: An Adaptive and Robust Intrusion Detection System Leveraging CSI from Commodity Wi-Fi

Shengjie Li[1,2], Xiang Li[1,2], Kai Niu[1,2], Hao Wang[1,2], Yue Zhang[1,2], and Daqing Zhang[1,2(✉)]

[1] Key Laboratory of High Confidence Software Technologies, Ministry of Education, Beijing 100871, China

[2] School of Electronics Engineering and Computer Science, Peking University, Beijing, China

{lishengjie,lixiang13,xjtunk,china7,zy.zhangyue,dqzsei}@pku.edu.cn

Abstract. Device-free human intrusion detection holds great potential and multiple challenges for applications ranging from asset protection to elder care. In this paper, leveraging the fine-grained Channel State Information (CSI) in commodity WiFi devices, we design and implement an adaptive and robust human intrusion detection system, called AR-Alarm. By utilizing a robust feature and self-adaptive learning mechanism, AR-Alarm achieves real-time intrusion detection in different environments without calibration efforts. To further increase the system robustness, we propose a few novel methods to distinguish real human intrusion from object motion in daily life such as object dropping, curtain swinging and pets moving. As demonstrated in the experiments, AR-Alarm achieves a high detection rate and low false alarm rate.

Keywords: WiFi · Device-free · Intrusion detection

1 Introduction

Device-free intrusion detection intends to inform whether there is a person breaking in the area of interests without attaching any devices. It is essential for various smart home scenarios such as asset protection, home security, child and elder care. In order to achieve device-free intrusion detection, various techniques have been proposed and studied, among which video-based [3] approach is one of the most popular methods. It utilizes cameras installed in the environment capturing image or video sequences for scene recognition. Its main problems include the privacy concern, inherent requirement for lighting condition and high false alarm rate. Other sensor-based approaches try to make use of information caused by human walking to detect intrusion but disturbance coming from the environment often causes a large portion of false alarms. Moreover, all these methods share the requirement of installing special hardware in the environment.

M. Mokhtari et al. (Eds.): ICOST 2017, LNCS 10461, pp. 211–223, 2017.
DOI: 10.1007/978-3-319-66188-9_18

Due to the limitations of the above-mentioned device-free intrusion detection methods, the low cost, easily available Wi-Fi devices are utilized to sense human intrusion. A typical WiFi based intrusion detection system consists of two phases: off-line calibration and online monitoring. During the off-line calibration stage, both data without human motion and with human motion are gathered to construct a normal profile and determine a detection threshold. Then in the online monitoring stage, once the deviation from the normal profile exceeds a pre-determined threshold, an intrusion event is detected.

Based on this principle, prior works [10,13,15] leverage the correlation of CSI (Channel State Information) measurements over time to infer intrusion occurrence. However, these methods are environment dependent and a labor-intensive learning process is often needed when the environment changes, i.e. furniture moves, WiFi device location changes, or deployment in another environment. Apart from the cumbersome environment dependent learning process, it is also intrinsically challenging for these systems to avoid false alarms caused by common scenes in daily life such as dropping object, swinging curtain and small pets' movement, which could also result in significant changes of CSI profile.

Aiming to overcome the limitations of state of art approaches, in this paper, we propose an adaptive and robust human intrusion detection system, called AR-Alarm. For the first time, AR-Alarm achieves real-time human intrusion detection in different environments without calibration efforts. To reach the goal, we firstly extract a robust feature using the ratio between the dynamic and static CSI profiles of the environment. And based on this feature, our system only needs to learn the static CSI profile through a self-adaptive mechanism when the applied environment changes. In order to further improve the robustness of the system, we consider the common scenes in daily life such as dropping object, swinging curtain and small pets' movement, and have proposed a series of schemes to distinguish human intrusion from these events.

The rest of the paper is organized as follows. We first review the related work in Sect. 2. Then we introduce some preliminaries about channel state information and our study about feature selection in Sect. 3. In Sect. 4, we present the detailed design of our proposed system, AR-Alarm, followed by the experiment evaluation in Sect. 5. Finally, we conclude the work in Sect. 6.

2 Related Work

In this section, we review the related work from two perspectives: research on passive intrusion detection and research on WiFi based intrusion detection.

Related work on passive intrusion detection. The earliest and most researched approach is based on vision techniques. For example, [3] utilized video-based algorithms to analyze sequences of images captured by cameras and to track moving people. However, these video-based systems still have a set of open issues to be resolved, such as privacy concern, intensive computation for real-time processing. Infra-based approaches [8] utilize human blocking of light beams to report an intrusion. They could preserve human privacy but are restricted to line-of-sight scenarios, and not be able to cover the entire area of an environment. Audio [6] and pressure [9] sensor information could also be used for intrusion detection, whose rationale is that intrusion activities will cause changes in acoustic noise or floor vibration. However, they are easily influenced by other sources of sound or pressure in the environment, leading to false alarms.

Related work on Wi-Fi based intrusion detection. Since RSS (Received Signal Strength) measurements are handily accessible in most existing wireless devices, it is widely studied to detect human presence and intrusion relying on RSS variance [7,16]. Despite its ease of access, RSS can fluctuate dramatically even at a stationary link [14], leading to unreliable detection results. Compared with RSS, CSI (Channel State Information) is a more fine-grained signal feature, that characterizes the multipath effect at the granularity of OFDM subcarrier in the frequency domain [2]. Similar to RSS-based systems, most CSI-based intrusion detection systems also leverage variations in CSI measurement to inform target presence or intrusion. Specifically, FIMD [15] leverages correlation of CSI amplitude over time to extract features and achieves device-free human motion detection. Further, PADS [10] extracts phase information from CSI and combines both phase and amplitude information to improve human detection accuracy. DeMan [13] not only utilizes temporal stability of CSI to detect dynamic human but also observes the periodic fluctuation of CSI due to human respiration to detect stationary human. An omnidirectional passive human detection system is proposed by Zhou [18], which virtually shapes the targeted coverage area by using PHY layer features. The paper [17] proposes a metric for commodity WiFi as a proxy for detection sensitivity to characterize the impact of human presence on wireless signals. However, all these works need on-site and environment-specific threshold calibration or model building when the target environment changes. Although in [4], a link sensitivity indicator is proposed to depict abundance of multipath propagation for accommodating to the environment change but multiple location attempts are still required to calibrate the system in advance.

Unlike existing intrusion detection schemes that require labor-intensive calibration or multiple location data collection when the target environment changes, our work aims to minimize such labor intensive overhead through adopting a robust feature and a self-adaptive learning mechanism. Moreover, we also take the easily confused daily events into account and propose effective schemes to distinguish real human intrusion from object motion, which are often ignored by existing work on human intrusion detection.

3 Preliminaries and Observations

In this section, we firstly introduce the Channel State Information (CSI) accessible on commodity Wi-Fi devices. Then based on intensive empirical study, we present a robust feature to characterize the change of CSI signal for intrusion detection.

3.1 Channel State Information

Channel State Information (CSI) is information that estimates the channel by representing the channel properties of a communication link. In the wireless communication system, the received baseband signal in frequency domain is:

$$y = Hx + n \tag{1}$$

where y and x are the received and the transmitted signal vectors respectively, n denotes the channel noise vector, H is the channel state information matrix. To estimate the channel state information matrix H, a predetermined pilot sequence is transmitted. According to the received sequence, receiver estimates the channel state information matrix by $H = y/x$, which contains the amplitude information and phase information. And CSI can be mathematically depicted as:

$$H = |H|e^{j\theta} \tag{2}$$

where $|H|$ and θ are the amplitude and phase, respectively. To increase communication capacity, current Wi-Fi standards (e.g., IEEE 802.11 n/ac) use orthogonal frequency division modulation (OFDM) technology in physical layer to split the whole spectrum band (20 MHz) into multiple (56) frequency sub-bands, transmitting data across multiple subcarriers in parallel. Each subcarrier can be viewed as an independent communication link and has its own CSI. In other words, every subcarrier CSI of all subcarriers gets together to form the CSI matrix of the system.

3.2 Robust Feature Selection

In typical indoor scenarios, Wi-Fi signals propagate from the transmitter to receiver through multiple paths such as floor, wall and furniture. When a person moves in the environment, additional signal paths are introduced by the reflection of human body. Correspondingly, the value of CSI will reflect the change of these paths. So the amplitude variation and phase in the CSI stream can be leveraged to detect human intrusion. In AR-Alarm, we utilize the phase difference over two antennas as the salient signal to sense the change of the environment,

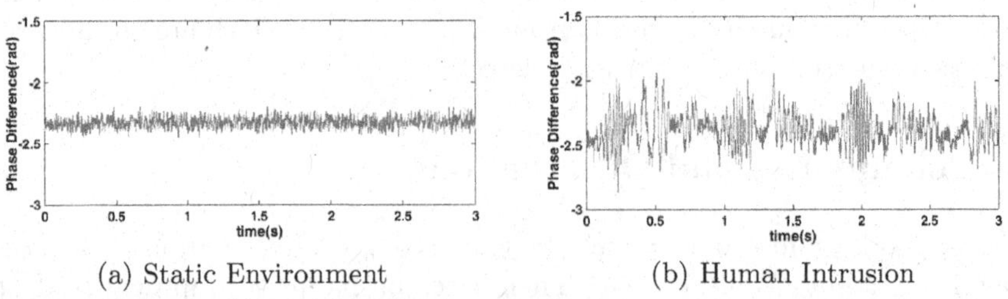

(a) Static Environment (b) Human Intrusion

Fig. 1. Phase difference of static and dynamic environment

for better sensitivity to signal variation [11]. Figure 1 shows the CSI phase difference in static and human intrusion environments. Whenever there is object movement in the environment, we can observe a change in the signal.

How do we mathematically characterize the signal variance of CSI phase difference? Intuitively, we can use the standard deviation to characterize the variance of the signal as shown in Fig. 2a. Unfortunately, like the fingerprint based solution, the threshold needs to be determined according to the environment change. Specifically, when we adjust the location of the receiver, the standard deviation of the signal variance is shown in Fig. 2b. If we change the room for experiment, the standard deviation changes as shown in Fig. 2c. As we can see, the threshold in scenario 1 (Fig. 2a) can't be applied directly to other scenarios. Through intensive experiment study, we find that if we use the maximum standard deviation of phase difference in static environment to normalize that in human intrusion scenarios, we don't need to learn a new threshold for a new scenario, as shown in Fig. 3. If σ is the standard deviation of CSI phase difference, then the robust feature can be selected as follows:

$$\mu_{motion} = \frac{\sigma_{motion}}{max(\sigma_{static})} \tag{3}$$

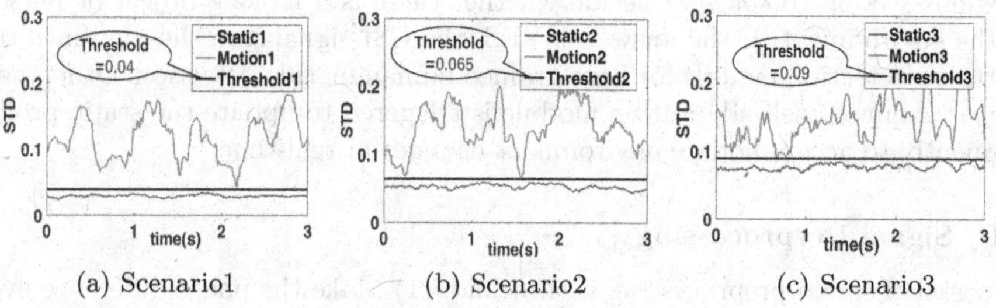

(a) Scenario1 (b) Scenario2 (c) Scenario3

Fig. 2. Standard deviation of phase difference in different scenarios

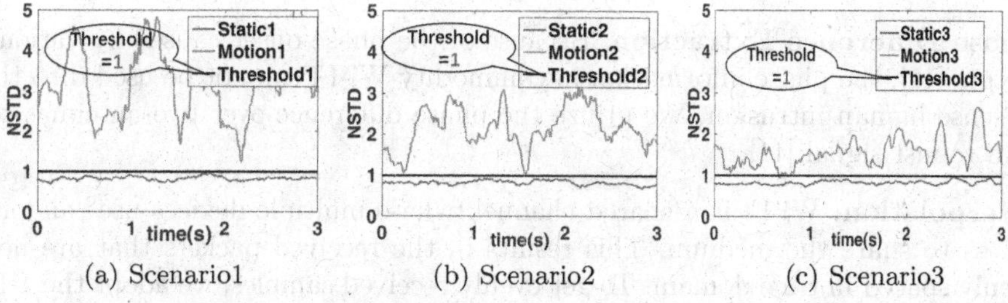

(a) Scenario1 (b) Scenario2 (c) Scenario3

Fig. 3. Normalized standard deviation of phase difference in different scenarios

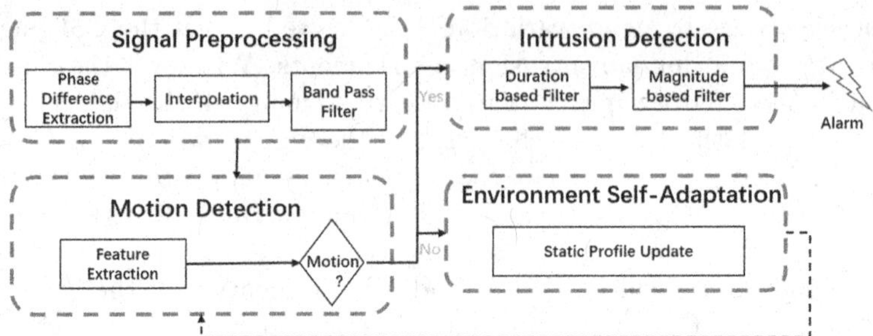

Fig. 4. Overview of the AR-Alarm

4 The AR-Alarm Human Intrusion Detection System

Our proposed real-time intrusion detection system, AR-Alarm, consists of four modules: signal preprocessing, motion detection, environment self-adaptation and intrusion detection. As shown in Fig. 4, the collected CSI signal streams are first fed into the signal preprocessing module to ensure the extracted phase difference continuous in a shared Wi-Fi channel and eliminate out-band interference. Then in motion detection module, we extract features as proposed in previous section to coarsely decide whether there is a moving object or person in the environment. If the answer is YES, the CSI signals are then fed into the intrusion detection module for finer-grained human motion detection. Otherwise, the environment self-adaptation module is triggered to update the static profile frequently to accommodate environment changes in real-time.

4.1 Signal Preprocessing

The goal of signal preprocessing is threefold: (1) Make the phase difference over two antennas as basic signal; (2) Deal with the uneven arrival of packets caused by the burst Wi-Fi transmissions. (3) Go through a band-pass filter to filter out non-human activities.

Phase Difference Extraction. Because of the phase offset caused by various factors [11], the phase information in commodity Wi-Fi can not be used directly to sense human intrusion. We utilize the phase difference over two antennas to be a robust signal [11].

Interpolation. Wi-Fi is a shared channel, where multiple devices use random access to share the medium. This results in the received packets that are not evenly spaced in time domain. To get evenly received samples, we adopt the 1-D linear interpolation algorithm to process the raw CSI readings. Since the duration of typical human intrusion is greater than one second, the above interpolation operation preserves the human intrusion information.

Band-pass Filter. According to work [12], the frequency of CSI amplitude variation could reveal the human motion speed. Similarly, from the time-frequency

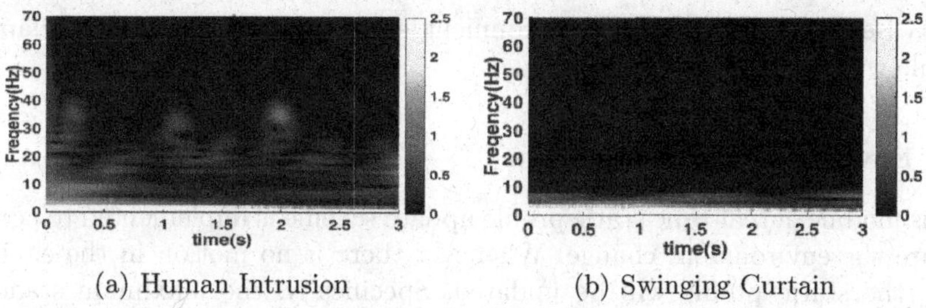

(a) Human Intrusion (b) Swinging Curtain

Fig. 5. Time-frequency analysis of different activities

analysis of phase difference in Fig. 5, we can see human intrusion induces obvious power profile in higher frequency than that caused by swinging curtain. And according to work [1], normal walking speeds ranges from 1.25 m/s to 1.5 m/s for human being. So we extract the signal whose frequency is in the range between 10 Hz (0.3 m/s) and 70 Hz (2 m/s) with a band-pass filter. By applying this filter, our system could filter out not only the high-frequency noise but also the low frequency disturbance caused by swinging curtain.

4.2 Motion Detection

In this module, we first extract feature from the filtered CSI phase difference signal, and then decide whether there is a moving object or human subject in the environment. This module contains two steps: (1) Feature Extraction (2) Motion Discriminant.

Feature Extraction. After the preprocessing in Sect. 4.1, we acquire the filtered phase difference signal as input for this step. Then based on the study in Sect. 3.2, we calculate the normalized standard deviation μ_{now} in a sliding window as the robust feature for further processing. It is depicted as follows:

$$\mu_{now} = \frac{\sigma_{now}}{max(\sigma_{static})} \tag{4}$$

σ_{now} means the standard deviation of current filtered CSI phase difference. $max(\sigma_{static})$ is the maximum value of standard deviation in the static environment which is updated with time. And its initial value was attained when the system was started for the first time. After calculation, both σ_{now} and μ_{now} will be used in next step for processing.

Motion Discriminant. Based on the extracted feature, we further propose a threshold-based method to decide whether there exists any motion in the environment, no matter what causes the motion. To check if the whole sliding window lies in the static state, we compare μ_{now} with a pre-defined threshold δ_{motion}. If it is larger than δ_{motion}, the feature μ_{now} will be passed to intrusion detection module to see if it is caused by human intrusion or object motion.

Otherwise, it implies a static environment and the environment self-adaption module will be triggered.

4.3 Environment Self-adaption

In this module, a real-time static profile update scheme is implemented to accommodate the environment change. Whenever there is no motion in the environment, the static profile will be updated. Specifically, the maximum standard deviation value of σ_{now} is computed, afterwards we update the previous result with $max(\sigma_{now})$ for later feature extraction in the motion detection module. Through this self-learning mechanism, our system could accommodate the environment change in real time and achieve the environment self-adaption.

4.4 Intrusion Detection

In this module, we develop two schemes to differentiate the intrusion from object motions in daily life. A duration based filter is used to get rid of very short-term object motions such as dropping objects, while a magnitude based filter is applied to eliminate the interference caused by small moving objects such as pets.

Duration-based Filter. In our daily life, moving objects in the environment could experience a high speed so that a band-pass filter could not filter them out, those objects could be falling coat hangers or dropping boxes. Through empirical study, we notice that these activities only last for a very short time. As shown in Fig. 6(a), the duration of a dropping object usually lasts less than 1 s, while human intrusion often lasts longer, say lasting for at least 2 s at a normal speed. In order to filter out those short-term activities, we measure the duration for $\mu_{now} > \delta_{motion}$. If the duration is less than 1 s, it implies object dropping;

Magnitude-based Filter. In consideration of different families, some may raise a small pet in their home. The motion of small pets not only could reach the same speed as human beings but also last for some time which could not be filtered out by the last steps. However, a small pet has a smaller size which often introduces less number of reflected paths than a human does, so the magnitude of signal fluctuation caused by the small pet movement is smaller than that by human intrusion as shown in Fig. 6(b). Inspired by this observation, we propose an area-based method to differentiate human intrusion from others. First, we calculate the integration when μ_{now} is larger than δ_{motion} in a time window (e.g. 1 s) and then compare the value with the threshold δ_{area} to determine if the motion it is human intrusion, which could be expressed as follows:

$$\begin{cases} \int (\mu_{now} > \delta_{motion}) dt > \delta_{area} & Human \quad Intrusion \\ \int (\mu_{now} > \delta_{motion}) dt < \delta_{area} & Not \quad Intrusion \end{cases} \tag{5}$$

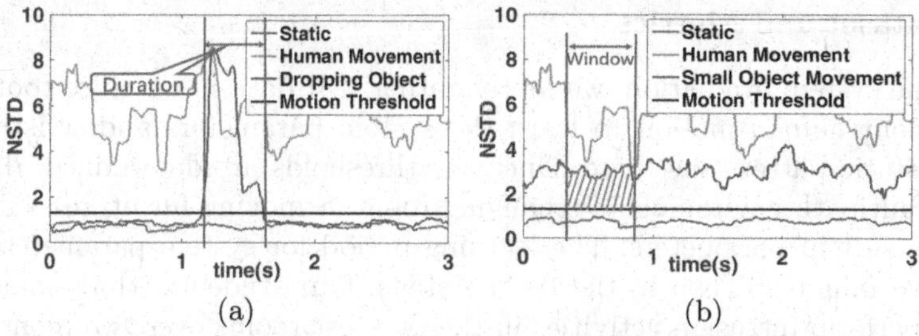

(a) (b)

Fig. 6. (a) Dropping object vs intrusion (b) Pet movement vs intrusion

5 Evaluation

In this section, we present the evaluation results of our AR-Alarm system using off-the-shelf WiFi devices. First, we introduce the experiment settings. Then we present the dataset and metrics for evaluation. Finally, we will report our system performance in various scenarios.

5.1 Experimental Setups

Our system only needs one Wi-Fi transmitter and one receiver. We employ two GIGABYTE miniPCs equipped with off-the-shelf Intel 5300 Wi-Fi cards as the transmitter and receiver. The CSI tool [5] developed by Halperin is installed on the miniPCs to collect the CSI from the receiver. The sampling rate of CSI in our experiments is set to 500 Hz to ensure that the human intrusion could be detected without much delay. We conduct experiments in two rooms of different sizes to test our proposed framework as shown in Fig. 7. (office room: 3 m × 4 m, meeting room: 6 m × 6 m).

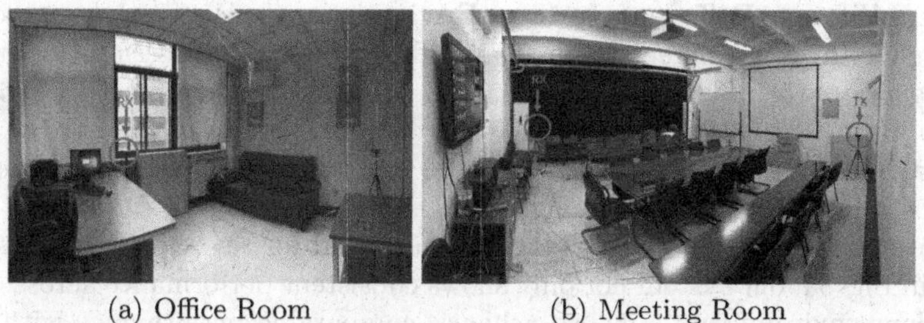

(a) Office Room (b) Meeting Room

Fig. 7. Test environments

5.2 Dataset and Metrics

Before the system evaluation, we firstly gather CSI data in an office room with and without human motion to learn the system parameters and construct an original static pattern database. Once the thresholds are determined, different indoor multipath environments (changing room or moving furniture) will share the same system parameters. The learning period for system parameters takes about two minutes. Then in the testing stage, four students (three males, one female) perform intrusion activities in the two test rooms over two months. We deploy a camera in each room to record the activities conducted as ground truth. And the metrics for evaluation are given below:

True Detection Rate (TDR) is the probability that the system can detect a human intrusion.

False Positive Rate (FPR) is defined as the proportion that the system generates an alarm when there is no human intrusion.

5.3 System Performance

In this section, we present the evaluation performance of our AR-Alarm system from two aspects. As the techniques proposed in previous work [10,13,15] are environment dependent, we first conduct experiments to see if our system can automatically adjust itself to adapt to the environments while achieving comparable results with previous work. Then to further evaluate the robustness of our system, we simulate several daily events which have not been considered in previous work.

5.3.1 Adaptability to the Environment

In order to test the adaptability of our system to the indoor environment changes, we design two challenging situations: (1) Different indoor environments, and (2) Different environment settings.

Adaptability to Different Indoor Environments. We firstly conduct the experiments in two different rooms (R1: Office Room, R2: Meeting Room) just like the prior work [4,10,13,15], the WiFi transmitters are placed at various heights from 1.2 m to 2 m. Diverse TX-RX distances from 2 m to 7 m are tested. Both LOS and NLOS conditions (when the transmitter is blocked by an object) are also evaluated. We divide the entire space into small grids of size $1.5\,\text{m} \times 1.5\,\text{m}$ and the intrusion activity takes place in every grid for several times. As shown below in Fig. 8a, our system not only shows consistent performance across different indoor environments but also achieves comparable performance with prior work [4,10,13,15]. Remarkably, in order to achieve such system performance, existing schemes [4,10,13,15] either require labor-intensive calibration or multiple location data collection to suit for a different environment. In contrast, our system is deployed in two environments without change of system parameters. So with its self-adaptive mechanism, it could accommodate different environments with no human efforts.

Adaptability to Environmental Setting Changes. Besides changing the indoor environments for experiments, we also evaluate the system against furniture movement. In each environment, we move big furniture such as bookcases, sofa, tables to different locations in order to simulate the setting changes. It is noted that our system performance is not affected much by the movement of these furniture. Specifically, Fig. 8b shows the performance when the sofa in R1 is moved to the window side and a big table in R2 is moved from the middle to the wall side. In all cases, AR-Alarm system shows excellent adaptability to the multipath environment changes.

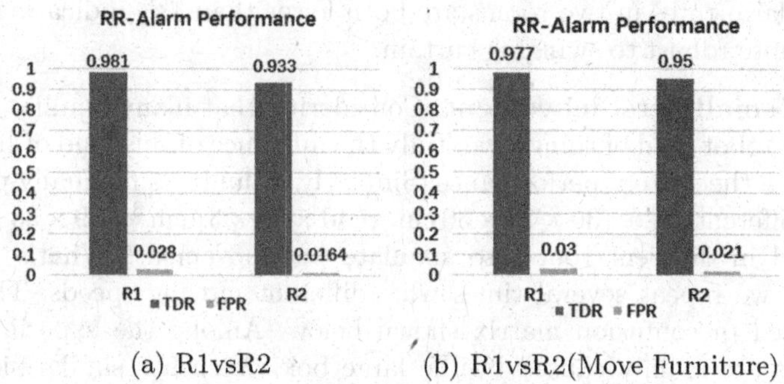

(a) R1vsR2 (b) R1vsR2(Move Furniture)

Fig. 8. AR-Alarm performance

5.3.2 Robustness to Daily Events

In this part, we further study the impact of daily events such as dropping object, swinging curtain and small pets‘ movement on the system performance, to see if we can distinguish human intrusion from these events.

Impact of dropping object. To study the influence of a dropping object to the system performance, we manually drop the object in different positions to simulate the dropping events happening in real life. To isolate the influence of human, volunteers stand firmly and hold the object in hand ahead of time which ensures the change of their posture is as little as possible in the whole dropping process. The influence of dropping event in two test environments is presented in Tables 1 and 2, respectively. In most cases, our system could resist influence of a dropping object. Sometimes, the object drops down and then rolls on the floor for a period of time. In this situation, our system might cause false alarm because of its long-lasting influence.

Impact of swinging curtain. To further test the system robustness, we evaluate the influence of swinging curtain. In the experiment, volunteers wave the curtain manually to simulate the effect of blowing wind. And for sake of excluding the interference from human, the subject is requested to stay outside the room with a cord connected to the curtain. Different waving strengths are applied to simulate different intensity of the wind. Results are shown in Tables 1 and 2, respectively.

Table 1. Confusion matrix of R1

G	P	
	Stationary	Intrusion
Dropping object	96.5%	3.5%
Swinging curtain	99.8%	0.2%
Moving pet	95.2%	4.8%

Table 2. Confusion matrix of R2

G	P	
	Stationary	Intrusion
Dropping object	98%	2%
Swinging curtain	99.5%	0.5%
Moving pet	94.5%	5.5%

The false-alarm rates in two rooms are both lower than 1%, indicating that the system is quite robust to swinging curtain.

Impact of small pets' movement. Considering that many families have pets or sweeping robot kind of things, we study the influence of this kind of small moving object on the system performance. Similarly, volunteers manually pull boxes of three different size ($30 \times 28 \times 30\,\mathrm{cm}^3$, $40 \times 30 \times 37\,\mathrm{cm}^3$, $59 \times 33 \times 44\,\mathrm{cm}^3$) with a cord in different routes to simulate pet movement. What's more, for each route, we repeat several times with different moving speeds. The results are presented in confusion matrix shown below. Among the experiments, the false alarms are mainly caused by the large box which has similar size with a human torso.

6 Conclusion

In this paper, we design and implement an adaptive and robust indoor human intrusion detection system, AR-Alarm. This is the first Wi-Fi based adaptive intrusion detection system which addresses two challenges, i.e., the multipath environment changes and common anomalous scenes in real life. Utilizing the commodity off-the-shelf WiFi devices, our system could achieve a very high detection rate and a low false alarm rate. Experimental results conducted in different multipath environments have demonstrated the adaptability and robustness of our system. It has the potential to become a practical and non-intrusive human intrusion detection system.

Human intrusion detection has long been a research topic in human activity sensing domain. Although we implemented quite an effective human intrusion detector using WiFi devices, the system still has a lot of room for further improvement. Considering that the intruders often break in from windows or doors, we could place transceivers properly to further improve the detection accuracy of our system. If we could take more daily events into account, our system will be further closer to practice. We are working on these questions and expect to deploy the system in real homes in near future.

Acknowledgments. This work is supported by National Key Research and Development Plan under Grant No. 2016YFB1001200.

References

1. Transafety. http://www.usroads.com/journals/p/rej/9710/re971001.htm
2. Bhartia, A., Chen, Y.C., Rallapalli, S., Qiu, L.: Harnessing frequency diversity in wi-fi networks. In: International Conference on Mobile Computing and Networking (MOBICOM 2011), Las Vegas, Nevada, USA, September, pp. 253–264 (2011)
3. Cai, Q., Aggarwal, J.K.: Automatic tracking of human motion in indoor scenes across multiple synchronized video streams. In: International Conference on Computer Vision, pp. 356–362 (1998)
4. Gong, L., Yang, W., Zhou, Z., Man, D., Cai, H., Zhou, X., Yang, Z.: An adaptive wireless passive human detection via fine-grained physical layer information. Ad Hoc Netw. **38**, 38–50 (2016)
5. Halperin, D., Hu, W., Sheth, A., Wetherall, D.: Tool release: gathering 802.11n traces with channel state information. ACM Sigcomm Comput. Commun. Rev. **41**(1), 53 (2011)
6. Iyengar, S.G., Varshney, P.K., Damarla, T.: On the detection of footsteps based on acoustic and seismic sensing. In: Asilomar Conference on Signals, pp. 2248–2252 (2007)
7. Kosba, A.E., Saeed, A., Youssef, M.: Rasid: a robust WLAN device-free passive motion detection system. In: 2012 IEEE International Conference on Pervasive Computing and Communications, pp. 180–189, March 2012
8. Liu, L., Zhang, W., Deng, C., Yin, S., Wei, S.: Briguard: a lightweight indoor intrusion detection system based on infrared light spot displacement. IET Sci. Measur. Technol. **9**(3), 306–314 (2015)
9. Orr, R.J., Abowd, G.D.: The smart floor: a mechanism for natural user identification and tracking. In: CHI 2000 Extended Abstracts on Human Factors in Computing Systems, pp. 275–276 (2000)
10. Qian, K., Wu, C., Yang, Z., Liu, Y., Zhou, Z.: Pads: passive detection of moving targets with dynamic speed using PHY layer information. In: IEEE International Conference on Parallel and Distributed Systems, pp. 1–8 (2014)
11. Wang, H., Zhang, D., Wang, Y., Ma, J., Wang, Y., Li, S.: RT-fall: a real-time and contactless fall detection system with commodity wifi devices. IEEE Trans. Mobile Comput. **PP**(99), 1 (2017)
12. Wang, W., Liu, A.X., Shahzad, M., Ling, K., Lu, S.: Understanding and modeling of wifi signal based human activity recognition. In: International Conference on Mobile Computing and NETWORKING, pp. 65–76 (2015)
13. Wu, C., Yang, Z., Zhou, Z., Liu, X., Liu, Y., Cao, J.: Non-invasive detection of moving and stationary human with wifi. IEEE J. Sel. Areas Commun. **33**(11), 2329–2342 (2015)
14. Wu, K., Xiao, J., Yi, Y., Gao, M., Ni, L.M.: Fila: fine-grained indoor localization. In: INFOCOM, 2012 Proceedings IEEE, pp. 2210–2218 (2012)
15. Xiao, J., Wu, K., Yi, Y., Wang, L., Ni, L.M.: FIMD: fine-grained device-free motion detection. **90**(1), 229–235 (2012)
16. Youssef, M., Mah, M., Agrawala, A.: Challenges: device-free passive localization for wireless environments. In: ACM International Conference on Mobile Computing and NETWORKING, pp. 222–229 (2007)
17. Zhou, Z., Yang, Z., Wu, C., Liu, Y., Ni, L.M.: On multipath link characterization and adaptation for device-free human detection, pp. 389–398 (2015)
18. Zhou, Z., Yang, Z., Wu, C., Shangguan, L.: Towards omnidirectional passive human detection. In: INFOCOM, 2013 Proceedings IEEE, pp. 3057–3065 (2013)

Short Contributions

Walking Pal: A Spatial and Context Aware System for the Visual Impaired

Hicham Elzabadani[1(✉)], Sara Eid[1], Lilan Haj Hussein[1], Bassel Hussain[1], and Adnan El Nasan[2]

[1] Electrical and Computer Engineering Department, American University in Dubai, Dubai, United Arab Emirates
helzabadani@aud.edu,
{sara.eid,lilan.hajhussain,bassel.hussein}@mymail.aud.edu
[2] Computer and Information Science Department, University of Massachusetts Dartmouth, Dartmouth, USA
aelnasan@umassd.edu

Abstract. People with visual impairment struggle to stay independent in unfamiliar places as they only have a sense of their immediate surroundings using the common available aids. The Walking Pal system aims to help the visually impaired become more independent in outdoor environments by being aware of both her immediate and extended surroundings. This would be achieved by describing points of interest, reading printed text, recognizing certain street features, and finally detecting obstacles. The Walking Pal system utilizes the power of smartphone technologies along with external hardware components to inform the user about the surrounding and guide her safely to her destination using audio messages.

Keywords: Visual impaired · Context aware · Spatial aware · Navigation · Recognition

1 Introduction

A person's ability to know information about her surrounding like location and nearby landmarks adds to her independence regardless whether she needs it directly or not. This spatial-context information may be taken for granted to most people; but for a blind person, it will hugely impact her capability to envision and understand her surroundings independently without the help of others. The blind's need for independence was emphasized by the great blind and deaf American author Helen Keller who said, "what a blind person needs is not a teacher, but another self.".

There have been many assistive technologies introduced in the past that would help guide people with visual impairments [1–3]. Most of these technologies require some kind of alterations to the existing environment. There are other solutions that require expensive proprietary devices to be used [5].

M. Mokhtari et al. (Eds.): ICOST 2017, LNCS 10461, pp. 227–232, 2017.
DOI: 10.1007/978-3-319-66188-9_19

In this paper, we propose a smartphone based application that helps the blind user learn about the surrounding and navigate safely. It is called The Walking Pal and doesn't require any modifications to the surrounding

The rest of the paper includes the related work in Sect. 2, the proposed solution in Sect. 3, testing and results in Sect. 4, and a conclusion in Sect. 5.

2 Related Work

There are many new innovations that aim to help the blind and increase their well-being through the implementation of new technologies. These devices vary from detecting obstacles using different sensors [6, 7] to describing objects in front of the blind through cameras and image processing methods [8]. There are numerous navigation systems that utilize GPS for outdoor localization [4, 10]. Other projects focused on indoor navigation that do not rely on GPS and involve adding some modifications to the surrounding to be recognized as the person is moving [5].

NavCog [3] propose a smartphone-based system that provides turn-by-turn navigation assistance based on accurate real-time localization over large spaces. In addition to basic navigation capabilities, our system also informs the user about nearby points-of-interest (POI) and accessibility issues (e.g., stairs ahead). Chumkamon et al. [9] propose an RFID-based system for navigation in a building for blind people or visually impaired. The system relies on the location information on the tag, a user's destination, and a routing server where the shortest route from the user's current location to the destination.

Other technologies like Bluetooth low-energy or BLE are becoming more popular in this field. Some of the projects utilize the beacon's Received Signal Strength Indication (RSSI) to estimate the distance to the user. Using the data from the RSSI and the location of the beacons, the system can give an estimate on the position of the user [3].

There are also commercial applications [11–13] and devices that help the blind navigate safely. Miniguide US is a portable electronic device that uses ultrasonic sensors to detect objects and gives feedback to the blind through vibrations. The device only detects obstacles without giving any information about the obstacle or the user's surrounding.

3 The Walking Pal System

There are three main functionalities provided by our system. First, describe the user's surrounding including street names, landmarks, and different points of interest and guide them to their destination if they wish so. Second, provide a text-to-speech mechanism to allow the user understand the words placed on different signs. Last is detect pedestrian traffic lights and crosswalks. We will describe the functions in the following sections.

3.1 Navigating and Describing Nearby Places

In this mode, we utilize an Android application that uses the phone's GPS in order to obtain the user's location. The user is able to utilize the Walking Pal system to navigate from one point to another. There are four buttons positioned on the four corners of the screen that can be used to operate the Walking Pal system. The top-left button is used to start/stop navigation. The top-right button is used to repeat the last navigation instruction. The bottom-left one is used to retrieve information about the surrounding area, and the bottom-right button is used to learn about the surrounding used text and image recognition as described in the next three sections.

The user can simply click the top-left button and say the destination. The app will analyse the audio message and confirm the destination. Next, the app will start the navigation process by giving audio instructions played in the earpiece. The app will give the user the distance to the next location they have to walk to. As the user starts walking, the app will beep in specific intervals. The beeping interval will shorten as the user comes closer to their next location.

At any time, the user can press the bottom-left button on the screen to retrieve information about the surrounding area. When the user reaches the desired destination, the Walking Pal system will notify her and would play an audio message and then stops the navigation process.

3.2 Text Recognition and Reading

The ability to recognize our whereabouts is highly dependent on our ability to read the roads and landmarks signs. These signs, in most cases, show some text that could indicate the road name, a landmark name, or any other names that would be helpful in guiding us to our destination. Walking Pal uses the phone camera to achieve this purpose.

As it is shown in Fig. 1, whenever the user requires guidance, she simply can use the phone and press the bottom-right button to scan the surrounding looking for any text that can be recognized. A timer will run asynchronously as a thread that will make the camera capture at a specified interval. The specified interval was set according to the approximate time required to process the captured image. Images are analysed and an Optical Character Recognition system is initiated to extract the text shown in these images. Using the same Text-to-speech engine we described earlier, the app would read the text through the earpiece or speaker.

3.3 Crosswalks and Pedestrian Traffic Lights Detection

Pedestrian traffic lights and crosswalks are detected through image processing methods using the phone's camera. The Walking Pal system utilizes various algorithms to detect crosswalks and pedestrian traffic lights.

The crosswalk detection algorithm starts by isolating the white bars and objects from the background. It first converts the RGB image to Gray scale then applies thresholding to isolate the white bars of the zebra crosswalk. Dilation is then applied several times to the resulted image followed by blurring to fill the gaps found in the detected white bars.

A canny edge detector is then used to obtain the edges of the rectangles. The Hough Line transform is applied to the resulted image to connect the edges and create straight lines which will create contours and also ignore the short unneeded lines. The system

Fig. 1. Text recognition process

then detects the contours of connected component that were previously created. Based on the area, contours are filtered to keep the sufficient rectangles of the crosswalk and ignore any small or large rectangles found in the image. The decision is then taken whether a crosswalk is detected or not only if three or more white bars are found in the captured image.

Whenever a cross walk is detected, the color of the traffic light is checked. The system simply checks for the round red or green signals, which is the most general shape for a traffic light. The algorithm starts by converting the image from RGB to Hue-Saturation-Value (HSV.) This will enable us to isolate the red or green color in the captured image. A Circle Hough Transform method is used to detect circles for the isolated image. If no signal is placed, it informs the user that no signal was found in that detected crosswalk. Similar to the previous function, the feedback is played using the earpiece to warn the user of the crosswalks and traffic lights ahead of her as shown in Fig. 2.

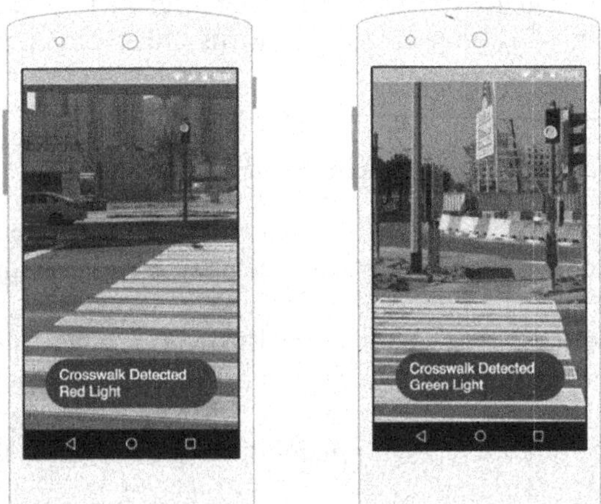

Fig. 2. Sample results of crosswalks and traffic light detection (Color figure online)

4 Testing and Results

To better understand how The Walking Pal system would perform in real life, we performed several tests and collected the results obtained.

Finding the nearby places was the simplest part of the system and it worked as expected. The crosswalk and traffic light detection functionality was tested in different places and circumstances to check the feasibility of the algorithms implemented.

We used the testing mode of the app to check the process of detecting crosswalks and traffic signals. Figure 3 shows the different stages a picture would go though in order to identify a crosswalk. The final result, whether a crosswalk is detected or not, is based on the last stage where the number of white bars is counted and if it is greater than three, the app will notify the user of the existence of a crosswalk.

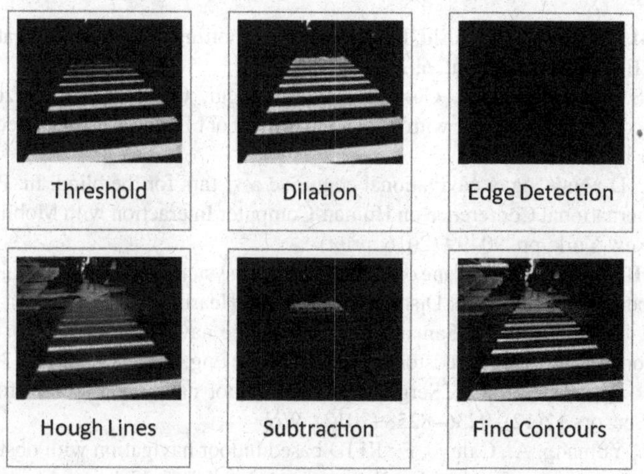

Fig. 3. Results of the crosswalks detection algorithm steps

4.1 Evaluation

We evaluated the system by recruiting five participants to use it around the university campus. We setup a starting point and a destination point that require turning and crossing a road. The participants were not familiar with the campus but they were all familiar with smartphone-based navigation. We then asked all the participants to use the Walking Pal system to navigate to the destination provided. We finished the evaluations by getting their feedback about the system and how it can be improved.

During the system evaluations, we walked alongside the participants and logged our observations to better understand the participants' ability to properly use the application. We noticed several common events that the participants encountered: repeating the instruction, turning more than is necessary, getting completely lost, and hitting an obstacle.

5 Conclusion

In this paper, we described the use of a smartphone-based system to help people with visual impairments navigate in unfamiliar places. The system uses the sensors and actuators provided by the phone to locate the user, give information about the surrounding, give instructions on how to reach the destination, and detect crosswalks and traffic light signals. It also uses an optional custom made glasses to detect obstacles. We tested the system with several participants and collected the results. Based on the results, the system was able to achieve the goal but still lacks some features that could make the experience more efficient.

References

1. Arikawa, M., Konomi, S., Ohnishi, K.: Navitime: supporting pedestrian navigation in the real world. IEEE Pervasive Comput. **6**, 21–29 (2007)
2. Mascetti, S., Ahmetovic, D., Gerino, A., Bernareggi, C.: ZebraRecognizer: pedestrian crossing recognition for people with visual impairment or blindness. Pattern Recogn. **60**, 405–419 (2016)
3. Ahmetovic, D.: NavCog: a navigational cognitive assistant for the blind. In: Proceedings of the 18th International Conference on Human-Computer Interaction with Mobile Devices and Services, New York, pp. 90–99 (2016, print)
4. Chaudary, B., Pulli, P.: Smart cane outdoor navigation system for visually impaired deaf-blind and blind persons. J. Commun. Disorders Deaf Stud. Hearing Aids **02** (2014)
5. Alhmiedat, T., Abutaleb, A., Samara, G.: A prototype navigation system for guiding blind people indoors using NXT Mindstorms. Int. J. Online Eng. (iJOE) **9**, 52 (2013)
6. Guerrero, L.A., Francisco, V., Sergio, F.O.: An indoor navigation system for the visually impaired. Sensors **12**(12), 8236–8258 (2012). Web
7. Sanchez, J., Yumang, A., Caluyo, F.: RFID based indoor navigation with obstacle detection based on A* algorithm for the visually impaired. Int. J. Inf. Electron. Eng. **5**(6), 428–432 (2015). Web
8. Voth, D.: wearable aid for the visually impaired. IEEE Pervasive Comput. **3**(3), 6–7 (2004). Web
9. Chumkamon, S., Tuvaphanthaphiphat, P., Keeratiwintakorn, P.: A blind navigation system using RFID for indoor environments. In: 5th International Conference on Electrical Engineering/Electronics, Computer, Telecommunications and Information Technology, Thailand, vol. 2, pp. 765–768 (2008)
10. Helal, A., Moore, S., Ramachandran, B.: Drishti: An integrated navigation system for visually impaired and disabled. In: Proceedings of the 5th IEEE International Symposium on Wearable Computers (ISWC 2001), p. 149. IEEE Computer Society, Washington, DC, USA (2001)
11. American Printing House for the Blind (2017). Aph.org. Accessed 13 Mar 2017
12. Brainport V100 Vision Aid (2017). BrainPort V100 Vision Aid. Accessed 13 Mar 2017
13. Be My Eyes | Bringing Sight to the Blind and Visually Impaired (2017). Bemyeyes.org. Accessed 13 Mar 2017

Integrating Prior Knowledge in Weighted SVM for Human Activity Recognition in Smart Home

M'hamed Bilal Abidine[1(✉)], Belkacem Fergani[1], and Anthony Fleury[2,3]

[1] Laboratoire d'Ingénierie des Systèmes Intelligents et Communicants, LISIC Laboratory, Electronics and Computer Sciences Department, University of Science and Technology Houari Boumediene (USTHB), 32, El Alia, Bab Ezzouar, 16111 Algiers, Algeria
abidineb@hotmail.com
[2] Mines Douai, URIA, Douai, France
[3] University of Lille, Lille, France

Abstract. Feature extraction and classification are two key steps for activity recognition in a smart home environment. In this work, we performed a new hybrid model using Temporal or Spatial Features (TF or SF) with the PCA-LDA-WSVM classifier. The last method combines two methods for feature extraction: Principal Component Analysis (PCA), and Linear Discriminant Analysis (LDA) followed by Weighted SVM Classifier. This classifier is used to handle the problem of imbalanced activity data from sensor readings. The experiments that were implemented on multiple real-world datasets, showed the effectiveness of TF and SF attributes combined with PCA-LDA-WSVM in activity recognition.

Keywords: Activity recognition · Feature extraction · PCA · LDA · Weighted SVM

1 Introduction

Several classification algorithms have been employed for Human Activity Recognition (HAR) tasks [1–4] to automatically recognize activities in intelligent manner about the occupants and ensure the comfort of older adults in smart home using sensor networks. In [5], we have developed a new classification method named PCA-LDA-WSVM based on a combination of Principal Component Analysis (PCA), Linear Discriminant Analysis (LDA) and the modified Weighted Support Vector Machines (WSVM). We demonstrated the ability of this method to achieve good improvement over the standard used methods such as HMM, CRF, SVM, WSVM.

Classifiers address the challenge of extracting information from raw sensor data through the use of features. In this paper, we wanted to improve the classification performances of the approach in [5] by introducing prior knowledge [6]. The 'Prepare breakfast' and 'Prepare dinner' activities share the same model as they involve the same set of object interactions. These two activities are distinguished by time of taking

M. Mokhtari et al. (Eds.): ICOST 2017, LNCS 10461, pp. 233–239, 2017.
DOI: 10.1007/978-3-319-66188-9_20

place, i.e. 'Prepare breakfast' takes place in the morning hours and "Prepare dinner" takes place in the afternoon or evening hours of the day. The location attribute can also discriminate between two different activity classes as 'Toileting' and 'Showering' that performed in two different locations.

2 The Proposed HAR System by Introducing the Prior Knowledge

2.1 Overview

The core idea of proposed method is as follows: A dataset is divided into training and testing sets. Having defined the activities to recognize and the list of potentially interesting features, we added both temporal and spatial features (TF and SF). We then extract the features that proved to be the most useful for activity recognition. These two sets are transformed independently with PCA and LDA methods. By adding those PCF it is possible to have more than the number of classes minus one extracted features by LDA. Then WSVM method, as the latter process as follow (Fig. 1).

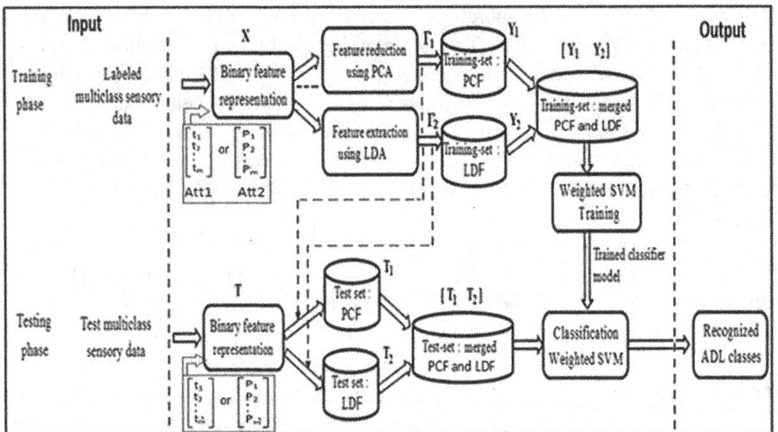

Fig. 1. Block diagram of the proposed activity recognition approach using the feature insertion. Att1 = TF, Att2 = SF.

2.2 Feature Representation

Sensors outputs are binary and represented in a feature space which is used by the model to recognize the activities performed. The raw data obtained from the sensors can either be used directly, or be transformed into a different representation forms (Fig. 2). We do not use the *raw* sensor data representation as observations; instead we use the "*Change point*" and "*Last*" representations which have been shown to give much better results in activity recognition [7].

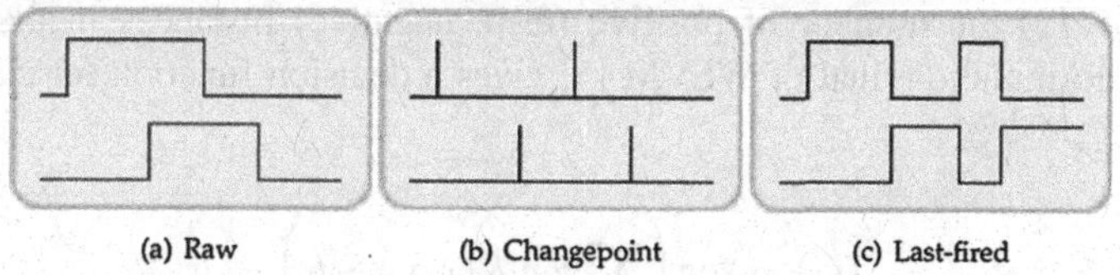

(a) Raw (b) Changepoint (c) Last-fired

Fig. 2. Different feature representations [8].

2.3 Feature Insertion

In this work, we improve the classification performances of class activities by introducing the feature insertion stage. We added two new features to the existent data matrix. The first attribute corresponds to the hour of beginning of the activity. We extract this feature directly from the data structure. The sensor activations are collected by the state-change sensors distributed all around the environment. To find out the second feature corresponding to the room label of performed activity, we search the different objects he is manipulating in the sensors, see the below Fig. 3. ID: is a number representing the sensor ID. Each sensor has its own unique ID.

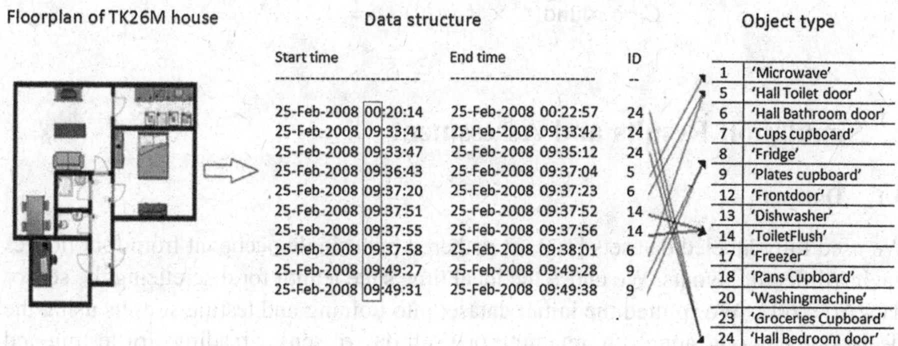

Fig. 3. TF and SF for TK26M dataset. In red, the hour of beginning activity. (Color figure online)

2.4 Weighted Support Vector Machines Classification (WSVM)

Osuna et al. [9] proposed a Weighted SVM (WSVM) algorithm by introducing two different cost parameter C_- and C_+ in SVM optimization problem for the minority ($d_i = -1$) and majority classes ($d_i = +1$), as follow

$$\min_{s,b,\zeta} \frac{1}{2} s \cdot s + C_+ \sum_{i|d_i=1}^{l_+} \zeta_i + C_- \sum_{i|d_i=-1}^{l_-} \zeta_i \tag{1}$$
$$\text{subject to } d_i(s \cdot \Phi(y_i) + b) \geq 1 - \zeta_i,\ \zeta_i \geq 0,\ i = 1, \ldots, l$$

l_+ *(resp.* l_-*)* the number of positive (resp. negative) instances in the database. Solving the formulation dual of WSVM [5] gives a decision function for classifying a test point $y \in R^{p+q}$

$$\mathrm{f}(x) = \mathrm{sgn}\left(\sum_{i=1}^{l_{sv}} \alpha_i d_i K(x, x_i) + b\right) \tag{2}$$

We used the Gaussian kernel as follows: $K(x, y) = \exp\left(-\|x - y\|^2/2\sigma^2\right)$. Huang et al. [10] raised a Weighted SVM algorithm. The cost coefficients are typically chosen as:

$$\frac{C_+}{C_-} = \frac{l_-}{l_+} \tag{3}$$

To extend Weighted *SVM* to the multi-class scenario in order to deal with N classes (daily activities), we used different misclassification C_i per class similar to [11]. By taking $C_- = C_i$ and $C_+ = C$, with l_+ and l_i be the number of samples of majority classes and number of samples in the ith class and C is the common cost parameter of the WSVM. The main ratio cost value C_i for each activity can be obtained by:

$$C_i = \mathrm{round}(C \times [l_+/l_i]) \quad i = 1, \ldots, N \tag{4}$$

3 Simulation Results and Assessment

3.1 Datasets

We used fully labeled datasets [1, 3, 7] gathered by a single occupant from four houses having different layouts. We chose the ideal time slice length for discretizing the sensor data $\Delta t = 60$ s. We splitted the initial dataset into training and testing subsets using the 'leave one day out' approach, retaining one full day of sensor readings for testing and using the remaining sub-samples as training data.

3.2 Results

We optimized the SVM hyper-parameters (σ, C) for all training sets in the range [0.1–2] and {0.1, 1, 5, 10, 100}, respectively, to maximize the error rate of leave-oneday-out cross-validation technique. The number of features after extraction for PCA and LDA is mentioned in [5]. Then, for WSVM classification method, we optimized locally the cost parameter C_i adapted to different classes.

In Table 1, the results show that the feature insertion set using either TF or SF contributes to significantly enhance the performance of PCA-LDA-WSVM classifier. One also notices that the TF is slightly better than SF for recognizing activities.

We report in Fig. 4, the classification results in terms of accuracy measure for each class. In TK26M dataset, our proposed combinations outperforms the other approaches

Table 1. Recall, Precision, F-measure and Accuracy results for all approaches in (%). Bold values are the results for our approaches for each dataset.

Datasets	Approach	Recall	Precision	F-measure	Accuracy
TK26M	PCA-LDA-WSVM [5]	78.8	80.1	79.4	95.6
	TF-PCA-LDA-WSVM	**82.0**	**82.8**	**82.4**	**93.8**
	SF-PCA-LDA-WSVM	**80.4**	**83.4**	**81.8**	**94.7**
TAP80F	PCA-LDA-WSVM [5]	41.4	49.6	45.1	75.8
	TF-PCA-LDA-WSVM	**43.2**	**51.3**	**46.9**	**65.4**
	SF-PCA-LDA-WSVM	**44.7**	**46.8**	**45.7**	**70.7**
OrdonezA	PCA-LDA-WSVM [5]	65.0	71.7	68.2	88.4
	TF-PCA-LDA-WSVM	**68.7**	**75.2**	**71.8**	**84.1**
	SF-PCA-LDA-WSVM	**68.0**	**73.0**	**70.4**	**86.5**

for 'Idle', 'Leaving', 'Toileting', 'Showering', 'Breakfast', 'Dinner' and 'Drink' activities. The majority activities are better for all methods over all datasets while the 'Idle' activity is more accurate for the proposed method compared to other methods. Additionally, the kitchen-related activities as 'Breakfast', 'Dinner' and 'Drink' are in general harder to recognize than other activities.

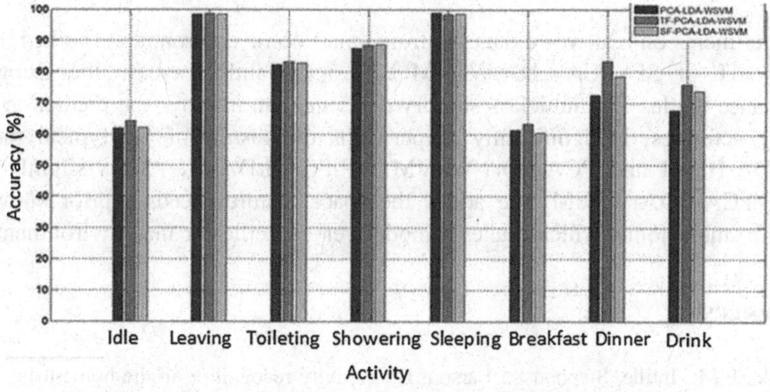

Fig. 4. Accuracy recognition rate for each activity on TK26M dataset.

In order to quantify the extent to which one class is harder to recognize than another one, we analyzed the confusion matrix of TF-PCA-LDA-WSVM for TK26M dataset in Table 2. One notices that the activities 'Leaving', 'Toileting', 'Showering', 'Sleeping', 'Dinner' and 'Drink' are better recognized comparatively with 'Idle' and 'Breakfast'. The kitchen activities seem to be more recognized using the proposed method combining TF with the PCA-LDA-WSVM classifier.

Given the considerations pointed out previously, the high performance obtained in the case of TK26M dataset, which seems to be less vulnerable to class-overlapping than others, as compared to other datasets. This overlapping between the activities is due to

Table 2. Confusion matrix (values in %) of activities for TF-PCA-LDA-WSVM on the TK26 M dataset.

Activity	Id	Le	To	Sh	Sl	Br	Di	Dr
Id	**64.3**	7.6	2.0	1.1	4.7	8.7	6.5	5.1
Le	0.6	**98.6**	0.2	0.5	0.0	0.0	0.1	0.0
To	7.8	5.2	**83.2**	2.1	0.7	0.6	0.1	0.3
Sh	5.2	0.0	4.2	**88.5**	0.0	0.0	0.9	0.2
Sl	0.3	0.3	0.4	0.5	**98.5**	0.0	0.0	0.0
Br	16.0	0.0	0.9	0.2	0.6	**63.4**	11.6	7.3
Di	5.0	0.7	0.3	0.0	0.5	2.6	**83.4**	3.5
Dr	6.8	0.0	0.0	0.2	0.2	6.2	1.7	**76.1**

the layout of the house. In the TK26M House, there is a separate room for almost every activity. The kitchen activities are food-related tasks, they are worst recognized because most of the instances of these activities were performed in the same location (kitchen) using the same set of sensors. Therefore the location of sensors strongly influences recognition performance.

4 Conclusion

Our experiments on real-world datasets from smart home environment showed that the strategy (TF or SF)-PCA-LDA-WSVM can significantly increase the recognition performance to classify multiclass sensory data, and can improve the prediction of the minority activities. It significantly outperforms the results of the typical methods PCA-LDA-HMM and PCA-LDA-WSVM. TF-PCA-LDA-WSVM is slightly better than SF-PCA-LDA-WSVM. We added the space features needs a prior knowledge about the smart home, which makes a model very specific for that environment.

References

1. Tapia, E.M., Intille, Stephen S., Larson, K.: Activity recognition in the home using simple and ubiquitous sensors. In: Ferscha, A., Mattern, F. (eds.) Pervasive 2004. LNCS, vol. 3001, pp. 158–175. Springer, Heidelberg (2004). doi:10.1007/978-3-540-24646-6_10
2. Logan, B., Healey, J., Philipose, M., Tapia, E.M., Intille, S.: A long-term evaluation of sensing modalities for activity recognition. In: Krumm, J., Abowd, Gregory D., Seneviratne, A., Strang, T. (eds.) UbiComp 2007. LNCS, vol. 4717, pp. 483–500. Springer, Heidelberg (2007). doi:10.1007/978-3-540-74853-3_28
3. Ordonez, F.J., de Toledo, P., Sanchis, A.: Activity recognition using hybrid generative/discriminative models on home environments using binary sensors. Sensors **13**, 5460–5477 (2013)
4. Abidine, M.B., Fergani, L., Fergani, B., Fleury, A.: Improving human activity recognition in smart homes. Int. J. E-Health Med. Commun. (IJEHMC) **6**(3), 19–37 (2015)
5. Abidine, M.B., Fergani, L., Fergani, B., Oussalah, M.: The joint use of sequence features combination and modified weighted SVM for improving daily activity recognition. Pattern Anal. Appl. 1–20 (2016). Springer-Verlag London

6. Fleury, A., Noury, N., Vacher, M.: Improving supervised classification of activities of daily activities of daily living using prior knowledge. Int. J. E-Health Med. Commun. **2**(1), 17–34 (2011)
7. Kasteren, T.V., Noulas, A., Englebienne, G., Krose, B.: Accurate activity recognition in a home setting. In: UbiComp 2008, pp. 1–9. ACM, New York (2008)
8. Kasteren, T.V.: Activity recognition for health monitoring elderly using temporal probabilistic models. Ph.D. thesis, University of Amsterdam, Amsterdam, The Netherlands, 27 April 2011
9. Osuna, E., Freund, R., Girosi, F.: Support vector machines: training and applications. Technical report. Massachusetts Institute of Technology, Cambridge, MA, USA (1997)
10. Huang, Y.M., Du, S.X.: Weighted support vector machine for classification with uneven training class sizes. In: Proceedings of the IEEE International Conference on Machine Learning and Cybernetics, vol. 7, pp. 4365–4369 (2005)
11. Chen, D.R., Wu, Q., Ying, Y., Zhou, D.X.: Support vector machine soft margin classifiers: error analysis. J. Mach. Learn. Res. **5**, 1143–1175 (2004)

Formal Test and Simulation Environment of Wireless Body Network

Khaldia Benahmed[1(✉)], Mostefa Belarbi[1(✉)], Abdelhamid Hariche[1(✉)], and Abou El Hassan Benyamina[2(✉)]

[1] LIM Research Laboratory, University of Tiaret, Tiaret, Algeria
benkhaldia@hotmail.fr, belarbimostefa@yahoo.fr, abdelhamid.hariche@univ-tiaret.dz
[2] LAPECI Research Laboratory, University of Oran ES-SENIA, Oran, Algeria
benyanabou@yahoo.fr
http://www.univ-tiaret.dz
http://www.univ-oran1.dz

Abstract. The general approach of this paper is to reduce the overall complexity in the context of nano-devices network and wireless body network (WBAN) based on NoC-FPGA (Network-on-Chip - field Programmable Gate Assembly) by applying an incremental formal approach. This research work treats a methodology that invokes the formal method based on validated Event-B theories: NoC Theory, wireless network theory, coloured graph theory and the VHDL theory (Very High Speed Integrated Circuit Hardware Description Language) and probabilistic properties to generate correctly the well-chosen context in terms of reliability, fault tolerance and more specifically to take this work as a very important validation criteria for our general approach.

Keywords: Nano-sensor network · NoC · Formal methods · Event-B · Theory concept · FPGA · VHDL · WBAN

1 Introduction

Several research works where the complexity is involved in the reconfigurable communicating architectures [1] (using Nano metric scale [1,2] without interference and ultra wide band (UWB) based on impulsion [1–5]) need formal technics to integrate correctly design flow of micro-electronic systems. Especially the liability and security of wireless sensors in the domain WBAN (low power consumption, low latency and high reliability communications [5]) which is nano-materials devices inside the human body (monitor the imbalance of cholesterol, the measurement of bone growth, etc. [3,5]). The WBANs determined by the stored energy that is always dissipated and can be reconstituted using certain energy recovery techniques (rhythmic vibration of the heart, body movement...), resulting in an energy fluctuation node aware of the time. Therefore, the lifetime of this type of network is longer.

Our suggestion consists of proposing a new approach of the design of sensors network using fault-tolerant platform [6] based on the reconfigurable technology

M. Mokhtari et al. (Eds.): ICOST 2017, LNCS 10461, pp. 240–246, 2017.
DOI: 10.1007/978-3-319-66188-9_21

of FPGA. This approach uses proved incremental refinement fashion in order to investigate formal proof using Rodin Tool associated to the Event-B Language [7]. The micro-architecture will be composed by two parts: the first part consists of the nano-device and the second part consists of the device constituted by SoC using FPGA technology [1]. This platform allows us to design and simulate wireless sensors by reducing time and reaching certain reliability. The paper structure is as follows: section two discusses the important part of the study consists of representing the network using several theories in Event-B [6,8,9] and the probabilistic properties [3,10]. Section three express the case study of modelling with Event-B the WBAN context with all details, where the section four discuss the result of simulating the WBAN system modelled and checked by Event-B, the last section take some conclusion from this work and the future perspectives token during this work.

2 Generic Modelling Approach

This paper introduces the new approach of Event-B modelling of a BAN nano-sensors system in the aim to create well-worked network (Fig. 1) by the mean of new construct of useful theories: NoC, graph, probabilistic properties and VHDL theory [11].

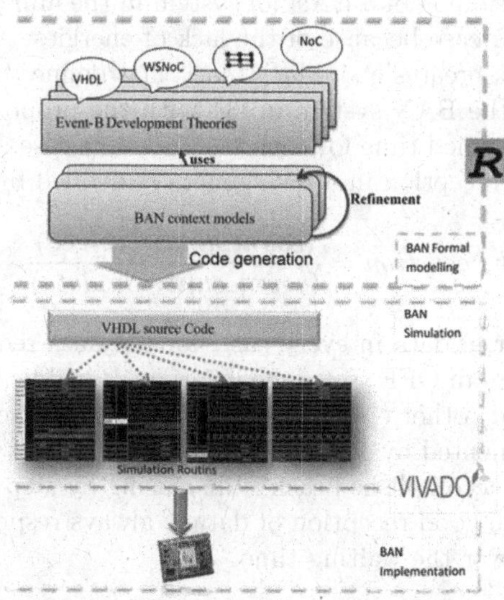

Fig. 1. The process of WBAN design during this work

2.1 Approch Motivations

In the follow here's some key points (Fig. 1) of this work:

- We present the WBAN context by means of the Theory plug-in which addresses the extensibility issues of Event-B to prove how our approach can be incorporated into the modelling and proof activity.
- this works is the introduction of new mechanism of recovering for the faulty nano-sensors thanks to the new strategy inspired from a previous work [11].
- Our work starts by the phase of modelling with Event-B theories already deployed and validated [11] in the mean of ensured the BAN context newly suggested.
- Associate properties from a probabilistic HMM model to the Event-B models.
- The token case study is for analysing the reasons of collision during multiple sending of data and propose a mechanism to detect the failure and solved it using a set of theories that help in the final step to generate a VHDL code thanks to VHDL theory.
- The carry out of some temporal properties in the modelling phase to make the proposed recovering strategy more convenient.

2.2 Probabilistic Properties

In this particular case of development in electronics systems design, validation is launched using HMM markovian (The number of received data under the variation of two important variants: the state of channels and the nodes) cycle to defines the best functioning of a BAN [5] system in the aim of avoiding in the worst mean the collision case because of the lack of energies.
With Event-B this work creates a similar theory that define the rules of probabilistic attribution for the BAN system in [3], with the proposition of carrying out of the factor of consumed time for each task in every case, knowing that the probability of coverage reception in a task generally defined by:

$$Prob\_reception = \frac{(count\_data\_received)}{(count\_emission\_data)}$$

to do count the number of data in every case, for the data reception where the channel and the node are in OFF state, the invariant P will be incremented by 1 (the event Well_received) other else. When the data are not received (the state is ON) Q will be incremented by 1 (the event Not_received).
In the time scale every accomplished task is increasing by step is covered by the invariant task_time. The good reception of data is always respecting the time of task and do not cross over the waiting time.

3 WBAN Context Development by Theories

The machine Event-B *BAN* has many theories (see Fig. 2) taking in consideration packet rates, time of energy consumption, the behaviour of the channel, and the fluctuation of the receiver's power in the probabilistic evaluation of nodes in order to detect a receiver node failure during a multi-transmission of data using the following invariants:

p: The number of receiving data during a single emission
q: The non-received data number during a single emission

if the number of received data by a node still less than the total data and the duration of the emission overpass the threshold of an ordinary emission task (model Ban_M0), then this faulty node will be coloured using Colored graph theory (Ban_M1). The multi emission of symbols is affected to the failure of the system, so the theory of WNoC nodes recovering helped to recover every node and uncoloured it till the end of all the faulty nodes which are in the waiting list (Ban_M2). The data flow in WBAN must not be randomly, but it must follow four case to check the behaviour of nodes in the suggested system by observing this behaviour using ProB Tool delivered in the Rodin toolset as a scenario of animation where multiple data must be received by a node:

- In the same time with a same rate (the arrival time to add for the Task_time will be the same even the time reserved for saving the data from a direction dir_buff_time).
- In the same time with different rates (the arrival time to add for the Task_time will be the same and we will add different times reserved for saving the data from a direction dir_buff_time).
- At different times with the same rate (the arrival time to add for the Task_time will be not the same but the time reserved for saving the data from a direction dir_buff_time will be the same).
- At different times with different rates (the arrival time to add for the Task_time will be not the same even the time reserved for saving the data from a direction dir_buff_time).

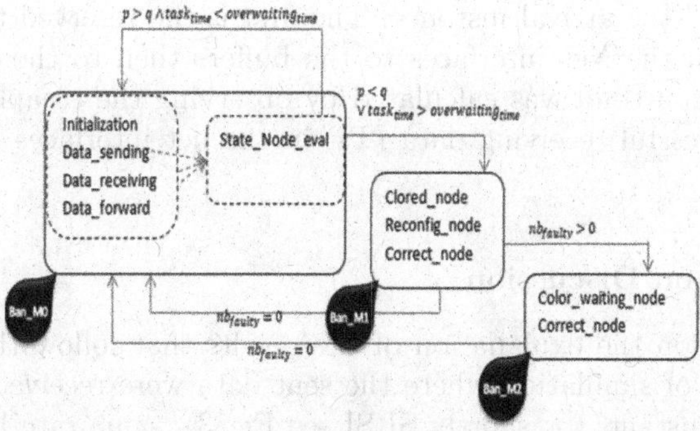

Fig. 2. The Model's description of WBAN during this work (Color figure online)

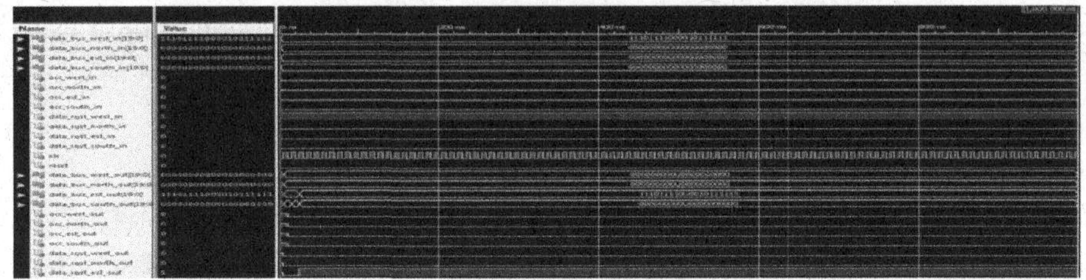

Fig. 3. The result of the first routine of simulation in VIVADO ISIM (SRSI).

4 Experimental Test and Results

The redefinition of *collision* in the context of BAN networks is not only about sequential collision of symbols of a same packet but also the sequential collision of symbols from different packets (the instance for arrival of data, and the rate to make it received by a node). Following the same line of argument just presented, we consider that the state of receiver node can be modelled using Event-B model in order to take the decision of how to give a recover signal to make the node in the state faulty become again a healthy node. Since that this model was interpreted to VHDL annotation thanks to the VHDL theory, we created four axes of simulation where the sent data were received at:

- Same rate (speed associated to distance which corresponds in our case to direction) and same time instant. (or shortly SRSI).
- Same rate but different at time instants, (or shortly SRDI).
- Different rates at same time instant, (or shortly DRSI).
- Different rates and different time instant, (or shortly DRDI).

The first question comes to the reader's mind is how the simulation routines had made in term of arrival time of data? We try to make a variation depends on arrival Rates and the arrival instance. The first is the reserved time for during the passage from the Net interfaces to the buffers then to the next interfaces calculated. When second was calculated by observing the escape time between the time of successful receiving data (Ts) in the net interfaces and the failure time (Tf).

4.1 Results and Discussion

In the next section the explanation of the results that follow the four created axes of sketches of simulation where the sent data were received at: same rate and same time instant. (or shortly SRSI see Fig. 3), same rate but different at time instants, (or shortly SRDI), different rates at same time instant, (or shortly DRSI), different rates and different time instant, (or shortly DRDI).

- **The first scenario(SRSI):** In this one the receiver node will treat only the first arrival Flit after the liberation and lose all the rest. This mean that the cross bar need a technique more carrying about how much space is required to store data received then go to the calculation of the next direction.

- **The second scenario(SRDI):** This scenario most of data will be received if every Flit arrived after a good time also this case could be treated if there is a mechanism let the arrival data wait a good time when the buffers still occupied. The result of multiple reception of data came from the four direction where the time window between every arrival of data is large (100 ns).
- **The third scenario(DRSI):** It have the similar number of received data as in the first one but the only difference rise in the order of receiving data following the time window linked to the rate of arrival data.
- **The fourth scenario(DRDI):** There's a loss of data in these nano-sensors which needs a scheduling mechanism to store and treat data. This mean also that the reception strategy need a mechanism for saving data from the loss of data especially in the case of multiple data coming to the node.

5 Conclusion and Perspectives

This suggested approach exploits the notion of refinement and incrementality mechanisms and formal proof. It allows us to improve the reliability and decrease the design time of high level specification. During this work, well-defined graph theory, auto-self organization network using reconfigurable FPGA and well-defined nano-sensors theory are taking all the attention. We show that our methodology can integrate several constraints like for example those associated to probabilistic model, or other concepts and technics associated to BAN network can be injected in future research such Multiple Input Output Orthogonal Frequency Demodulation Modulation MIMO-OFDM [12], as new level of the refinement process. The methodology used the coupled tools, at one hand RODIN tool based Event-B language and at the other hand Simulation Xilinx environment and VHDL language. Code generation and integration system will be performed in the last step of the methodology.

Acknowledgments. This Works is a part of research project supported by the thematic research agency (ATRST) of research direction (Algerian Ministry of High Education and Scientific Research).

References

1. Haymar, K., et al.: Self-organized mobility in nanosensor network based on particle swarm optimization and coverage criteria. In: Proceeding NCM08 Proceedings of the 2008 Fourth International Conference on Networked Computing and advanced Information Management, vol. 01, pp. 636–641 (2008)
2. Ferrand, P., Maman, M., Goursaud, C., Gorce, J.-M., Ouvry, L.: Performance evaluation of direct and cooperative transmissions in body area networks. Ann. Telecommun. **66**, 213–228 (2011)

3. Islam, N., Misra, S.: Catastrophic collision in bio-nanosensor networks: does it really matter? In: 2013 IEEE 15th International Conference on e-Health Networking, Applications & Services (Healthcom), October 2013
4. Coussy, P., Baganne, A., Martin, E., Casseau, E.: Intégration Optimisée de Composants Virtuels orientés TDSI par la Synthése d'Architecture Colloque sur le Traitement du Signal et de l'Image (GRETSI) (2004)
5. Sudjai, M., Tran, L.-C., Safaei, F.: Adaptive space-time-frequency-coded UWB system for wireless body area network. EURASIP J. Wireless Commun. Networking **2015**, 36 (2015)
6. Hariche, A., Belarbi, M.: Towards code generation of reconfigurable MPSoC network using vertex coloring algorithms. University of Oran, 28–29 Sepp. 2014. Journées systémes embarquées et paralléles (2014)
7. Daoud, H., Tanougast, C., Belarbi, M.: Formal specification and verification of an architecture based wireless network oriented NoC. In: codit 2014, Metz-France (2014)
8. Hariche, A., Belarbi, M., Daoud, H.: Based B extraction of QNoC architecture properties. In: International Workshop on Mathematic and Computer Sciences, Tiaret, MOMAJ, vol. 2, issue 01, pp. 8–13, December 2012
9. Andriamiarina, M.-B., Méry, D., Singh, N.-K.: Revisiting snapshot algorithms by refinement- based techniques. Comput. Sci. Inf. Syst. **11**(1), 251–270 (2012)
10. Hariche, A., Belarbi, M., Daoud, H.: A new operators-based approach for the event-B refinement: QNoC case study. In: IEEE International Conference on Mechatronics IEEE ICM 2013, Beirut, December 2013
11. Hariche, A., Belarbi, M., Chouarfia, A.: Embedded systems design using event-B theories. Int. J. Comput. Digital Syst. **5**(2), March 2016. http://dx.doi.org/10.12785/ijcds/050207
12. Marchetti, N., Rahman, M.I., Kumar, S., Prasad, R.: OFDM: principles and challenges. In: Tarokh, V. (ed.) New Directions in Wireless Communications Research, pp. 29–62. Springer, Boston (2009). doi:10.1007/978-1-4419-0673-1_2

Comparison of Machine Learning Algorithms to Increase Prediction Accuracy of COPD Domain

Lokman Saleh[1(✉)], Hamid Mcheick[2(✉)], Hicham Ajami[2(✉)], Hafedh Mili[1(✉)], and Joumana Dargham[3(✉)]

[1] Computer Science Department, Université du Québec à Montréal, Case postale 8888, Succursale Centre-ville, Montréal, QC H3C 3P8, Canada
Saleh.Lokman@courrier.uqam.ca, Mili.Hafedh@uqam.ca

[2] Computer Science Department, Université du Québec à Chicoutimi, 555, Boul De l'Université, Chicoutimi, QC G7H 2B1, Canada
{Hamid_Mcheick,Hicham.Ajamil}@uqac.ca

[3] Department of Computer Science, University Balamand, Tripoli, Lebanon
Joumana.Dargham@balamand.edu.lb

Abstract. Medicine and especially chronic diseases, like everything else on earth is filled with ambiguity. This is why, identifying patients at risk present a big challenge to human brain. Poor control and misdiagnosis of chronic diseases has a great impact quality of life of patients, the expenses and performance of health care system. The global economic cost of chronic diseases could reach $47 trillion by 2030, according to a study by the World Economic Forum (WEF). Beside this economic burden, such treatment failure increases the risk of progression of disease which inevitably leads to premature death or further illness and suffering. Today, health informatics is reshaping the research in the medical domain due to its potential to concurrently overcome the challenges encountered in the traditional healthcare systems. Uncertainty, accuracy, causal attributes and their relationship, all have their places in this new technology through contemporary machine learning algorithms. Prediction of exacerbation of Chronic Obstructive Pulmonary Disease (COPD) is considered one of the most difficult problems in the medical field. In this paper, we will leverage unused machine learning methods to increase prediction accuracy in COPD. To this end, we compared three of the most common machine learning algorithms (decision tree, naive Bayes and Bayesian network) based on ROC metric. Furthermore, we used discretization process for the first time in this context.

Keywords: Machine learning · Chronic Pulmonary Disease COPD · Exacerbation · Select relevant attributes · Accuracy · Prediction

1 Introduction

One of the most important issues treated by machine learning algorithms are the uncertainty and the prediction of relevant attributes. These issues appeared clearly with COPD. In this work, we focus on the Bayesian belief network, naïve Bayes and decision

M. Mokhtari et al. (Eds.): ICOST 2017, LNCS 10461, pp. 247–254, 2017.
DOI: 10.1007/978-3-319-66188-9_22

tree techniques to support the uncertainty, while Wrappers and filters methods has been used to select the relevant attributes. Moreover we highlighted both supervised and no supervised discretization algorithms for continuous data. On the other hand, we implemented TAN and K2 algorithms to realise dependency between the relevant attributes. These steps help us to predict the exacerbation in COPD with high accuracy.

COPD infections are a combination of small airway obstruction and alveolar destruction, phenomena known as chronic bronchitis and emphysema. Unfortunately, there is no treatment for COPD, or rather there is no cure to reverse the damage done to the airways and lung function, but therapy can slow its progress, reduce complications, improve quality of life [2], and surely avoid exacerbation. This latter is the main reason leading to worsening of health conditions [3].

This modest contribution, seeks to predict exacerbation. In general, exacerbation is defined as an impaired lung function, acute event, or sudden worsening of COPD symptoms likely to cause death [4]. Moreover, exacerbation may contribute to degradation of quality of life [13], and respiratory function [5]. This situation can last for several days to several weeks [6], and no treatment has been found to cure, stop, or prevent exacerbation. The existing medication only dilates the bronchi allowing more air into the alveolus [3]. Therefore, early detection of exacerbation can reduce its effects, facilitate lungs recovery [7], and avoid their transition to the higher level of COPD disease. Thus, daily monitoring of COPD is an essential step to prevent the occurrence and the risk of exacerbation, by using machine learning algorithms.

The real cause of exacerbations is not fully understood [4]; each one has different signs and symptoms [8], even biomarkers cannot be relied upon to distinguish between COPD cohort at stable state and at exacerbation [9]. Thus, because the diversity and the fluctuation of this symptoms or signs, predicting frequent exacerbations is needed to plug the uncertainty gap where logical processing [If-Else] does not work. In this context, Bayesian network, naïve Bayes and decision tree have proven their efficiency to handle uncertainty in intelligent environments, more particularly those involving medical applications(fluctuation of symptoms) [10], it follows that, Wrappers and Filters methods to select the relevant attributes, and resolve the diversity of symptoms.

In this article, we highlighted and compared many algorithms in the machine learning field; to present a model effectively can select the relevant attribute, and detect the exacerbation with high accuracy compared to the existing wok in the COPD domain. A discretization step and the dependency between the relevant attributes have added also.

2 State of the Arts

Remote monitoring of COPD patient is an interesting topic, but the published works in this domain lack of the automation (automatic data processing) [11, 12]. Over the past months, we examined the current kinds of information system in order to propose a new improved solution. During this review, we distinguished three types of monitoring systems, (i) telehealth communication systems, (ii) automatic alerts systems (automatic data processing), and (iii) systems that address the selection of relevant attributes in COPD.

Telehealth technology aims to create better-informed environment of personalized health care like [12–14]. All these systems do not take exacerbation problem into consideration, but only focus on COPD generally, and they require a persistent connection to the network [12]. In addition, these systems making treatments quite expensive as a manual analysis is needed to complete the medical test [13, 14]. Moreover, [15–17] assured that this kind of healthcare was ineffective because the mortality rate has increased with the use of these kind of systems.

The automated systems could eliminate the need for physicians' intervention to accomplish the primary tasks of detecting the disease. So far, there is no appropriate and immediate response to each patient. On the other hand, the predictive capacity of exacerbation in [18] is moderate with AUC (*Area Under Receiver Operating Characteristic*) = 76%. Likewise [11] was not fully autonomous because the authors have recourse to experts (pneumologists) to define the dependency between the attributes, which limit the future evolution of the predictive model. Similarly, [19] did not consider exacerbation, and the prediction accuracy was very modest and did not exceed 69% by using AUC.

Thirdly, the ambiguity and the presence of unknown and large exacerbation factors induce the bioinformatics systems to select relevant factors or attributes. Recently, [20] identified the relevant factors, but this study don't take into account the exacerbation of COPD. Furthermore, the predictive capacity of the final model of Raghavan et al. [21] was moderate, AUC = 77%. In the same manner [22], the AUC of this system was also moderate AUC = 0.75% and it does not deal with exacerbation.

2.1 Discussion

The previous section shows that the attributes can be categorized either by the experts or by the classifier itself (e.g. the naïve Bayes) that checks the continuous attributes separately. For example, patients cohort were divided by the expert into four age groups: 18–44 years, 45–64 years, 65–74 years and 75 years and over [20]. Also, in [11], all variables except FEV_1 (Forced expiratory volume) are binary. FEV_1 is divided into five categories based on expert opinion [19]. Presented another possibility to treat continuous attributes without any categorization through using naïve Bayes. The result in this study (AUROC = 69%) is poor according to the [23] evaluation. Thus, automatic categorization or discretization in the absence of an expert in the context of COPD is a new contribution in COPD research field.

Moreover, the automatic selection of attributes, [20] uses the Bayesian network and the Markov Blanket, but this latter has a strong relationship with the Bayesian network [24], which limits its use with other learning methods, like naive Bayes and decision tree. In addition, other studies covering the selection of relevant attributes in COPD, such as [21, 22], did not perform well, with an AUROC of 77% and 75%, respectively. This situation prompts us to highlight and use new methods for selecting relevant attributes in the field of COPD.

To ensure good prediction accuracy, we note that the ordering of these methods (Selection of relevant attributes and discretization) is indispensable because: (I) According to our research, no researcher asserts that discretization has to be done before the selection of attributes, or the opposite. (II) The methods for selecting relevant attributes can support continuous attributes, such as CFSsubsetEval. Therefore, it is not necessary to make discretization firstly. In other words, selection methods may not require discretization where it can be used only for the processing algorithm, such as Bayesian network or decision tree.

Moreover, a comparison between decision tree (ID3 and C4.5 algorithm), Bayesian network, and naïve Bayes, is not achieved in the field of the COPD.

In this context, the next section compare between the using algorithms, and choice an order based on the prediction capacity of each combination. And last part discusses the future work (Sect. 4).

3 Experimentation and Results

During this experiment, we used a learning base that consists of 61 attributes and 1985 patients suffering from COPD. This learning base is available on the github website [25] from the CrowdANALYTIX [26]. This source is a web page organizes regular contests around the prediction in scientific data. The drawback with this learning base is that the exact name of each column is hidden. This learning database contains many attributes like Exacer (is the attribute), Demographics (age, gender, height, weight, etc.), Lung Function (including 20 continuous attributes that have been derived from spirometry), etc.

The evaluation metric used in the comparison is the *area under the receiver operating characteristic (ROC) curve*, which is summarized by Area under ROC (AUC). AUC is the metric that widely adopted in machine learning communities, e.g. [8, 11, 20, 27], etc. Moreover, in this study, we will use 10-Fold CrossValidation stratified. Weka [28] by default uses stratified cross validation. Weka is the software system used during our experimentation.

Table 1. Results obtained by the AUROC metric by applying the discretization that precedes the selection of relevant attributes

10 Cross Validation	Discretization → Selection attributes	The initial attributes are mixed (continuous and discrete)			
		61 attributes and 1985 patients using Weka			
	AUROC	Naïve bayes	Bayes network (K2)	ID3	C4.5
EWD 10 Intervals	CFSsubsetEval	0.780	0.780	0.550	0.496
	Gain Ratio Attribute Eval	0.730	0.729	0.522	0.496
	WrapperBestFirst	0.796	0.796	0.734	0.675
	WrapperGenetic	0.791	0.791	0.614	0.658
EFD 10 Intervals	CFSsubsetEval	0.771	0.771	0.555	0.496
	Gain Ratio Attribute Eval	0.719	0.719	0.552	0.496

(continued)

Table 1. (*continued*)

10 Cross Validation	Discretization → Selection attributes	The initial attributes are mixed (continuous and discrete)			
		61 attributes and 1985 patients using Weka			
	AUROC	Naïve bayes	Bayes network (K2)	ID3	C4.5
	WrapperBestFirst	0.799	0.801	0.757	0.562
	WrapperGenetic	0.792	0.791	0.623	0.496
Fayyad & Irani's MDL	CFSsubsetEval	0.795	0.795	0.547	0.664
	Gain Ratio Attribute Eval	0.768	0.768	0.605	0.673
	WrapperBestFirst	**0.802**	**0.802**	0.759	0.688
	WrapperGenetic	0.800	0.802	0.758	0.660
Kononenko's MDL	CFSsubsetEval	0.791	0.791	0.580	0.663
	Gain Ratio Attribute Eval	0.769	0.769	0.609	0.658
	WrapperBestFirst	0.800	0.800	0.763	0.692
	WrapperGenetic	0.798	0.801	0.756	0.670

Table 1 shows that, using the Bayesian network or naïve bayes, applying the discretization method (Fayyad & Irani's MDL) and then selecting the relevant attributes (Wrapper-BestFirst) on the learning base, give us the best result(AUROC = 80.2%) comparing to the other algorithm in the Table 1. With the genetic algorithm the result is promised also, but the number of the relevant attributes is bigger. Also we found, the discretization before the selection attributes can significantly increase the accuracy and decrease the number of relevant attributes.

Table 2. Learn the belief network from the learning base, by using Weka explorer.

	A - The variables are discrete, with Fayyad & Irani's MDL	
	B - Selection using wrapper with best first search algorithm	
10 - Cross Validation	*Area Under Roc Curve - AUC*	*Nb of relevant attributes*
BN(K2) – 1 parent	80%	11
BN(K2) – 2 parents	80.9%	15
BN(K2) – 3 parents	80.20%	14
BN(TAN)	**81.50 %**	**17**

Because the homogenous result between naïve bayes and Bayesian network, Table 2 shows that, using the Bayesian network, applying the discretization method (Fayyad & Irani's MDL) and then selecting the relevant attributes (Wrapper-BestFirst) on the learning base, by the TAN algorithm to realize the dependency between the relevant attributes is powerful prediction system to detect exacerbation with AUROC = 81.5%.

Thus, from 61 attributes at the beginning, with AUC = 76.8% (without discretization, and selection attributes, but only by using Bayesian network and K2 – 1 parent, this is the default configuration of Weka), we arrive at 17 relevant attributes with AUC = 81.5%.

4 Conclusion

Machine learning algorithm is still considered to be relatively new. It may offer different types of services such daily monitoring activities. In the medical domain, these algorithms allow COPD patients to make health decisions for himself through low cost rapid platform. These algorithms constitute the basic components of our ongoing context-aware application.

Many infections are detected in the existing solutions to predict exacerbation. These approaches: (i) focus only on the general aspect of COPD, (ii) have moderate accuracy of prediction, (iii) are not autonomous, and (iv) select the relevant attributes of COPD in an insufficient way (Markov Blanket, filters methods, etc.).

To solve these issues, we applied and compared set of machine learning methods and algorithms. The proposed model has the following features (i) concentrate on pulmonary crises or exacerbations, (ii) our prediction model has a good AUC = 81.5%, (iii) Our system is autonomous by using Fayyad & Irani's MDL algorithms (discretization and TAN) that describe relation between the attributes, rather than refer to experts, (iv) selection of relevant attributes through Wrapper-BestFirst.

For future work, we would like to increase the accuracy of prediction, by using neural network, or deep learning methods, and improve Wrappers-BestFirst algorithm.

References

1. Funtowicz, S.O., Ravetz, J.R.: Uncertainty and Quality in Science for Policy, vol. 15. Springer, Dordrecht (1990). doi:10.1007/978-94-009-0621-1
2. MPOC, bronchite et emphysème, Québec, A.p.d. (2016)
3. Le fardeau humain et financier de la MPOC - Une des principales causes d'hospitalisation au Canada, Thoracologie S.C.D., Février 2010. http://www.lignesdirectricesrespiratoires.ca/sites/all/files/MPOC_report.pdf
4. Lareau, S., Moseson, E., Slatore, C.G.: Patient information series. Am. J. Respir. Crit. Care Med. **189**(6) (2014)
5. Burt, L., Corbridge, S.: COPD exacerbations. AJN Am. J. Nurs. **113**(2), 34–43 (2013)
6. Seemungal, T.A., et al.: Time course and recovery of exacerbations in patients with chronic obstructive pulmonary disease. Am. J. Respir. Crit. Care Med. **161**(5), 1608–1613 (2000)
7. Wilkinson, T.M., et al.: Early therapy improves outcomes of exacerbations of chronic obstructive pulmonary disease. Am. J. Respir. Crit. Care Med. **169**(12), 1298–1303 (2004)
8. Van der Heijden, M., Velikova, M., Lucas, P.J.: Learning Bayesian networks for clinical time series analysis. J. Biomed. Inform. **48**, 94–105 (2014)

9. Hurst, J.R., et al.: Use of plasma biomarkers at exacerbation of chronic obstructive pulmonary disease. Am. J. Respir. Crit. Care Med. **174**(8), 867–874 (2006)
10. Simões, P.W., et al.: Metanálise do uso de redes bayesianas no diagnóstico de câncer de mama. Cadernos de Saúde Pública **31**(1), 26–38 (2015)
11. Van der Heijden, M., et al.: An autonomous mobile system for the management of COPD. J. Biomed. Inform. **46**(3), 458–469 (2013)
12. Trappenburg, J.C., et al.: Effects of telemonitoring in patients with chronic obstructive pulmonary disease. Telemed. e-Health **14**(2), 138–146 (2008)
13. Maiolo, C., et al.: Home telemonitoring for patients with severe respiratory illness: the Italian experience. J. Telemed. Telecare **9**(2), 67–71 (2003)
14. Vontetsianos, T., et al.: Telemedicine-assisted home support for patients with advanced chronic obstructive pulmonary disease: preliminary results after nine-month follow-up. J. Telemed. Telecare **11**(suppl 1), 86–88 (2005)
15. Berkhof, F.F., et al.: Telemedicine, the effect of nurse-initiated telephone follow up, on health status and health-care utilization in COPD patients: a randomized trial. Respirology **20**(2), 279–285 (2015)
16. Polisena, J., et al.: Home telehealth for chronic obstructive pulmonary disease: a systematic review and meta-analysis. J. Telemed. Telecare **16**(3), 120–127 (2010)
17. McLean, S., et al.: Telehealthcare for chronic obstructive pulmonary disease: cochrane review and meta-analysis. Br. J. Gen. Pract. **62**(604), e739–e749 (2012)
18. Halpin, D.M., et al.: A randomised controlled trial of the effect of automated interactive calling combined with a health risk forecast on frequency and severity of exacerbations of COPD assessed clinically and using EXACT PRO. Prim. Care Respir. J. **20**, 324–331 (2011)
19. Ryynänen, O.-P., et al.: Bayesian predictors of very poor health related quality of life and mortality in patients with COPD. BMC Med. Inform. Decis. Mak. **13**(1), 1 (2013)
20. Himes, B.E., et al.: Prediction of chronic obstructive pulmonary disease (COPD) in asthma patients using electronic medical records. J. Am. Med. Inform. Assoc. **16**(3), 371–379 (2009)
21. Raghavan, N., et al.: Components of the COPD Assessment Test (CAT) associated with a diagnosis of COPD in a random population sample. COPD: J. Chronic Obstr. Pulm. Dis. **9**(2), 175–183 (2012)
22. Amalakuhan, B., et al.: A prediction model for COPD readmissions: catching up, catching our breath, and improving a national problem. J. Community Hosp. Intern. Med. Perspect. **2**(1) (2012)
23. Sandelowsky, H., et al.: The prevalence of undiagnosed chronic obstructive pulmonary disease in a primary care population with respiratory tract infections-a case finding study. BMC Family Pract. **12**(1), 122 (2011)
24. Sinoquet, C., Mourad, R.: Probabilistic Graphical Models for Genetics, Genomics, and Postgenomics. Oxford University Press, Oxford (2014)
25. Rajasekaran, S.: Database about COPD exacerbation (2015). https://github.com/sibrajas/data-python/blob/master/CAX_COPD_TRAIN_data.csv
26. CrowdAnalytix (2015). https://www.crowdanalytix.com/contests/predict-exacerbation-in-patients-with-copd
27. Van den Berge, M., et al.: Prediction and course of symptoms and lung function around an exacerbation in chronic obstructive pulmonary disease. Respir. Res. **13**(1), 1 (2012)
28. Weka: Data Mining Software in Java (2011)
29. Porkodi, R.: Comparison of filter based feature selection algorithms: an overview. Int. J. Innov. Res. Technol. Sci. **2**(2), 108–113 (2014)

30. Bangsuk, J., Cheng-Fa, T.: A comparison of filter and wrapper approaches with data mining techniques for categorical variables selection. Int. J. Innov. Res. Comput. Commun. Eng. (2014)
31. Kohavi, R., John, G.H.: Wrappers for feature subset selection. Artif. Intell. **97**(1–2), 273–324 (1997)

Medical Semantic Question Answering Framework on RDF Data Cubes

Usman Akhtar, Jamil Hussain, and Sungyoung Lee(✉)

Department of Computer Science and Engineering,
Kyung Hee Univerity, Seoul, South Korea
{usman,jamil,sylee}@oslab.khu.ac.kr

Abstract. In this paper, we have proposed a framework to support the semantic question answering over the RDF data cube that is published according to the Linked Open Data (LOD) principles. As statistical data published all over the Internet there is a need to empowers the non-experts to query in the form of the natural language. But, the existing question answering system unable to support query on the statistical data in the form of the RDF cube. The current research is motivated by the need of the clinical organizations, who wish to develop a platform for analyzing the clinical data across multiple clinical sites. Linked open data (LOD) provides a support to published statistical data in the form of the RDF cube. Our proposed framework will provide a support to interact in the form of the natural language question answering that will produce the SPARQL query to extract the answer from the RDF data cube. In future, we will develop the benchmark to calculate the accuracy of the answer.

Keywords: Semantic question answering (SQA) · RDF data cubes · Question answering framework

1 Introduction

An increasing amount of the statistical data is published on the Linked Open Data (LOD) cloud. Getting insights from the data in more intuitive ways are becoming important. Systems for the Semantic Questions Answering (SQA) plays a vital role to connect with linked open data and provides an intuitive interface by translating natural languages queries into SPARQL syntax. Statistical data need more advanced querying methods to empowers non-experts users to draw their own conclusions. Semantic question answering is extremely important in the following application involving Linked Data to access public data sources.

- **Healthcare and Life Sciences (HCLS):** Statistical data in the form of the RDF data cubes influence decisions in a domain such as health care and life sciences. Many clinical datasets are often composed of the numerical observations as well as statistical information such as clinical trial data which is often composed of patient attribute [3].

M. Mokhtari et al. (Eds.): ICOST 2017, LNCS 10461, pp. 255–260, 2017.
DOI: 10.1007/978-3-319-66188-9_23

- **Biomedical Question Answering:** In biomedical, workers want to express their information needs in natural language. BIOASQ [5] encourages the participant to adopt semantic indexing as a mean to combine the information from the multiple sources of different types such as biomedical articles and ontologies. But, this system typically lacks supports for the RDF data Cubes, where clinical data represented in the form of multi-dimensional data.

We have motivated the need of the semantic question answering, where statistical data in the form of the RDF data cubes. However, there exist some important challenges that need to be tackled by the Semantic questioning answering system, including the following:

- **Lack of processing RDF cubes by SQA systems:** One of the major limitations of SQA system is a lack of processing of the statistical data in the form of the RDF data cube. Statistical data is different than other data and can not be queried by the existing linked open data querying approaches. However, the current SQA system provide translating natural language into SPARQL, which is a native language to query the RDF knowledge bases [2,3]
- **Enabling Access Over Statistical Data:** Current query federation approaches enables the integration of the multiple data sources but they do not consider the methods to access the statistical data while maintaining the good performance [5].

Although, there are a number of benefits to publishing data in multi-dimensional, such as statistics in Linked Open Data (LOD) cloud using LOD publishing principles. First, the data become web addressable and allow a consumer to annotate and link the data. Secondly, data can be flexible and combined with the other data using Linked data technology. Finally, data can be reusable and access by using the SPARQL, one of the example is linkedspending[1], which contains government spendings from all over the world as linked data.

In this paper, we have proposed a framework to handle the statistical data natural language query that works on the RDF data cube using SPARQL query template. In Sect. 2, we have discussed the preliminaries related to the RDF data cube and what operations are allowed in the RDF data cube. In Sect. 3, We have explicitly mentioned the problem of the existing SAQ system while dealing with the RDF data cube. In Sect. 4, we have proposed the framework to handle statistical queries. Finally, we have discussed the initial results in the discussion and give directions to the future work.

2 Preliminaries

Statistical data can be expressed in the form of the RDF data cube[2], also called as an OLAP cube or hypercube, which usually consist of the multi-dimensional datasets. Data cube represent the multidimensional numerical data and consist

[1] http://linkedspending.aksw.org/.

[2] https://dvcs.w3.org/hg/gld/raw-file/29a3dd6dc12c/data-cube/index.html.

of the array of cells. And each cell is identified by the associated dimension and mostly sparse.

Definition 1. *RDF data cube format: In linked open data, RDF data cube vocabulary*[3] *allows expressing the data cube. Each RDF data cube consists of model and observations. RDF data cube supports three main operations dicing, slicing and rolling which create a subcube of the main data cube.*

Definition 2. *There is a difference between the Question Answering (QA) and the Semantic Question Answering (SAQ). In QA, users ask questions in natural language using their own terminology. In SQA, the natural language question is transformed into the formal query using SPARQL.*

3 Problem

In summary, from the prior work, we can represent the medical statistical data as RDF data cube. However, how to execute the SPARQL queries over the data cubes is still the challenging issue. We have not seen any work looking at putting all aspect of RDF Cubes together. As argued in the introduction we can not use existing Question Answering (QA). Since they do not provide the query template to match the RDF cube.

3.1 Solution Strategies

Question answering over the linked data is an active research area but there are only a few solutions exists in the semantic question answering over the RDF data cube. From the literature, we have shortlisted the two strategies that can be implemented on the current problem, but each strategy has its own strength and weakness.

***Template Based Question Answering*:** In this approach, domain independent and domain dependent lexicon and it use SQA pipeline. First, users supplies a natural language question and then the tagger identifies the part of the speech such as nouns and lexicon is created which parse the question. Then the construction of the semantic representation and transformed into the SPARQL query. For indexing, Apache Solr is used which perform faster on statistical data. Finally, the answer is presented as a list to improve the SPARQL query using the AutoSPARQL [4] algorithm. The work is limited in support the RDF data cube, the generated SPARQL query do not provide the accurate results. We decide to use this approach in order to reduce the complexity. But, in our algorithm, we have used the modified version.

***Extracting RDF from Text*:** A bootstrapping strategy that extracts the RDF from the text, the main focus is to extract the natural language patterns from the unstructured data. A similar type of approach such as BOA [1] the goal of

[3] https://www.w3.org/TR/vocab-data-cube/.

this approach is to extract the structured data as RDF from unstructured data. BOA approach uses the Linked data web for knowledge. First, this approach will extract the natural language pattern from the Linked Data Web making the use of the data web as a background knowledge. Secondly, BOA generates RDF and that can be queried easily via SPARQL. On the statistical data, this approach can solve the problem but the current SPARQL syntax generated by BOA will not work on RDF cube.

4 Our Proposed Approach

We propose a framework by combining different approaches to Semantic Question Answering (SQA) over RDF data cube, where natural language questions convert into SPARQL query and work on the statistical data. To design, we take into the account of the existing SAQ architecture over the linked data. In the following, we will explain our proposed framework in detail. But one of the biggest challenges that we face in realization how to combine the different approaches in order to work on RDF data cube. The framework has a main three main states (Interpretation, Matching, Execution). As shown in the Fig. 1, a user posted the natural language question over the Linked open data cube that is stored in the triple store. The framework generates the equivalent SPARQL query and generates the answer.

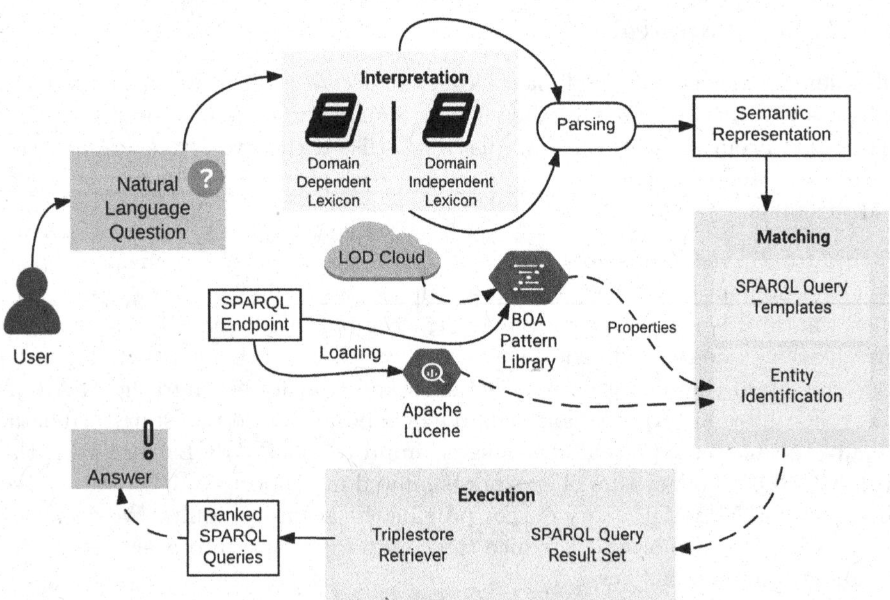

Fig. 1. Our proposed framework handle the naive user question and produce equivalent SPARQL query to run over the RDF data cube.

4.1 Interpretation Phase

The first step is a crucial step of the core module when the natural language question comes then this phase referring to the RDF cube operations are detected. Normally, these operations are detected by certain key phrases and are detected using the regular expressions. In this phase, it is determined that how the input questions will be identified by rest of the framework. In the pre-processing step dataset index that is initialized by using Apache Lucene[4] and then the terms can be found by the index. At the end, of this step, a syntactic parse tree is generated for the question.

4.2 Matching Phase

After the interpretation of the given question is generated, the question is then split into the phrases and mapped to the RDF data cube. The matching phase extracts the answers from the sources according to the delivered interpretation content. The output of the interpretation can be SPARQL query which can be handled by the RDF data cube store. In the statistical data, the answer type can be a countable, uncountable or temporal example such as integer is countable and double is uncountable and a year is temporal.

4.3 Execution Phase

After the answer is extracted from the RDF data cube then it can be ambiguous and redundant. In the simplest example, question explicitly mentions in a dataset description such a "located hospitals in 2017", for this case it can be found by matching. Finally, the highest ranking query will be executed first and the final ranking is based on the returned answer.

5 Discussion

As more and more Question Answering system is emerged every year to support the statistical data access of the RDF data cube, there is a need of the query builder, that select and combine the SPARQL features to access the linked open data sets that are published over the cloud.

5.1 Research Findings

We believe that the RDF data cube will be a strong baseline in the new research sub-field. Accessing statistical medial data is still challenging. Over the past years, a lot of research focusing on the interaction paradigms that allow the end user to easily access the interface and use natural language in a more intuitive way. Although, the key challenges are in translating the user's information using the standard web query processing technique and evaluate the accuracy.

[4] https://lucene.apache.org/core/.

On the other hand, multilingual questions have become an issue for the semantic web community, there is a need of the system that can help in overcoming the language barriers by facilitating the multilingual access to semantic data.

6 Conclusion and Future Work

We have introduced the framework to support the question answering over the RDF data cube. This work is motivated by the need of the clinical organizations who wish to develop a platform for analyzing the clinical dataset in the form of the natural language questions. Our framework will support the question answering over the Linked Data. One of the strengths of the proposed approach is to generate the SPARQL query template that can extract the answer from the RDF data cube. In the future work, we plan to continue contributing the development the full system and open source along with the benchmarks. We will investigate, how to integrate the Semantic question answering technique to the existing question answering system.

Acknowledgments. This work was supported by the Industrial Core Technology Development Program (10049079), Develop of mining core technology exploiting personal big data) funded by the Ministry of Trade, Industry and Energy (MOTIE, Korea).

References

1. Gerber, D., Ngomo, A.-C.N.: Extracting multilingual natural-language patterns for RDF predicates. In: Teije, A., Völker, J., Handschuh, S., Stuckenschmidt, H., d'Acquin, M., Nikolov, A., Aussenac-Gilles, N., Hernandez, N. (eds.) EKAW 2012. LNCS, vol. 7603, pp. 87–96. Springer, Heidelberg (2012). doi:10.1007/978-3-642-33876-2_10
2. Höffner, K., Lehmann, J.: Towards question answering on statistical linked data. In: Proceedings of the 10th International Conference on Semantic Systems, pp. 61–64. ACM (2014)
3. Höffner, K., Lehmann, J., Usbeck, R.: CubeQA—question answering on RDF data cubes. In: Groth, P., Simperl, E., Gray, A., Sabou, M., Krötzsch, M., Lecue, F., Flöck, F., Gil, Y. (eds.) ISWC 2016. LNCS, vol. 9981, pp. 325–340. Springer, Cham (2016). doi:10.1007/978-3-319-46523-4_20
4. Lehmann, J., Bühmann, L.: AutoSPARQL: let users query your knowledge base. In: Antoniou, G., Grobelnik, M., Simperl, E., Parsia, B., Plexousakis, D., Leenheer, P., Pan, J. (eds.) ESWC 2011. LNCS, vol. 6643, pp. 63–79. Springer, Heidelberg (2011). doi:10.1007/978-3-642-21034-1_5
5. Tsatsaronis, G., Schroeder, M., Paliouras, G., Almirantis, Y., Androutsopoulos, I., Gaussier, E., Gallinari, P., Artieres, T., Alvers, M.R., Zschunke, M., et al.: BioASQ: a challenge on large-scale biomedical semantic indexing and question answering. In: AAAI fall Symposium: Information Retrieval and Knowledge Discovery in Biomedical Text (2012)

Author Index

Printed in the United States
By Bookmasters